The Japanese Submarine Force and World War II

The Japanese Submarine Force and World War II

Carl Boyd and
Akihiko Yoshida

BLUEJACKET BOOKS

Naval Institute Press
Annapolis, Maryland

This book has been brought to publication by the generous assistance of Marguerite and Gerry Lenfest.

Naval Institute Press
291 Wood Road
Annapolis, MD 21402

© 1995 by Carl Boyd and Akihiko Yoshida

All rights reserved. No part of this book may be reproduced or utilized in any form or by any means, electronic or mechanical, including photocopying and recording, or by any information storage and retrieval system, without permission in writing from the publisher.

First Bluejacket Books printing, 2002
ISBN 1-55750-015-0

Library of Congress Cataloging-in-Publication Data

Boyd, Carl.
    The Japanese submarine force and World War II / Carl Boyd and Akihiko Yoshida.
        p. cm. — (Bluejacket books)
    Includes bibliographical references and index.
    ISBN 978-1-55750-015-1 (alk. paper)
        1. World War, 1939–1945—Naval operations—Submarine.
2. World War, 1939–1945—Naval operations, Japanese. 3. Japan. Kaigun—History—World War, 1939–1945. I. Yoshida, Akihiko, 1943– II. Title. III. Series.
D783.6 .B89 2002
940.54′5952—dc21   2001057970

Printed in the United States of America on acid-free paper ∞

6 5 4 3 2 1

TO ALL SAILORS WHO HAVE SERVED
BENEATH THE SEAS

Contents

List of Illustrations	ix
Preface	xi
Introduction: Basic Concepts of Submarine Strategy and Tactics	1
1 Submarines of the Imperial Japanese Navy	8
2 Weapons, Equipment, Personnel, and Shore Support for the Submarine Force	36
3 War in the Pacific and Submarine Operations, 1937 to Mid-1942: Successes and Missed Opportunities	53
4 New Submarine Operational Patterns and New Devastation in the Second Half of 1942	92
5 The Attrition of War and Submarine Operations	113
6 Submarine Operations and Plans for the Decisive Battle, 1944	134
7 Submarine Operations Near the War's End	158
Appendixes	
1 Imperial Japanese Navy Instructions for Submarine Warfare and the Decisive Battle	191

2 The Pearl Harbor Carrier Strike Force 196
3 Reconnaissance Operations with Submarine-Borne Aircraft, November 1941 through November 1942 198
4 Southern Expeditionary Main Force (Second Fleet) 200
5 Imperial Japanese Navy Task Force Organization (*Guntai-Kubun*) against Midway, the Aleutians, and Port Moresby 201
6 Sixth Fleet Submarines in the Eastern Solomons, Late 1942 203
7 Leadership of the Sixth Fleet, Mid-1943 204
8 Task Force Organization for Operation *A-Gō sakusen* 206
9 Summary of Japanese Submarine Losses in World War II and the Surviving Submarines 208
10 Biographies of Key Members of the Imperial Japanese Navy Submarine Force 219

Notes 227
Bibliography 243
Index 259

Illustrations

Photographs

A Japanese *Holland*-type submarine, circa 1908	10
The *I-71* looking forward from the quarterdeck, April 1939	25
A two-man Japanese midget submarine found in June 1960 near the entrance to Pearl Harbor	60
The midget submarine rammed and depth-charged by the USS *Monaghan* in December 1941 used as filling for a new sea wall at Pearl Harbor	62
Sakamaki's midget submarine at Mare Island, September 1942	63
The *I-68* under way at 23 knots in 1934	85
The sinking of the USS *Yorktown* (CV-5), 7 June 1942	85
The wreck of the *I-1* being examined by U.S. Army intelligence personnel, 11 February 1943	106
The wrecked hulk of the *I-1* in Kamimbo Bay, Guadalcanal	106

x Illustrations

A *RO-100*-class submarine photographed near Rabaul
by an Allied aircraft in March 1943 107

The port auxiliary engine room of the *I-14* 176

The water-tight hangar door on the *I-400* 177

Inside the *I-400*'s hangar designed to hold three seaplanes 177

Looking forward from the bridge of the *I-14* 178

The forward torpedo room of the *I-58* 181

The *I-14*, *I-401*, and *I-400* at Guam, November 1945 186

The snorkel device of the *I-400*-class submarine 186

Japanese submarines tied up at the Pearl Harbor Submarine
Base, 27 February 1946 187

The sinking of a Japanese submarine off Sasebo in April 1946 188

Maps

1 Japanese submarines in Hawaiian waters, December 1941 56
2 Submarine deployment on the west coast of the United
   States, December 1941 66
3 First picket lines "A" and "B" 80
4 The shift of picket lines westward 82
5 First submarine picket lines near Guadalcanal 94
6 Shift of submarine picket lines near Guadalcanal 96
7 Maneuvers of the USS *Wasp* and *I-19* 100
8 Submarine picket lines in the vicinity of Tarawa 125
9 The Great Triangle 139
10 Submarines of "A (*Kō*)" Unit 140
11 Submarine redeployment on picket lines after U.S. invasion 142
12 Submarine initial deployment as ordered
   on 18 October 1944 154
13 Submarine deployment, 20–24 October 1944 155
14 Final deployment of submarines, 27 October 1944 156

Preface

The performance of the Imperial Japanese Navy's submarine force in World War II fell far short of prewar expectations. The Japanese naval high command was inaccurate in its anticipation of the type of war it would embark upon in 1941, and the submarine force, in particular, quickly became a victim of unrealistic military planning and preparation. First designed to weaken a U.S. fleet of 21-knot battleships en route to an anticipated massive clash with Japanese dreadnoughts in the western Pacific, the submarine force was from the outset of the war confronted by much faster U.S. aircraft carriers after the successful Japanese attack on battleship row in Pearl Harbor. The submarine force was left groping for an effective strategic and operational plan of action while a sophisticated U.S. Navy undersea force quickly hardened to the reality of wartime conditions.

The lackluster performance of Japanese submarines in Hawaiian waters in December 1941 did not compel the high command to modify prewar plans for the submarine force. The formidable undersea arm of the Imperial Navy operated aimlessly and without a coherent strategy in the opening months of 1942. Inflexible prewar battle objectives usually held sway, or any new ones were often ill-conceived and incomplete. Moreover, in the battles of the Coral Sea and Midway the Japanese submarine force again failed to measure up to prewar expectations, but opinion of the navy high command continued to hold that submarines should be used chiefly to assist in the decisive battle of capital ships. Then came the surprise American offensive at Guadalcanal, and the crisis situation after late 1942 seemed to require the use of submarines in particularly dangerous supply and evacuation missions. The fate of the Japanese submarine force was sealed.

The force often operated helter-skelter during the war, being constantly obligated to commit submarines in unanticipated and ever increasing and dangerous crises. Submarines undertook a wide variety of assignments; for example, they were deployed along picket lines in an attempt to ambush and pursue enemy naval forces, only to be ordered and sometimes reordered to dash elsewhere when enemy forces were discovered beyond the original picket lines. Submarines were assigned to reconnoiter heavily guarded enemy ports and advance anchorages. There they sometimes launched midget submarines, human-piloted torpedoes, and aircraft, with minimal results. Submarine aircraft also dropped a few incendiary bombs on Oregon forests, and submarine deck guns fired on other minor targets on the American mainland and various islands. In addition to supply and evacuation operations with bypassed Japanese island garrisons, submarines transported highly explosive gasoline for refueling seaplanes. Moreover, the Japanese undertook other dangerous submarine transport operations with their German allies on the other side of the globe, with whom they exchanged personnel and small amounts of strategic goods, such as quinine and tungsten, and blueprints and prototypes of war machinery. There were also various forays into the Indian Ocean, but crises in the Pacific often forced the boats to concentrate there against strong and rapidly advancing Allied forces. These highly dispersed operations characterized much of Japanese submarine strategic and operational activity throughout the war. The occasional entreaty advocating concentration against enemy sea communications and extended U.S. supply lines, particularly to the South Pacific and Australia, was always played down and usually rejected.

Further explanation for the failure of the submarine force has its roots in the shortcomings of Japanese naval doctrine. The Imperial Navy's neglect of antisubmarine warfare (ASW) before the war proved deadly to the wartime Japanese merchant marine, but the Japanese submarine force was also adversely affected. Japanese submarines were poorly prepared to cope with U.S. Navy ASW operations.

During months of work against German U-boats in the Atlantic before the attack on Pearl Harbor, the U.S. Navy had the experience of escorting convoys, experience that sharpened ASW skills. The Japanese navy had no such wartime experience. When war came, Japanese submariners were unaware that they could be so effectively and systematically pursued on the surface by enemy radar and beneath the sea by sonar. Japanese submarines made little deliberate effort to avoid detection by such sophisticated sensors; moreover, Japanese submarine-borne radar and active sonar used later in the war were primitive by U.S. Navy standards and of little consequence. With no significant ASW doctrine, Japanese submariners, unlike their American and German counterparts, had little understanding of the theories of sound promulgation in relation to temperature layers or water stratification. Careful maneuvering while submerged could reduce the chance of detection, but deeply submerged Japanese submarines usually ascended directly to periscope depth to reconnoiter in a quick 360-degree sweep and then surfaced, fearing only the possibility of being spotted directly and visually by an enemy patrol. Japanese submarines were usually large, powerfully armed, and fast on the surface, but once detected they made good targets because of their slow submerged speed, poor maneuverability, and limited diving depth. Finally, a lack of concern about ASW manifested itself in submarine designs that failed until late in the war to emphasize noise-reduction features.

In spite of the enormous hardships and losses suffered by Japanese submariners (127 of about 160 large submarines in service during the war were lost), their spirit never faltered. Loyalty and unit cohesion remained strong among the elite members of the submarine force. Many of them, especially enlisted men, came from poor farm families; these young men frequently volunteered for submarine duty, in part, for the extra pay submariners received. They were thus able to send more money home to help their families. The special pay, however, also made submariners the envy among surface sailors. Therefore, these circumstances and the prestige associated with submarine service reinforced Japanese submariners' sense of pride and commitment to their service and fellow undersea comrades. Japanese submariners, like submariners in the American and German navies during the war, were loyal and dedicated sailors who functioned courageously and competently in the most trying of circumstances.

* * *

This book owes its genesis in 1988 to Dean C. Allard, who was then Director of Naval History, Naval Historical Center, and to Kanji Akagi, then Visiting Scholar, School of Advanced International Studies, Johns Hopkins University. These two scholars, quite independently, offered encouragement and facilitated the initial meeting of the authors at the Admiral Nimitz Foundation symposium, "Submarine Operations in the Pacific, 1941–1945," in Fredericksburg, Texas, May 1989. Thereafter, the work took shape slowly over the next few years through additional meetings of the authors, frequent correspondence, and much research in an array of sources in Japan and the United States.

The authors are indebted to many people for their help in writing this book. Mary Jo Valdes at the Pacific Fleet Submarine Memorial Association kindly made available some important submarine materials. We are grateful to Admiral Kennosuke Torisu, a retired veteran submariner of the Imperial Japanese Navy, and to Dr. Christopher W. A. Szpilman, a Japanese scholar formerly at Old Dominion University. Malcolm Muir Jr., Professor of History at Austin Peay State University, and the late Captain Paul R. Schratz, a retired U.S. Navy submariner, provided much useful information. The late Professor David C. Evans read an earlier version of the manuscript, and his generous and insightful criticisms proved invaluable to the authors as we made revisions. This volume has also benefited from the assistance and reflection of several Old Dominion University students, particularly David A. Kohnen, Sheryl L. Mednik, Toshiaki Kaneko, and Chiyoko T. Quasius. The maps drawn by Pamela Wheary, a graduate student of cartography, represent a special effort to help illustrate the text.

We are also indebted to the staff members of the Naval Institute Press, whose labor and imaginative suggestions have helped immeasurably to make our work easier. Moreover, Patricia E. Boyd has been an extremely insightful copy editor, and Robert J. Richardson has created a smart and sensitive index—to these independent professionals go our special thanks.

The Japanese Submarine Force and World War II

Introduction

Basic Concepts of Submarine Strategy and Tactics

The sudden arrival of U.S. Navy Commodore Matthew Perry with four steam-powered warships in Japan in 1853 was a show of force that highlighted the vulnerability of Japan's insular society and its minuscule navy. Japanese naval strategists recognized their weakness and soon became convinced that Japan could best resist foreign demands with a modern naval force. Thus, Perry's arrival gave impetus to a new naval defense policy. By the turn of the century Japan's navy had grown into a reasonably sophisticated steam-powered force; indeed, Japanese warship tonnage increased from a modest 14,002 in 1872, to 65,582 in 1894, to 256,816 in 1902, to 579,877 in 1912.[1]

Tactical and strategic operational plans for fighting an enemy's battle fleet grew similarly. Operational plans were in their infancy by the early 1890s, but the new Imperial Navy's baptism of fire and victory in the war with the Chinese in 1894–95 gave great incentive for further planning. More significantly, the sweeping naval victory over the Russians in 1904–5 proved a just reward and was particularly decisive in the future of the Japanese navy. After these wars the Japanese were optimistic and devoted much effort to developing a viable national defense policy. The time was right, then, for Japan, as an increasingly industrialized and ambitious nation, to set up a formal process for estimating military requirements and their close associations with the needs of foreign policy.

The first of a series of strategic plans was developed early in the new century. In the Imperial Defense Policy (*Kokubō hōshin*)—published first in 1901 with new editions appearing in 1910, 1912, 1920, 1928, and 1934—national strategic planners designated the United States as the probable enemy. Consequently, the U.S. Navy became the chief rival of the Imperial Japanese Navy in an anticipated struggle over hegemony in the western Pacific. Updating was a constant process in each edition of the Imperial Defense Policy, but intense study to meet new contingencies was undertaken particularly in 1918 near the end of World War I, in 1923 after the Washington Naval Treaty, and in 1936 after the Japanese government terminated its obligations under the earlier naval treaties and arms limitation agreements.[2] In each of these updated revisions the U.S. Navy remained the Japanese navy's foe.

In spite of significant changes in the international balance of power by the eve of World War II, the basic strategy of the Imperial Navy did not change after 1907. A decisive battle with a weakened U.S. Navy in Asian waters was the goal. This would be achieved in part by repeated attacks on the American battle fleet during its anticipated crossing of the Pacific to the vicinity of the Mariana Islands, as the plan eventually developed from the late 1920s into the 1930s. Japanese occupation and use of American bases in the Philippines and on Guam would also help weaken the American fleet while it was steaming westward; obviously, the Americans would also be denied support from those bases.[3]

In 1936 Japanese naval strategic planners estimated their requirements for a successful battle with the U.S. Navy: 12 battleships, 10 aircraft carriers and their air groups, 28 heavy and light cruisers, 6 torpedo squadrons with 6 light cruisers as flagships and 96 destroyers, 7 submarine squadrons (each with a light cruiser to serve as squadron flagship and 10 submarines), and 65 land-based air groups. Impressive though this force was, the Japanese estimated that it would probably be 70 to 80 percent of the strength of the U.S. Navy.[4] The Japanese knew that as the Pacific War approached, the American navy was heavily involved in the Atlantic, so there was almost a balance between Japanese and American naval forces in the Pacific. In some categories, for example, in aircraft carriers available for Pacific operations, the Japanese navy could claim superiority. On the other hand, although no longer restricted by treaties after the mid-1930s, Japan found that the weakness of its own economic, industrial, and technological base inhibited the strengthening of the navy. Thus, as war with the United States drew nearer in the late 1930s, many Japanese naval officers were uneasy, seeing that it was their destiny to fight against a superior navy, as fate had befallen the Japanese earlier in their battles against the Chinese and Russian navies.[5]

Operations for the Systematic Reduction of the Enemy Fleet

The leaders of the Japanese navy fully understood that because they would have to fight a stronger American navy (they anticipated that U.S. Navy ships in the Atlantic would reinforce the Pacific fleet), they had to reduce American battleship strength—the mainstay of all navies of the day—before it could be concentrated against them in the western Pacific. Accordingly, they developed elaborate tactics to wear down the American battle line.

Navy Battle Regulations (*Kaisen yōmurei*) evolved as a preliminary work. The writings of Lt. Comdr. (later Vice Adm.) Shinshi Akiyama, a brilliant naval strategist and tactician, provided the foundation for the first edition of the regulations in 1901. These regulations were of great value to the Japanese during the Russo-Japanese War, and later they served as a significant backdrop for the more far-reaching and aggressive plans of the 1930s. However, Akiyama's heyday was on the eve of World War I, largely before submarines and other important technological innovations like air power came into play in later decades. Thus, his specific comments about submarines were understandably limited. For example, he wrote that

> The submarine, a newly emergent type, has begun to transform what up to now has been the surface tactics of naval warfare into three-dimensional, subsurface warfare. It [the submarine] *will become a formidable weapon in the future,* but because its development is still in its infancy it is a bit early to rank it as battle-worthy. Instead, we may properly regard it now as a mobile subsurface mine.[6]

Akiyama's estimate of the worth of the submarine at the time is understandable; his strategic thinking focused on the decisive battle that was to end a naval war, a battle in which submarines of the day could not provide assistance.

With the precedent of Akiyama's instructions and naval success at Tsushima in 1905, new and increasingly elaborate and comprehensive plans were developed, particularly starting in the mid-1920s. At that time American maneuvers in Hawaiian waters convinced Japanese admirals, as one American historian has argued, that "the United States Navy appeared to be rehearsing a decisive battle for the distant waters in the western Pacific." Officers of Japan's Navy General Staff "divided their strategy into two parts: the attrition stage and the decisive battle."[7] Auxiliary forces, defined in the Imperial Navy as essentially all naval units other than battleships, chiefly held the role of carrying out systematic reduction or protection operations. During a nighttime destroyer torpedo attack on enemy battleships, heavy cruisers were to prevent or check any attack from enemy forces. In all torpedo attacks the destroyers were also expected to provide an effective antiair and antisubmarine screen for the main force. Moreover, while maintaining a tactical advantage, the heavy cruisers were to guide Japanese battleships to the enemy's main force. In such anticipated battle action the light cruisers would reconnoiter in advance of the Japanese main force. Carrier airplanes were to fly reconnaissance missions near the battle as well as maintain air superiority above the battle fleet and attack the enemy with torpedoes and bombs whenever possible. Finally, available land-based air-area groups would establish wide air surveillance.[8]

The Role of Submarines in the Decisive Battle

By the 1930s battle instructions for submarines far exceeded Akiyama's earlier reflections. Modern long-range submarines received crucial and complex assignments. Indeed, on the eve of the Pacific War, as one scholar states succinctly, "Japan's admirals planned to use their newly developed submarines and bombers to grind the American fleet down as it crossed the Pacific."[9] Submarines were to reconnoiter the enemy bases and anchorages. Then they would track and pursue the enemy fleet after its sortie, radio news of the enemy's activities to the Japanese fleet commander, and repeatedly ambush and torpedo the enemy's main force while it sailed westward to the Marianas for the decisive battle. Thus Japanese submarines, like most other auxiliary units in the Imperial Navy, had the main task of weakening the enemy battle fleet as much as possible before the decisive clash of dreadnoughts. However, submarines were expected to have far more direct contact with the enemy over a longer period of time than would any other type of Japanese warship, and this expectation heightened the sense of their importance.[10]

A more complete delineation of the instructions outlining the role of submarines in the decisive battle is essential to understand the prewar mind-set of Japanese admirals (see appendix 1 for the general battle instructions of 1934 and Combined Fleet Tactical Instructions of 1943). Broad instructions in 1934 stipulated that submarines attack the enemy's main force, independently or in coordination with other Japanese units. Submarines were generally to aid the battle line in any way possible, including action to prevent enemy battleships from maneuvering to a position for launching a surprise attack on the Japanese main force. But aspects of the prewar mind-set were carried over into the more specific instructions of the war years. Although the 1943 instructions anticipated many operational and tactical situations in elaborate detail, one cannot escape the impression that these instructions were rigid, stilted, and somewhat artificial. The experience of two years of war had little benefit on the design of specific instructions for the submarine force in 1943, as will be discussed later in this book.

* * *

Although the chief goal of submarine prewar doctrine always sought first to serve the interests of the battle fleet, a brief flirting with an alternative submarine doctrine came early in the interwar period. When Japan was an Allied power in World War I, the Imperial Navy gained valuable experience by escorting Allied forces in the Pacific and Indian Oceans and, late in the war, in the Mediterranean Sea as well. Japanese officers clearly saw the importance of providing reliable protection of sea communications during World War I. Thus, the Japanese submarine force was initially built in the 1920s with the intention of deploying it against enemy sea communications *as well as* against the enemy's main fleet in a decisive battle. But the submarine force was small, too small to be divided between the two missions. Furthermore, there was little interest in the doctrine advocating destruction of enemy sea communications because the destruction of the enemy's battle fleet was crucial and such a difficult problem. Once the enemy's fleet was crushed, Japanese planners assumed that a battle-seasoned submarine force would then find it easy to destroy enemy sea communications. Therefore, the subject was studied very little in naval schools and during training exercises. Only one paragraph was devoted to the subject of enemy lines of communication in the 1943 edition of Combined Fleet Tactical Instructions. The few submarines assigned specifically to attack sea communications during the Pacific War were also always ordered to seek and attack the enemy warships. Only secondarily were submarine commanders encouraged to attack convoys and individual supply ships along major sea routes or at entrances of protective harbors or anchorages. Emphasis was placed instead on proper deployment of Japanese submarine forces to support the battle line most effectively.[11]

There were also strong historical reasons behind the Japanese battle fleet doctrine. Japanese naval planners and strategists were held captive by their past success. In their analysis of the naval war of 1914–18, they emphasized surface clashes—the battle of Jutland was an example—and played down the effectiveness of U-boat warfare against British seaborne commerce. Some U-boat accomplishments early in the war, such as the *U-9*'s sinking of three British 12,000-ton armored cruisers within three hours on 22 September 1914, left an indelible impression with Japanese naval planners. The same submarine sank another cruiser nearly three weeks later, and the *U-27* damaged the seaplane carrier *Hermes* in a torpedo attack at the end of October. The Japanese studies also emphasized the cooperation of German U-boats with the High Seas Fleet in the Jutland operation, particularly in what the British feared was a "U-boat trap."[12] This Japanese perspective suffered from the lingering influence of the Japanese great victory at Tsushima in 1905. The victory was so impressive that it predetermined strategic thinking in the Imperial Navy—later Japanese admirals could think only of duplicating Admiral Heihachirō Tōgō's great feat.

A Japanese naval observer assigned to the Royal Navy during World War I, Comdr. (later Adm.) Nobumasa Suetsugu (1880–1944) was a strong advocate of submarine interaction with fleet strategy, and in his studies of the German example and the debate in the British press, he emphasized that the submarine was a dreaded weapon for use against warships. As one Japanese historian has recently written, Suetsugu, as commander of the First Submarine Squadron (1923) and head of the First Section (Planning) of the First Department (Operations) of the Navy General Staff (1923–25), was responsible for working out the "'attrition strategy' . . . [that] assigned to large, high-speed submarines the important mission of wearing down the enemy's main fleet on its transpacific passage, in addition to patrolling and defending the Western Pacific."[13] In various lectures in the 1920s, for instance at the Navy War College, Suetsugu, then vice chief of Navy Staff (1928–30), stressed that Japanese submarines should attack the American fleet as it left Pearl Harbor.[14] Called *yōgeki sakusen* (interceptive operations), this new submarine element that was appended to the traditional concept of a decisive battle was expected to reduce the combat abilities of the American battle fleet by 30 percent by the time it reached the western Pacific.[15] Suetsugu, later commander in chief of the Combined Fleet (1933–34) and eventually minister of home affairs in the First Konoe Cabinet (December 1937 to January 1939), had considerable influence in naval matters, particularly in the late 1920s and in the 1930s.[16] He was also a right-wing extremist, particularly regarding war against China. Evidence suggests that he held only slightly less radical views regarding war against the United States. When asked by a representative of the Army General Staff whether the navy was seriously considering war with the United States, Suetsugu answered, "Certainly, even that is acceptable if it will get us a budget."[17]

* * *

A rapidly changing Japan brought with it a number of traditional Japanese values and attitudes into the twentieth century, yet late in the nineteenth century through the 1930s the government increasingly pursued an expansionist mission. The Japanese military became an instrument of policy, and the major component of expansionism in the nation's foreign policy rested heavily upon the armed forces. Powerful Anglo-American interests had established themselves earlier in the areas the Japanese were beginning to regard as their rightful spheres of interest. These conflicting interests were ominous. Nevertheless, this reality did not deter the Japanese. Many believed the supposed degeneracy and pacifism of Americans would keep the United States from fighting, particularly if the war was long and costly. On the other hand, many Japanese believed in an older and superior source of inner strength, the famed "Japanese spirit," that could overcome the West's industrial and military superiority.

The odd and strained relationship between Japanese traditional isolationist values and modern expansionism proved to be a formula for disaster. The ensuing struggle resulted in a crushed Japanese nation in August 1945, but in the interim, Japanese naval strategy was designed to produce unchallengeable Japanese hegemony in the western Pacific. Planners of the war envisaged great sacrifice on the part of all units of Japan's armed services, but within the Imperial Navy the submarine force was the first to suffer. Physical damage inflicted by the enemy at the outset of the war was only one type of damage sustained by the submarine force; perhaps more important was the failure of Japanese submarines to live up to the naval high command's prewar expectations. Thus, the Japanese submarine force was never able to escape the influence of the battleship mind-set.

1
Submarines of the Imperial Japanese Navy

Japan's twenty-five large submarines in Hawaiian waters in the first week of December 1941 represented a long and sophisticated effort to develop a modern and powerful submarine force. The oldest of the Japanese submarines around Oahu was fifteen years, and the newest was five weeks.

As part of the Imperial Japanese Navy's quest to become a modern fighting force, naval leaders decided in May 1904, three months after the outbreak of the Russo-Japanese War, to experiment with the new undersea craft. Thus, nearly two decades before the Japanese developed strategic plans in which the U.S. Navy was named the Imperial Navy's chief rival, Japan purchased five *Holland*-type submarines from the Electric Boat Company in Groton, Connecticut. The specially constructed, disassembled sections of these boats and additional materials were shipped by rail to Seattle, Washington, where they were loaded aboard the *Kanagawa Maru,* which sailed for Japan on 5 November 1904. The submarines were then secretly assembled at Yokosuka Navy Yard.[1] Thus the beginnings of the Japanese submarine force were rather inauspicious and in keeping with Shinshi Akiyama's views before the war that the submarine was an infant and not yet battle-worthy.

The Japanese navy was careful and systematic in its investigation of the *Holland*-type submarine. The U.S. Navy had bought the new submersible craft, the sixth of the submersibles designed and built by John P. Holland, and then commissioned the boat as the USS *Holland* in April 1900. The preceding year, however, Lt. Kenji Ide, who was studying in the United States, made a test dive in the *Holland* model. Ide enthusiastically reported the following statistics of the American vessel to his naval superiors in Japan and emphasized the boat's practical use for port and coastal defense.

Displacement: 64 tons surfaced; 74 tons submerged
Dimensions: 53 feet 10 inches × 10 feet 2 inches × 8 feet 6 inches
Machinery: Single-shaft Otto gasoline engine plus electric motor, 45 brake horsepower, 50 shaft horsepower = 8 knots surfaced, 5 knots submerged; diving depth 75 feet
Armament: One 18-inch torpedo tube (bow; three torpedoes)[2]

By the summer of 1901, the Japanese navy, with Ide acting as its agent, sought to purchase some *Holland* craft. Negotiations were started with the Electric Boat Company, successor of the Holland Torpedo Boat Company, but the parties were unable to agree on terms, and negotiations were broken off by the end of the year.

However, Japanese interest in submersibles did not wane. News that *Holland*-type submarines were also being adopted by the British was of special interest to Japanese admirals, who had long admired the Royal Navy. In Great Britain Lt. Comdr. Kōzaburō Oguri watched British experimentation and sea trials and, like Lieutenant Ide, reported strongly in favor of submarines to his superiors in Japan. Both officers returned to Japan by the time of the Russo-Japanese War to champion the case for adoption of the submarine in the Imperial Navy. Thus, by the time the Japanese navy placed an order for construction of five *Holland*-type boats in 1904, three years of careful investigation convinced Japanese admirals of the growing sophistication of submersibles and the need to develop a submarine force in the Imperial Navy.[3]

The Japanese *Holland*-type boats were larger than the earlier craft and were further modified for diving to a maximum depth of 125 feet. The specifications follow.

Displacement: 103 tons surfaced; 124 tons submerged
Dimensions: 67 feet overall × 11 feet 11 inches × 10 feet 3 inches
Machinery: Single-shaft four-cylinder gasoline engine, 180 brake horsepower; electric motor, 70 horsepower = 8 knots surfaced, 7 knots submerged; range 184 nautical

	miles at 8 knots surfaced, 21 nautical miles at 7 knots submerged
Armament:	One 18-inch torpedo tube (bow; two torpedoes)
Complement:	Thirteen[4]

Known only by their hull numbers one through five, the first Japanese *Holland* was completed in August 1905 and commanded by Oguri, who before the Russo-Japanese War had gained experience with the British *Holland*-type boats. Numbers 2 and 3 were completed a month later; 4 and 5 went into service in October 1905. At that time Commander Oguri was appointed commandant of the corps—this was the beginning of the infant Japanese submarine force. On 23 October 1905, these five small submarines participated in a naval review with the Combined Fleet off Yokohama, where they astonished observers, particularly civilian, when the boats submerged and later surfaced. These boats were used for extensive training until they were stricken and broken up in 1921.[5]

While the Japanese anticipated that the continued purchase of for-

A Japanese *Holland*-type submarine under way on the surface, circa 1908. In the background is the former Chinese battleship *Chin Yen* (launched in 1882, 7,200 tons), captured by the Japanese in the Sino-Japanese War, 1894–95. (Naval Historical Center, NR&L [M] 24584-A)

eign submarines would be necessary, they were also eager to build their own submarines. Their first two boats bore the hull numbers 6 and 7. Indeed, the first of these Imperial Japanese Navy (*Kaigun*) *Holland*-type boats was laid down at Kawasaki Shipyard, Kobe, when the other *Holland* boats were en route from Seattle in November 1904. John Holland personally sent Kenji Ide, whom the American designer knew well, blueprints for these two smaller (63 tons submerged for number 6 and 95 tons for number 7) experimental craft.[6] However, these two submarines were inferior to the earlier *Holland* types, and the Japanese navy recognized the weakness of Japan's submarine technology.[7]

The Japanese submarine force suffered an early tragic accident that later served as a noble example of submariner character. Boat number 6 was running submerged on its gasoline engine while sucking air through an extended air induction tube (later called the snorkel). The induction valve mechanism failed to close when on 15 April 1910, waves of water unexpectedly poured into the boat and caused it to sink to the bottom. Crew members recognized that they faced certain death as the boat filled with the sea and isolated pockets of air vanished. The next day the little boat was located and raised. Apparently, all members of the crew died serenely at their stations—their brave behavior deeply moved the Japanese public. Thus, the Japanese submarine force developed an early tradition of self-sacrifice as a backdrop for later trying conditions, particularly in World War II.

After purchasing the original American *Holland*-type submarines, the Japanese purchased four additional types from Great Britain, France, and Italy. They carefully studied their newly purchased vessels to learn as much as possible about submarine technology; the Japanese often made improvements and modifications as they developed a distinctive technology of their own. In little more than fifteen years, the Japanese were prepared to design and build their own submarines in Japan.

* * *

By the end of World War I the following types of submarines had been purchased from Western countries:

Holland type from the United States
Vickers "C" and "L" types from Great Britain
Schneider-Laubeuf type from France
Fiat-Laurenti type from Italy

The Vickers "L" type was the last of Japanese purchases of foreign submarines, but naval analysts gained much insight in modern submarine technology after studying the designs of all of these foreign boats. More significant, however, were the German U-boats that Japan, an Allied power in World War I, acquired after the war.

Japan received seven U-boats as German reparations in 1919; they were studied and tested in preparation for the construction of larger Japanese-built submarines of the "I" class. "I" is a romanization of the first letter in the traditional Japanese syllabary (written as the Greek lambda), "RO" is the second, and "HA" the third. Therefore, under three separate classes established in 1924, an I-boat was a first-line class A submarine, the RO-type submarine was a somewhat smaller class B boat, and the HA-type Japanese submarine was a small coastal class C boat with an appreciably more limited range and displacement. Midget submarines were later listed in the HA series.

Although German influence in the modernization of various Japanese institutions—legal, medical, educational, military—was particularly important after the Germans won the Franco-Prussian War, 1870–71, British influence was traditionally foremost in the Japanese navy until the end of World War I. With Germany's defeat and the scuttling of the German High Seas Fleet at Scapa Flow in June 1919, the Imperial Japanese Navy stood third in the world after the British and American navies. But British influence decreased rapidly, especially in the Japanese submarine force. The technology of German U-boats was clearly superior. Moreover, the wide-ranging U-boats received much attention during the war; their involvement in fleet strategy had already been delineated by Capt. Nobumasa Suetsugu, a member of the Japanese delegation at the Washington Conference in 1921. Anglo-American treatment of Japan at that conference on arms limitations outraged many prominent Japanese naval officers, not least of whom was Suetsugu, promoted to the rank of rear admiral on 1 December 1923. Japan's capital ship ratio of six to the American ten (also the British ten) would result in a Japanese naval force significantly inferior if attacked by the whole weight of the U.S. Navy. No limits were placed, however, on submarine strength at the Washington Conference. Therefore, after the war when Japanese shipbuilding facilities were considerably modernized and relations with Anglo-American powers were in some respects becoming strained, the arrival of seven German U-boats offered a special opportunity. Some Japanese believed that they could help redress the naval balance by changing the character of their submarine force for potential use as a powerful arm of the battle fleet.

On 25 June 1919, the American naval attaché in Tokyo was given a special opportunity to survey the U-boat precursors to a new generation of Japanese submarines. The aide-de-camp to the Japanese naval minister took the Allied and Associated powers' naval attachés to Yokosuka to inspect the newly arrived submarines. The seven ex-German U-boats were given new names in the Japanese navy: the *U-125* became *O-1*, *U-46* became *O-2*, *U-55* became *O-3*, *UC-90* became *O-4*, *UC-99* became *O-5*, *UB-125* became *O-6*, and *UB-143* became *O-7*.[8] The American naval attaché was impressed by several especially significant features of the ex-German submarines and reported to the Military Intelligence Division in Washington in July:

(1) Excepting the *UC-90*, they have a mast for radio, which can be erected or dropped down from the inside of the submarine by an electrical apparatus.

(2) Excepting the *U-46*, they are all provided with two sawlike torpedo net cutters, one on deck and the other on the bottom.

(3) In order to prevent the projecting parts of submarines [from] getting tangled with lines or cords, while sailing under water, steel wires are stretched from the top of the conning tower to the bow and two from the conning tower to the stern. These wires can, by special device, be utilized for radio signaling to short distances. The vertical and horizontal rudders, and propellers are protected by strong frames around them.

(4) In order to purify the air inside the submarine, there are provided apparatuses which purify the air by means of chemicals, and others that give out compressed oxygen.

(5) In order to show the site of the submarine when stuck to the bottom, they have buoys which are attached to the submarine by chains, which can be floated from the submarine. There are also rubber tubes through which the salvaging vessel can send down air or liquid food. They are also equipped with apparatus for telephonic communication.[9]

The Japanese were quick to recognize the need for foreign assistance as they prepared to assimilate features of these U-boats into their own schemes of building submarines; naturally they sought German submarine designers, technicians, and former U-boat officers. Indeed, shortly after Japan received the German U-boats, Capt. T. Godo of the Japanese navy was named head of a naval mission to Germany. The

American military attaché in Tokyo reported to the War Department on 9 October 1919 that the Japanese were "now in Berlin for the purpose of studying submarine construction from German naval designers.... Captain Godo expects to obtain German patents and designs for submarines, and also expects to bring German naval mechanics back with him to Japan."[10]

The first German submarine specialists had already arrived in Japan a few months earlier during the summer of 1919. One engineer, who had helped build U-boats at Germaniawerft in Kiel during the war, was taken to Kure "by the Japanese government especially to train officers and men, and to explain the ex-German submarines to the Japanese navy," as an American intelligence report declared.[11]

The number of German submarine specialists working for the Japanese reached a high point soon after the war and then tapered off dramatically. Probably several hundred German submarine designers, technicians, and former U-boat officers were brought to Japan under usually five-year contracts—one Office of Naval Intelligence (ONI) report originating in Germany claimed that by 1920 "over 800 submarine building specialists, etc. have gone to Japan."[12] Engineers and ex-U-boat officers were most sought after, commanding the highest salaries. Annual salaries of ¥25,000 (about $12,000), plus a yearly bonus ranging from ¥5,000 to ¥10,000, were not uncommon. Additionally, Germany-Japan round-trip travel expenses were guaranteed by the Japanese. These Germans were usually employed directly by the Kawasaki Shipyard in Kobe.

Knowledge of German activity in Japan was widespread. For example, the American military attaché in Venezuela learned of the Japanese-German association through his German counterpart in Colombia and offered the following observation in a memorandum to the U.S. Army assistant chief of staff, G-2 (Intelligence) in 1927: "The acquisition by Japan of what might be termed the best professional talent in a special arm is a point worthy of our immediate attention." The American attaché further recommended that the services of the German submarine specialist, Robert Bräutigam, under contract in Japan since 1923, "might be acquired by us, not only as an interesting expert of unquestioned efficiency in his special arm, but as a means to keep track of Japanese activities, through him and his connections with former colleagues, now in the Japanese service."[13] Similar German activity in Japan was claimed in 1929 in a letter to G-2 in Washington from the American military attaché in Berlin.[14]

However, by late in the decade few German specialists remained employed by the Japanese, and immediate German influence in general had all but vanished. In 1928 another ONI report, this one originating in Japan, declared confidently that no more than twenty-eight German submarine specialists had been employed in the Kobe area during the last five years. "As various submarines were completed, . . ." wrote a U.S. Navy lieutenant in Japan in November 1928, "the Japanese staffs gradually took over the work, until finally a distinctly Japanese type of submarine was evolved. Consequently, during the past two or three years, the influence of the German designers with the Japanese lessened to such a degree that at present it is practically nil."[15]

* * *

Shifting Japanese submarine tactical and strategic thinking helped to create different classifications of boats. The same lieutenant in Tokyo concluded in 1928 that "German [technical] influence . . . is overrated. . . . Japanese submarine design is tending almost entirely towards large fleet submarines, capable of operating with the fleet."[16] Various new tactical and operational concepts about how submarines ought to be used also started to take shape in the navy. However, the dominant view remained unshakable—the chief purpose of the submarine was to intercept the enemy battle fleet and systematically weaken it through repeated attacks.

Before this time the submarines in the Japanese navy were small (less than 1,000 tons) with limited firepower, slow speed, and short cruising range. These conditions changed when a new era of construction started after the conclusion of the Five-Power Naval Treaty coming out of the Washington Conference in 1922. Compared with Japan's standard RO-class submarines intended for coastal defense, the new I-class submarine had nearly twice the displacement and operational range as well as a speed advantage of 2–5 knots. The new submarines were fast enough to operate with dreadnoughts of the 1920s or to scout ahead, and they had sufficient range and provisions for a sixty-day cruise across the Pacific or Indian Oceans.

However, the Japanese had plans to build a series of large submarines before they received the seven German U-boats. Two prototypes were actually completed. These experimental boats were two different types and were originally intended to serve as models for the systematic construction of large I-boats. One prototype was derived from the British K class submarine of 1917. Laid down under the naval program of 1919, launched in 1921, and completed in 1924, the *I-51* (ex–hull number *44*) was the first fleet-type submarine in the Japanese navy—the *Kaigun-dai* (large fleet type), abbreviated as *Kaidai*. The large features of the *I-51* were very attractive to the Japanese and a decided departure from the various Vickers-class submarines then in the Japanese navy. Nevertheless, plans changed, and this experimental boat served chiefly as a backdrop and not as a model for future designs. This Type 1 submarine, the first of a series of *Kaidai* types, was used largely for training until it was decommissioned on 1 April 1940.

One *Kaidai* Type 1

The *I-51* was the only *Kaidai* Type 1 submarine. Specifications: displacement of 1,500 tons surfaced, 2,430 tons submerged; length 300 feet; 5,200 horsepower; four shafts, four Sulzer diesel engines (two shafts and two diesels after 1932); 20 knots surfaced, 10 knots submerged, with a cruising range of 20,000 nautical miles at 10 knots surfaced, 100 nautical miles at 4 knots submerged; eight torpedo tubes; twenty-four torpedoes; one 4-inch deck gun; diving depth of 200 feet.

One *Kaidai* Type 2

The other prototype, the subsequent experimental *I-52* (Type 2), had a little more influence on future design. It was employed very extensively in fleet training exercises during the interwar years when data were collected for refinements of design in the new *Kaidai* types in service by 1941.

The *I-52* (ex–hull number *51*) was the only *Kaidai* Type 2 submarine. Although its specifications were similar to those of the *I-51*, this experimental boat was modeled after the *U-139*, whose specifications in brackets follow those of the *I-52:* displacement of 1,500 [1,930] tons surfaced, 2,500 [2,483] tons submerged; length 331 [302] feet; 6,800 [3,300] horsepower; 22 [15.3] knots surfaced, 10 [7.6] knots submerged, with a cruising range on the surface of 10,000 [12,630] nautical miles at 10 [8] knots surfaced, 100 [53] nautical miles at 4 [4.5] knots submerged; eight [six] torpedo tubes; sixteen [nineteen] torpedoes; one 4.7-inch and one single-mount 3.1-inch [two single-mount 5.9-inch] deck guns; diving depth of 175 [230] feet.

The *I-52* was the second experimental *Kaidai* submarine built by the

Japanese. It was laid down under the naval program of 1920, launched in 1922, completed in 1925, and decommissioned on 1 August 1942. Its double-hull design, like the German cruiser-type submarine of 1917 (*U-139*), had considerable design significance. The *I-52* had a notably higher surface speed than the *U-139*, a characteristic in keeping with the new role I-boats were to play vis-à-vis the Combined Fleet. Several additional *Kaidai* Type 2 submarines were planned, but they were cancelled in 1922 before contracts were issued, building materials were assembled, or the keels were laid down. The chief reason for this change in submarine construction plans was the earlier arrival of the German reparation submarines.

The famed naval journalist Hector Bywater explained something of the turmoil and reevaluation that seized Japanese submarine planners between the end of the war and the eve of the Washington Conference:

> Eight new submarines—four sea-going and four coastal boats—covered by the naval programme of 1919, were to have been commenced the following year, but before they were laid down an event had occurred which is believed to have brought about an important modification in Japanese ideas on submarine design. This event was the arrival at Yokosuka on the 20th June 1919, of seven ex-German submarines, which had been allotted to Japan for experimental and propaganda purposes, by the Inter-Allied Naval Council in Paris. These seven vessels had previously been closely examined by Japanese experts in Europe, and were, indeed, selected by them as representing the most useful types from the Japanese point of view.[17]

Plans and preparation for the construction of the *I-51* and *I-52* were well-defined before the Japanese could fully analyze various features of the seven U-boats and then formulate and agree upon new I-boat designs. The presence of German submarine specialists in Japan was also significant; nevertheless, the process of determining naval needs and submarine capabilities was complex and time-consuming. Bywater, as a contemporary naval analyst, observed that no knowledgeable person would expect that "Japan will slavishly follow the German model. . . . It has been made clear that her constructors have original ideas on the subject, and that they have already succeeded in evolving a particular type of submarine which conforms to the special requirements of Japanese naval strategy."[18] Indeed, when Bywater published these observations in 1921, the Japanese scrapped four of the former

German U-boats, and the next year the remaining three U-boats were scrapped.

In general, the seven German reparation submarines served as a backdrop for future Japanese submarine development, but only the *UB-125* specifically led to the development of a new type of I-boat. A minelaying U-boat, the *UB-125* was the largest of the original reparations submarines.

Four *Kirai sen* Type

The *Kirai sen* (*Kirai fusetsu sensuikan*, abbreviated *Kirai sen*) was the only minelaying-type submarine in the Japanese navy; there were four boats of this type (*I-21* to *I-24*, renamed *I-121* to *I-124* on 20 May 1942). These boats were completed in 1927 and 1928 and then modified and fitted with gasoline tanks in 1940 to serve as seaplane-refueling submarines early in the war; thus, the scope and range of reconnaissance flights were increased. However, these four boats retained their minelaying capability. The *Kirai sen* type was slightly larger than the German model; specifications in brackets following those of the Japanese minelayers are for the *UB-125*. Displacement of 1,383 [1,163] tons surfaced, 1,768 [1,468] tons submerged; length 279 [269] feet; two diesel engines, 2,400 [2,400] horsepower; 14.5 [14.7] knots surfaced, 7 [7.2] knots submerged, with a cruising range of 10,500 [11,470] nautical miles at 8 [8] knots surfaced, 40 [35] nautical miles at 4.5 [4.5] knots submerged; four [four] torpedo tubes; twelve [fourteen] torpedoes; forty-two [forty-two] mines; one single-mount 5.5-inch [5.9-inch] deck gun; diving depth of 200 [250] feet.

* * *

A genuinely Japanese submarine force started to develop the physical characteristics that were thought to complement the battleship. In addition to the large fleet-type (*Kaidai*) submarines, in the 1920s the Japanese introduced an ocean-cruising type of submarine, the *Junyō sensuikan*, abbreviated as *Junsen*. Thus, the *Kaidai* and *Junsen* submarines were designed intentionally large with considerable endurance for oceangoing fleet operations. They were also designed to have a good surface speed, powerful armament, and extensive communication facilities in order to coordinate attacks.

Submarines of the *Junsen* type were designed specifically to patrol and reconnoiter independently in distant enemy waters. Like the

Kaidai-type submarines, the *Junsen* was intended primarily for launching attacks on the enemy's battle fleet. Attacks on enemy non-capital ships always assumed a very low priority in the minds of Japanese submariners. With large hulls and extremely long cruising ranges, *Junsen*-type submarines could operate for long periods at sea and, if needed, could also act as submarine squadron flagships. (Usually the submarine squadron flag was assigned to a light cruiser.) The first *Junsen*-type I-boat in the 1920s began its numbering system with number one, whereas the *Kaidai* type of I-boat continued with number fifty-three, following the experimental *I-51* and *I-52*. However, this system was not always adhered to later in the war.

Four *Junsen* Type 1

The initial four *Junsen*-type boats (*I-1* to *I-4*) were completed between 1926 and 1929. Specifications: displacement of 2,135 tons surfaced, 2,791 tons submerged; length 320 feet; two diesel engines, 6,000 horsepower; 18 knots surfaced, 8 knots submerged, with a cruising range of 24,400 nautical miles at 10 knots surfaced, 60 nautical miles at 3 knots submerged; six torpedo tubes; twenty torpedoes; two single-mount 5.5-inch deck guns; diving depth of 265 feet. The *I-1*, like most large I-boats, was designed with a double hull, whereby the pressure in the tank space between the heavy-pressure hull and the thinner outer hull was always equalized with that outside, at whatever depth the submarine was operating.

As the construction of I-boats, both *Junsen* and *Kaidai* types, was emphasized in the 1920s, several improvements were made. In general, however, they became larger, faster, and more heavily armed, a trend clearly discernible in the modifications that appeared in the *Kaidai* submarines between 1927 and 1932.

Four *Kaidai* Type 3a

The *Kaidai* Type 3a was the first mass-produced fleet-type Japanese submarine: *I-53* to *I-55* and *I-58*. These four boats were completed between 1927 and 1928. Specifications: displacement of 1,800 tons surfaced, 2,300 tons submerged; two diesel engines, 6,800 horsepower; 20 knots surfaced, 8 knots submerged, with a cruising range of 10,000 nautical miles at 10 knots surfaced, 90 nautical miles submerged at 3 knots; eight torpedo tubes; sixteen torpedoes; one single-mount 4.7-inch deck gun; diving depth of 200 feet.

Five *Kaidai* Type 3b

The *Kaidai* Type 3b was a modified Type 3a: *I-56, 57, 59, 60,* and *63.* These five boats were completed between 1928 and 1930. Their specifications were almost identical to those of Type 3a. Modifications concerned mainly the shiplike bow (unlike the rounded bow of the Type 3a), greater length (331 versus 330 feet), and different conning tower configurations.

Three *Kaidai* Type 4

The three *Kaidai*-Type 4 submarines (*I-61, 62,* and *64*) were modernized Types 3a and 3b and were completed between late 1928 and 1930. Specifications: displacement of 1,720 tons surfaced, 2,300 tons submerged; length 320 feet; 20 knots surfaced was possible because of new and more efficient 6,000-horsepower MAN (*Maschinenfabrik Augsburg-Nürnberg*) diesel engines, 8.5 knots submerged, with a cruising range of 10,800 nautical miles at 10 knots surfaced, 60 nautical miles at 3 knots submerged; six newly designed torpedo tubes; fourteen torpedoes; one single-mount 4.7-inch deck gun; diving depth of 200 feet.

Three *Kaidai* Type 5

The three boats of the *Kaidai* Type 5 (*I-65* through *I-67*) were completed in 1932, the product of much study and experimentation with earlier fleet-type submarines. Specifications: displacement of 1,705 tons surfaced, 2,330 tons submerged; length 320 feet; two diesel engines, 6,000 horsepower; 20.5 knots surfaced, 8.25 knots submerged, with a cruising range of 10,000 nautical miles at 10 knots surfaced, 60 nautical miles at 3 knots submerged; six torpedo tubes; fourteen torpedoes; one new-type 3.9-inch deck gun; diving depth of 230 feet.

* * *

The increasingly large Japanese I-boats in the 1920s offered an array of opportunities to extend the submarine arm of the Imperial Navy. Aviation was an important technical innovation that received much attention during World War I, and further developments in aviation were carefully studied by Japanese strategic planners. Not surprisingly, therefore, the Japanese were among the early pioneers in investigating the possibilities of linking aviation and submarine technology.

Somewhat before the first Japanese aircraft-carrying I-boat was completed in 1932, there was great speculation by foreign observers about the aerial innovation and its possible association with the rapidly growing Japanese submarine force. An American military attaché in Tokyo, for example, reported in August 1924 that he believed the recent story in an Ōsaka newspaper was correct: "Special investigations are now in progress at the Oppama (Yokosuka) Aviation Corps about airplane carrying submarines. For experimental purposes a German airplane of the Heinkel type has been imported."[19] The report continued with the observation that the "plane carrying submarine will be equipped with a large calibre" antiaircraft gun for protection when the craft was launched in enemy waters. Speculation continued throughout the decade. By January 1927, another American military attaché reported from Tokyo that a German airplane engineer, "Dr. Theodor Carlman, . . . an authority on airplane construction, arrived in Japan Jan[uary] 12th. He has come to this country under a two year contract with the Kawanishi [Aircraft Company in Kobe]."[20] By May 1929, an American observer in Tokyo was convinced that "the Japanese navy, after long investigation and tests, has developed a special airplane at the Kure arsenal for use on the larger type submarines."[21] Indeed, funds were already allocated for the construction of an aircraft-carrying submarine (*I-5*); materials were assembled, and its keel was laid down at Kawasaki Shipyard in Kobe on 30 October 1929.

One *Junsen* Type 1M

The *I-5* was an experimental aircraft-carrying I-boat. Two tubular hangars, one to port and one starboard, were fitted immediately aft of the conning tower. One hangar was used to store the fuselage and twin floats; the other stored the wings. The tubular hangars were retracted into the deck when the seaplane was not in use. In training exercises in the early 1930s the Japanese realized that in wartime conditions, the submarine would be extremely vulnerable to attack while the scout plane was being assembled. This was an awkward procedure. Still more time was required to prepare the plane for launching on the catapult extending aft on top of the hull. Despite these difficulties this was the basic design of Japanese aircraft-carrying submarines throughout the 1930s. In 1940, however, by which time a new design was being built, the *I-5*'s aircraft and aerial equipment were removed, and a second single-mount 5.5-inch gun was added instead.

Launched in June 1931 and completed in July of the next year, the *I-5* was generally similar to the *Junsen* Type 1 submarines, although displacement of the *I-5* was a little greater. Specifications: displacement of 2,243 tons surfaced, 2,921 tons submerged; length 320 feet; two diesel engines, 6,000 horsepower; 18 knots surfaced, 8 knots submerged, with a cruising range of 24,000 nautical miles at 10 knots surfaced, 60 nautical miles at 3 knots submerged; six torpedo tubes; twenty torpedoes; one single-mount 5.5-inch gun; one floatplane (until 1940); diving depth of 260 feet.

In spite of the weaknesses in the design of Japan's first aircraft-carrying submarine, particularly concerning the tubular hangars, Japanese naval planners quickly appreciated the potential of such I-boats. Hence, a series of aircraft-carrying submarines was launched that culminated in the *I-400* class with three aircraft, the world's largest submarine when the first of the class was completed at the end of 1944. The aircraft-carrying submarines generally got larger in the 1930s while work continued to design better aircraft-carrying arrangements and equipment.

One *Junsen* Type 2

Type 2 was an improved Type 1M. There was only one Type 2 boat (*I-6*). Laid down three months after the *I-5* was completed (October 1932), the *I-6* was launched in March 1934 and completed in May 1935. Although intended from the outset as an aircraft-carrying boat, its aerial configuration was similar to *I-5*'s. Specifications: displacement of 2,243 tons surfaced, 3,061 tons submerged; length 323 feet; two diesel engines, 8,000 horsepower; 20 knots surfaced, 7.5 knots submerged, with a cruising range of 20,000 nautical miles at 10 knots surfaced, 60 nautical miles at 3 knots submerged; six torpedoes tubes; seventeen torpedoes; one single-mount 5-inch deck gun; one floatplane; diving depth of 265 feet.

Two *Junsen* Type 3

The two Type 3 boats (*I-7* and *I-8*) were designed and specially equipped as submarine squadron flagships. Completed in 1937 and 1938, the boats' specifications were as follows: displacement of 2,525 tons surfaced, 3,583 tons submerged; length 358 feet; two diesel engines, 11,200 horsepower; 23 knots surfaced, 8 knots submerged, with a reduced cruising range of 14,000 nautical miles at 16 knots surfaced, 60 nautical miles at 3 knots submerged; six torpedoes tubes; twenty torpedoes; one single-mount 5.5-inch deck gun (*I-8*'s deck gun was replaced with a twin-mount 5.5-inch gun shortly before sailing for German-occupied France in 1943). Each of these submarines had a seaplane, hangars, and catapult similar to the *I-6*'s.

The *Junsen* Type 3s were the last aircraft-carrying submarines to have the hangar and catapult aft of the conning tower; new types most prevalent during the 1940s all featured the hangar and catapult forward of the conning tower.

Three New *Junsen* Type A1

The first of the New *Junsen* Type A1 submarines was laid down in January 1939. Based on the *Junsen* Type 3, the three boats of this type (*I-9* through *I-11*) were completed in 1941 and 1942. They were especially fitted and equipped to act as submarine squadron flagships, with extra telecommunication equipment and additional accommodations for a squadron commander. Specifications: displacement of 2,919 tons surfaced, 4,149 tons submerged; length 373 feet; two diesel engines, 12,400 horsepower; 23.5 knots surfaced, 8 knots submerged, with a cruising range of 16,000 nautical miles at 16 knots surfaced, 60 nautical miles at 3 knots submerged; six torpedo tubes; eighteen torpedoes; one single-mount 5.5-inch deck gun; one floatplane; diving depth of 330 feet. The hangar was faired into the forward part of the superstructure, and the catapult extended forward on top of the hull.

With the completion of the *I-9* in February 1941, the Japanese had seventeen years of valuable experience in building large I-boats. In those seventeen years the horsepower of individual diesel engines used in the largest of Japanese submarines increased many times, from 1,300 (*I-51* in 1924) to 6,200 (*I-9* in 1941). Surface displacement, in this example, increased some 1,419 tons (from 1,500 to 2,919 tons), and top speed increased 3.5 knots (from 20 knots for the four-engine experimental *I-51* to 23.5 knots for the two-engine *I-9*). New I-boats coming into service in 1941 were among the best submarines in any navy at the time.

The *Kaidai*-type I-boats, like the *Junsen* types, became more sophisticated in the interwar years while their designs continued to emphasize greater speed, size, and range. The Imperial Navy developed plans for building a new series of *Kaidai* submarines after the London Naval Treaty was concluded in 1930. Vessels built under the naval programs in the first part of the decade fell within the treaty limitations, but in December 1936, by which time Japan had withdrawn from the Washington and London naval agreements, the Japanese government assumed a new attitude toward the earlier arms limitation agreements and prepared to build more powerful vessels.

Six *Kaidai* Type 6a

The six boats of this type (*I-68* through *I-73*) were completed between 1934 and 1937; they featured the new Japanese diesel engine *Kansei honbu* (Naval Technical Bureau), abbreviated as *Kanpon*. Specifications: displacement of 1,785 tons surfaced, 2,440 submerged; length 336 feet; the two new *Kanpon* engines produced 9,000 horsepower; 23 knots surfaced, 8.25 knots submerged, with a cruising range of 14,000 nautical miles at 10 knots surfaced, 65 nautical miles at 3 knots submerged; six torpedo tubes; fourteen torpedoes; one single-mount 3.9-inch deck gun for the *I-68* through *I-70*, one single-mount 4.7-inch deck gun for the *I-71* through *I-73*; diving depth of 245 feet.

Two *Kaidai* Type 6b

With modifications made to Type 6a, there were only two boats of this type, the *I-74* and *I-75*. Completed in 1938, these boats were a foot longer (344 versus 343 feet), had a greater displacement (1,810 tons surfaced, 2,564 tons submerged), and had a different surfaced range (10,000 miles at 16 knots); otherwise, specifications were the same. (These old *Kaidai*-type hull numbers were increased by 100 each on 20 May 1942; thus the *I-74* was renamed *I-174*.)

Twenty New *Junsen* Type B

A new Type B, based in part on the *Kaidai* Type 6a, was laid down in January 1938. Like the *Junsen* types and the *Junsen*-based Type A1, Type B submarines carried aircraft. With the exception of the *I-17*, all boats of this type had the hangar and catapult forward.

Most of the mass-produced Japanese submarines were New *Junsen* Type B; there were twenty boats (*I-15, 17, 19, 21, 23,* and *25* through

Submarines of the Imperial Japanese Navy 25

The *I-71* (later named *I-171*) looking forward from the quarterdeck, April 1939. This submarine was completed at Kobe on 24 December 1935. (Naval Historical Center, NH 73055)

39). They were completed between 1940 and 1943, with seven of them in service before the attack on Pearl Harbor. Specifications: displacement of 2,584 tons surfaced, 3,654 tons submerged; length 350 feet; two diesel engines, 12,400 horsepower; 23.5 knots surfaced, 8 knots submerged, with a cruising range of 14,000 nautical miles at 16 knots surfaced, 96 nautical miles at 3 knots submerged; six torpedo tubes;

seventeen torpedoes; one single-mount 5.5-inch deck gun; diving depth of 330 feet.

Five New *Junsen* Type C

Completed in 1940 and 1941, the five boats of this type (*I-16, 18, 20, 22,* and *24*) also evolved from the *Kaidai* Type 6a and were noted for their heavy torpedo armament. Specifications: displacement of 2,554 tons surfaced, 3,561 tons submerged; length 350 feet; two diesel engines, 12,400 horsepower; 23.5 knots surfaced, 8 knots submerged, with a cruising range of 14,000 nautical miles at 16 knots surfaced, 60 nautical miles at 3 knots submerged; eight torpedo tubes; twenty torpedoes; one single-mount 5.5-inch deck gun; diving depth of 330 feet. This type did not carry a seaplane.

The maze of different types of large I-boats was continued during the war years. However, characteristics of various submarines started to change in response to the lessons and challenges of fighting a war with an industrially more powerful United States.

Ten New *Kaidai* Type A

The ten New *Kaidai* Type A boats (*I-176* through *I-185*) were launched in 1941–43, and the last one completed, the *I-183*, entered service in November 1943. These boats were improved *Kaidai* Type 6a submarines. Specifications: displacement of 1,833 tons surfaced, 2,602 tons submerged; length 346 feet; two *Kanpon* engines produced 8,000 horsepower; 23.1 knots surfaced, 8 knots submerged, with a cruising range of 8,000 nautical miles at 16 knots surfaced, 50 nautical miles at 5 knots submerged; six torpedoes tubes; twelve torpedoes; diving depth of 260 feet.

Three New *Kaidai* Type C1

The *I-46* through *I-48* were the only New *Kaidai* Type C1 submarines. Completed in 1944, these boats were similar to the New *Junsen* Type C. Specifications: displacement of 2,557 tons surfaced, 3,564 tons submerged; length 350 feet; two diesel engines, 11,000 horsepower; 23.5 knots surfaced, 8 knots submerged, with a cruising range of 14,000 nautical miles at 16 knots surfaced, 60 nautical miles at 3 knots submerged; eight 21-inch torpedo tubes; twenty torpedoes; diving depth of 330 feet.

One New *Junsen* Type A2

The *I-12* was the only New *Junsen* Type A2 boat. Launched in 1943, this submarine was similar to the New *Junsen* Type A1 boats, but its diesel engines had less horsepower. Other propulsion dimensions were also modified. Thus, the *I-12*'s two diesel engines produced 4,700 horsepower. Top surface speed was 17.7 knots; 6.2 knots submerged, with a cruising range of 22,000 nautical miles at 16 knots surfaced, 75 nautical miles at 3 knots submerged. Diving depth was 330 feet.

Two Modified New *Junsen* Type A

The *I-13* and *I-14* were further modifications of the New *Junsen* Types A1 and A2 submarines, the *I-9* through *I-12*. They were completed in late 1944 and early 1945. Specifications: displacement of 3,603 tons surfaced, 4,762 tons submerged; length 372 feet; two diesel engines, 4,400 horsepower; 16.7 knots surfaced, 5.5 knots submerged, with a cruising range of 21,000 nautical miles at 16 knots surfaced, 60 nautical miles at 3 knots submerged. These two larger submarines could carry two aircraft each; the hangar was on the centerline, and the conning tower was offset to port. A snorkel device was also fitted on these boats. Diving depth was 330 feet. The external surfaces of this class of submarine were covered with anechoic coating, an anti-sound-reflecting substance made of a resilient base of synthetic rubber and sand with a thin cement or plastic covering.

The *I-12* through *I-14* represented a new trend in wartime construction of large submarines. New models often emphasized greater operating radius; therefore, they had less powerful diesel engines and slower speeds. In spite of the doctrine insisting that submarines serve the interests of the battle fleet in a decisive battle, challenges to the submarine force during the war often illustrated the need for greater endurance—the high speeds of earlier designs appeared less important in most wartime conditions after 1943. Moreover, the new trend placed less strain on scarce wartime precision materials used to build engines.

Six New *Kaidai* Type B1

The six New *Kaidai* Type B1 boats (*I-40* through *I-45*) were completed in 1943 and early 1944, but with only slightly less powerful diesel engines (11,000 versus 12,400 horsepower.) Otherwise, these boats were similar to the mass-produced New *Junsen* Type B. In mid-1944, the *I-44* was the first Japanese submarine equipped with radar. Diving depth was 330 feet.

Three New *Kaidai* Type B2

The successor to the New *Kaidai* Type B1, i.e. Type B2, continued the general wartime trend with emphasis on less powerful machinery to allow greater endurance. The *I-54, I-56,* and *I-58* of this type were originally designed to carry an airplane, but late in the war, the *I-56* and *I-58* were modified to carry six suicide torpedoes (the *kaiten*) on deck. Their hangars and catapults were removed. Specifications: displacement of 2,607 tons surfaced, 3,688 tons submerged; length 350 feet; two diesel engines produced 4,700 horsepower; 17.7 knots surfaced, 6.5 knots submerged, with a cruising range of 21,000 nautical miles at 16 knots surfaced, 105 nautical miles at 3 knots submerged; six 21-inch torpedo tubes; nineteen torpedoes; diving depth of 330 feet.

Three New *Kaidai* Type C2

Another large submarine was the New *Kaidai* Type C2. The three boats of this type (*I-52, I-53,* and *I-55*) were completed in 1944; they were very similar to the earlier New *Kaidai* Type C1, yet, in keeping with the wartime construction trend, less powerful machinery was used to give these submarines greater range. Specifications: displacement of 2,564 tons surfaced, 3,644 tons submerged; length 350 feet; two diesel engines, 4,700 horsepower; 17.7 knots surfaced, 6.5 knots submerged, with a cruising range of 21,000 nautical miles at 16 knots surfaced, 105 nautical miles submerged at 3 knots; six 21-inch torpedo tubes; nineteen torpedoes; two single-mount 5.5-inch deck guns; diving depth of 330 feet.

Three *Sen-toku* Type

The *I-400*-class submarines were the largest submarines built by any nation prior to the close of World War II. This special submarine type

(*Sensuikan toku*, abbreviated *Sen-toku*) was first projected in 1942 when eighteen boats were planned, but only five were laid down, and three (*I-400* through *I-402*) were completed by the end of the war. These giant seaplane-carrying submarines were intended for attack on the Panama Canal or ports along the Pacific coast of the continental United States. Specifications: displacement of 5,223 tons surfaced, 6,560 tons submerged, with two cylindrical inner hulls side by side; length 394 feet; four Japanese-built MAN diesel engines, 7,700 horsepower; 18.7 knots surfaced, 6.5 knots submerged, with a cruising range of 37,500 nautical miles at 14 knots surfaced, 60 nautical miles at 3 knots submerged; eight 21-inch torpedo tubes; twenty torpedoes; one single-mount 5.5-inch deck gun, three triple-mount 1-inch antiaircraft guns; diving depth of 330 feet. Similar to the smaller *I-13* and *I-14*, the *Sen-toku* type had a larger hangar (110 feet long) and a powerful catapult for launching its three *Seiran* seaplanes, converted *Suisei* dive bombers. The *I-400* class was fitted with a snorkel, a device for supplying air to a submerged submarine. This particular type of snorkel was fitted on the starboard side of the conning tower. It was raised hydraulically and included exhaust and intake masts for auxiliary engines only. Like the *I-14*, the *I-400*-class submarines had an anechoic coating to impede sonar detection.

Three *Sen-taka* Type

Completed in February and May 1945, the *I-201*, *I-202*, and *I-203* were designed as fast submarines (*Sensuikan taka*, abbreviated *Sen-taka*) with a welded streamlined hull. Five other fast submarines were laid down, but they were incomplete at the end of the war. The *Sen-taka* submarines were modern attack boats capable of high underwater bursts of speed to break contact with enemy ASW ships. Specifications: displacement of 1,291 tons surfaced, 1,450 tons submerged; length 257 feet; two MAN diesel engines, 2,750 horsepower; 15.8 knots surfaced, 19 knots submerged, with a cruising range of 5,800 nautical miles at 14 knots surfaced, 135 nautical miles submerged at 3 knots or 17 miles at 19 knots; four 21-inch torpedo tubes; ten torpedoes. A snorkel was fitted on the *I-201* class; however, it had been completely installed and operated only on the *I-202* by the end of the war. The snorkel was in the after end of the conning tower fairwater and the mast could be raised about 10 feet. The induction through the snorkel cut into the ventilation supply line, so that no additional hull opening was required. This Japanese snorkel was unlike the most common German snorkel: a tube, hinged to the U-boat's deck, that was raised for use. No operational patrols were made by the *I-201*-class boats.

Supply and Transport I-Boats

Several additional types of I-boats designed largely for replenishing operations were built during the Pacific War. Only one support submarine (*Sensuikan ho*, abbreviated *Sen-ho*), the *I-351*, was completed by 1945, but this 3,512-ton vessel was of no consequence before it was sunk by an American submarine in July 1945.

Only slightly more promising was the Type D transport I-boat (*Sensuikan tei*, abbreviated *Sen-tei*). Eleven of the Type D1 (*I-361* through *I-371*) were completed in 1944. Specifications: displacement of 1,779 tons surfaced, 2,215 tons submerged; length 239 feet; two diesel engines, 1,850 horsepower; 13 knots surfaced, 6.5 knots submerged, with a cruising range of 15,000 nautical miles at 10 knots surfaced, 120 nautical miles at 3 knots submerged; diving depth of 250 feet. These boats were designed to carry two special 42-foot landing craft in wells aft of the conning tower. The landing craft were specially designed to resist water pressure when the submarine submerged. In addition to the submarine's complement, 110 landing troops could be carried, along with some 65 tons of cargo inside the hull and 20 tons outside. Several of the Type D1 boats were modified late in the war into *kaiten*-carrying submarines. Each submarine could carry five of these suicide torpedoes.

The *Sen-tei* Type D2 was a modified Type D1. The *I-372* (converted into a *kaiten* carrier) and *I-373* were the only two boats of this type completed before the war ended. Specifications: displacement of 1,926 tons surfaced, 2,240 tons submerged; length 241 feet; two diesel engines, 1,750 horsepower; 13 knots surfaced, 6.5 knots submerged, with a cruising range of 15,000 nautical miles at 10 knots surfaced, 100 nautical miles at 3 knots submerged; one single-mount 5.5-inch deck gun; diving depth of 330 feet. The Type D2 was fitted with a snorkel device and was originally designed to transport one landing craft, 110 tons of cargo, and 150 tons of gasoline.

* * *

The Japanese were most eager to develop the strategic strength of their submarine force after the I-RO-HA classification was introduced in 1924. In spite of the emphasis on the construction of large fleet-type and ocean-cruising I-boats, the other two classes of submarines—the RO and HA types—had a distinctive place in the Imperial Japanese Navy. Near the end of 1924, a group of older and smaller boats just beneath the I-boat classification was reclassified as the Medium Fleet type (*Kaigun chūgata,* abbreviated as *Kaichū*).

The first of the medium-size RO-boats were of foreign design, but modified and built in Japanese shipyards. The *RO-1* and *RO-2* were completed in 1920 and at the time were known simply by their hull numbers, *18* and *21,* respectively. They were of the Italian Fiat-Laurenti F1 design (717 tons surfaced). Further modification of this Italian design led to numbers *31, 32,* and *33;* they were completed in 1922 and renamed *RO-3, RO-4,* and *RO-5* in 1924. Thirty-seven other second-class submarines with surface displacements of 665–996 tons were launched or completed before the end of 1926. Their RO designations were *RO-11* through *RO-32, RO-51* through *RO-53,* and *RO-57* through *RO-68.*[22] These boats were used extensively for training during the interwar years. Most of them were scrapped by the late 1930s, although some of them saw combat in the Pacific War.

Because the Japanese were concentrating on the construction of large I-boats during the interwar years, only two RO-boats were built in the 1930s. They were experimental prototypes for a wartime type of submarine that, it was assumed, could be built rapidly in an emergency. These two boats were of a wholly Japanese design.

Two *Kaichū* Type 5

The *RO-33* and *RO-34* were completed in 1935 and 1937, respectively. Specifications: displacement of 940 tons surfaced, 1,200 tons submerged; length 239 feet; two diesel engines, 2,900 horsepower; 19 knots surfaced, 8.25 knots submerged, with a cruising range of 8,000 nautical miles at 12 knots surfaced; 90 nautical miles at 3.5 knots submerged; four 21-inch torpedo tubes; ten torpedoes; one 3-inch single-mount deck gun; diving depth of 250 feet. Improved RO designs were employed in the construction of two series of medium submarines during the war.

Eighteen *Kaichū* Type 6

Eighteen second-class *Kaichū* Type 6 submarines (*RO-35* through *RO-50* and *RO-55* and *RO-56*) were completed in 1943 and 1944. An improved *Kaichū* Type 5, the Type 6 boat was far more maneuverable than the large I-boats and was designed to accommodate the Type 95 torpedo, the submarine version of the so-called Long Lance. Specifications: displacement of 1,115 tons surfaced, 1,447 tons submerged; length 259 feet; two diesel engines, 4,200 horsepower; 19.7 knots surfaced, 8 knots submerged, with a cruising range of 5,000 nautical miles at 16 knots surfaced, 45 nautical miles at 5 knots submerged; four 21-inch torpedo tubes; ten torpedoes; diving depth of 260 feet.

Eighteen *Kaishō* Type

The *Kaigun shō* type (abbreviated *Kaishō*) was a small naval coastal and island defense submarine that could be built in about twelve months. The *RO-100* through *RO-117* were completed between 1942 and 1944. Specifications: displacement of 601 tons surfaced, 782 tons submerged; length 194 feet; two diesel engines, 1,100 horsepower; 14.2 knots surfaced, 8 knots submerged, with a cruising range of 3,500 nautical miles at 12 knots surfaced, 60 nautical miles at 3 knots submerged; four 21-inch torpedo tubes; eight torpedoes; diving depth of 250 feet. None of this type survived the war.

* * *

The HA type was the smallest of Japanese submarines; originally they were intended for coastal defense only. Like the RO-boats, the first of the HA-boats were of foreign design. Indeed, the *HA-1* and *HA-2*, known before 1924 as hull numbers 8 and 9, were British built. They displaced only 286 tons surfaced. Similarly, hull number 15 was French built and renamed *HA-10* in 1923. By that time there were only ten of these largely experimental craft in the Imperial Navy and all were stricken from the navy list by 1929.

The Japanese also constructed an experimental high-speed submarine in August 1938, at the time the world's fastest undersea craft. Based on experience with fast short-range midget submarines, number 71, as this one boat was designated, had the following specifications: displacement of 213 tons surfaced, 240 tons submerged; length 140 feet; one diesel engine, 1,200 horsepower; 13.2 knots surfaced, 21.2 knots submerged, with a cruising range of 3,830 nautical miles at 12 knots surfaced, 38 nautical miles at 7 knots submerged; three non-reloadable torpedo tubes; diving depth of 265 feet. Although this prototype sought to meet the Japanese requirements for local defense of outlying island bases, it was abandoned for various technical and operational reasons and scrapped in 1941. However, extensive evaluation of this craft produced valuable data for the design of the high-performance *I-201* and *HA-201* classes laid down in 1944 and completed in 1945.[23]

Seven *Sen-taka shō* Type

The small and fast *Sensui-taka shō* (abbreviated *Sen-taka shō*) submarines came late in the war; they were intended for coastal operations and defense of the home islands. Seven boats (*HA-201* through *HA-205* and *HA-209* and *HA-210*) were completed before surrender, but they were not fully fitted out. The specifications included a displacement of 377 tons surfaced, 440 tons submerged; length of 146 feet; one diesel engine, 400 horsepower; 10.5 knots surfaced, 13 knots submerged, with a cruising range of 3,000 nautical miles at 10 knots surfaced, 100 nautical miles at 2 knots submerged; two 21-inch torpedo tubes, four torpedoes; diving depth of 330 feet.

* * *

By the mid-1930s, the Japanese very secretly started to experiment with midget submarines. Known only by their hull numbers, *1* and *2*, the first two units each displaced 46 tons submerged, were 78 feet long, and were completed in 1934. With hulls shaped like a torpedo, no conning tower, and two muzzle-loaded torpedoes tubes forward, the experimental Type A midget submarines had an original submerged speed of 24 knots. Named "A-targets" (*Kō hyōteki*), their successor prototypes of 1936, the *HA-1* and *HA-2*, were fitted with a conning tower; thus, their submerged speed was reduced to 19 knots. The Type A (*Kō-Gata*) craft had no means of recharging its electric storage batteries; its range of operation was thereby limited to 80 nautical miles at 6 knots. Later wartime successive versions, Types B (*Otsu-Gata*) and C (*Hei-Gata*) and D (*Kōryū*), were fitted with a small diesel engine for surface propulsion and for charging the battery.

Japanese naval planners became convinced after extensive tests and exercises in the late 1930s that the midget A-targets could be used effectively against the U.S. battle line as part of the decisive battle strategy. "Included in these exercises," a former member of the wartime Japanese Naval Censorship Bureau has written, "were several 'push-off' experiments from the [seaplane tender] *Chitose*, which proved the feasibility of their utilization in long range operations."[24] In this manner the midget submarines were to reach the vicinity of the battle. According to plans, once launched through hinged doors at the stern of the seaplane tenders *Chitose* and *Chiyoda* (converted in 1941 to transport twelve boats each), the prewar midget submarines were to swarm about and destroy enemy capital ships. The *Mizuho* and *Nisshin* were similar midget submarine carriers. About fifty Type A midget submarines were secretly built at a special factory near Kure before the Pearl Harbor attack. However, specifically for that attack the five New *Junsen* Type C submarines—*I-16*, *I-18*, *I-20*, *I-22*, and *I-24*—were refitted to transport one midget A-target each to the entrance of Pearl Harbor. This is an example of how prewar plans had to be modified to accommodate the requirements of the bold air strike against American warships in the harbor.

No more than 100 of the Types A through C *Kō hyōteki* midget submarines were ever built, but many more of the Type D *Kōryū* were planned and built very late in the war. The *Kōryū* were intended for coastal defense. About 570 Type Ds were planned, and estimates projected building 180 boats each month. However, production was much more limited because of damage to shipyard shops during B-29 air raids. Nearly 115 boats were completed and more than 400 were under construction at the time of surrender in 1945. Specifications of the Type D boats included a displacement of 59 tons submerged; length of 86 feet; one diesel engine and generator; 8 knots surfaced, 16 knots submerged, with a cruising range of 1,000 nautical miles at 8 knots surfaced, 125 nautical miles at 2.5 knots submerged; two 18-inch muzzle-loaded torpedoes; diving depth of 330 feet.

The *Kairyū* was a much smaller version of the Type D *Kōryū* midget submarine. The *Kairyū* had a displacement of only 19 tons submerged and a length of 56 feet. While this craft was designed to carry two 18-inch torpedoes outside the pressure hull, the shortage of torpedoes in the summer of 1945 meant that some of these boats were intended for use as suicide weapons with a 270-pound explosive charge in the nose. Production of the *Kairyū* kept pace with that of the *Kōryū*—there were nearly two hundred of these midget submarines completed by September 1945 and a similar number under construction. Nevertheless, the war ended before the Type Ds and the *Kairyū* became fully operational.

* * *

A study of the characteristics and specifications of the various types of submarines in the Imperial Navy from 1905 through the Pacific War demonstrates that Japanese submarines were increasingly modern and effective weapons. They usually enjoyed a significant advantage in surface speed over their foreign counterparts, and the torpedoes they used were vastly superior. The designs of the various classes of undersea craft were always modern by the standards of the day, and some, particularly late in the Pacific War, were quite innovative. The designs all sought to meet the needs of national defense. Increasingly during the interwar years, however, as the role of submarines in plans for a decisive battle became more articulated, submarine designs were specifically tailored to the needs of the battle fleet. No matter what the size of undersea craft, from less than 100 tons for the midget A-targets to over 5,000 tons surfaced displacement for some of the larger I-boats, the chief purpose was largely the same, to help grind down the American battle fleet before the anticipated decisive battle. Only late in the war, particularly with the introduction of smaller and faster submarines, were designs changed somewhat when the fortune of the Combined Fleet had long eclipsed and the defense of the home islands was foremost and inescapable.

2

Weapons, Equipment, Personnel, and Shore Support for the Submarine Force

Various components of the submarine force will be investigated and discussed in this chapter, mainly up to the eve of the Pacific War. Analysis of their overall significance will largely be addressed in later chapters. While the quality of Japanese submariners and their equipment improved steadily early in the twentieth century, it was during the interwar period that the Japanese submarine force systematically developed into a thoroughly creditable arm of the Imperial Navy. All components of the navy's submarine force were designed to mold the best qualities of the fighting sailor and submarine matériel into a distinguished and quite viable silent service. Yet, the tremendous dimensions and overwhelming circumstances of Allied numerical force in the coming war would prove devastating to the Japanese submarine force.

Submarine Armament

Japanese submarines carried an array of weapons; some of them were unusual, but the traditional torpedo was the most important. Torpedoes in the Imperial Japanese Navy were originally foreign, purchased particularly from the Whitehead Company of Great Britain. The initial submarine torpedoes were 18 inches in diameter, but when a Vickers

"L" type submarine was contracted for in 1918, a new torpedo, 21 inches in diameter, was required. The new torpedo was called the Type 6 submarine torpedo, named after the sixth year of the reign of Emperor Taishō (1917).[1]

The types and performances of Japanese submarine torpedoes are outlined below.

Type 6 (1917): 21-inch diameter; 37 knots; range 7,000 meters (7,700 yards); weight of warhead 205 kilograms (451 pounds); kerosene fuel; compressed air drive.

Type 89 (1929): 21-inch diameter; 45 knots; range 5,500 meters (6,050 yards); weight of warhead 295 kilograms (649 pounds); kerosene fuel; compressed air drive.

Type 92 (1932): 21-inch diameter; 30 knots; range 5,000 meters (5,500 yards); weight of warhead 300 kilograms (660 pounds); battery drive.

Type 95 (1935): 21-inch diameter; 49 knots; range 9,000 meters (9,900 yards); weight of warhead 405 kilograms (891 pounds); kerosene fuel; pure oxygen drive. (The Type 95 torpedo was similar to the Type 93, sometimes called "Long Lance," used by cruisers and destroyers, but there was considerable danger in handling pure oxygen used by this torpedo in the confined quarters of a submarine. This torpedo had nearly three times the range of the Mark 14 torpedo carried by U.S. submarines.)

Type 95 (1935): aviation, 18-inch diameter; 42 knots; range 2,000 meters (2,200 yards); weight of warhead 200 kilograms (440 pounds); kerosene fuel; compressed air drive.

Significantly, an early decision was made in the Imperial Navy to introduce the 21-inch torpedo; obviously, a comparable innovation was essential in the design of torpedo tubes. Extensive experiments were conducted. Thus, hull number 46 (later named *RO-57*), the first Japanese submarine designed with 21-inch torpedo tubes, was laid down under the 1919–20 naval program and completed in July 1922. The 21-inch torpedo tube was introduced in U.S. Navy submarines at about the same time.

The various torpedo tubes in Japanese submarines after the adoption of the 21-inch torpedo are listed below.

Type 10 (1921) and Type 15 (1926): British patent, air ejection type.
Type 88 (1928): Japanese design, water ejection type; thus, no air bubble was released when a torpedo was fired.

Type 95 (1935): Japanese design, compressed-air ejection type, but little air was released when this torpedo was fired. Compressed air used for ejection was recovered inside the submarine's hull just before the tail of the ejected torpedo cleared the outer end of the tube. By using a two-stage air ejection valve, torpedoes could be fired at considerable depth and were sometimes fired at depths up to 40 meters (132 feet).

TORPEDO FIRING DATA COMPUTER AND PERISCOPE

The standard torpedo data computer (TDC) for Japanese submarines was the Type 91 (1931). This torpedo firing computer, located in the conning tower, was connected directly with the periscope, gyro compass, and ship's log. Basic operations included (1) pre-set data—torpedo speed, ship speed, firing interval; (2) input data before firing—target speed, target angle on the bow, target range, train angle of line of sight; and (3) output data—torpedo angle deviation, train angle of fire, torpedo run (range and time). Three improved types of TDCs were later developed: Type 92 (1932), Type 98 (1938), and Type 3 (1943). Japanese TDCs were generally quite reliable, but like similar equipment in U.S. Navy submarines in the 1930s, torpedo firing solutions were only as good as the input data provided to the TDC; estimates of a target's speed and range, in particular, depended largely on the "seaman's good eye."[2] Thus, throughout the war Japanese TDCs were incapable of *generating* the range or bearing, but they effectively solved the firing problem in accordance with the input data.

The most commonly used periscope was Type 88 (1928); Model 3 was employed for attack purposes while the Model 4 was for reconnaissance. Initially, the Type 88 periscope was 7 meters (23 feet) long; later it was lengthened to 10 meters (33 feet).[3]

DECK GUNS

Deck guns aboard Japanese-built submarines were originally converted from various types of guns used on certain surface ships. The 5.5-inch deck guns on ocean-cruising submarines were from the secondary battery of battleships or the main battery of light cruisers. Such large guns were thought appropriate because these large submarines were often expected to operate independently in enemy waters.[4] Thus, large guns were part of an integrated design of Japanese I-boats; moreover, the guns were conveniently available. The 4.7-inch deck guns on fleet-type submarines were from old destroyers. Some of these submarines had 4-inch single-mounted antiaircraft (AA) guns from old heavy cruisers. Coastal defense boats mounted a 3-inch AA gun. After the threat of air attack on Japanese boats became more serious during the war, many submarines started to carry 1-inch triple-mount or 1-inch single-mount AA automatic guns.

MINES

Only one type of mine was designed for submarine minelaying operations. The Type 88 (1928) contained explosives weighing 180 kilograms (396 pounds) and had a maximum arming depth of 350 meters (1,155 feet). As observed previously, there were only four minelaying submarines, the *Kirai sen* type. In addition to minelaying operations, these submarines were often employed for refueling flying boats or for transport purposes during the Pacific War. Japanese minelayers, like some American submarines in the late 1930s, used regular torpedo tubes from which mines were dropped to the ocean floor.

SPECIAL ATTACK (SUICIDE) WEAPONS

Unusual weapons carried by Japanese submarines included special attack (*tokkō*) suicide weapons produced late in the war, especially after the Japanese defeat at the battle for Leyte Gulf. (*Tokkō* is an abbreviation formed by combining *toku* and *kō*.) By October 1944, the *kaiten* project was given a high priority. Only one type of suicide torpedo was completed and became fully operational before the end of the war: a human torpedo, the *kaiten* (the word means revolution, but during the war this was understood to mean that impending defeat would be turned into victory). The original *kaiten* (Type 1) displaced 8.3 tons; its fuel was kerosene and pure oxygen; its operational range at 30 knots was about 4 miles (13 miles at 12 knots); and the weight of its warhead was 3,400 pounds. Two improved types of *kaiten* (Types 2 and 4) displaced about 18.3 tons each; they had a range of more than 8 miles at 30 knots or about 14–17 miles at 20 knots. The weight of the warhead was 3,400 pounds, although the Type 4 was designed to carry more explosives. Only a very limited number of the Types 2 and 4 were built before the end of the war, but nearly 400 Type 1 *kaiten* were completed. These suicide torpedoes were frequently launched from the deck of a submarine. However, *kaiten*-carrying I-boats did not become fully operational until early 1945.

PLANES FOR AIRCRAFT-CARRYING SUBMARINES

Also significant to Japanese submarine armament were specially designed airplanes. The specifications of two of these planes follow:

Aichi Aircrafts made the two-seater *Seiran* seaplane dive bomber for the *I-400* class of submarine, although it was never used operationally. Specifications include the following: 1,400 horsepower; maximum speed 255 knots; cruising range 600 miles; load capacity a 250-kilogram (550-pound) bomb. The capacity of this dive bomber could be increased to carry an 800-kilogram (1,760-pound) bomb by removing the main aircraft float.

The *Zero*-Type small reconnaissance plane also carried the designation E14Y1. The Bureau of Air (*Kōkū gijutsu shō*) built this very small, easy-to-handle, two-seater plane. The aircraft was officially adopted for use aboard submarines at the end of 1940. Specifications included the following: 300 horsepower; maximum speed 190 knots. Planes with the E14Y1 designation normally did not carry any armament, but they were sometimes fitted with a 7.7-millimeter machine gun. They had a relatively long cruising range of 570 miles, with a flight duration of approximately four hours. The Japanese navy placed a high value on these aircraft because of the greatly extended range of reconnaissance they provided.

Submarine Propulsion Systems

DIESEL ENGINES

Diesel engines used in Japanese submarines, like the designs of early submarines, initially came from a variety of foreign countries. However, the more reliable diesel engines from Germany were eventually adopted by the Japanese. The various diesel engines purchased by the Japanese are shown in the following list:

Schneider-Laubeuf, 2,000 horsepower (1915).
Vickers, 600 horsepower (1916).
Fiat-Laurent, 2,600 horsepower (1919).
Sulzer Type 2, single-action, two-cycle, air injection, 1,300 horsepower. The patent was purchased and the engine was made in Japan from 1918 to 1923 for use originally in the experimental *I-51*.
Sulzer Type 3, single-action, two-cycle, air injection, 3,400 horsepower. This diesel engine was built between 1921 and 1933 for use in various *Kaidai*-type submarines.

MAN Type 1 (*Maschinenfabrik Augsburg-Nürnberg*), single-action, four-cycle, air injection, 1,200 horsepower. This engine was made from 1925 to 1927 for use in the (*Kirai sen*) minelaying-type submarine.

MAN Type 2, single-action, four-cycle, air injection, 3,000 horsepower. This engine was used in several *Kaidai* and the early *Junsen*-type submarines.

After learning foreign diesel technology and gaining considerable experience with diesel engines, the Imperial Japanese Navy was able to make its own diesel propulsion systems for submarines. The Naval Technical Bureau (*Kansei honbu*), abbreviated *Kanpon*, took the initiative for designing and manufacturing diesel engines for use in Japanese submarines. Also, because of *Kanpon*'s guidance and assistance, private machinery companies started to build submarine engines. Japanese-designed diesel engines were quite sophisticated for the time and had several special features, including double action, non–air injection, and high power in various models. Some of the diesel engines originally designed and manufactured by the Japanese are listed below. The increasing size and sophistication of these engines were symptomatic of other modern developments taking place in the Japanese submarine force.

Kanpon Type 1a, Model 7, double-action, two-cycle, air injection, 4,500 horsepower. This engine was made in 1935 for the improved *Junsen*-type submarine.

Kanpon Type 1b, Model 8, double-action, two-cycle, air injection, 5,000 horsepower. Produced from 1933 to 1942, this engine was used in various *Kaidai* submarines.

Kanpon Type 1a, Model 10, double-action, two-cycle, air injection, 6,300 horsepower. This diesel engine was made from 1936 to 1938 for the *Junsen* submarines.

Kanpon Type 2, Model 10, double-action, two-cycle, air injection, 7,000 horsepower. This engine for the large *Junsen* submarines was produced between 1939 and 1943.

Mitsubishi Type 21, Model 8, single-action, four-cycle, non–air injection, 1,450 horsepower. This engine was made in 1935 for the *Kaichū* submarine.

Kanpon Type 22, Model 10, single-action, four-cycle, non–air injection, 2,600 horsepower. This engine was produced in 1943 to the end of the war for various submarines, but mainly for the *Kaichū* boats.

ELECTRIC MOTORS AND BATTERIES

Japanese submarines used a diesel-electric propulsion system. An electric generator that could also be used as a motor was connected by a shaft to the aft end of each of two diesel engines. Clutches separated the engines in one compartment from the generator-motors in the adjacent compartment. The shafts from the propellers were also connected to the generator-motors with clutches. When surfaced and under way on diesel power, all clutches were engaged. Batteries could also be charged in this mode by diverting some electrical current to storage cells or by running on the surface with one diesel engine applied to propulsion and one engaged solely for charging batteries. A similar operation was possible late in the war in those submarines fitted with the snorkel device, a subject discussed in a later chapter. When submerged and using battery power, the clutches between the diesel engines and generator-motors were disengaged. If batteries were charged while a submarine was at mooring, the clutches between the generator-motors and the propeller shafts were disengaged.

This propulsion system was extremely awkward; thus, Japanese submarines, large I-boats in particular, were generally slow diving not only because of their large hulls, but also because of the cumbersome linkage arrangement in the propulsion system. For example, in an emergency dive requiring swift action, the enginemen would first stop the engines. Then they would disengage two clutches between the pairs of generator-motors and the two diesel engines. An electrician would then switch the electrical circuits of the generators, thus changing their function into motors. Electrical current from the batteries would then rotate the armature of the motors, and engaged clutches would continue to force the propellers to turn.

Electric generators were direct current (DC) with a low 220-volt output. There were three types of motors: one (660 kilovolt-amperes) produced 900 horsepower for the *Kaidai* submarines; a second type (880 kilovolt-amperes) produced 1,200 horsepower for the *Junsen* and *I-400*-class submarines. The third type (440 kilovolt-amperes) produced 600 horsepower for the *Kaichū* submarines.

Batteries were the ebonite-clad type made by the Yuasa Battery Company. A group (118 lead-acid batteries) generated 240 volts. The number of groups in a submarine depended on the size and power requirements of the particular class of submarine. Associated with these batteries were hydrogen detectors and electrolytic-type ampere-hour meters—in late 1945, U.S. Navy investigators found these two Japanese instruments to be "far superior to those observed on German submarines."[5]

Submarine Personnel

OFFICER VOLUNTEERS

The physical and mental standards were high for the dedicated officers of the Japanese submarine force. Regular line and engineer officers for the submarine force were selected from young volunteer junior officers. In peacetime these officers were usually lieutenants junior grade having two or three years of service in surface ships. However, during the Pacific War the need for officers increased so sharply that volunteer officers from among ensigns with limited service experience were accepted; they were often very recent graduates from the Naval Academy at Etajima or from the Naval Engineering Academy at Maizuru. Nevertheless, the morale and fighting spirit of officers in the Japanese submarine force, in spite of tremendous destruction, never weakened during the war.

ENLISTED VOLUNTEERS

Enlisted men in the Japanese submarine force formed an elite group. They were selected from among young, highly rated volunteers who had the devotion and physical characteristics similar to those of submarine officers. In peacetime the volunteers selected for submarine service were mostly third class petty officers or leading seamen. They were usually torpedomen, minemen, sonarmen, signalmen, radiomen, enginemen, or electricians. During the war, enlisted volunteers were selected for service in submarines immediately after completion of only a basic rating course at a naval service school.

VOLUNTEERS FOR SPECIAL ATTACK (SUICIDE) UNITS

Volunteering for special attack suicide service was different from volunteering for the regular submarine program. The program leading to duty in a *tokkō* special attack unit started in the fall of 1944 after the battle for Leyte Gulf. Training was brief; there was a large number of volunteers from among professional submariners as well as from other groups of Japanese servicemen. These groups included (1) volunteer reserve officers who graduated from the Merchant Marine Academy, (2) reserve officer volunteers from among college students who completed basic reserve officer training, (3) enlisted petty officer aviation cadets who completed pre-flight training, and (4) unusual young enlisted men of exceptional ability and character. Indeed, *tokkō* mentality was sweeping the nation as a whole. The suicide tactics were rational, given the near-total destruction of Japan's conventional naval forces late in the war. The willingness of Japan's young men to sacrifice themselves was nearly the only, somewhat intangible, national resource left by the end of 1944.

OFFICER EDUCATION

Education courses for submarine officers were held at the Submarine School in Kure starting in the early 1920s, although the curriculum was not fully in place until 1924. The curriculum included torpedo tactics, submarine technical subjects, and engineering. There were four different courses of study for submarine officers:

"Submarine Command Course" (*Kōshu gakusei*). Students were selected from among lieutenant commanders or senior lieutenants for this most demanding course at Submarine School, which constituted a six-month course of instruction. Students completed the *Otsushu* curriculum (discussed below) for more junior officers in addition to the following main curriculum: (1) principles of submarine strategy and tactics, including torpedo attack techniques, (2) specific submarine ship-handling and navigation techniques, and (3) submarine hull construction and engineering.

"Submarine Officer Course" (*Otsushu gakusei*). Students were selected from among lieutenants and ensigns who completed the Advanced Torpedo Officer Course at the Torpedo Naval Service School. Successful students were usually eligible for later assignment as submarine executive officers. The curriculum for this four-month course of instruction included (1) submarine tactics, operations, and communications, (2) submarine diving techniques, and (3) submarine hull construction and engineering.

"Submarine Engineering Course" (*Kikan gakusei*). Students were selected from among engineering officers who completed the Advanced Engineer Course at the Marine Engineering Naval Service School. The curriculum for this six-month course of instruction included (1) specific submarine engineering, (2) submarine hull construction and trimming techniques, and (3) submarine tactics.

"Basic Submarine Officer Course" (*Sensuikan kōshū-in*). This course for young officer volunteers was two months long. Basic submarine technology and tactics were taught.

ENLISTED EDUCATION

"Submarine Operating Technique Training" (*Senkōjutsu renshūsei*). In this six-month course of instruction that emphasized basic submarine operating technology, the enlisted students were volunteers who completed their basic rating course, for example, for torpedoman's mate, at a naval service school. After serving in submarines for some time, these enlisted submariners became eligible to enroll in an advanced rating course at a naval service school.

TRAINING

Training for regular submariners was entirely on-the-job training aboard submarines. A few old submarines were assigned to the Submarine School for student training cruises during the course of instruction; nevertheless, experience in submarines was very limited before graduation. Thorough on-the-job training always took place on the submarine to which a Submarine School graduate was initially assigned, not as a result of brief cruises made while a student.

Training for officers and enlisted men for special attack (suicide) units after mid-1944 was different from that pursued by regular submariners; training facilities differed as well. Special training units were under the administrative control of special attack air training groups. The length of instruction varied with the assignment for either a midget submarine mission or a *tokkō* (special attack) weapon mission. There were two midget submarine units and one special attack weapon training unit: (1) midget submarine (*Kō hyōteki* or *Kōryū*): Ōurazaki, Kure; (2) midget submarine (*Kairyū*): Oppama, Yokosuka; and (3) *Kaiten*: Ōtsu-Jima, in Tokuyama Bay, Inland Sea.

Submarine Logistics Support

BASES AND FACILITIES

Before the war there were no base facilities designated specifically for the submarine force. Submarines, like surface ships, were supported by ordinary naval base facilities—the Navy Yard Submarine Department carried out repair and overhaul, and the Supply Depot took care of supply matters. At the beginning of the interwar period these navy yard and supply depot facilities for submarines were available only at the main naval bases of Yokosuka, Kure, Sasebo, and Maizuru. The growth of the submarine force and the threat of war necessitated the establishment of additional logistics support systems, particularly ones designed specifically to serve submarines. Thus, Submarine Base Support Units (*Sensuikan kichitai*) were organized at several naval bases. These units were organized more extensively after the outbreak of the war in 1941. In addition to the aforementioned four main naval bases, new advanced Submarine Base Support Units were organized at Ōminato (situated in Aomori Bay on the south side of Tsugaru Straits), Kwajalein, Rabaul, Penang, Surabaya, Palau, Cebu, and Truk. The logistics support provided by these bases included repair, overhaul, and service to hull machinery and weapons; supply of parts, goods, and food; and administrative assistance, welfare, and medical care for the crews.

NAVY YARDS AND PRIVATE SHIPBUILDING COMPANIES

Submarine construction required heavy industrial shipbuilding facilities with advanced technology; such facilities were relatively limited in the 1930s. Nonetheless, submarines were built at three navy yards and by a few private facilities before the war. These included (1) Navy Yards at Yokosuka, Kure, and Sasebo; (2) Mitsubishi Heavy Industry Company, Kōbe and Yokohama Shipyards; and (3) Kawasaki Heavy Industry Company, Kōbe Shipyard. After the outbreak of war, additional submarines, mainly medium and transport types and midget boats, were constructed at the following navy and private facilities: (1) Maizuru Navy Yard; (2) Mitsui Shipbuilding Company; (3) Uraga Shipbuilding Company; (4) Fujinagata Shipbuilding Company; and (5) Hitachi Manufacturing Company.

SUBMARINE TENDERS AND SUBMARINE SQUADRON FLAGSHIPS

It was common for a Japanese submarine squadron to include a surface ship, frequently a light cruiser, to serve as squadron flagship. Usually an additional surface vessel served as a submarine tender for support during special missions and activities. In the early days of the development of the submarine force, the tenders were converted from old troop transport ships captured from the Russians in the war of 1904–5. However, two new submarine tenders were built in 1923 and 1924: the *Jingei* ("Fast whale") (8,500 tons) and the *Chōgei* ("Long whale") (5,160 tons). In 1934, a more modern 10,000-ton tender, the *Taigei*

("Great whale"), was built. Subsequently, after Japan withdrew from the Washington Naval Treaty, the *Taigei* was converted into a light aircraft carrier and renamed the *Ryūhō*.[6] Submarine tenders were used mainly at advance submarine bases, for example, Kwajalein, Rabaul, and Truk. When the submarine fleet (the Sixth Fleet) was first organized in 1941, the light cruiser *Katori*, formerly a midshipmen training vessel, was assigned as the submarine force flagship. The *Katori* sometimes also served as a mission support tender, but mainly for carrying out administrative support.[7]

Naval Communication Systems

JAPANESE LAND COMMUNICATION STATIONS

Japanese submarine communication systems fell into two categories: (1) shore-to-submarine communications, in which transmissions were broadcast from network control stations, and (2) submarine-to-shore communications, in which submarine transmissions were made to the nearest network control station. In the latter instance an original message would be relayed to the addressee.[8]

Radio communications were intricate and, in general, not fully reliable for communicating with individual submarines on distant war patrols. Very low frequency (VLF) broadcast waves could be used only during the daytime, and transmissions were always weak. High frequency (HF) transmissions could be made during the day and night. Broadcasting took place at even hours of the day; to ensure their receipt during the night, even hours were used for retransmitting earlier daytime messages.

The chief network control and broadcast transmitting land station was the Tokyo Communication Group, which used both VLF and HF. However, radio relay stations had to be employed for HF messages. There were several local land communication HF relay stations in service at various stages of the war. The chief relay stations were (1) the Sixth Communication Group at Kwajalein and the First Communication Group at Saigon, which were active from December 1941 to February 1942; (2) the Fourth Communication Group at Truk and the Tenth Communication Group at Singapore, which were used from March 1942 to June 1944; (3) the Third Communication Group at Saipan (destroyed by U.S. bombardment by mid-June 1944) and the Tenth Communication Group at Singapore, which were used in June and July 1944; and (4) the Kure Communication Group, operating from July 1944 to the end of the war.[9] In an effort to reduce the distances of communications, these various stations were generally established as close to the zones of combat as possible.

SUBMARINE COMMUNICATIONS

Restrictions placed on submarine communications were so severe that they sometimes inhibited the effectiveness of submarine operations, as will be discussed in later chapters. For the most part, however, communications aboard submarines were limited to receiving broadcasts and to transmitting a submarine's own messages to land communication stations. It was essential, in order to avoid D/F detection, to keep submarine transmissions to shore networks as brief as possible. Acknowledgment of the receipt of a submarine's message was made by the land communication station's rebroadcast of the original message. The sending of specific receipts or the broadcasting of recognition signals was usually prohibited because of the dangers of being detected by the enemy.

Submarines were permitted to send radio messages for no more than five minutes in any particular transmission. Standing instructions also advised submarine skippers that soon after such a transmission, their submarine should move swiftly out of the immediate vicinity to avoid possible detection resulting from enemy direction finding (D/F) operations.

Japanese submarines carried a considerable variety of modern communication equipment. Most submarines were equipped with Type 99, Special Model 3 or 4, LF and HF transmitters; Type 92, VLF receivers; and ordinary all-band receivers. VLF antennae were used; they were either the rectangular frame type or the type fixed to the submarine bridge structure. Japanese submarine radio equipment, like that in American submarines, received various improvements throughout the war, but no fundamental advances were made.[10]

Various codes were used for submarine radio communications. The "D" code was used until late June 1942; thereafter, the "RO" code was used for ordinary operations. The "OTSU" code was used during naval combat, and the "BO" code was used for various local operations.[11] These and various other Japanese military and diplomatic codes and ciphers were largely solved by American and British cryptanalysts during the war.

Radar was probably the most dramatic wartime development for submarines. But not until the final stage of the war, starting in mid-1944, were some Japanese submarines fitted with the new electronic warning equipment. Although breakdowns were frequent and the systems proved generally unreliable, one type of air and surface-search radar included electric countermeasure and warning devices. Nevertheless, the Japanese radar program as it applied to the submarine force was unsuccessful.

As the Japanese navy sought to develop more sophisticated radar apparatus, much assistance was received from Germany, particularly in 1942–44, when numerous radar sets, cases of parts, and blueprints of electronic equipment reached Japan in blockade runners. However, facilities for producing essential high-quality radar vacuum tubes in Japan were extremely limited and inadequate to meet military requirements. Japanese scientists estimated in 1945 that the life expectancy of radar vacuum tubes was no more than a month of continuous service.[12]

Development of the Submarine Force

The Japanese submarine force was always plagued with serious problems. There was no independent submarine organization in the Imperial Japanese Navy until the Sixth Fleet was organized for the submarine force in 1941. Previously, the largest submarine organization was the squadron, which was part of the fleet organization—the First Submarine Squadron was part of the First Fleet, and the Second Submarine Squadron was part of the Second Fleet. The flag officers for the submarine force were the two squadron commanders and the superintendent of the Submarine School. This troika consisted of three rear admirals who formed the leadership for tactical development of the Japanese submarine force.[13]

There were several submarine staff officers at various senior commands. For example, submarine staff officers were assigned to the Operations Section of the Operations Department, Navy General Headquarters, the Bureau of Naval Affairs of the Navy Ministry, and the Combined Fleet Headquarters. The rank of these submarine staff officers was usually no higher than commander; the submarine officer's influence at the senior commands was thus slight. These officers were regarded as mere liaisons whose chief duty was to arrange for the adjustment of submarine tactical development to suit the needs of the surface fleet.[14]

The lack of an effective voice with which to represent submarine interests was a major explanation for why the Imperial Navy failed to promote sound tactical development of the submarine force. Of course, the organizational structure that relegated submarine matters to a position of insignificance was a product of the battleship orientation of the Imperial Navy. Even in 1942, after it became apparent that the submarine force did not achieve its prewar expectations, the Sixth Fleet had little success in coming to grips with the problems that had long plagued aspects of its development. The Sixth Fleet commander did not have the full range of command prerogatives, nor were all submarines necessarily under his command. The tactical development of the Japanese submarine force remained hampered throughout the war.

SUBMARINE TECHNOLOGY

The Seventh Department of the Naval Technical Bureau (*Kansei honbu*) was responsible for submarine technological development, but its authority was limited to matters concerning submarine hulls and hull fittings. The bureau had to work with several different naval divisions. These included the Third Department when weapons were under consideration, the Fifth Department for machinery concerns, and the Bureau of Naval Aviation (*Kaigun kōkū honbu*) for plans for aircraft-carrying submarines. Such a troika system for the technological development of submarines was as inefficient as the troika for the tactical development of the submarine force, especially when basic concepts of design and supervision of construction were the concern. To make matters worse, the troika arrangement also applied to lower administrative levels. For example, for the construction of submarine hulls and hull fittings, the Submarine Department of the Navy Yard was involved, but the Torpedo or Gunnery Departments also participated if weapons were the topic. Furthermore, only the Machinery and Electrical Departments had authority concerning machinery. Obviously, such complicated, uncontrollable systems were inefficient; naval administrative weaknesses had a direct impact on submarine technology, but the navy high command failed to make appropriate corrections.

These chaotic systems lasted throughout the war, significantly weakening the submarine construction program. Rather than concentrating on the construction of a few tried and true submarines, the construction of several different types of submarines was undertaken late in the war when industrial productivity was overtaxed and greatly reduced. Moreover, the availability of good construction material was sharply reduced and the quality of construction was poorer than during earlier times.

The Imperial Navy placed various submarine construction orders with navy and private contractors, depending on their shipyard capabilities and the priority of other outstanding building programs. At the beginning of 1945, for example, the navy halted construction of merchant and larger naval vessels and ordered instead the wholesale building of a new type of five-man midget submarine called the Kōryū (see chapter 1). Over 500 of the boats were scheduled to be built by the end of September 1945, and 180 boats each month thereafter. Contracts were placed with eleven different navy and private shipyards, but production was extremely limited, in part because of the damage of Allied air raids. The performance of the Mitsubishi Nagasaki Works illustrates the limited production: When the war ended, this shipyard had completed only 3 Kōryū submarines, 69 other boats were half completed, and the remainder were in various stages of prefabrication.[15]

ESTABLISHMENT OF THE BUREAU OF SUBMARINES (KAIGUN SENSUIKANBU)

The many problems of the Japanese submarine force worsened later in the war. Some submarine officers advocated reform. Represented by Rear Adm. Shigeaki Yamazaki, superintendent of the Submarine School, they emphasized the need for establishing the Bureau of Submarines. Although there was some objection by conservatives, the new bureau was in fact established in May 1943. Vice Adm. Shigeyoshi Miwa served as the bureau's first chief; later Admiral Yamazaki was appointed to the post. The bureau was mainly responsible for (1) planning for submarine readiness, (2) research and planning for tactical and technological development, and (3) liaison with senior commands. The reformers had good intentions, and the new bureau held much promise, even so late in the war, a year and a half after the attack on Pearl Harbor. Nevertheless, the new Bureau of Submarines lacked sufficient power to implement the needed reforms, a condition made more difficult by the pressures of war when senior bureaus could make stronger claim to limited war materials. If old problems could not be resolved in good times, there was very little chance that improvement could be instituted in bad times; thus, there was no resolution to these administrative problems in the last two years of the war.

* * *

The Japanese submarine force has frequently been misrepresented in Western literature. Overall, against their respective enemies, Japanese submarines were not as effective as German U-boats in the Atlantic and American submarines in the Pacific. Nevertheless, Japanese submarines commanded a lot of attention and respect during the war, and American intelligence, in particular, was wary of their prowess. A 1944 Office of Naval Intelligence (ONI) report cautioned that although to date "the Japanese submarine fleet has not been employed as a major tactical weapon," the future appeared ominous. "As allied forces advance upon the inner defense ring of the Japanese home islands and their supply lines become further extended, it is anticipated that the submarine will become one of Japan's most important defensive weapons."[16] American naval analysts clearly appreciated the potential of the Japanese submarine force more than most strategists in the Imperial Japanese Navy.

After August 1945, U.S. investigators rushed to interrogate Japanese submariners and took several of their submarines, including three aircraft-carrying boats—*I-400, I-401,* and *I-14*—and the high-speed *I-200* class of submarine, to Pearl Harbor for thorough study. Several of their technological features, including the snorkel, were of much interest to the U.S. Navy.[17]

Japanese submarine technology was advanced enough by wartime standards, and Japan's professional, highly dedicated submariners were obviously brave enough to do their duty. However, the Allies achieved a huge superiority in numbers and resources that weighed heavily on Japan. Thus, the attrition of war gradually wore down the Imperial Japanese Navy, and the submarine force, always wedded to the interests of the battle fleet, was an early victim and notable sacrifice.

3

War in the Pacific and Submarine Operations, 1937 to Mid-1942: Successes and Missed Opportunities

The terms of war were not ideal from the point of view of the Japanese submarine force, although there had been several decades of painstaking development of submarine matériel, personnel, institutions, and strategic and tactical doctrines. The decisive battle was pivotal in contingency planning, and such a confrontation was always emphasized in elaborate fleet maneuvers of the Japanese navy in the 1930s. Predictably, the role of submarines in these maneuvers conformed to the needs of the battle fleet. During the decade of Japan's military advances in China, the navy as a whole had only limited opportunities to gain combat experience, whereas the submarine force missed out almost entirely on the chance to carry out war patrols.

* * *

The Sino-Japanese War spread to Shanghai by August 1937, after beginning in a clash between the Japanese and Chinese forces at the Marco Polo Bridge near Peking a month earlier. Inevitably, Japanese naval forces became involved, but the small Chinese navy was no match for the powerful naval forces of Japan. Most Japanese naval combat involvement focused on operations carried out by the Navy Special Landing Force, the so-called Japanese marines. Fleet Air Force operations supported army and marine operations. Thus, the navy's combat role was small and military conditions in the war practically excluded submarines, although two submarine squadrons were assigned to China waters.[1]

Submarines carried out only a few patrols during the war with China. The tenders *Taigei* and *Chōgei* of Submarine Squadron 1 and six ocean-cruising boats (*I-1* through *I-6*) were assigned to the Third Fleet (China Theater Fleet) in September 1937. Their mission was to patrol and blockade the central and southern Chinese coasts. The squadron was based at Hong Kong until the fall of 1938. Similarly, boats of Submarine Squadron 3 patrolled and blockaded the northern Chinese coast.[2] Four minelaying submarines (*I-21* through *I-24*) of this squadron were organized around the light cruiser flagship *Kuma* in December 1937. Attached to the newly organized Fourth Fleet, Submarine Squadron 3 was based at Tsingtao until the fall of 1938.

Although Japanese submarines were not heavily involved in the war, surface ships attached to the submarine force saw considerable transport service. Since the Imperial Japanese Army required reinforcements in northern China, many different types of vessels, including submarine tenders, were engaged in a major sea lift to transport troops. The submarine tenders *Chōgei* and *Jingei*, escorted by the light cruiser flagship *Isuzu*, participated in extensive troop transport operations between Japan and Tsingtao in 1937.

The legacy of very limited experience in 1937–38 was of no import to submarine force operations in the next war, which started in December 1941. Indeed, the ethos of military furor that gripped the Japanese nation during the Sino-Japanese War served mainly as a psychological backdrop for the young but proud submarine force. Moreover, all Japanese submarines were withdrawn from Chinese waters in December 1938 as part of the Japanese government's effort to mitigate international tension over the war. Thus, it was a highly inexperienced Japanese submarine force that was thrown into a catastrophic and demanding war in late 1941. The unexpected hardships of the reality of combat in a prolonged war proved devastating.

The Japanese advance into Southeast Asia, in particular, produced rapidly increasing tension between the United States and Japan after September 1940, so that by the summer of 1941, with the Japanese military buildup throughout French Indochina and the American trade embargo against Japan, the Tokyo government made the fateful decision for war with the United States. Adm. Osami Nagano, chief of Navy General Staff, argued convincingly that time was running out for

Japan. The embargo would progressively weaken Japan, and the estimated tonnage of U.S. Navy ships on the launching ways in 1941 and future construction of American warships would jeopardize and eventually overwhelm Japanese hegemony in the western Pacific. With this manifest dilemma before Japanese strategists, Adm. Isoroku Yamamoto, commander in chief, Combined Fleet, proposed an initial air strike against the American battle fleet at Pearl Harbor, where its headquarters had been moved from San Diego in July 1941. The objective was to damage U.S. forces sufficiently to keep them temporarily on the defensive and to prevent the American battle fleet from intervening with the Japanese southern advance.

Long-range prewar strategy was suddenly upset. The decisive battle and the strategy of attrition against the American fleet had remained largely unchanged since the late 1920s. The chief innovation came in the 1940 plan, when the site of the projected battle was moved nearly 2,000 miles eastward from the Marianas to the Marshalls.[3] An entirely new role for submarines was hammered out. In general, more than twenty submarines were to precede the carrier strike force to Hawaiian waters and there check on possible American fleet movements. If warships were sighted, the submarines would track, but not fire on, the ships until the start of the air strike. Thereafter, the submarines were to lurk outside of Pearl Harbor and between the Hawaiian Islands and the U.S. mainland to attack any warships attempting to escape from the air strike, to finish off any damaged ships trying to limp back to mainland ports, and to prevent any reinforcements from reaching Oahu.

Hawaiian Waters

With high risks but great expectations, Admiral Yamamoto issued the operational orders on 5 November 1941 for the air assault on Pearl Harbor. The operational plan included an elaborate command structure for the powerful armada (see appendix 2).

THE DEPLOYMENT OF SUBMARINES OUTSIDE OF PEARL HARBOR

Submarines sortied from their home ports in Japan between 11 and 21 November; many of them sailed via Kwajalein, where they came under American intelligence surveillance. On 26 November U.S. Navy intelligence estimated that there was gathered "probably one-third of the [Japanese] submarine fleet."[4] All submarines were on station in

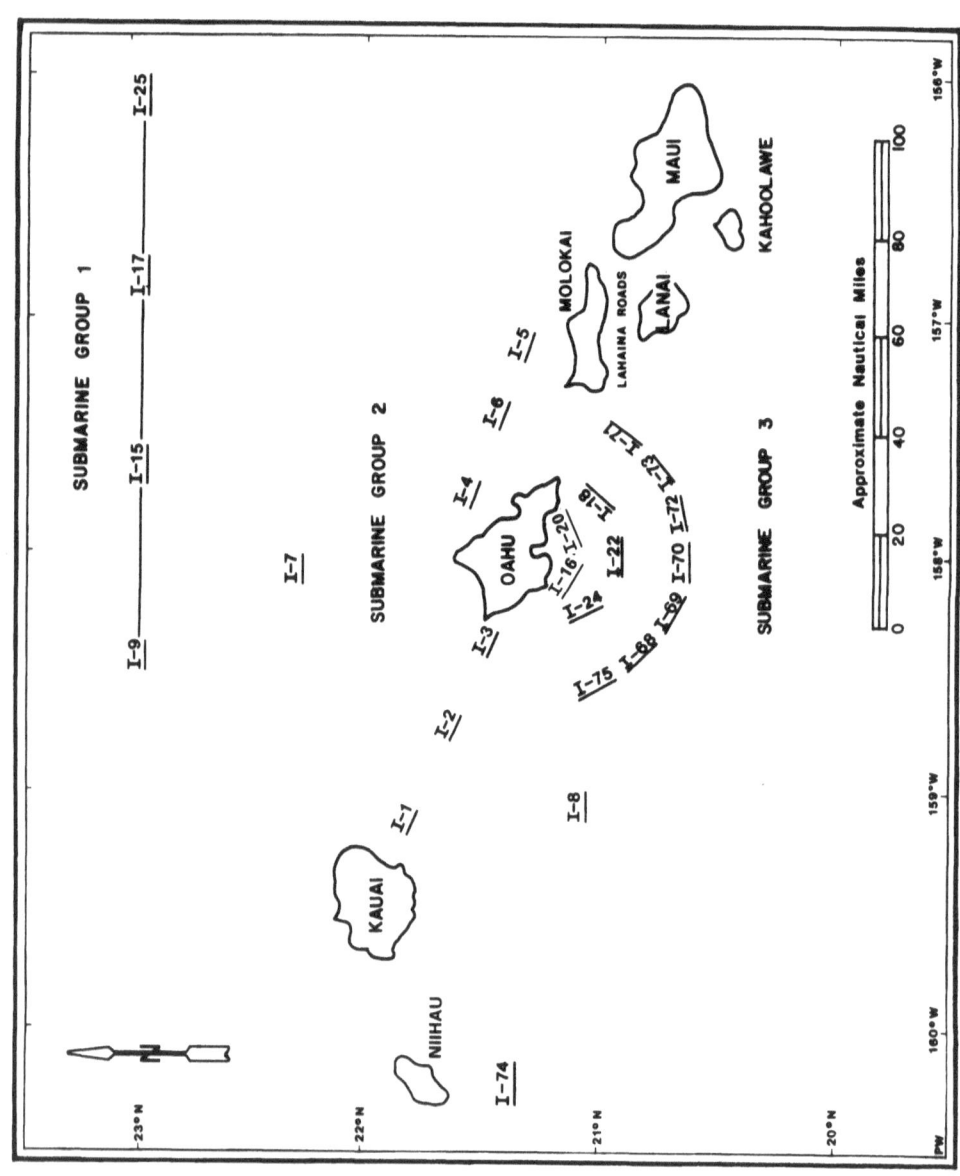

War in the Pacific, 1937 to Mid-1942   57

Hawaiian waters by "X" day minus one (6 December, Western Hemisphere).[5] (See map 1 for the disposition of Japanese submarines in Hawaiian waters at the time of the attack.)

Failure was prevalent, and the reasons are several. U.S. Navy antisubmarine warfare (ASW) forces were effective against the Japanese. For example, the *I-68*, some 30 miles from the entrance to Pearl Harbor, came under heavy depth-charge attack and suffered minor damage. The *I-69*, after launching an unsuccessful torpedo attack against a cargo ship on the night of 7 December, was near Barbers Point in southern Oahu when the submarine became caught in what the Japanese thought was an antisubmarine net.[6] (The *I-69* probably became entangled in some sort of stray American tow line or was caught in a harmless drill minefield used by U.S. Navy minesweepers for practice against dummy mines.) The submarine was also heavily depth charged. Capt. Nobuki Nakaoka, commander of Submarine Division 12, on board the *I-69*, recalled later that a depth-charge explosion under the hull produced a very hard shock, and the boat had to dive as deeply as possible. Leaks were dangerous, and it was impossible to use the ejection pump at such great depths. The Japanese sailors were determined to fight to the end, but they also feared defeat. Thus, they armed demolition explosives before making a final attempt to escape from their entanglement. At a depth of 250 feet, the *I-69* slipped out of the net by going full astern and blowing main tanks. The *I-69* was lucky to escape undetected on the surface after some 40 hours of struggle.[7]

Other boats of the Third Submarine Group were also depth charged and had little success. The *I-72* sank a small cargo vessel some 250 miles south of Oahu on 8 December, and the *I-75* made a similar claim 100 miles south of Kauai on 17 December. Having caused no damage to U.S. warships, plagued by failure and missed opportunities, the remaining submarines of the Third Submarine Group left Hawaiian waters on 17 December to return to Kwajalein.

Some fourteen other Japanese submarines patrolling in Hawaiian waters were no more effective. The three submarines assigned originally as an advance screening unit for the Carrier Strike Force joined four

Map 1. (*Opposite page*) Japanese submarines in Hawaiian Waters, December 1941. (Source: Japan, Bōeichō Bōeikenshūjo Senshibu, ed., *Sensuikan shi* (History of submarines), Senshi Sōsho (War history series), vol. 98 [Tokyo: Asagumo Shimbunsha, 1979], 95)

ocean-cruising submarines of the First Submarine Group to continue patrol operations in Hawaiian waters. Of these seven submarines, only the *I-9*, the flag submarine of Rear Adm. Tsutomu Satō, commander of Submarine Squadron 1, sank a cargo vessel—the U.S. steamer SS *Lahaina* (5,645 tons)—several hundred miles northeast of Oahu on 11 December. The seven older ocean-cruising submarines of the Second Submarine Group also continued patrols in Hawaiian waters until 11 January 1942. The flag submarine, *I-7,* launched its seaplane for a completely successful dawn reconnaissance flight around Pearl Harbor on 17 December. This flight occurred in spite of tightened defenses of Pearl Harbor. Thus, the high command in Tokyo received a full report of the damage caused by the air attack. In another minor action, the *I-4* sank one cargo vessel, the 4,858-ton Norwegian motorship *Hoegh Merchant,* off Makapuu Point, Oahu, on 14 December.

Japanese submarines in Hawaiian waters were plagued by mishaps and failure. Naval planners anticipated that the nine fleet-type submarines of the Third Submarine Group would have the best chance to attack the enemy. With their vantage point some 40 miles from Pearl Harbor, these submarines formed a dense line capable of concentrated attack on American warships off Oahu. The chief of staff to Admiral Yamamoto when the Pearl Harbor attack was planned noted that he "expected that more damage would be inflicted by submarine attacks, which would be continued over a longer period, than by the air attacks, which would be of comparatively short duration."[8] Given prewar expectations, the submarines' failure in early December was particularly surprising and disappointing to the Japanese high command.

Part of the reason for the failure of the I-boats in Hawaiian waters concerned the manner of directing operations from afar. The commander of the Sixth Fleet, Vice Adm. Mitsumi Shimizu at Kwajalein, filled the air each night shortly before the air strike with radio messages to his submarines around the Hawaiian Islands. A U.S. Navy intelligence officer, then stationed at Pearl Harbor, wrote twenty-five years later that "port authorities in Hawaii were thus made conscious of the magnitude and to some extent the location of the Japanese submarine menace. They were consequently cautious in routing ships, and this had some bearing on the Japanese lack of success."[9]

Capt. Kyūgorō Shimamoto, commander of Submarine Division 7, criticized submarine operations in Hawaiian waters at the outset of the war because there was no basic and coordinated plan of action. For example, when a submarine sighted an enemy ship and was ordered to give chase and attack if possible, the submarine's originally assigned area of patrol was left unguarded while the attack was being pursued. Such operations were particularly ineffective if the submarine's top speed did not enable it to overtake its prey quickly. Moreover, Captain Shimamoto lamented the fact that Japanese submarines always had to contend with strong enemy ASW operations.[10]

Another submarine operation was carried out far from Hawaii, although still associated with the main attack. Several days before the attack on Pearl Harbor, two submarines were involved in elaborate air reconnaissance operations. (The Japanese made a determined effort, particularly during the first year of the war, to utilize submarine-borne aircraft in reconnaissance operations—see appendix 3.) Observing strict radio silence, the *I-10* reconnoitered Suva, Fiji, where its seaplane was lost on 30 November. Then the *I-10* proceeded to Pago Pago, Samoa, arriving by 4 December. This I-boat sank the 4,473-ton Panamanian motorship *Donerail* in the South Pacific on 10 December before sailing to the west coast of the United States. The other submarine of the Reconnaissance Unit, *I-26*, sank the SS *Cynthia Olsen*, a 2,140-ton lumber freighter, about 900 miles northeast of Hawaii on 8 December. But these results were extremely modest for the grand north-south sweep of these two submarines.

THE SPECIAL ATTACK UNITS—MIDGET SUBMARINES

Five ocean-cruising submarines, each with a piggyback midget submarine Type A Target (*Kō hyōteki*), did not become part of the grand plans to attack U.S. forces until the fall of 1941. The five submarines were on their assigned stations near the entrance to Pearl Harbor on the night of 6 December (Hawaii time). In spite of trouble with the gyro compass of the *I-24*'s two-man midget submarine, its commanding officer, Ens. Kazuo Sakamaki, was determined to disembark in his little submarine as scheduled. The other four midget submarines were more easily launched before dawn on the day of the air attack. Nevertheless, almost no information was received from the five midget submarines after they sortied. Lt. (jg) Masaji Yokoyama in the *I-16*'s midget submarine reported *"tora, tora, tora"* (meaning surprise attack succeeded) at 2241 on 7 December. Thus, Japanese submariners believed that an explosion sighted near midnight was caused by a torpedo launched from Yokoyama's midget submarine. But this is not con-

A two-man Japanese midget submarine found in June 1960 in about 75 feet of water some 2,000 yards off Keehi Lagoon near the entrance to Pearl Harbor. The submarine was depth-charged in December 1941. (USN photograph, USS *Bowfin* Submarine Museum & Park)

firmed by U.S. Navy evidence; moreover, it is obvious that the error-riddled operation was poorly executed and that exaggerated reports of success were often based on modest evidence.

All five midget submarines were lost in spite of the efforts of the parent submarines. The five large I-boats patrolled the waters south of Oahu during the day of the air attack on Pearl Harbor; then they shifted to the area south of Lanai, which was the designated area for recovery of the midget submarines. The area was searched in vain before the parent submarines left Hawaiian waters en route to Kwajalein on the night of 11 December.

Ensign Sakamaki's midget submarine from the *I-24*, plagued by a defective gyro compass, wrecked on a reef—he was captured by U.S. service men from Bellows Field, Oahu.[11] Thus, Sakamaki became the first Japanese prisoner of war of the United States; his crewman drowned in the surf.[12] The submarine was used as a display to sell war bonds during a nationwide tour of more than forty states and some two thousand cities. This one little boat was responsible for raising enough money to pay for the repairs at Pearl Harbor necessary in the aftermath of the Japanese attack.[13]

The other midget submarines were no more lucky. The second midget submarine was rammed and depth charged inside Pearl Harbor by the destroyer USS *Monaghan* (DD-354) during the air attack. Within two weeks during the cleanup of the harbor, the badly mangled little submarine was raised, taken to the nearby submarine base, and soon rolled into a hole where a new pier was being built. In June 1960, a third midget submarine was found at the bottom of Keehi Lagoon outside of Pearl Harbor in about 75 feet of water by a U.S. Navy scuba diver. After its bow, which contained two torpedoes, was removed and disposed of at sea, the rest of the hull was given to the Japan Maritime Self-Defense Force.[14] The midget craft, with a new bow attached, remains at the Etajima Navy Museum as a memorial. The other two midget submarines remain lost.[15] The failure of the five midget submarines to achieve the results anticipated by the high command was the first in a series of submarine force failures.

THE RACE TO SHIFT PATROL AREAS

Shortly after the Pearl Harbor attack, Japanese submarines in Hawaiian waters started to receive radically different operational orders. This was the beginning of a pattern of a long series of similarly confusing orders. Unforeseen circumstances forced the high command to place new and unexpected operational demands on submarines.

The Japanese high command was greatly disappointed that U.S. Navy carriers were not inside Pearl Harbor on the morning of the air attack; thereafter, no opportunity was missed to catch the elusive enemy carriers. Submarines bore the brunt of this largely haphazard pursuit.

The Japanese were encouraged by new information reported by the *I-9* on 9 December. The I-boat sighted an American carrier group east of Oahu on that date and reported: "Sighted *Lexington* type carrier and two cruisers in east channel off Oahu: course—060 degrees; speed—20 knots; appears to be proceeding to the West Coast." Because of this message and because submarines had not been effective in Hawaiian waters, Adm. Mitsumi Shimizu, commander, Sixth Fleet, aboard his flagship anchored at Kwajalein, received the first evidence from his own submarines that part of the U.S. Navy forces, particularly the aircraft carriers, had survived the air assault. He assumed that they had already sortied and were en route to the safety of west coast ports on the U.S. mainland. This conformed to the scenario anticipated in recent prewar Japanese planning. Thus, Shimizu decided to give chase and to shift the submarine patrol area to the east.[16]

New orders were issued from Admiral Shimizu's flagship. The First Submarine Group, along with two submarines of the Reconnaissance Unit, the *I-10* and *I-26*, were instructed to pursue the enemy eastward and patrol offshore of the mainland. With a few additional submarines the total number of Japanese submarines patrolling off the west coast reached nine by 19 December. The patrol areas stretched from Cape Flattery, Washington, in the north, to San Diego, California, in the south. However, Japanese submarines were acting on erroneous information about U.S. Navy operations in the immediate aftermath of the

The midget submarine rammed and depth-charged by the USS *Monaghan* (DD-354) in December 1941, recovered and here about to be used as filling for a new sea wall at Pearl Harbor. Visible in the background are sections of Kazuo Sakamaki's midget submarine, which had wrecked on a reef some distance away near Bellows Field. Soon afterward, this craft was assembled and displayed throughout the United States for war bond drives until 1945. (USN photograph, USS *Bowfin* Submarine Museum & Park)

air attack at Pearl Harbor. The carrier group sighted was the USS *Enterprise* (CV-6) and escorts on ASW patrol. There was no eastward evacuation of U.S. carriers, as Shimizu had assumed.[17] Indeed, U.S. carrier strength in Hawaiian waters was soon to increase.

The *I-70* was among the submarines ordered to pursue a U.S. carrier and other warships "fleeing" eastward to the safety of the U.S. mainland. The carrier group referred to in the Japanese report was likely Task Force 8, built around the *Enterprise*. The fast carrier entered Pearl Harbor near sunset on 8 December and left after refueling a little more than nine hours later to patrol north of Oahu. On 10 December, some 200 miles northeast of Oahu, *Enterprise* pilots sighted three I-boats in widely separated areas and making good speed on the surface. The *I-70* fell victim to dive-bombing, and the *Enterprise* was credited with the first combatant ship destroyed by U.S. forces in the war.[18]

A view of Sakamaki's midget submarine in September 1942 at Mare Island Naval Shipyard, California, one of several stops during President Roosevelt's 9,000-mile trip around the country. As Secret Service agents stand guard, the president talks with Vice Adm. John W. Greenslade, commander Twelfth Naval District, and Rear Adm. Wilhelm L. Friedell, who commanded the shipyard at Mare Island. (Naval Historical Center, NH 47036)

Submarine Attack on the USS *Saratoga*

The USS *Saratoga* (CV-3) became the victim of a hastily formed submarine picket line a month after the Pearl Harbor attack. Three submarines of the earlier special attack midget submarine mission, the *I-18, I-22,* and *I-24,* were ordered to return to Hawaiian waters after they were resupplied at Kwajalein. They sortied on 3 January 1942. On the morning of 9 January, the *I-18* sighted a *Lexington*-class carrier and a cruiser steaming westward near Johnston Island. Rear Adm. Shigeaki Yamazaki, commander of Submarine Squadron 2, immediately ordered all available submarines in the area to establish a north-south picket line and to commence reconnaissance operations westward. At 1740 (local time) on 11 January, Comdr. Michimune Inaba, in the *I-6*, the third boat from the north in the extended picket line, sighted a *Lexington*-class carrier, one cruiser, and two destroyers about 270 miles from Johnston Island. Some time later, after maneuvering for a firing position, Inaba fired three torpedoes at the carrier target with an 80-degree angle on the bow and at a range of 4,700 yards. He heard two explosions and estimated that a large U.S. Navy aircraft carrier was sunk. The *I-6* survived a heavy depth-charge attack and surfaced at 2200, but no enemy ships were then in sight.[19]

The attack on the *Saratoga* caused some Japanese officers to reflect on the status of the submarine force. For example, the chief of staff of the Combined Fleet, Adm. Matome Ugaki, noted in his diary at the time that

> Quite a few of our submarines are sweeping the area. So, even if the crippled carrier escaped sinking, other subs would easily catch her again and the heavy cruiser too, if lucky.
>
> The officers and men of the submarine service have gone through endless hardship up to now. . . . They also have proved that submarines are indispensable.
>
> I shall be very happy because I have regretted the growing trend to underestimate their [submarine] ability, dazzled by the brilliance of the air activity.[20]

Nevertheless, Admiral Ugaki had grave doubts that the American carrier was in fact sunk, in spite of the naval high command's claim. "The navy is not supposed to lie," he wrote, and he hoped that such enemy ships that were claimed as sunk would never again appear in newspaper stories "or on the sea in the future."[21] An exaggerated claim or not, the *Saratoga* was badly damaged but did not sink; nevertheless, the absence of the *Saratoga* early in the Pacific War was alarming to American naval strategists.

By January 1942, there were only four U.S. Navy fast heavy carriers in the Pacific—the *Lexington* (CV-2), *Saratoga* (CV-3), *Yorktown* (CV-5), and *Enterprise* (CV-6). The *Hornet* (CV-8) reached the Pacific in March, and the *Wasp* (CV-7) arrived in June. Thus, American carrier strength in the Pacific suffered considerably by the temporary removal of the *Saratoga*. Indeed, the strategic balance early in the Pacific War remained precarious with the losses of the *Lexington* in early May in the battle of the Coral Sea and the *Yorktown* a month later, although the Japanese also suffered heavy losses, particularly at Midway.

* * *

On balance, the record of Japanese submarines in Hawaiian waters at the time of the air strike and for at least a month afterward was more one of missed opportunities than successes. During this time hundreds of American warships—including the *Enterprise, Lexington, Saratoga,* and *Yorktown* and their cruiser and destroyer escorts—steamed in and out of Pearl Harbor, but none was hit by a Japanese submarine-launched torpedo. Only a few minor cargo vessels were sunk. Otherwise, some night bombardments of various islands—Maui, Hawaii, and Kauai, for example—were carried out, an indication that the submarines were about to conclude their patrols and start homeward. An intelligence officer at Pearl Harbor later wrote that "none of these bombardments caused much damage. A bombardment was a fairly reliable indication that the submarine was departing from the area and this information was useful in ship routing."[22] Thus, Japanese submarines were a serious nuisance in Hawaiian waters to be taken seriously, but in their operations they pretty well unmasked themselves and caused no strategic damage to the ability of the United States to respond to Japan's attack on American territory.

Submarine Patrols off the West Coast, December 1941 to January 1942

In the aftermath of the Japanese navy's failure to bag the American carriers, the high command was particularly alarmed about the possibility of enemy reinforcements being sent from the U.S. mainland to Pearl Harbor. Thus, in December 1941, nine new ocean-cruising submarines took up patrol stations off the west coast of the United States.

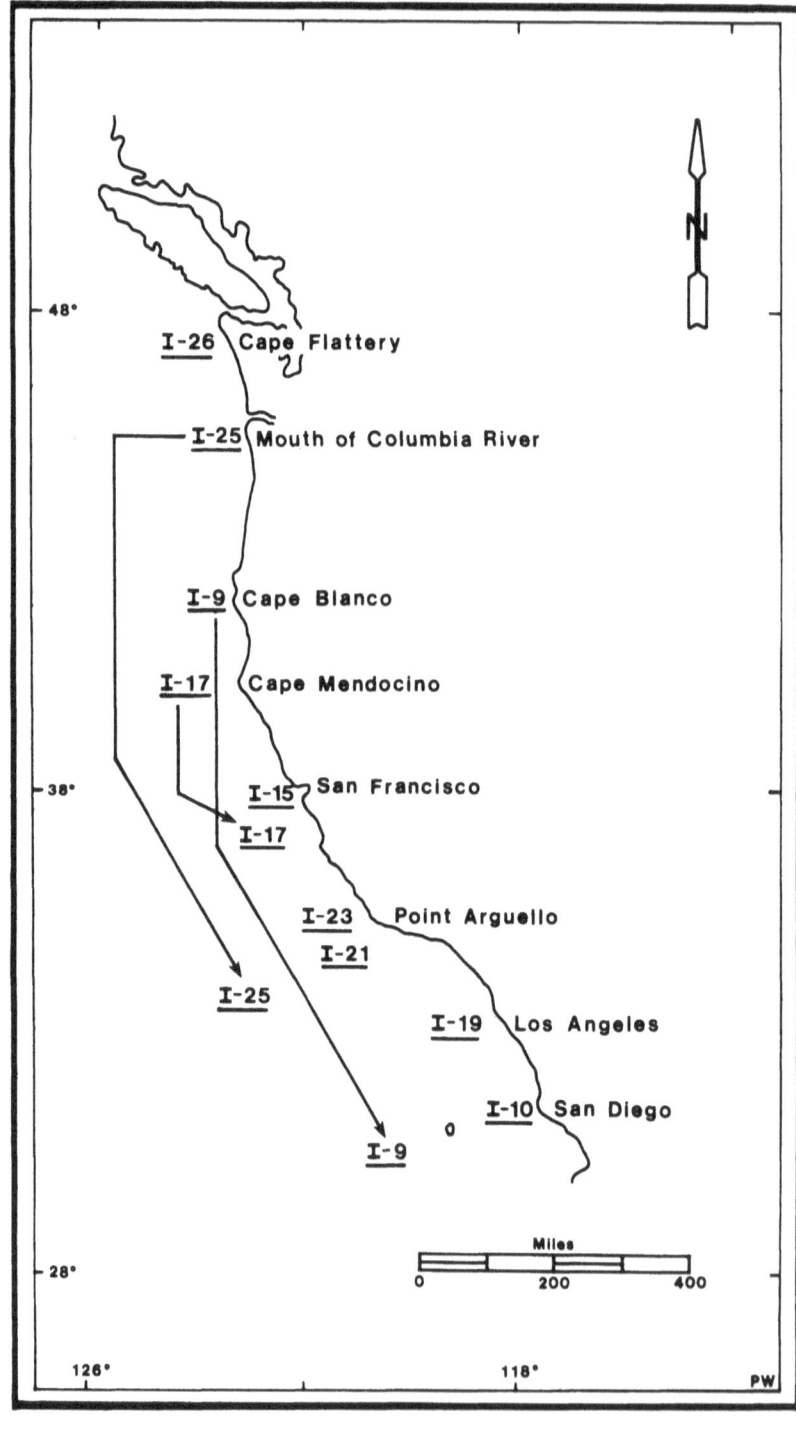

Their assigned patrol areas (north to south) were clearly delineated: *I-26*, off Cape Flattery, Washington; the *I-25*, off the mouth of the Columbia River, Oregon; the *I-9*, off Cape Blanco, Oregon; the *I-17*, off Cape Mendocino, California; the *I-15*, off San Francisco, California; the *I-23*, north of Point Arguello, California; the *I-21*, off Point Arguello, California; the *I-19*, off Los Angeles, California; and the *I-10*, off San Diego, California. Later, on 21 January 1942, as a result of information from Navy General Headquarters that a U.S. Navy battleship group had passed through the Panama Canal and was proceeding, presumably, to California ports, Rear Adm. Satō, in the *I-9*, ordered a shift southward for new patrol stations.[23] The *I-25* moved from off the mouth of the Columbia River to off Point Arguello; the *I-9* shifted from off Cape Blanco to off San Diego; and the *I-17* moved from off Cape Mendocino to off San Francisco (see map 2).[24]

The material results of this far-reaching operation in enemy home waters were insignificant—U.S. naval forces were not damaged, and the toll taken on American merchant shipping was modest, especially when compared to the sizable number of submarines committed by the Japanese. None of these submarines had any difficulty reaching their assigned areas, and a certain leisure then characterized their initial patrols and the return of the I-boats westward to Kwajalein. The *I-17* reported sighting an enemy cruiser group east of Hawaii on New Year's Day, and the seaplane from the *I-19* made a night reconnaissance flight over Pearl Harbor on 4 January 1942. Most of the submarines from this first major west coast operation returned to Kwajalein between 11 and 15 January.

The Japanese official history estimates that these submarines sank only five cargo ships totaling 30,370 tons and damaged five others (34,299 tons). Although none of the Japanese submarines that reached the west coast was lost and little shipping was destroyed, the psychological impact of Japanese men-of-war so close to the Washington-Oregon-California coast caused Americans in those states enormous anguish and consternation.[25] But the Japanese failed to take advantage of American anxiety, a subject to be discussed at a later point.

Some Americans feared invasion. As a U.S. Navy study concluded in March 1945, the initial performance of Japanese submarine operations

Map 2. (*Opposite page*) Submarine deployment on the west coast of the United States, December 1941. (Source: Bōeichō Bōeikenshūjo Senshibu, ed., *Sensuikan shi*, 107)

was scanty, although the operations appeared to be preliminary to possible invasion. Their "operations during the period under consideration [5 December 1941 to 25 March 1942] were mostly defensive in nature, with remarkably few claimed sinkings of Allied vessels, and greatly increased reconnaissance activity and investigation of invasion possibilities of American Territories and Island bases."[26] Nevertheless, the actual behavior of Japanese submarines seemed to belie the existence of the dire war between Japan and the United States.

The Japanese had what they themselves called a victory disease (*senshō-byō*), the florid expectations in 1942 of a mighty vanquisher. The victory disease infected the Japanese civilian population and military personnel alike.[27] A civilian sample is seen in various press reports. For example, Radio Tokyo concluded on 3 March 1942 that "sensible Americans know that the submarine shelling of the Pacific coast was a warning to the nation that the Paradise created by George Washington is on the verge of destruction."[28] But the military example of the victory disease was the result of deliberate propaganda to contribute to public euphoria. Minor shelling by the *I-17* lasted twenty minutes and damaged only a pier and an oil well derrick near Santa Barbara, California.[29] Nevertheless, such action was described by a Japanese navy captain of the Naval Information Department as a "bombardment" that inflicted "heavy damage in California" and "unnerved the entire Pacific coast." In April the same naval office announced that "as the Imperial Navy now controls all the Pacific and Indian oceans, the day is imminent when these will be called the New Sea of Japan."[30] As a contemporary U.S. naval officer wrote later, an early symptom of the victory disease was the Japanese "decision to reduce submarine surveillance in Hawaiian and west coast waters" in favor of operations in the southwest Pacific. "This forced the Japanese to rely on radio intelligence" about U.S. naval movements while their own naval strength was spread widely.[31] However, a Japanese submarine school instructor had another, less plausible explanation for the submarine failure off the American coast. In August 1942, Commander Muraoka told students that the failure was due to peculiar circumstances and technological factors. Several of the merchant vessels were in shallow water, navigating close to the coast, Muraoka declared. Because Japanese torpedoes would dive to about 100 feet immediately after firing and run at that depth for the first 500 yards before leveling off, several merchantmen got away unharmed.[32] In fact, the casualness of submarine operations east of Hawaii was not recognized as particularly harmful to Japanese wartime goals until it was too late and the urgencies of the war in the South Pacific and elsewhere demanded undivided commitment from the submarine force.

* * *

The war moved along at a rapid pace during the last days of 1941 and the opening months of 1942, yet submarines showed little assertive or decisive action. The submarine operations associated with the occupation of Wake demonstrate this point. The operation for the occupation of Wake Island was one of the missions of Vice Adm. Shigeyoshi Inoue, commander of the Fourth Fleet (and of the South Pacific Force in this particular operation); Rear Adm. Tadamichi Kajioka was responsible for the actual occupation. His Wake Island Occupation Group consisted of the light cruiser *Yūbari*, eight destroyers, and two transport ships with a Navy Special Landing Force battalion. In addition, three coastal-defense-type submarines (*RO-65*, *RO-66*, and *RO-67*) of Submarine Division 27 were initially assigned to patrol and blockade operations around Wake.[33]

The three submarines under division commander Capt. Sōkichi Fukaya sailed confidently from Kwajalein on 6 December 1941. They conducted reconnaissance operations in the vicinity of Wake, but the boats failed to discover any significant information about the defenders. Accurate fire from 5-inch U.S. Marine Corps gun batteries beat back the attacking forces. The Japanese lost two destroyers, and the occupation group was forced to return to Kwajalein. The group was then reinforced before resuming the operation. The *Sōryū* and *Hiryū*, on return from the air attack at Pearl Harbor, formed the carrier strike group. The Heavy Cruiser Support Group was made up of the *Aoba*, *Kinugasa*, *Furutaka*, and *Kako*. The submarine patrol and blockade units were reassigned to Yoshiyasu Matsuo, commander of Submarine Division 26. The renewed operation included the *RO-60*, *RO-61*, and *RO-62*, as well as *RO-66*, which remained off Wake after the first occupation operation failed.

On 12 December, Matsuo's submarines sailed from Kwajalein to a debacle of their own making. The second assault on Wake started at dawn on 23 December; this time the defending Americans were quickly overwhelmed. Nevertheless, the submarine operations were badly bungled. Two submarines were lost needlessly: the *RO-66* sank after colliding with the *RO-62*, some 25 miles southwest of Wake at 2230 (local time), 17 December, and the *RO-60*, when returning from the Wake operation, ran into a reef at the northern end of Kwajalein Atoll and sank at 0200 (local time) on 29 December.

Similarly, some 1,400 miles to the southwest, Japanese submarines associated with the occupation of the Bismarck Islands were of no consequence. Capt. Sōkichi Fukaya, commander of Submarine Division 27 (*RO-65* and *RO-67*) and Capt. Takeo Nagai, commander of Submarine Division 33 (*RO-63, RO-64,* and *RO-68*) were responsible for submarine operations near Rabaul, New Britain. The five submarines carried out general surveillance patrols in the second half of January 1942, and then returned to Truk without incident. Thus, the operations of these five submarines were singularly insignificant; they yielded no vital information and inflicted no damage whatsoever on U.S. forces.

Submarine Operations in the Java Sea and around the Malay Peninsula, December 1941 to February 1942

The leadership of the Japanese navy was enthusiastic about expansion into the "Southern Important Territories" (*Nampō yōiki*)—the Philippines, Malaya, Burma, and the Dutch East Indies—to conquer vast lands and to control the source of rich raw materials. The operations had long been studied and examined as part of the General Plan for the Employment of the Empire's Forces (*Teikoku yōhei kōryō*). Submarine squadrons were attached to each of the forces taking part in the southern expansion operation (see appendix 4).

THE MALAYA INVASION

The Malaya Invasion Force, with a troop convoy, succeeded in landing the 25th Army Corps at the neck of the Malay Peninsula at dawn on 8 December 1941 (local time). The British intended to counterattack, but on 10 December, bombers of the General Support Land Based Air Force sank the chief British capital ships—the new battleship HMS *Prince of Wales* and the older battle cruiser HMS *Repulse*. Thus, the Japanese navy was assured sea and air superiority in the area of Malaya. Notably, in this instance, the role of the submarine force had some significance.

Two submarine squadrons (sixteen boats) were attached to the Malaya Invasion Force. Rear Adm. Setsuzō Yoshitomi, commander of Submarine Squadron 4, had six old fleet-type submarines (*I-53, I-54,*

I-55, I-56, I-57, and *I-58*); two coastal-defense-type submarines (*RO-33* and *RO-34*); and two minelaying-type submarines (*I-21* and *I-22*). Rear Adm. Tadashige Daigo commanded Submarine Squadron 5, which consisted of six old fleet-type submarines (*I-59, I-60, I-62, I-64, I-65,* and *I-66*).

These two submarine squadrons were to support troop landing operations, attack enemy ships, and lay mines. Most significantly, however, the submarines established picket lines to help detect any British reinforcements. The *I-53, I-54,* and *I-55* formed a 100-mile east-west picket line off the east coast of the central Malay Peninsula. The *I-57, I-58, I-62, I-64, I-65,* and *I-66* formed a 200-mile east-west picket, 100 miles north of the aforementioned three-boat line.

* * *

Submarine reconnaissance operations during the Malaya invasion proved to be vital for the early Japanese success, for submarines first spotted the two British capital ships. Japanese submarine commanders were always particularly anxious to locate enemy capital ships. At 1415 (local time) on 9 December, the *I-65*, in the northern picket line, sighted the *Prince of Wales* and *Repulse* proceeding to the northwest at 14 knots. The submarine tracked the British ships until they disappeared in a rain squall at 1722. Rear Admiral Yoshitomi, commander of Submarine Squadron 4, ordered all submarines in the general vicinity to search for the elusive enemy ships, and shortly after midnight on the tenth, the two ships were again sighted, this time by Lt. Comdr. Sōshichi Kitamura in the *I-58*. He fired five torpedoes, but they missed. The *I-58* surfaced and gave chase while reporting enthusiastically: "Sighted enemy at 057 degrees, 140 miles from Kuantan; enemy course—180 degrees, speed—22 knots, time—0241." By 0325, the *I-58* reported that the enemy course was 240 degrees and that the ships were proceeding to Kuantan, but Commander Kitamura lost contact with the enemy two hours later. These submarine reports gave focus to daylight air searches and the subsequent air attacks and sinking of the British ships, in spite of the fact that the last report, the 0325 message from the *I-58*, was not relayed to the senior command. Submarines of Squadrons 4 and 5 continued to patrol Malay waters until 27 December, but only two submarines claimed any success: the *I-56* sank a small cargo ship, and the *I-66* sank a Dutch submarine, probably *O-16* or *K-XVII*. However, the *I-21* and *I-22* laid mines at the eastern end of the Johore Strait, Singapore, and then patrolled in the general vicinity.

THE INVASION OF THE PHILIPPINE ISLANDS

Whatever degree of success submarines enjoyed during the Malaya invasion, their role in the invasion of the Philippines was more in keeping with the rather lackluster pattern that characterized submarine patrols off the U.S. mainland and elsewhere in the Pacific. On 8 December, air groups of the General Support Land Based Air Force struck at U.S. forces around Manila and Cavite. With Japanese air superiority achieved at the outset, the 16th Army Corps succeeded in landing at Lingayen on 22 December, but only two minelaying submarines (*I-23* and *I-24*) of Submarine Squadron 6 (Rear Adm. Chimaki Kōno) were attached to the Philippines Invasion Force. Their mission was to patrol the waters around Luzon, to support air assaults by rescuing any Japanese pilots shot down, and to lay mines. The *I-23* laid forty mines at the east end of Manila Bay, and the *I-24* laid thirty-nine in Balabac Strait between Palawan and Borneo. Only the *I-24* sank an enemy vessel, a small cargo ship on 10 December.

THE INVASION OF THE DUTCH EAST INDIES

The naval dimensions of initial Japanese operations in the Philippines and the Malay Peninsula were swift, and thus plans for implementing the next step of the scheme for expansion into the Southern Important Territories were undertaken without delay. On 26 December Vice Adm. Nobutake Kondō, commander of the Southern Expeditionary Main Force (Second Fleet) reorganized the Philippines Invasion Force (Third Fleet) into the Dutch East Indies Invasion Force. The new force was under the command of Vice Adm. Ibō Takahashi. Submarine groups were also reorganized for these operations. Several submarines, including the *I-1* through *I-7*, were brought back from Hawaiian waters to become part of the Dutch East Indies offensive. These particular submarines steamed thousands of miles to reach their newly assigned areas of operation in the third week of the war. However, the average number of cargo vessels they sank was only one each. This is a specific example of the reduction of the submarine force around Hawaii and a symptom of the victory disease: reassigning groups to a new area before the original area of operation was free from threat. The Japanese opportunity to keep careful watch for any U.S. Navy resurgence was greatly weakened while undertaking new offensives.

Three new submarine groups were formed as the Dutch East Indies Invasion Force.

1. Submarine Group "A (*Kō*)"—Rear Adm. Setsuzō Yoshitomi, commander of Submarine Squadron 4 and Rear Adm. Chimaki Kōno, commander of Submarine Squadron 6. This submarine group included six old fleet-type submarines, two coastal-defense-type submarines, and four minelaying submarines.
2. Submarine Group "B (*Otsu*)"—Rear Adm. Tadashige Daigo, commander of Submarine Squadron 5. There were six old fleet-type submarines in this group.
3. Submarine Group "C (*Hei*)"—Rear Adm. Hisashi Ichioka, commander of Submarine Squadron 2. The seven old ocean-cruising submarines in this group were the *I-1* to *I-7*.

The mission of these groups was simply to patrol their designated areas, particularly for the purpose of detecting enemy retreats or the arrival of reinforcements. They were, of course, ordered to attack any enemy ships they sighted. Submarines of Group "A" were deployed in the Java Sea and in the vicinity of the Sunda Strait; Group "B" was assigned to the Bay of Bengal; and submarines of Group "C" were originally assigned to patrol along the eastern coast of the Celebes, but they shifted generally to the waters between Java and Australia.

This was one of the most extensive submarine operations early in the war, and it met with considerable success. The specific activity of the twenty-five submarines participating in this operation is summarized in table 1.

The potential of the Japanese submarine force was clearly demonstrated by the activities of the submarines of the Dutch East Indies Invasion Force. During the invasion, submarines were far more effective than a comparable number of I-boats in Hawaiian waters or off the west coast of the United States. Japanese records state that some forty cargo vessels were sunk and at least another six ships were damaged. However, the successes were not without setbacks: two submarines were lost, the *I-60* and *I-24*.

The potential of the submarine force was still not fully exploited in these operations. The primary mission was reconnaissance in the interests of invasion and fleet operations. With the exception of the four minelaying submarines, no specific offensive goals were assigned to the submarines from the outset. Moreover, the submarines scored no tor-

Table 1. Japanese submarine operations in Southeast Asian-Australian waters, January–March 1942

Boat	Activity	Damage to enemy
	Submarine Group "A (Kō)"	
I-53	Patrolled east of Singapore; then in the Lombok Strait along eastern Java	Three cargo vessels sunk
I-54	Patrolled south of Sunda Strait near western Java	One cargo vessel sunk
I-55	Patrolled north of Sunda Strait; then south of Lombok Strait	Two cargo vessels sunk
I-56	Patrolled south of Java; then in Lombok Strait	Four cargo vessels sunk; two others damaged
I-57	Patrolled Lombok Strait	One cargo vessel sunk
I-58	Patrolled north of Lombok Strait; then south of Sunda Strait	Four cargo vessels sunk; one other damaged
RO-33, RO-34	Patrolled south of Java	—
I-21	Patrolled near Timor; laid mines off Darwin, Northern Territory, Australia	One cargo vessel sunk
I-22	Laid mines and patrolled in Torres Strait between Cape York, Queensland, and New Guinea	—
I-23, I-24	Laid mines off Darwin; later, I-24 came under heavy surface and air attack and was sunk primarily by depth charges from minesweeper HMAS *Deloraine*, 20 January 1942	—
	Submarine Group "B (Otsu)"	
I-59	Patrolled north of Sunda Strait; then Bay of Bengal	Two cargo vessels sunk
I-60	Patrolled the area south of Sunda Strait; was sunk during surface engagement with British destroyer HMS *Jupiter*, 17 January 1942	One oil tanker sunk
I-62	Patrolled in the Bay of Bengal	Two cargo vessels sunk; three others damaged

(continued)

Table 1. (*Continued*)

Boat	Activity	Damage to enemy
I-64	Patrolled in the Indian Ocean	Five cargo vessels sunk; another damaged
I-65	Patrolled in the Indian Ocean	Five cargo vessels sunk
I-66	Patrolled in the Indian Ocean off Ceylon	Four cargo vessels sunk
	Submarine Group "C (*Hei*)"	
I-1	Patrolled off northwestern Australia	One cargo vessel sunk
I-2	Patrolled west coast of Australia	One cargo vessel sunk
I-3	Patrolled west coast of Australia	One cargo vessel sunk; another damaged
I-4	Patrolled south of Java	Dutch steamer *Ban Ho Guan* (1,693 tons) sunk, 28 February
I-5	Mistakenly fired on by Japanese aircraft; obligated to abandon its patrol	—
I-6	Patrolled off the southern coast of Java	Two cargo vessels sunk
I-7	Patrolled off the southern coast of Java	One cargo vessel sunk, probably the 3,271-ton Dutch steamer *Le Maire*, on 4 March

pedo hits against Allied warships; rather, their successes were against generally smaller and slower cargo vessels sailing independently. And maritime captains were not trained expressly in taking evasive action during submarine attacks until later in the war.

The circumstances of the attacks on the two submarines lost during these operations also shed some light. The old 1927 *I-24* was detected in relatively shallow water (about 140 feet) by a recently commissioned Australian minesweeper equipped with the most modern of sonar apparatus. Rocked by the concussion of repeated depth-charge explosions, the I-boat wallowed briefly to the surface before taking its final plunge. U.S. Navy divers later discovered that one hatch had been blown wide open and its steel dogs bent, and the gaskets of two other hatches were blown out.[34] The *I-60* was also blown to the surface at the outset of a depth-charge attack. In fact, the emerging submarine was so close to HMS *Jupiter* that the British destroyer's 4.7-inch guns could not be depressed far enough to take aim. But the range opened, and in a running gun duel the Japanese were finally overwhelmed by the destroyer's firepower. One *Jupiter* officer later summarized this first sinking of a Japanese submarine by a British warship in World War II and concluded that "one can say in retrospect about the action that the [Japanese] Submarine Commander was inexperienced, as we should not have brought him to the surface so easily, when he had plenty of depth and sea room."[35] Thus, it was clear that Allied ASW equipment was generally the best available and that early experience in combat was a cruel and often unforgiving teacher.

Submarine Reconnaissance for Carrier Strike Force Operations in the Indian Ocean

Vice Adm. Chūichi Nagumo's Carrier Strike Force returned to Japan for supplies after the air assault on Pearl Harbor to prepare quickly for the next operation—a dash into the Indian Ocean with air attacks planned against Trincomalee and Columbo, Ceylon. This came as no surprise to U.S. Navy intelligence. A few days before Nagumo's force entered the Indian Ocean, Combat Intelligence at Pearl Harbor reported on 26 March that "all evidence points to very definite plans for offensive action in the Indian Ocean in the immediate future." Four days later, naval intelligence reported "continuing indications" of the coming Japanese air, surface, and submarine strike. Finally, on 31 March a report declared that "predicted enemy operations appear to have started."[36]

Combined Fleet Headquarters wanted submarines to reconnoiter enemy waters around Ceylon and along the western coast of India.[37] Submarine Squadron 2 (*I-1* to *I-7*), commanded by Rear Adm. Hisashi Ichioka, was assigned the mission. The *I-1* did not participate, but the other six old ocean-cruising submarines of the squadron sailed for the Indian Ocean. The performance of this squadron was undistinguished.

None of these boats had a clear-cut mission other than to reconnoiter for air strike operations. The *I-7* was assigned to launch its seaplane for reconnoitering Trincomalee and Columbo two days before the air attack. However, strong British air and naval ASW forces prevented the *I-7* from carrying out its aerial reconnaissance mission; the submarine could only patrol the waters southeast of Ceylon until the day of the air attack on 9 April. Despite its curtailed mission, the *I-7* managed to sink one vessel, the 9,415-ton British motorship *Glenshiel*, on 3 April. The *I-2*, commanded by Hiroshi Inada, acted as a weather report vessel off Trincomalee; this boat also sank one cargo vessel, probably the British steamer SS *Chilka* (4,360 tons). Another weather vessel, off Columbo, was the *I-3*, which sighted an enemy convoy on 7 April, immediately damaged the 4,872-ton British steamer *Elmdale* in surface deck-gun action, and the following day sank the British motorship *Fultala* (5,051 tons). The *I-4*, *I-5*, and *I-6* carried out reconnaissance operations along the western coast of India and in the vicinity of the Maldive Islands—the *I-4* sank a cargo ship near the Maldive Islands; *I-5* patrolled near Cape Comorin at the southern tip of India; and *I-6* patrolled off Bombay and sank two British steamers, the 5,897-ton *Clan Ross* and the 5,424-ton *Bahadur*.[38] Again, submarine performance was lackluster, accounting only for the destruction of seven cargo ships; however, Admiral Nagumo's forces launched very effective air attacks against Trincomalee and Columbo, and they sank the old 1919 light aircraft carrier HMS *Hermes* and two heavy cruisers, HMS *Cornwall* and HMS *Dorsetshire*.[39] The reconnaissance support provided by the boats of Submarine Squadron 2 was but a small factor in Nagumo's success. Nevertheless, Allied strategic strength in the Indian Ocean was enormously weakened in April 1942. Clement Attlee, then British secretary of state for dominion affairs, summarized the situation for Prime Minister John Curtin of Australia. There was no effective British naval shield to cover the western and northwestern approaches to Australia. Moreover, in a report dated 27 April 1942, Attlee estimated that "action against Malaya barrier involving large scale combined operations is beyond our resources until Germany has been defeated."[40]

The Midway and Aleutian Operations

The Japanese navy lacked a definitive strategic plan after the "Southern Important Territories" were occupied in April 1942. Elaborate discussions were belatedly undertaken. The Imperial Army suggested that the best policy would be to adhere to the prewar "National Defense Policy of the Empire" by withdrawing some army forces and consolidating Japan's defensive strength. However, Adm. Isoroku Yamamoto, commander in chief, Combined Fleet, argued strongly that the old naval strategy—interception operations and systematic reduction of the enemy fleet as it reached out to the western Pacific—ought to be abandoned once and for all. The strategy had at the outset been temporarily abandoned in favor of the Pearl Harbor strike, but since that attack failed to destroy the American carrier forces and new battleship units were supplementing the U.S. Pacific Fleet, the old Japanese naval strategy became dominate again in early 1942. Yamamoto advocated more offensive operations, such as the invasion and occupation of the Hawaiian Islands. Navy General Headquarters opposed Admiral Yamamoto, maintaining that the weaker Imperial Navy would be unable to invade Hawaii. Moreover, keeping an invasion force adequately supplied at such great distances would be impossible. Rather, the Navy General Headquarters advocated expansion to the southeast. The occupation of Fiji and the Samoan Islands would enable the Japanese to cut sea communications between the United States and Australia, although the use of submarines for this purpose was not specifically envisaged. After much debate and discussion, naval strategic planners decided to undertake *both* expansion operations—in the central Pacific toward Hawaii and in the South Pacific for the occupation of Fiji and Samoa. The initial goals of these operations included the occupation of Port Moresby in Papua, New Guinea, as well as the occupation of Midway and the Aleutians. The purpose was to establish a defensive perimeter at considerable distances from the heart of the Japanese Empire.[41]

In these circumstances the "Doolittle Raid" on Tokyo and other Japanese cities in April 1942 should have been viewed as an ominous sign of the enemy's tenacity and capability. A defensive strategy, if implemented immediately, would probably have been a more prudent move for fighting a war of attrition. But the attack by Col. James Doolittle's B-25 bombers from the newly commissioned carrier *Hornet* (CV-8) had just the opposite effect on Japanese navy strategic leadership. Since modern naval air power enabled U.S. forces to launch aggressive strikes deep into the heart of the Japanese Empire, a defensive strategy quickly became impossible. Yamamoto maintained that Japanese naval strategy had to be offensive, at least in the short run until a defensive perimeter could be established at greater distance from Tokyo. Thus, the decision was made to embark upon Operation "MI" for Midway, Operation "AL" for the Aleutians, and Operation "MO" for Port Moresby. Massive forces were assembled (see appendix 5).

Ten submarines of the Third and First Submarine Groups were assigned to picket lines "A" and "B" for reconnaissance and interception of U.S. naval forces en route to Midway (see map 3). Submarines were scheduled in the original plan to arrive on their assigned picket line station by D-day minus five, that is, 30 May (Midway time), but they were late because of deployment delays. They arrived piecemeal and independently between D-day minus three and D-day itself (1–4 June). Picket line "A" stretched 200 miles along meridian 166-30 W, about 700 miles southeast of Midway. Picket line "B" stretched 200 miles, about 700 miles east of Midway along a northeast-southwest line (163-10 W to 165-30 W). The ten submarines deployed on these two lines failed to detect any U.S. naval forces en route to the battle of Midway, and, therefore, the Japanese high command operated blindly to a large degree until it was too late to change the course of the battle.

The Japanese submarine deployment plan was based on the expectation that the enemy would behave predictably. Japanese planners of Operation "MI" anticipated that they would enjoy the element of surprise during their attack on Midway, and that the U.S. Navy Carrier Task Force would sortie from Pearl Harbor *after* the Japanese assault on Midway began. It was expected that submarines of picket lines "A" and "B" would have the opportunity to intercept U.S. Navy carriers en route to the vicinity of Midway after 4 June. The Japanese naval high command was convinced that the enemy's carriers were still operating in the South Pacific. At a minimum, if by chance U.S. carriers were steaming north from the South Pacific on the eve of the attack on Midway, they would have to put into Pearl Harbor for fuel and provisions before rushing on to the vicinity of Midway. Invariably in this worst-case scenario Japanese submarines would arrive on their assigned picket lines sometime *before* U.S. Navy aircraft carriers could possibly pass through their patrol areas, or so the Japanese high command was convinced. Thus, Combined Fleet Headquarters was not worried about the deployment delays. In fact, however, the U.S. Navy Carrier Task Force passed through the areas where Japanese submarines would *later* establish picket lines "A" and "B."

Most accounts, particularly in western studies, of the Japanese defeat at Midway frequently cite the weakness of I-boat deployment as a major factor leading to defeat. The submarines could not report on the location of the U.S. Navy's carriers and their cruiser and destroyer escorts. Yet the Japanese high command did not know that American

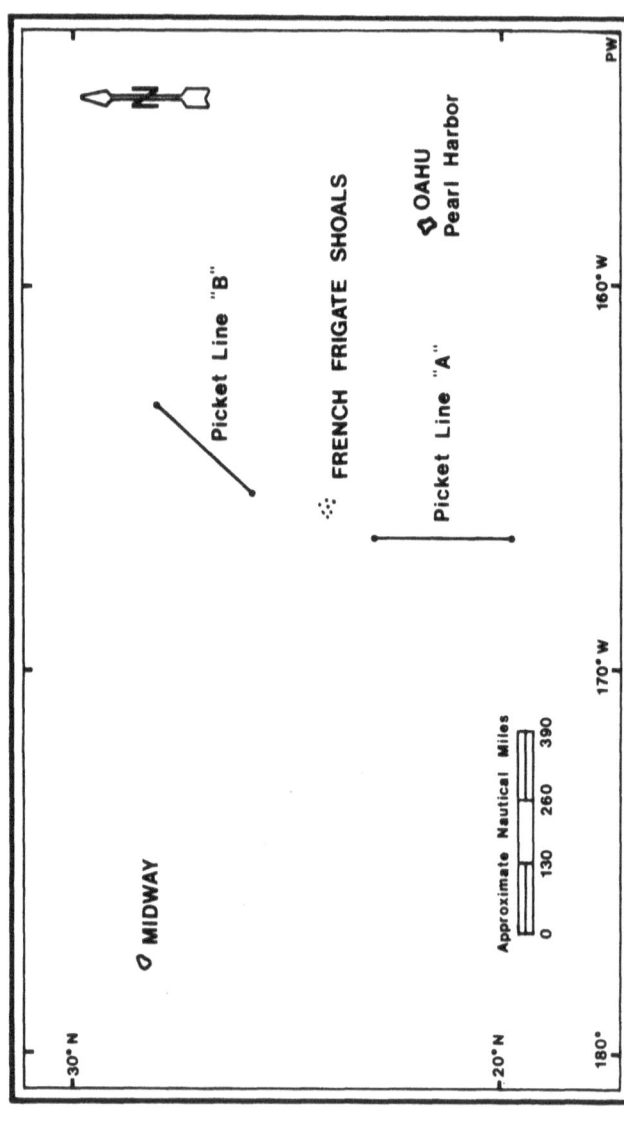

Map 3. First picket lines "A" and "B." (Source: Bōeichō Bōeikenshūjo Senshibu, ed., *Sensuikan shi*, 149).

cryptanalysts were making significant progress toward solving several Japanese codes and ciphers. The timetable behind the high command's rationale for the deployment of submarines was no doubt incautious; on the other hand, it appeared logical.

SUBMARINE REFUELING OPERATIONS FOR THE FLYING BOATS

Two Navy Type 2 Flying Boats, Kawanishi H8K (nicknamed "Emily" by American servicemen) were scheduled for reconnaissance missions over Pearl Harbor on 30 May after refueling at the French Frigate Shoals. With a range of nearly 4,000 miles, the Emily was one of the most outstanding water-based combat aircraft of World War II. The *I-121* and *I-123* (formerly named *I-21* and *I-23* before 20 May) arrived loaded with aviation fuel at the French Frigate Shoals late during the night of 28 May, but the *I-123* sighted two American ships at the shoals. The submarine's report caused the commander of Submarine Division 13 to postpone the refueling operation for one day. When the *I-123* observed an American flying boat landing in the shoals on 30 May, the refueling operation was canceled altogether because the Japanese assumed that U.S. forces were already in control of the French Frigate Shoals. Nevertheless, the *I-121* and *I-123* continued to patrol the area until the conclusion of Operation "MI."

The failure of this particular submarine refueling operation was specifically due to the insightful work of U.S. Navy intelligence. Japanese flying boats had received fuel from submarines in the lee of the French Frigate Shoals before flying to Oahu earlier in the year. American intelligence analysts solved an important puzzle in March by eventually discovering in the Japanese syllabaries the *kana* call signals for certain submarines and air units and by observing through D/F fixes that Japanese submarines had always been near the shoals when reconnaissance aircraft appeared near Pearl Harbor. Adm. Chester Nimitz, commander in chief, U.S. Pacific Fleet, reacted swiftly by sending the seaplane tender *Ballard* (AVD-10), a converted World War I destroyer, to the crucial area to prevent similar Japanese refueling operations in the future. By the end of May, a minelayer joined the *Ballard* and started to use the lee of the shoal as an anchorage.[42] Thus, the submarine-to-aircraft refueling operation on the eve of the battle of Midway was foiled by American intelligence. Indeed, a wartime intelligence officer soon concluded that "every Japanese campaign has been

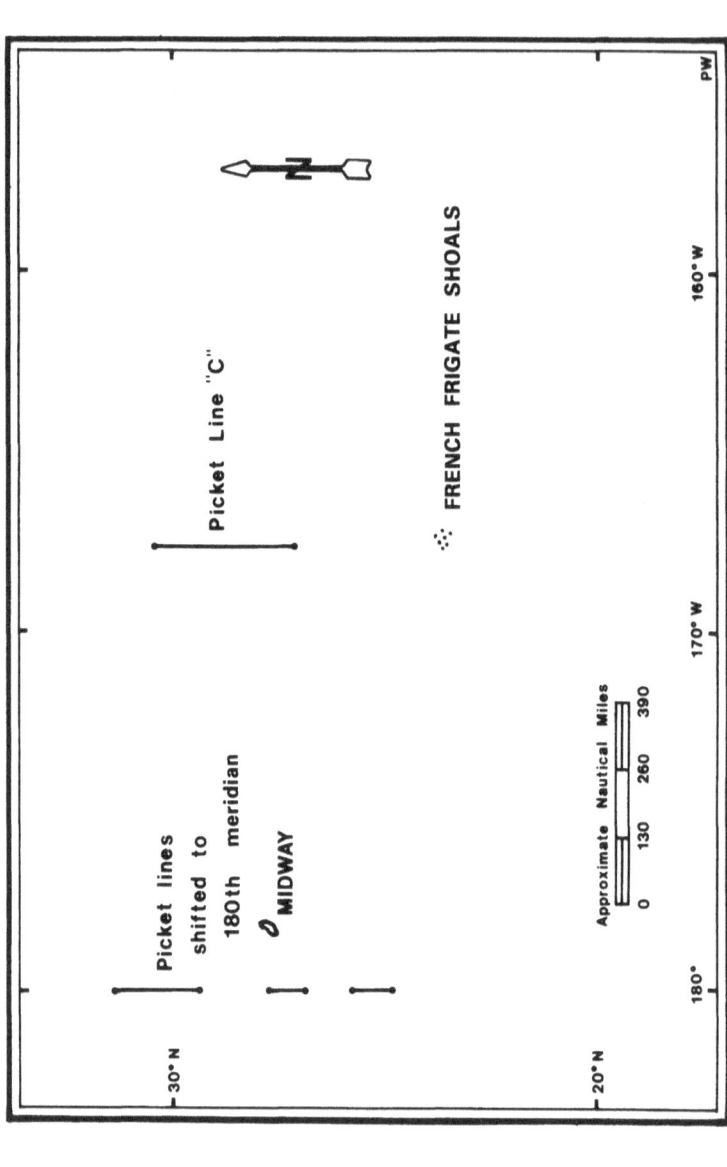

Map 4. The shift of picket lines westward. (Source: Bōeichō Bōeikenshūjo Senshibu, ed., *Sensuikan shi*, 149)

marked by similar close cooperation between air and submarine fleets."[43]

SUBMARINE RECONNAISSANCE OF THE MIDWAY AND ALASKA AREAS

Initial submarine reconnaissance missions were widespread. The *I-168,* for example, reconnoitered near Kure Island (some sixty miles northwest of Midway) on 31 May and carried out a similar mission near Midway on 1 June. Thereafter, the *I-168* continued to patrol in the vicinity and provided Combined Fleet Headquarters with important weather information. Submarines of the First Submarine Group proceeded to the northern Pacific and to the coast of Alaska to carry out reconnaissance operations: the *I-25* was off Kodiak by 24 May, *I-19* was near Dutch Harbor by 28 May, *I-15* was off the central Aleutians, and *I-17* was off the western Aleutians. These submarines remained on their respective stations until Operation "AL" was concluded—then they started to shift their patrol areas toward the west coast of the United States.

THE SHIFT WESTWARD OF SUBMARINE PICKET LINES AFTER ATTACKS ON JAPANESE AIRCRAFT CARRIERS

A comprehensive account of the battle of Midway is not necessary in the context of this book; suffice it to say that the loss of four aircraft carriers on 4 June was a devastating shock to the Imperial Japanese Navy. The decision to abandon Operation "MI" was made by midnight on the fourth, but Admiral Yamamoto hoped that submarines could still deliver a decisive blow against U.S. carrier forces around Midway. From Kwajalein, Vice Adm. Teruhisa Komatsu, the new commander of the Sixth Fleet, ordered all fleet-type submarines to shift their picket lines in order to establish the newly designated picket line "C" by the morning of 5 June (see map 4). The new line, some 200 miles long and 500 miles east of Midway, ran along meridian 168-40 W. Also, the two minelaying submarines, *I-121* and *I-123,* in the vicinity of the French Frigate Shoals, were ordered to proceed westward. By the afternoon of 6 June, Admiral Yamamoto, fearful that the American carriers were pursuing him, ordered all submarines around Midway to shift their deployment to the west of Midway, on meridian 180 W.[44] Those submarines receiving the newest order dashed westward on the surface, but the majority of the boats were unable to take up their newly assigned stations until the tenth or eleventh (Western Hemisphere dates). Finally, the Combined Fleet Headquarters received new information that U.S. carrier forces were still east of Midway, and the submarines were ordered back east again. But it was too late to entrap the carriers *Hornet* (CV-8) and *Enterprise* (CV-6), and the two carriers escaped to the safety of Pearl Harbor.

The Japanese high command was a victim of its own indecision. Another high-speed dash to entrap the elusive American forces would have been impossible for most of the I-boats because of insufficient fuel supply after the earlier dashes. Thus, submarines assigned to the original picket lines accomplished nothing of consequence in Operation "MI." Only the *I-169* sighted U.S. forces northeast of Midway on the night of 7 June, but no attack could be launched and contact was soon lost.[45]

The shock of heavy losses and the fog of battle obviously dimmed various assessments of conditions by the Japanese high command. Submarines were sought in the hope that they could deliver an eleventh-hour victory, yet they were misdirected by faulty intelligence concerning the enemy. The Japanese failure at Midway was due to imperfect intelligence as much as the American victory was due to amazingly insightful intelligence.[46]

THE SINKING OF THE USS *YORKTOWN* (CV-5) BY THE *I-168*

One piece of Japanese tactical intelligence resulted in the sinking of the only U.S. aircraft carrier lost in the June clash between the two navies. On 5 June a Japanese reconnaissance aircraft sighted and reported an enemy carrier drifting about 150 miles north-northeast of Midway. U.S. Navy intelligence intercepted the following Japanese enciphered message from the First Air Fleet to Yamamoto at 0340, 6 June: "Enemy carrier of *Yorktown* class suffered great damage, listing to starboard and drifting in position 39-30 N 176-10 W." The error in the *Yorktown*'s position was soon corrected in another message, "Probably 30-30 N 176-10 W."[47] Thus the commander of the Sixth Fleet, Admiral Komatsu, ordered the nearest submarine, the *I-168* commanded by Lt. Comdr. (later Comdr.) Yahachi Tanabe, to attack the damaged carrier as soon as possible. The *I-168* was on patrol in the vicinity of Midway (it had bombarded Midway during the afternoon of the fourth and later during the evening bombarded nearby Eastern Island as well). Sighting the American carrier nearly dead in the water on the morning of 6 June, Commander Tanabe calmly maneuvered his boat to the best firing position and, at 1305, almost abeam of the damaged carrier and at a range of about 1,000 yards, launched four

War in the Pacific, 1937 to Mid-1942   85

The *I-68*, completed at Kure Navy Yard on 31 July 1934, here under way at 23 knots during its sea trials. Renamed *I-168* in May 1942, this submarine was responsible for sinking the USS *Yorktown* (CV-5) at Midway in June 1942. (Naval Historical Center, NH 73054)

The sinking of the USS *Yorktown* (CV-5) on the morning of 7 June 1942, as seen from an accompanying destroyer. Note the damage to the hull caused by torpedoes from *I-168* on the previous day. (Naval Historical Center, NH 95575)

torpedoes. Tanabe heard four explosions before U.S. destroyers started a series of very heavy depth-charge attacks. The *I-168* was under attack for about seven hours. Eventually obliged to surface, Commander Tanabe expected the worst in a deadly duel with the enemy destroyers. He was relieved to find the destroyers some distance away, and he made good a surfaced escape from the scene under the cover of dusk.[48] Tanabe later recalled his lucky escape: the *I-168*'s batteries were damaged so badly that the boat could no longer remain submerged. Thus, Tanabe decided to surface and engage the enemy in what was certain to be a suicidal gun duel. Once on the surface, however, Tanabe sighted two enemy destroyers steaming away—the Japanese submariners were happy to dash into the mist of dusk.[49] Tanabe's survival was not typical in the Japanese submarine service as a whole. Generally, remarkably good American ASW tactics were enormously effective against Japanese submarines.

Submarine Patrols off the West Coast of North America, June–July 1942

After the conclusion of Operation "AL," five ocean-cruising submarines of the First Submarine Group shifted patrol stations to the waters off the west coast of North America in much the same manner as did their predecessors. They were relieved in mid-June by seven old ocean-cruising submarines of the Second Submarine Group. Compared to the considerable number of submarines deployed during these patrols, damage to the enemy was very modest. In mid-June the *I-25* damaged the Canadian freighter *Fort Camosun* and bombarded Astoria, Oregon, on the twenty-first, and the *I-26* sank a cargo ship on 7 June and bombarded a radio station on Vancouver Island, British Columbia, on the twentieth. The *I-7* also sank one cargo vessel before the Second Submarine Group patrol ended in mid-July.[50] Capt. Tomejirō Tamaki, commander of Submarine Division 7, recalled that the surveillance of specific enemy harbors, which were well protected by ASW forces, proved to be very difficult and not very effective, especially under conditions of poor visibility. He recommended the deployment of many submarines against enemy lines of communications in areas of dense shipping.[51] However, Captain Tamaki's recommendation went largely unheeded while the Japanese naval high command was preoccupied with offensive operations still going on in the South Pacific. These surveillance operations in the distant waters of North America were not undertaken systematically; the engagements of the First and Second Submarine Groups after Operation "AL" were little more than nuisance patrols.

Special Attack Units at Sydney, Australia, and Diégo Suarez, Madagascar

In March 1942, a second special attack two-part operation was planned for midget submarine missions in the Indian Ocean and in Australian waters. The overall operation was carried out by units of the newly organized Eighth Submarine Group (Submarine Squadron 8) commanded by Commodore Noboru Ishizaki.[52]

Originally, two submarine units were assigned to Australian waters. Capt. Haruo Katsuta, commander of Submarine Division 14, commanded Submarine Unit "B" with three ocean-cruising submarines. The original plan was for these submarines, the *I-27* (with a midget submarine aboard), *I-28*, and *I-29*, to carry out a mission off the southern coast of Australia. The second group of three submarines, the *I-22*, *I-24* (each carried a midget submarine), and *I-21*, formed Submarine Unit "C," commanded by Capt. Hanku Sasaki, commander of Submarine Division 3. The group was ordered to destroy enemy shipping off the eastern coast of Australia and in the waters around New Zealand. However, before Unit "B" reached the southern coast of Australia and the submarines of Unit "C" arrived on their stations, they were united and renamed the Eastern Unit under the command of Captain Sasaki.

Submarines of the Eastern Unit were initially ordered to support Operation "MO," the invasion of Port Moresby, but they were dismissed from this mission after the Japanese setback in the battle of the Coral Sea in early May 1942 interrupted invasion plans. The submarines were then allowed to resume their mission designed to destroy enemy commerce and to launch special midget submarine attacks. However, the *I-28* was lost south of Truk as it was returning from the Coral Sea—the U.S. submarine *Tautog* (SS-199) torpedoed the Japanese submarine on 17 May. At about the same time, the *I-21* reported sinking two enemy cargo vessels, but on balance the *I-21*'s success was small compensation for the loss of the *I-28*, a new submarine in service for less than three months.

Most of the submarines of the Eastern Unit stopped at Truk for supplies and to take aboard the midget submarines and then sortied for the mission to Australia on 18 May. The *I-29*, which maintained a watch off Sydney, reported that enemy warships were in the harbor. Therefore, the unit's commander, Captain Sasaki, decided to concentrate midget submarines outside of Sydney Harbor. Concentration of his force was completed on the twenty-ninth, and three midget submarines were launched at the harbor entrance on the afternoon of 31 May. Not unlike the earlier experience of the Special Attack Unit in Hawaiian waters, the parent I-boats searched and waited in vain to recover the midget submarines. Without a sign of the midget submarines, the parent boats eventually left the designated recovery area on 3 June.

Australian sources confirm that one midget submarine launched torpedoes at the USS *Chicago* (CA-29), fresh from the battle of the Coral Sea and anchored in Sydney Harbor. The torpedoes missed the American cruiser and passed under the Dutch submarine *K-9*, but one torpedo exploded under HMAS *Kuttabul,* a converted harbor ferry docked at Garden Island. Some nineteen sailors were killed, and others were injured. The other torpedo ran ashore at Garden Island but failed to explode. Two of the little submarines were sunk, but they were raised from the seabed off George's Head and at Taylor Bay in Sydney Harbor. The Royal Australian Navy held a military funeral and buried the bodies of Lieutenants Keiu Matsuo and Katsuhisa Ban and their crewmen, Petty Officers Masao Tsuzuki and Mamoru Ashibe.⁵³ One midget submarine was placed on public display in Australia during the war in an effort to stimulate the sale of war bonds, not unlike the use Americans made of the *I-24*'s midget submarine after it wrecked on a reef off Oahu six months earlier. Some parts of the midget submarines sunk in Sydney Harbor were also sold as souvenirs to the public to assist the war effort.⁵⁴ Today one of the submarines is on display at the Australian War Memorial at Canberra. The third midget submarine failed to get inside Sydney Harbor but was caught in an antitorpedo net. The submarine's crew (Lt. Kenshi Chūman and PO Takeshi Ōmori) set off demolition charges to destroy themselves and their craft near 2230 on 31 May.⁵⁵

Another special attack was carried out by the new ocean-cruising I-boats of Submarine Unit "A." The five new ocean-cruising boats—*I-16, I-18, I-20* (each carried a midget submarine), *I-10,* and *I-30* under the command of the squadron head, Commodore Ishizaki—sortied westward from Penang, Malaya, on 30 April. The trip across the Indian Ocean was uneventful; moreover, no enemy ships were sighted in East African ports by the *I-30* during the reconnaissance patrol in late May. However, the reconnaissance plane from the *I-10* spotted a British battleship group at Diégo Suarez, Madagascar, on 30 May. Ishizaki sought to concentrate his midget submarines on these targets of opportunity, but his efforts were not without complications. The launching machinery aboard the *I-18* failed to work properly; thus, the small vessel was unable to participate in the special attack, and eventually the large I-boat had to return to base with its midget submarine on board. On the other hand, the *I-16* and *I-20* launched their midget submarines during the evening of 30 May (local time).[56]

The special attack had some success. The old battleship HMS *Ramillies* (28,000 tons) was damaged by a torpedo from the *I-20*'s midget submarine at 2035 on 30 May, the largest victim of any Japanese midget submarine attack during the war. (The *Ramillies* remained out of service for nearly a year.) An hour after the *Ramillies* was hit, the oil tanker *British Loyalty* (6,993 tons) was sunk by the same Japanese craft, commanded by Lt. Saburō Akeida. He and his crewman, PO Masami Takemoto, were forced to abandon their craft after it grounded on an outer reef. They then set out on a fifty-nine-hour trek across the parched country of northern Madagascar. The two Japanese submariners were shot when they refused to surrender to a party of fifteen British soldiers. Their graves remain near the harbor. The British, in order to help protect their Middle East convoys, had recently stormed and occupied Diégo Suarez for fear that the anticipated Japanese arrival would not be effectively resisted by the governing Vichy French.[57]

The overwhelming failure of midget submarines in special attack operations following the Pearl Harbor attack was persuasive evidence to the Submarine Force Headquarters that the use of midget submarines desperately needed to be reexamined. New targets were selected, but special attack midget submarines continued to be ineffective when employed against enemy transports in the anchorages off Guadalcanal in late 1942.[58] Nor were they effective later in the war around Lunga and Guadalcanal, Solomon Islands (November 1942), Aleutian Islands (June 1942 to August 1943), Okinawa (August to October 1944), Philippines (January to March 1945), and Japan (January to August 1945).[59]

Submarine Patrols in the Indian Ocean and the Southeast Coast of Australia, Mid-1942

Submarines of Unit "A" and the Eastern Unit continued to patrol their respective areas after the special attacks. The results were considerable. The I-boats of Unit "A" operated mainly in the Mozambique Channel and off the eastern coast of Madagascar until mid-July. The *I-10* sank eight cargo ships:

5 June 1942	Panamanian steamer *Atlantic Gulf* (2,639 tons)
5 June 1942	American motorship *Melvin H. Baker* (4,999 tons)
8 June 1942	British motorship *King Lud* (5,224 tons)
28 June 1942	British motorship *Queen Victoria* (4,937 tons)
30 June 1942	American steamer *Express* (6,736 tons)
6 July 1942	Greek steamer *Nymphe* (4,504 tons)
8 July 1942	British steamer *Hartismere* (5,498 tons)
9 July 1942	Norwegian steamer *Alchiba* (4,427 tons)

The *I-16* sank four, the *I-18* sank three, and the *I-20* sank seven cargo vessels of various sizes. The fifth submarine, the *I-30*, carried out a reconnaissance mission along the eastern coast of Madagascar, but no enemy ships were sighted. At the same time, however, two Japanese armed merchant cruisers (*Aikoku Maru* [10,437 tons] and *Hōkoku Maru* [10,438 tons]) were operating in the central and western parts of the Indian Ocean. They, as well as Submarine Squadron 8 I-boats, were under the operational control of then Rear Admiral Ishizaki, who was recently promoted. The two Japanese cruisers, which supported various I-boats in the area, attacked and sank the British ship *Elysia* (6,757 tons) and captured two other cargo ships. Thus Japanese presence in the Indian Ocean was widely felt by retreating and regrouping Allied forces in mid-1942.

Japanese submarines in Australian waters were also reasonably successful at this time. Five submarines of the Eastern Unit patrolled off the New South Wales coast. The *I-21* sank three cargo vessels and bombarded Newcastle, New South Wales, on 8 June. The *I-24* and *I-27* each sank one enemy cargo ship, and the *I-29* damaged a similar vessel. During this deployment the *I-22* conducted reconnaissance operations off Wellington and Auckland, New Zealand.[60] However, Australian records suggest that Japanese submarines caused more damage than official Japanese accounts seem to claim. Ships attacked by Japanese submarines but not sunk between 16 May and 3 August totaled eight (*Murada, Wellen, Allara,* the 4,734-ton coastal vessel *Age,* the 7,748-ton *Orestes,* the 3,362-ton cargo ship *Echunga,* the *Coolana,* and the 4,240-ton cargo ship *Barwon*). Seven ships were sunk during the same period (the 5,967-ton *Guatemala,* the 4,812-ton iron ore carrier *Iron Chieftain,* the *G.S. Livanos, Coast Farmer, Dureenbee, William Dawes,* and the 3,353-ton iron ore carrier *Iron Crown*).[61]

These submarine operations were aimed primarily at the destruction of enemy shipping in the Indian Ocean and off southeastern Australia —and they were reasonably successful, not unlike a few similar operations earlier in the war. This destruction in a war of attrition—thirty cargo vessels (nearly 150,000 tons) sunk, two cargo ships captured, and many others damaged—was not without significance. Only the *I-28* was sunk in the group of I-boats, and none was lost during the operations against commerce in June and July 1942. However, the mounting pressure of the war, especially with the coming of the struggle for Guadalcanal, would not permit the submarine force to pursue operations aimed mainly at the destruction of enemy shipping. The powerful Navy General Headquarters and Combined Fleet Headquarters were confronted with immediate military dangers; thus additional demands were made of the submarine force. Submarines had to operate as an arm of the battle fleet and serve directly the needs of naval surface craft of the Imperial Navy. But a worse fate awaited the submarine force: Japanese submarines would soon be required to serve the needs of Imperial Japanese Army units isolated on bypassed islands.[62]

4

New Submarine Operational Patterns and New Devastation in the Second Half of 1942

Submarine Operations in the Struggle for Guadalcanal

Heads of the Japanese army and navy were shocked by news of the Allied amphibious landings on 7 August 1942. These successful landings were against the Yokohama Air Group (flying boat) based at Tulagi, Florida Island, and an airfield under construction on Guadalcanal (captured and named Henderson Field in honor of Marine Major Lofton R. Henderson, a dive-bomber squadron commander killed in the battle of Midway). Japanese forces in the vicinity were quickly reorganized. The Outer Southern Pacific Force (Eighth Fleet) and the Twenty-Fifth Land Based Air Squadron (*Dai nijūgo kōkū sentai*) (parts of the Eleventh Air Fleet) were thus created and placed under the command of Vice Adm. Gunichi Mikawa. But no submarines formed a part of the initial reorganization of Japanese forces in the Guadalcanal campaign. Admiral Mikawa soon launched counterattacks (the battle of Savo Island, shortly after midnight, 9 August 1942), and land-based air groups continued to launch strong attacks against Allied forces in the air, at sea, and on land. The bitter struggle for Guadalcanal had started and was to last until February 1943.[1]

THE FIRST DEPLOYMENT OF SUBMARINES IN THE SOLOMON SEA

While enemy landings on Guadalcanal came as a surprise to Admiral Yamamoto, he did not disregard the seriousness of the setback; accordingly, he ordered all available forces, including submarines, to concentrate around Guadalcanal. Yamamoto himself moved forward to Truk in the battleship *Yamato*.

The submarine force responded as quickly as possible to the crisis. Six submarines of the Third Submarine Group and five of the Seventh Submarine Group had been operating in the South Pacific during July, but not all of them could respond immediately to Admiral Yamamoto's orders. Several of them needed supplies or repairs. It was a little more than two weeks after the initial landings that the commander of the Sixth Fleet, Vice Adm. Teruhisa Komatsu, was prepared to launch his submarine offensive. He (like Admiral Yamamoto) and his headquarters moved forward to Truk to direct the operations of the Third and Seventh Submarine Groups. There were also nine submarines of the First Submarine Group under Komatsu's command. Thus, with the chief exception of the ten submarines of the Eighth Submarine Group based at Penang and in the Indian Ocean, the vast majority of operational ocean-cruising and fleet-type submarines in the Japanese navy was concentrated in the Pacific by the final months of 1942 in waters of the eastern Solomons for the struggle of Guadalcanal (see appendix 6).[2]

Surprisingly, the first submarines deployed in the eastern Solomons failed to interfere with the Allied landings and buildup on Guadalcanal. The *I-169* and *I-171* patrolled those waters briefly in mid-August, but they failed to make contact with the enemy. The *I-174* and *I-175* carried out similar operations off New Caledonia, and the *I-121*, *I-122*, *I-123*, *RO-33*, and *RO-34* patrolled east of Guadalcanal and in the vicinity of Indispensable Strait. These nine submarines represented a major commitment to check the enemy, but they were misdirected and not used effectively at the crucial early stages of the American buildup in the Solomons. The Japanese were too slow to focus their forces in order to come to grips with military reality.[3] Three weeks after the initial landings, Adm. Matome Ugaki, chief of staff of the Combined Fleet, lamented in his diary entry of 31 August 1942, "So far our submarines have done nothing to enemy reinforcements."[4]

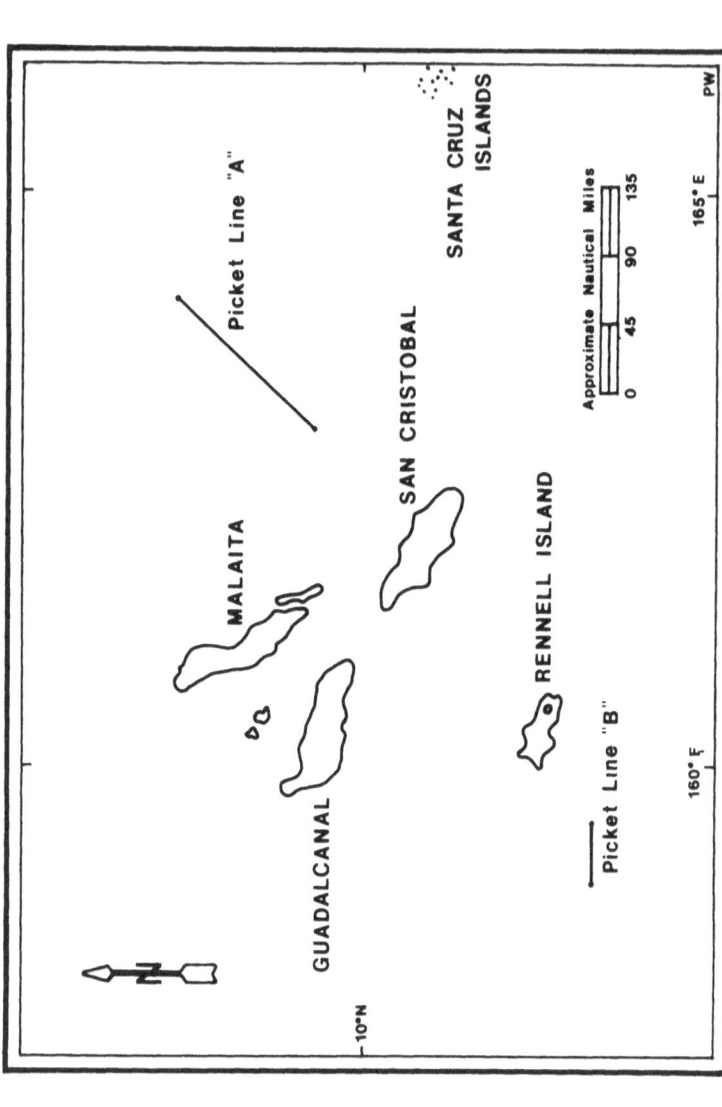

Map 5. First submarine picket lines near Guadalcanal. (Source: Bōeichō Bōeikenshūjo Senshibu, ed., *Sensuikan shi*, 183)

THE REDEPLOYMENT OF SUBMARINES FOR INTERCEPTING AMERICAN OPERATIONS

The arrival of reinforcements and U.S. carriers was crucial to American success after the initial landings. Sixth Fleet Headquarters at Truk estimated that U.S. carriers would operate in the waters off the eastern Solomons in support of land and air operations on Guadalcanal. Therefore, Admiral Komatsu wanted to establish submarine picket lines to intercept enemy carriers en route to their Guadalcanal support areas. In late August, seven submarines of the First Submarine Group established picket line "A," 200 miles east of Malaita Island and northeast of Guadalcanal. The formidable 100-mile long line ran in a northeast-southwest direction. A second picket line, "B," comprised three submarines along a 30-mile line some 50 miles southwest of Rennell Island, about 150 miles south of Guadalcanal (see map 5). Furthermore, three minelaying submarines of the Seventh Submarine Group were deployed east of Malaita, and two coastal defense submarines maintained reconnaissance patrols, one off Port Moresby and one in the 35-mile-wide Indispensable Strait between Guadalcanal and Malaita. It was obviously important to the Japanese high command to obtain information from these submarines about movements of enemy carriers and reinforcement units.[5]

SUBMARINES AND THE BATTLE OF THE EASTERN SOLOMONS, AUGUST 1942

From the outset Americans saw Guadalcanal as a watershed and an objective for which a strong stand had to be taken, but Japanese reaction was slow to change from piecemeal attacks against the invaders to all-out assaults at Henderson Field. After the failure of the first counterattack by Col. Kiyotaka Ichiki's battalion, Imperial General Headquarters (*Daihon-ei*) planned to launch a larger force under the command of Maj. Gen. Kiyotake Kawaguchi. Japanese makeshift troop transports approached Guadalcanal with the support of two carrier groups.[6] However, U.S. naval intelligence knew about impending Japanese reinforcements; thus, three U.S. carrier groups were deployed. Kawaguchi's movements were known in advance, and failure soon followed. A key officer assigned to the Combat Intelligence Unit in Hawaii explained:

> Until the Battle of Midway, communications intelligence completely dominated combat intelligence, but when the action shifted to the Solomons there was also a change in the nature of combat intelligence.

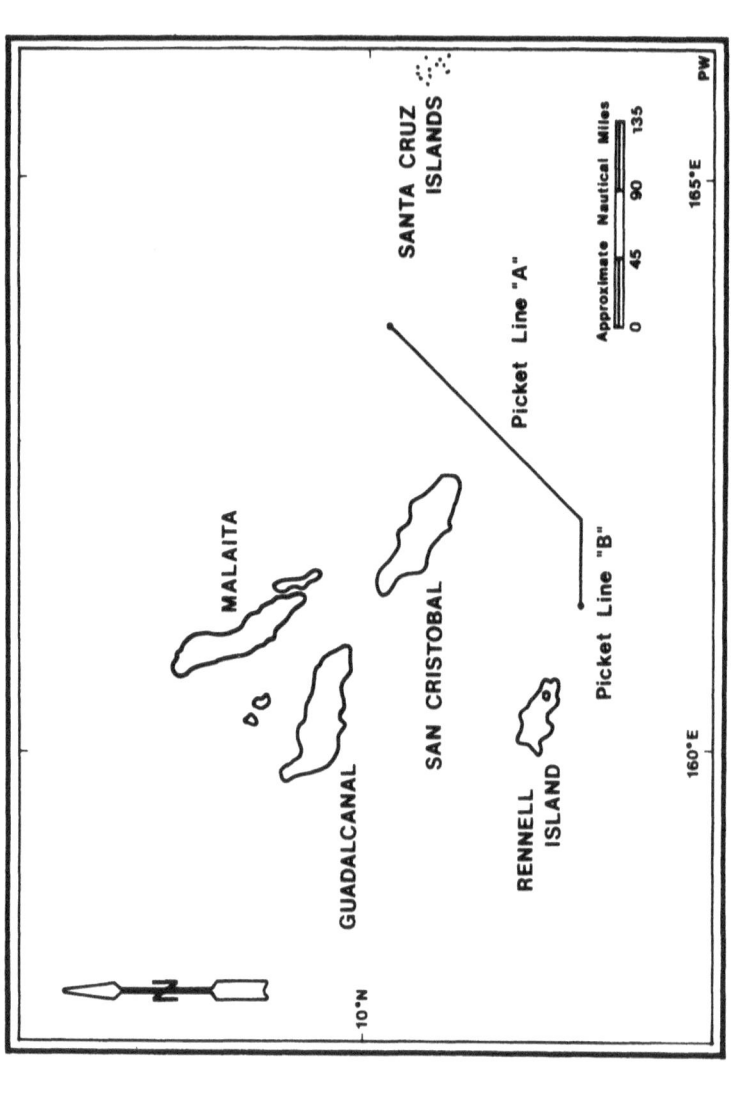

Map 6. Shift of submarine picket lines near Guadalcanal. (Source: Bōeichō Bōeikenshujo Senshibu, ed., *Sensuikan shi*, 183)

The Japanese, being now on the defensive and having their forces concentrated in Rabaul, no longer needed to transmit plans by radio and this, together with the change in their code, made it impossible for radio intelligence to determine specific details of their dispositions and timing. We could still read some minor codes including the local one used in the Marshalls and Carolines. The port director at Truk continued to use that code to report arrivals and departures of combat vessels. With this information and traffic analysis, it was frequently possible to detect a buildup of Japanese naval strength at Truk or Rabaul, which usually preceded a naval move against Guadalcanal.[7]

Although extensive radio intelligence was received from Pearl Harbor, the commander of the South Pacific Force relied heavily on naval reconnaissance, coastwatchers, and aerial photographs. Thus the scene was set for the battle of the eastern Solomons at dawn on 24 August.

The submarines in picket line "A" failed to detect U.S. carriers—the confusion was not unlike that plaguing Japanese submarines at the battle of Midway nearly ten weeks earlier. Again, orders were issued repeatedly to shift the picket lines. The submarine command headquarters reacted dramatically to every significant development during the struggle. For example, by the evening of the twenty-fourth, the light aircraft carrier *Ryūjō* was sunk; at this time the USS *Enterprise* suffered some damage and lost some fifteen planes. The seven submarines on picket line "A" were then ordered to shift southward at least 100 miles while maintaining the same northeast to southwest direction (see map 6). The three submarines on picket line "B" also received new orders to shift eastward until the eastern end of the new line "B" touched the southwestern end of the new line "A." During the shifting maneuvers, the *I-15* and *I-17* sighted an enemy aircraft carrier at midnight on the twenty-fourth, but the submarines were unable to launch attacks. Soon thereafter Admiral Komatsu ordered all submarines to pursue the enemy carrier, but to no avail. By the evening of the twenty-fifth, Komatsu ordered all submarines to return to their previously assigned picket lines, renamed lines "E" and "F." Within twenty-four hours an air reconnaissance flight reported that a U.S. carrier group was steaming eastward some 200 miles south of Guadalcanal—two submarines were belatedly ordered to pursue the high-speed enemy force. Obviously, the Japanese again suffered from enormous mismanagement of their submarine forces.[8]

The Sixth Fleet accomplished very little before 31 August; the American buildup had gone on for three weeks without submarine interference. This lack of interference was crucial to the initial survival of American forces at Henderson Field, which was completed at first by using a lot of captured Japanese construction equipment. (Only one American bulldozer was landed before cargo ships departed in August.) Yet submarines of the Sixth Fleet sustained heavy casualties. The *RO-33* was redeployed and, having completed a supply mission to Guadalcanal, was patrolling off Port Moresby when it was sunk by the Australian destroyer *Arunta* on 29 August. The day before, the *I-123* was sunk off Savo Island by the USS *Gamble* (DM-15), a light minelayer converted from a 1919 flush-deck destroyer. And two boats on picket line "A," later called line "E," were damaged by ASW attacks and obligated to retire from the Solomons for repairs. On 31 August Admiral Komatsu ordered the picket lines rearranged once again, and a new line was established between Santa Cruz Island in the east and San Cristobal Island in the west. This picket line held promise.[9]

THE SUBMARINE ATTACK ON THE USS *SARATOGA* (CV-3)

Fresh from repairs in Bremerton, Washington, after the January attack, the veteran carrier *Saratoga* once again came under submarine attack. At dawn on 31 August, Cmdr. Minoru Yokota of the *I-26* sighted a carrier well east of San Cristobal Island and launched six torpedoes with a 120-degree angle on the bow and a 3,800-yard range.[10] One torpedo hit, causing some damage to the *Saratoga*, but it was less damage than that caused by the *I-6*'s attack some eight months earlier. A witness to the attack from aboard the *Saratoga* later recalled that

> The Japanese submarine fired several torpedoes at us and quickly dived deeper in an attempt to avoid the destroyer *MacDonough* [some 30 yards from the submarine] and the depth charges she was certain to drop. On the way to the depths the submarine apparently scraped the destroyer's hull. One of the torpedoes hit us amidships, starboard side. The damage was not as severe as that caused by the blast in January, and we limped off for Tongatapu [an advance base in the South Tonga island group] where the hole was filled with concrete. The *Saratoga* then sailed to Pearl Harbor for permanent repairs, where I was transferred to the *Enterprise,* my home for the next twenty-seven months, as it turned out.[11]

The *I-26* was unable to confirm the effects of its attack at the time because of a four-hour ASW heavy counterattack.[12]

THE SINKING OF THE USS *WASP* (CV-7)

U.S. carriers were highly valued prey for Japanese submarines in the eastern Solomons. On the afternoon of 13 September, Japanese air reconnaissance sighted a U.S. carrier group some 200 miles southeast of the southeastern tip of San Cristobal Island. At the time, the nine submarines deployed on a picket line between San Cristobal Island and Santa Cruz Island were alerted that an enemy carrier group was in the general vicinity. Carrier *Wasp* fell prey to Comdr. Takaichi Kinashi in the *I-19*, stationed near the center of the picket line, about 140 miles southeast of the eastern end of San Cristobal Island. At noon (local time) on the fifteenth, Kinashi heard several propeller sounds; fifty minutes later he sighted a carrier, a cruiser, and escorting destroyers at a distance of about 8 miles. The range and position of the target ruled out an attack at the time. On two occasions, however, the U.S. carrier group altered its heading on the inside, thus reducing the range while also presenting a more favorable angle on the bow (see map 7). Finally, at 1345, the *I-19* fired six torpedoes at the carrier target, with a 50-degree angle on the bow and a range of 1,000 yards. Commander Kinashi thought he heard four explosions. (The *I-19* was unable to confirm the results of the attack because of heavy ASW counterattacks. However, at dusk the nearby *I-15* confirmed that a badly damaged and drifting enemy aircraft carrier had sunk.[13]) Three of *I-19*'s Type 95 torpedoes hit the *Wasp*, and three others approached another carrier group built around the *Hornet* (CV-8) some 12 miles away—one torpedo hit and slightly damaged the battleship USS *North Carolina* (BB-55). (The slight damage nonetheless knocked the new fast battleship out of the war for two months for repairs.[14]) Then another torpedo hit the destroyer USS *O'Brien* (DD-415), causing the ship later to break in two and sink on 19 October while en route to the United States for refitting. The sixth torpedo from the *I-19* ran its long course without hitting any ships.[15] Undoubtedly Commander Kinashi's attack was one of the more effective among Japanese submariners in the war. Although the element of chance, always present in war, favored Kinashi's hits on the *North Carolina* and *O'Brien*, this remarkable salvo offers ample evidence of the superiority of Japanese torpedoes.

SUBMARINE OPERATIONS IN SEPTEMBER

The failure of the second counterattack by Maj. Gen. Kiyotake Kawaguchi's brigade on Guadalcanal in September was extremely dis-

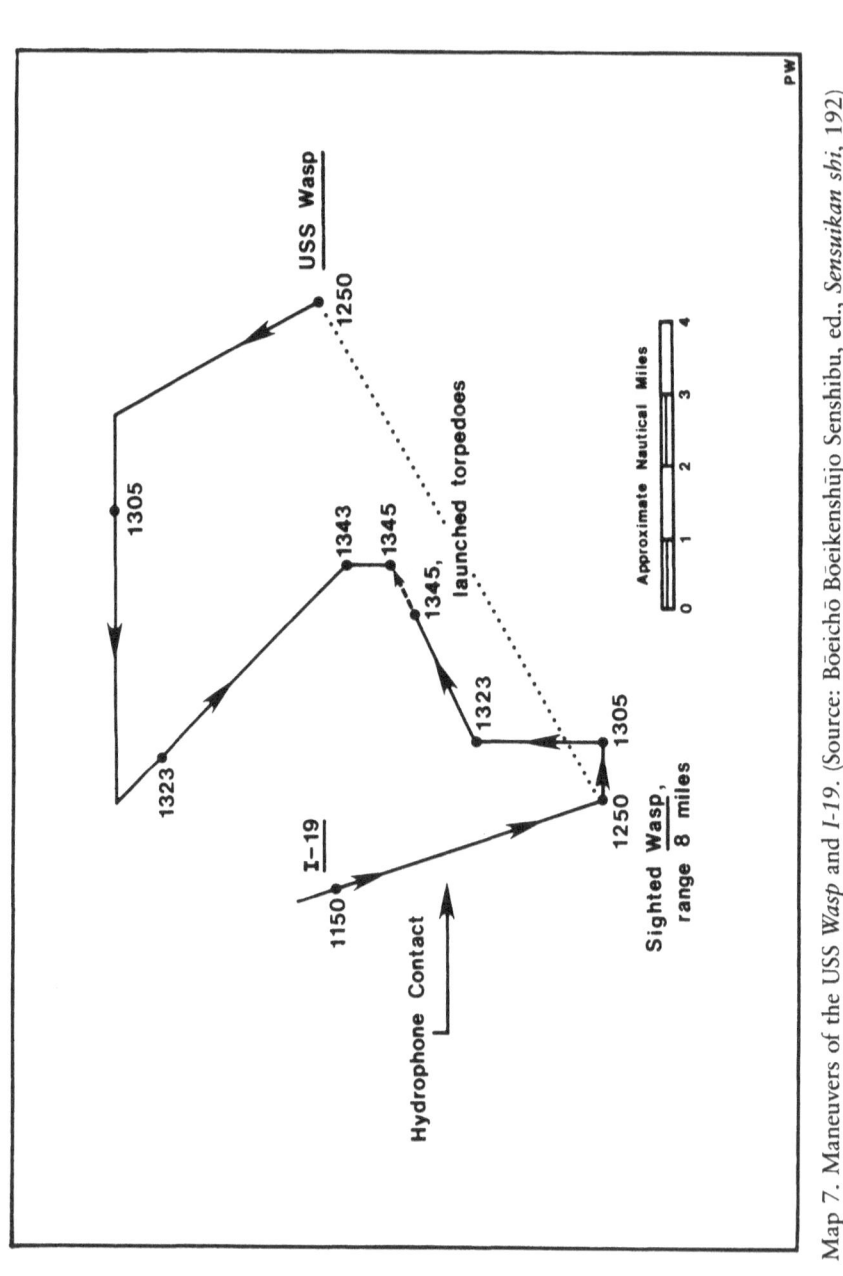

Map 7. Maneuvers of the USS *Wasp* and *I-19*. (Source: Bōeichō Bōeikenshūjo Senshibu, ed., *Sensuikan shi*, 192)

turbing to the senior command at Army and Navy Imperial Headquarters. Determined not to lose Guadalcanal, the decision was made to escalate the struggle by sending the Second Division, fresh from the conquest of Java, to confront U.S. marines on Guadalcanal. Combined Fleet Headquarters ordered all available naval forces to support the transport of these veteran troops and their supplies to the besieged island.[16]

Pressure was increased on submarine operations to prevent U.S. reinforcements from reaching the island. All submarines near the Solomon Islands were placed under the unified command of Rear Adm. Shigeaki Yamazaki, commander of Submarine Squadron 1. However, Japanese submarine interference with the U.S. buildup on Guadalcanal remained marginal. With the notable exception of the sinking of the *Wasp*, submarine activity was moderate during this period and largely ineffective. In effect, most submarine activity had little bearing on the high command's chief concern, securing Guadalcanal as a Japanese bastion. For example, the *I-31* bombarded an enemy flying boat base in a nuisance raid at San Cristobal Island on 12 September, and five days later this boat reconnoitered bases on Espiritu Santo Island. Again, on 2 October, Espiritu Santo was the subject of a reconnaissance mission, this time carried out by a seaplane launched from the *I-21*—an American airstrip under construction was observed. And while the *I-4* damaged the 7,440-ton American cargo ship *Alhena* on 29 September, more significantly, U.S. forces on Guadalcanal continued to hold on.[17]

SUBMARINE OPERATIONS IN OCTOBER

The struggle for Guadalcanal became more intense in October. In preparation for the arrival of Japanese reinforcements on 15 October, the battleships *Kongō* and *Haruna* bombarded Henderson Field at midnight on the thirteenth, destroying some forty-eight of the ninety U.S. aircraft there. The Japanese planned a "total attack" for 22 October, then postponed the attack to the twenty-fifth. Carrier task forces from both sides, intending to support or to prevent the great Japanese attack, clashed violently on 26 October in the battle of the South Pacific, called the battle of Santa Cruz by the Allies. The Japanese fleet was considerably larger than the American, and the margin of the Japanese naval victory was considerable as well. The carrier *Hornet* was sunk, and the only other U.S. carrier in the battle, the *Enterprise*, was damaged. The Japanese carrier *Shōkaku* and the light carrier

Zuihō were damaged as well—significantly, the Japanese lost more planes than the Americans and the Japanese Second Division failed to take Henderson Field from the First Marine Division. However, the struggle for Guadalcanal continued.[18]

At sea the role of the Japanese submarines became more important because of the heavy damage both carrier air groups sustained. Ten of Admiral Yamazaki's submarines were assigned generally to reconnaissance missions with the hope that they would be as successful as the *I-19* had been in sinking the *Wasp*. There were four ocean-cruising submarines in one group—*I-15, I-17, I-19, I-26*—and five ocean-cruising-type submarines and one fleet type in the other: *I-4, I-5, I-7, I-8, I-22*, and *I-176*. These boats were to conduct patrols around Guadalcanal and prevent the arrival of enemy reinforcements. (At the time, a few other submarines were undergoing repair at Truk or Rabaul.[19])

Although Japanese submarines constituted a powerful undersea force and were of enormous concern to Allied commanders, their potential was undermined because of continued mismanagement. In particular, the effectiveness of submarine operations in October was hampered because of frequently changing orders from the high command. The commander of submarines in the eastern Solomons, Admiral Yamazaki, never had a clear picture of the intentions of U.S. battle forces until it was too late for his submarines to implement intercept operations very effectively. Picket lines were frequently shifted. For example, with the aerial sightings of an American carrier group on 13 October, northeast of San Cristobal Island and southwest of Rennell Island, submarines were ordered to dash north from a previously established picket line over 200 miles away. Only the *I-176* was able on this occasion to sight the enemy—it launched torpedoes and damaged the USS *Chester* (CA-27) during the night of the twentieth. The heavy cruiser withdrew from the Pacific for repairs in Norfolk, Virginia, and rejoined the Pacific Fleet several months later in 1943. With the impending battle of Santa Cruz (South Pacific) at hand, on 19 October submarines were ordered to take up new picket line stations west of Espiritu Santo Island. Nine submarines dashed southwestward to the wrong site, as it turned out, for the battle of Santa Cruz would take place north of the island, starting at dawn on the twenty-sixth. Admiral Yamazaki again ordered his submarines to shift, this time to an area about 300 miles north. In this instance, the *I-15, I-21*, and *I-24* sighted the U.S. forces steaming south from Santa Cruz at a point 200 miles west of Espiritu Santo. They fired torpedoes, but no hits were scored against the fast-moving targets. In other submarine action, the *I-7* reconnoitered Espiritu Santo on 13 October and bombarded the island the following night, and the *I-15* acted as a refuel boat for seaplane reconnaissance operations. The *I-22,* however, was lost after its final communication on 4 October.[20]

Submarine commanding officers were critical of the frequent change of orders, but their criticisms were ignored by the high command. In the pressing circumstances of the struggle for Guadalcanal and other islands in the Solomons, submariners were to receive even more objectionable orders. They were soon to supply or evacuate Japanese army units on isolated islands.[21]

SUBMARINE OPERATIONS FROM NOVEMBER 1942 UNTIL THE EVACUATION OF GUADALCANAL IN FEBRUARY 1943

After the Second Division failed to capture Henderson Field, Imperial Headquarters continued to refuse to give up the struggle for Guadalcanal. The Thirty-Eighth Division, conqueror of Hong Kong, was ordered to "Starvation Island," as Guadalcanal would soon be known, but transport and supply of Japanese troops were made extremely difficult by growing American air strength. Combined Fleet Headquarters conducted November's campaign for Guadalcanal as it had the previous month. Reinforcements were run in to the island by fast destroyers, and naval strength was enhanced by the big guns of Japanese battleships. By 15 November two major battles took place off Guadalcanal, with the Japanese losing two battleships, *Hiei* and *Kirishima,* while two U.S. light cruisers were sunk. A critically important Japanese convoy was annihilated on 13 November (nine thousand of the fourteen thousand reinforcing troops failed to reach the island), and Guadalcanal started to become a desperate island for the poorly supplied Japanese soldiers there. At about the same time, the Japanese were confronted with another successful Allied counterattack in New Guinea.[22]

Submarine missions remained crucial in the Japanese struggle. The First Submarine Group was now commanded by Rear Adm. Hisashi Mito, who relieved Admiral Yamazaki on 22 October. Three submarines —*I-16, I-20,* and *I-24*—had the mission of launching midget submarine attacks against enemy convoys off Guadalcanal. Others (*I-15, I-17,* and *I-26*) were to patrol waters southwest of San Cristobal Island to prevent enemy reinforcements from reaching Guadalcanal. Similarly, another group of submarines under the command of Rear Adm. Setsuzō Yoshitomi (*I-122, I-172, I-175,* and *RO-34*) was to patrol waters northeast of San Cristobal Island for the same crucial purpose, to prevent enemy reinforcements from reaching Guadalcanal. Three additional submarines under the command of Capt. Hanku Sasaki were assigned reconnaissance missions in the vicinity of Noumea, New Caledonia. (At this time a few other submarines, under the direct command of Vice Adm. Teruhisa Komatsu, commander of the Sixth Fleet, were undergoing repair at Truk.[23])

The relative ineffectiveness of submarine operations in November was accentuated by the losses the submarine force suffered. Eight midget submarines, brought from Japan to Truk by the tender *Chiyoda* and then transported to the Shortland Island advance base south of Rabaul, were again employed, as *Kō hyōteki* midget submarines had been earlier at Pearl Harbor, Sydney, and Madagascar. The results were negligible. Only *I-20*'s midget submarine damaged a transport off Guadalcanal on 7 November. The other midget submarines were lost.[24]

The larger submarines were no more successful than the midgets at this time. The only enemy ship sunk by an I-boat in November was the cruiser *Juneau* (CL-52).[25] Damaged badly earlier in the first battle of Guadalcanal, the light cruiser was steaming south during the morning of the thirteenth when one of *I-26*'s torpedoes caught it port side under the bridge. An enormous explosion caused the ship to disintegrate and sink almost immediately. Almost seven hundred men, including the five Sullivan brothers, went down with the *Juneau* or died in the open sea. (As a result of this sinking, the U.S. Navy issued regulations forbidding relatives from serving in the same ship.[26]) Other submarines participated in reconnaissance operations: the *I-7* off Vanikoro Island, Santa Cruz; *I-9* off Espiritu Santo; *I-21* off Noumea; and *I-31* off Pago Pago, American Samoa. The *I-17* and *I-122* acted as refueling boats for seaplane reconnaissance missions. The high price paid for carrying out these operations was the loss of the *I-15* and *I-172*. These boats were patrolling in the vicinity of San Cristobal Island when Japanese naval authorities received their final communications in early November.[27] The *I-172* was sunk by the USS *Southard* (DMS-10). The ratio of Japanese submarines lost to U.S. vessels sunk by submarines became worse for the Japanese, and after almost one year into the war, there seemed to be little hope that the much-respected and powerful prewar Japanese submarine force would ever be able to recover.

SUBMARINE TRANSPORT OPERATIONS

The hardship of the Sixth Fleet was further intensified less than a year after the attack on Pearl Harbor, when many boats were assigned transport duty. On 16 November 1942, Admiral Yamamoto ordered the use of submarines for transportation missions because of the critical conditions faced by Japanese forces on Guadalcanal and at Buna in eastern New Guinea. Admiral Komatsu initially ordered thirteen ocean-cruising and fleet-type submarines to participate in the dangerous transportation missions.

These submarines transported about 1,115 tons of cargo to Guadalcanal while they also evacuated over two thousand troops (several more thousand troops were evacuated by fast destroyers); however, the submarine force suffered badly. As with the fast destroyers of the so-called Tokyo Express, the place and hour of arrival of various I-boats were often known in advance through U.S. cryptologic intelligence.[28] The *I-3* was lost on 9 December when attacked by *PT-59* near Cape Esperance, Guadalcanal; *I-4* was lost soon after its final communication was received on 20 December; and *I-1*, after being badly damaged in an attack by two New Zealand corvettes, was successfully beached in Kamimbo Bay at the northwestern end of Guadalcanal and abandoned on 29 January 1943. The *I-1* yielded valuable code books, which, as a senior U.S. Navy intelligence officer wrote after the war, were "as precious as a moon rock to an astronomer."[29] The *I-18* was lost in early February after completing its supply mission to Guadalcanal. Because of these overwhelming casualties and the continued deterioration of Japanese positions on the island, by mid-February 1943, submarines were finally withdrawn from the transportation operations at Guadalcanal.[30]

The failure of submarines in this ill-conceived operation was also due to poor planning by the high command. As Comdr. Yoshimitsu Sekito, Submarine Squadron 7 staff operations officer, later recalled,

> In spite of the use of many submarines in these transportation operations, they were not very effective. The transportation operations failed because of slipshod planning by the senior command and because of the confusion resulting from rapidly deteriorating military conditions. Sometimes submarine sailors were ordered to transport unnecessary supplies while risking their lives; sometimes they transported troops alone, without appreciable supplies, only later to be required to evacuate the same troops. Furthermore, there

106   The Japanese Submarine Force

The wrecked *I-1* being examined by U.S. Army intelligence personnel as the USS *PT-65* stands by, 11 February 1943. The Japanese submarine was damaged during an attack by New Zealand corvettes and forced to beach in Kamimbo Bay, Guadalcanal, on 29 January 1943. The *I-1* was completed at Kobe on 10 March 1926. (National Archives, SC 243966)

The wrecked hulk of *I-1* in Kamimbo Bay, Guadalcanal. Beached and sunk near the northwest tip of Guadalcanal by HMNZS *Kiwi* and *Moa* in January 1943, the hulk of *I-1* yielded documents of great intelligence value. (National Archives, SC 166454)

was little coordination between the army and the navy in these operations.[31]

All in all, the struggle for Guadalcanal was a costly experience for the Japanese submarine force. Nine submarines were lost since the American landings in August, which were very serious losses if not devastating to the future of the Japanese submarine force. During the same period submarines were responsible for the sinking of the *Wasp*, *Juneau*, and *O'Brien*, and the *Saratoga*, *North Carolina*, and *Chester* were damaged by submarine torpedoes. These warships represented no inconsiderable loss to the Allies at a crucial stage in the Pacific War. Yet, when one considers the large number of submarines committed to the Guadalcanal campaign and the strategically critical nature of that campaign, one could reasonably expect that considerably more enemy naval ships would have been sunk. It is perhaps too easy to suggest that Japanese submarines were misused during the supply and evacuation operations at Guadalcanal, but the strength and determination of the enemy and the tradition of Japanese armed forces never to surrender left Japanese submariners with no alternatives.[32]

A *RO-100*-class Japanese submarine photographed near Rabaul by an Allied aircraft in March 1943. (National Archives, 80-G-63995)

Axis Relations and the Submarine Connection

Another dimension of Japanese submarine operations starting in 1942 was communication with Japan's European allies. In September 1940, Japan concluded the Tripartite Pact, a military alliance with Germany and Italy. A few days after the Pearl Harbor attack in December 1941, the two European Axis powers joined Japan in the war against the United States. In fact, they were not obligated to do so under the terms of their alliance. Despite the alliance, the navies of the three Axis powers had no common strategy; in particular, the German and Japanese navies had no significant communications concerning the coordination of naval strategies and operations. However, the Japanese navy wanted German items such as aircraft engines, submarine homing torpedoes, and electronic devices. Mutual economic assistance was an integral part of the 1940 Axis Pact. Germany, on the other hand, wanted important raw materials from Japanese occupied territories, for example, natural rubber, tin, and tungsten. But the connection by surface blockade runners was coming under heavy Allied attack, and after the summer of 1942, the operations of Atlantic-Pacific surface runners became extremely hazardous. The surface blockade runner system for maintaining the East-West Axis exchange was dangerously unreliable. Thus, the use of submarines was planned in operations designed to maintain this vital link.[33] This type of long-distance transportation operation also proved extremely dangerous for Japanese submarines, particularly later when they fell sometimes inescapably within the shadow of Allied cryptologic intelligence operations.

The first submarine to make the long trip to Axis Europe was the *I-30*, commanded by Comdr. Shinobu Endō. At the conclusion of its operations in the Indian Ocean with the *I-10*, *I-16*, *I-18*, and *I-20* in June 1942 (see chapter 3), the *I-30* took on supplies and fuel from a Japanese armed merchant cruiser south of Madagascar and started the long and hazardous voyage to Europe. The big boat rounded the Cape of Good Hope by 30 June and, under an escort of German minesweepers in the Bay of Biscay, reached the safety of German harbor facilities at Lorient, France, during the first week of August. Grand Admiral Erich Raeder, commander in chief of the German Navy, greeted the Japanese sailors amid much fanfare.[34]

The *I-30* carried a modest amount of strategically important goods on its maiden voyage into the Atlantic, for it had previously been on a war patrol in the Indian Ocean. However, the Japanese boat left France in late August with a prize cargo of German technical equipment, such as radar, rocket and glider bombs, and antitank guns, intended for Japanese armed forces. This 350-foot I-boat reached Penang safely and then sailed to Singapore. On 13 October, however, the *I-30* struck a British mine near Keppel Harbor, Singapore, losing much of the valued cargo (some was salvaged) and thirteen of the hundred-man crew.[35] Admiral Ugaki, chief of staff, Combined Fleet, wrote extensively of this event in his diary entry of 14 October 1942:

> The most regrettable incident was the sinking of the submarine *I-30*. After the Indian Ocean operation she was sent to Europe and, after sailing around South Africa, arrived safely at a German submarine base in France where she delivered the documents and things entrusted to her. A big welcome given to her was made public in radio photos and announcements by Imperial headquarters. On her way back, she reached Singapore at 0930 yesterday, the 13th. After finishing business she left there for Yokosuka at 1600. But she struck a mine at the end of the swept channel south of the commercial port and sank.
>
> All those aboard were rescued except about a dozen petty officers and men, but the new arms and parts which our navy needed most were lost. Their transportation to our homeland was the main object of her being sent to Europe. After covering more than eighty percent of the whole trip, she met this disaster in our occupied port. Nothing could be more regrettable. I also felt my responsibility to the high command and especially to the German authorities for the loss. At least the arms on board her should be salvaged by all means.[36]

It was an ominous beginning for submarine blockade running. The next I-boats to sail for Europe would not depart until the next year, when the conditions of the Pacific War were more demanding of Japan and the Allied communications intelligence grid was more widespread. Both of these conditions jeopardized the Axis submarine connection.

Submarine Patrols in the Northern Pacific and off the West Coast of North America

While the chief deployment of Japanese naval forces in the second half of 1942 was in the South Pacific, the Northeast District Force (Fifth Fleet) was engaged in carrying out operations in the northern Pacific and in Aleutian waters. After the occupation of the islands of Attu and Kiska in the Aleutian chain in June, there was much debate in the high command about whether to try holding both islands. Their strategic value to the Japanese was greatly reduced because of the American pivotal victory at Midway. Nevertheless, the initial decision was made to keep and reinforce both islands, and for more than nine months the Japanese struggle to hold on proved costly, particularly to the submarine force. A submarine garrison force attached to the Fifth Fleet was based at Kiska. Comdr. (later Capt.) Yoshinosuke Katō, commander of Submarine Division 33, had an old ocean-cruising type and seven coastal-defense-type submarines: the *I-6, RO-61, RO-62, RO-63, RO-64, RO-65, RO-67,* and *RO-68*.[37]

The northern waters proved disastrous for Japanese submarines in late 1942; Japanese attacks on American ships were very limited. For example, the *RO-61* damaged the seaplane tender USS *Casco* (AVP-12) in a torpedo attack at dusk on 30 August, but the next day this small submarine was sunk during an ASW attack by U.S. aircraft and the destroyer *Reid* (DD-369). In September at least two submarines were damaged in American and Canadian bombing raids against the Kiska anchorage, and in early November the *RO-65* was lost accidentally in an emergency dive during an air raid. Other submarines were also dispatched to Aleutian waters in late 1942, and many more arrived in the spring of 1943 to participate in evacuation operations, not unlike their assignments in the South Pacific.

A Japanese submarine again carried out attacks against the mainland of the United States. The *I-25,* one boat of the First Submarine Group not actually sent to Guadalcanal, arrived off Cape Blanco, Oregon, in late August 1942 to exact vengeance for the humiliating Doolittle air raid on Japanese cities the previous April. The lone submarine launched its seaplane on 9 September and again on the twenty-ninth, each time dropping two 170-pound incendiary bombs on the forests of Oregon. The Federal Bureau of Investigation (FBI) started to investigate the attack within four hours of the first explosion, and soon Lt. Gen. John L. DeWitt, commander of the Fourth Army and the Western Defense Command, sent staff officers to Washington, D.C., to obtain permission to add to his defense forces, including a small air squadron of P-38s.[38] These were only nuisance attacks, however, and they caused very little damage—only one bomb exploded to start a small fire on Wheeler Ridge, approximately four miles southeast of Mount Emily. Nevertheless, the *I-25* sank two oil tankers, the 6,600-ton SS *Camden* not far from Seattle in early October and the SS *Larry Doheny* near Cape Sebastian at about the same time, 5 October. With one torpedo left, the *I-25* started the long voyage back to its base at Yokosuka when on 11 October, two submarines, which the Japanese assumed to be American, were sighted on the surface sailing southward. The Japanese torpedo struck the foreign submarine, sinking it in about twenty seconds with all hands. Postwar records reveal, however, that *I-25*'s victim was the *L-16*, one of two Russian submarines en route at that time from Vladivostok to Panama. Since Japan and the Soviet Union were not at war in 1942, this attack, had its facts been known at the time, might have had serious diplomatic consequences. On 24 October the *I-25* reached Yokosuka after a seventy-day, 12,000-mile war patrol. It was an operation with several odd dimensions, nevertheless, *I-25*'s primary mission, the bombing of the U.S. mainland in retaliation for the Doolittle raid, was accomplished with much skill and bravery.[39]

Submarine Patrols in the Indian Ocean, August–November 1942

The other main group of Japanese submarines not engaged in the struggle for Guadalcanal was the Eighth Submarine Group (Submarine Squadron 8), commanded by Rear Adm. Hisashi Ichioka, who relieved Admiral Ishizaki in August. Two ocean-cruising and three old fleet-type submarines of this squadron (*I-27, I-29, I-162, I-165,* and *I-166*) were assigned communications destruction missions out of Penang. Their patrols lasted until the end of November. The *I-27* sank one cargo ship in the Arabian Sea; *I-29* sank four cargo vessels on the African side of the Indian Ocean; *I-162* sank two cargo ships and damaged another in the Bay of Bengal; and *I-165* and *I-166*, patrolling in the same general area, sank a total of three cargo ships and damaged another. Thus, five boats sank ten cargo vessels (totaling nearly 60,000 tons) without suffering damage to themselves. It was a kill-survival ratio not frequently enjoyed by the Japanese submarine force.

When this operation was concluded, the three fleet-type submarines were transferred from the Indian Ocean to the Arafura Sea and to the waters off eastern Australia, where the pace of war was far more demanding. However, they did not sink any enemy vessels. The two ocean cruising-type submarines of the Eighth Submarine Group remained in the Indian Ocean, where they sank two additional cargo ships. All in all, these operations against enemy lines of communication were relatively successful in late 1942, at least when compared with the performance-loss ratio of other Japanese submarines during the same period and for much of the first year of the war. But the bitter struggles, in the Aleutian and particularly in the Solomon Islands, dominated the high command's guidance of war as the Allies assumed an unrelenting offensive in the latter part of 1942. Submarines, like all other Japanese forces, were increasingly called upon in attempts to check the ever-growing advances of enemy forces.

5

The Attrition of War and Submarine Operations

The South Pacific Early in 1943

In spite of various shortcomings of Japanese submarine operations in 1942, their performance that year, in comparison with their performance in the rest of the war, was their best. The breadth and pace of their operations wore heavily on the silent service by 1943, and the Imperial Navy seemed unable to regain the initiative after failures at Midway and Guadalcanal. Furthermore, the overall performance of Japanese submarines was insufficient to deter the ever-growing strength of Allied forces.

In the aftermath of the struggle for Guadalcanal many submarines were laid up for repair and overhaul, and many of the officers and crew were rotated or relieved by fresh sailors. As a result, at least in part, submarine operations were relatively modest early in 1943. One such operation was carried out by then *I-6* when six acoustic mines brought from Germany were laid off Brisbane, Australia, on 13 March. (These new acoustic mines were shaped much like torpedoes and were discharged from the submarine through the ordinary 21-inch torpedo tube.) The *I-6*'s enciphered radio communications had been intercepted by American intelligence, and three U.S. submarines—*Stingray* (SS-186), *Trigger* (SS-237), and *Halibut* (SS-232)—were ordered to lie in wait for the Japanese submarine. But the U.S. submarines failed to spot the *I-6*.[1] Although this particular mission was a failure, this type of cryptologic intelligence, namely, ULTRA, was increasingly used with good results in 1943. Originally, ULTRA was the name the British gave to information obtained from breaking German wireless traffic enciphered on the Enigma machine. However, distinct nomenclature broke down, and by 1943 the term "Japanese ULTRA" was commonly used by Americans for information obtained from reading Japanese navy, army, and air systems. ULTRA intelligence was sent from Commander of Submarines, Pacific, to U.S. submarines on station in the western Pacific through special internal code and communications channels available only to submarine commands.[2]

Other Japanese submarines were engaged in search and rescue operations because of another disaster that befell Japanese forces. Japanese army reinforcements headed for New Guinea were attacked in the Bismarck Sea by U.S. Army aircraft on 2 March. ULTRA had given the Americans two weeks' advance notification of the Japanese convoy routes and destinations.[3] Eight transport ships and four destroyers were sunk—about 3,000 soldiers were lost. The Japanese deployed several submarines to search the area for survivors, including the *I-17*, which picked up 156 soldiers, and the *I-26*, which rescued 54. Soon afterward, the *I-26* proceeded to the eastern coast of Australia and there sank two cargo vessels.[4] The offensive quality of these submarine operations was of no major consequence, as they inflicted little damage on Allied forces. This was an alarming state of affairs for the Japanese, especially considering it was the beginning of a crucial year, 1943, when Japan's fortune waned more appreciably.

Yet in the same year there appeared briefly some new enthusiasm for operations aimed at the destruction of enemy sea communications. The newly appointed commander of the First Submarine Group (Submarine Squadron 1), Rear Adm. Takerō Kōta, ordered such an operation in the vicinity of Fiji and Samoa. His four ocean-cruising submarines (*I-17, I-19, I-25,* and *I-32*) made patrols in April and May; all of them returned safely. The *I-17* sank one cargo vessel, *I-19* sank two and damaged another, and *I-25* sank one cargo ship. Similarly, the newly appointed commander of the Third Submarine Group (Submarine Squadron 3), Rear Adm. Katsumi Komazawa, sent his new fleet-type submarines to search for enemy merchantmen near the Solomons and eastern New Guinea in May and June. The *I-174* sank a cargo vessel and damaged another as well, and *I-177* sank two cargo ships.

The *I-178* also sank a cargo ship; however, after stopping briefly at Truk in early June, this boat was not heard from after the seventeenth, and the Sixth Fleet presumed that it was lost. The fourth submarine of this squadron, *I-180,* also sank two cargo vessels and damaged another two. Thus, one of the eight submarines was lost during these operations against enemy shipping, and at least fifteen cargo ships were sunk or damaged from April to June.[5]

The Seventh Submarine Group (Submarine Squadron 7) also briefly emphasized the destruction of enemy shipping, but its success was more limited. Rear Adm. Kaku Harada, appointed squadron commander in January, was attached to the fleet command based at Rabaul. There were eight submarines in his command: *I-122, RO-34, RO-100, RO-101, RO-102, RO-103, RO-106,* and *RO-107.* Of these submarines, the *RO-101* rescued forty-five survivors in the aftermath of the March U.S. Army air attack on troop transports in the Bismarck Sea. The *RO-103* was scheduled to assist in the rescue mission, but slight damage from hitting a reef prevented it from operating with the *RO-101* on this occasion. Later, on 23 June, the *RO-103* sank two transport ships near Guadalcanal, but the *RO-34* and *RO-102* were sunk in the same area. The American destroyer *O'Bannon* (DD-450) was responsible for the destruction of the *RO-34* on 5 April, and *PT-150* and *PT-152* sank *RO-102* on 14 May. Thus, Submarine Squadron 7 lost two boats, whereas only two enemy transport ships were sunk.[6]

SUBMARINE TRANSPORT OPERATIONS FOR NEW GUINEA

After the evacuation from Guadalcanal, the Japanese army and navy intended to check the Allied advance at the "Bismarck Barrier." Accordingly, reinforcements were sent to the central Solomons and to the eastern New Guinea area. But the enormous setback suffered in early March in the Bismarck Sea made it clear to the high command that transport operations could not be continued by ordinary surface transport ships. Instead, small landing craft (*Dai hatsu*) were substituted in what was called "ant carrying transport" operations. The small 55-foot *Dai hatsu* landing craft, built since about 1935, was highly versatile for island-to-island hauling, but its cargo capacity was no more than 16 tons. Experiments were also conducted with a 135-foot submergible stores vessel (*Unkatō*) designed for one-way replenishment missions. Towed underwater by a large submarine to coastal waters of isolated island garrisons, a loaded *Unkatō* was then cut loose and beached, to be unloaded by island garrison troops. But these operations were unreliable and extremely difficult to control—very few vessels of this type reached their destination.[7] In general, these types of transport operations proved inadequate for possibly checking the advance of Douglas MacArthur's forces at Lae, the most important point in eastern New Guinea. As a result, submarines and fast destroyers of the Tokyo Express were again called upon for transport and reinforcement operations.[8] The mission for Lae was assigned to the Seventh Submarine Group under Admiral Harada, who sent out numerous submarines from mid-March to mid-June with much misgiving about this type of mission. Nevertheless, in forty-eight sorties, one thousand troops and 1,400 tons of supplies were transported by submarines and, surprisingly, without any submarines being lost or damaged.[9] But the reinforcement operation failed to strengthen the land forces sufficiently to halt MacArthur's forces, and by the end of September, the Lae army garrison was overwhelmed. Forces of MacArthur's Southwest Pacific Command started then to advance along the northern coast of New Guinea.[10]

The Indian Ocean in Early 1943

Eight ocean-cruising submarines of the Eighth Submarine Group (Submarine Squadron 8), commanded by Rear Adm. Noboru Ishizaki, were not caught up in the struggle for Guadalcanal or New Guinea. Operations against commerce held the most potential in the Indian Ocean, where merchant shipping was rarely escorted, although this Allied practice started to change in 1943. Indeed, in January 1943 the navy distributed a new publication titled "Strategic Reference for the Destruction of Marine Traffic by Submarine." The key purpose of this brief submarine doctrine was to destroy enemy merchant shipping; however, the doctrine was never wholeheartedly implemented, "due to the traditional idea for the decisive battle by the fleet," as a Japanese naval historian has recently written.[11]

Another reason the doctrine was not implemented in the Indian Ocean was because squadron submarines, pressed into hard service since the beginning of the war, were forced to undergo long overhauls and extensive repair during much of early 1943. Thus, effective operations in the Indian Ocean at this time were limited to the activities of only three submarines (*I-27*, *I-37*, and *I-29*). They sank or damaged eight ships: the *I-27* (commanded by Lt. Comdr. Toshiaki Fukumura) succeeded in sinking five cargo ships (totaling 25,000 tons) and damaging another, and the *I-37* sank two cargo vessels.[12]

The most unusual operation in the Indian Ocean in early 1943 was the one carried out by the *I-29* in its meeting with the *U-180*. On 9 February 1943 the *U-180* left Kiel with blueprints of various military weapons (V-2 rockets and jet engines, for example). The German submarine refueled from the *U-462* on 3 March and proceeded to the Indian Ocean. Two passengers were also aboard the *U-180*, Subhas Chandra Bose and his adjutant, Dr. Habid Hassan, a former student at Oxford University. As part of a deception plan, prerecorded interviews between Hitler and Bose were broadcast from Berlin while the *U-180* was still in the Atlantic during the first two weeks of the long voyage. Bose, India's revolutionary Nationalist leader, had escaped in early 1941 from prison to flee into Afghanistan, through the Soviet Union, and thence to Berlin. There, as the guest of the Hitler government from March 1941 to early 1943, he recruited supporters for rather modest Indian troop formations, presumably to be used against the British in India once the Germans conquered the Caucasus and were ready to link up with the Japanese. But by early 1943, when there was no prospect of an Axis linkup, Bose decided to throw in his lot with the Japanese, and the Germans facilitated his return to Asia by sending the *U-180* on this peculiar passenger-transport mission.[13] The *I-29* had been sailing westward through the Indian Ocean to rendezvous with the *U-180* at a prearranged point southeast of Madagascar. It carried two Japanese passengers whose purpose was to go to Germany to observe the techniques of U-boat construction. The *I-29* also carried three *kaiten* and secret information about Japanese torpedoes intended for the German navy and two boxes of gold specifically for the Japanese embassy in Berlin. The rendezvous took place on 23 April, and after a ten-hour meeting and the exchange of passengers and cargoes, the Axis submarines parted. The *U-180* returned safely to the Atlantic, arriving eventually at Bordeaux, and the *I-29* took Bose directly to Singapore.[14] In general, however, this elaborate and rather daring operation held very little military promise.

The Aleutians in Early 1943

OPERATIONS FOR THE DEFENSE AND SUPPORT OF ATTU

Japan's earlier decision to keep and reinforce both Attu and Kiska soon had to be changed when U.S. forces stepped up efforts in early

1943 to recapture the American territory. However, the exhausting March clash of U.S. and Imperial Navy cruiser groups in the battle of the Komandorskis (southwest Bering Sea) obligated the Japanese to cancel efforts to reinforce and supply the isolated garrison forces with ordinary surface transport ships. Thus, submarines were called upon again, but in severe weather conditions far worse than at Guadalcanal or New Guinea. Submarines of the Northern District Force (Fifth Fleet) were assigned the treacherous mission. Two old and three new ocean cruising–type submarines and three old fleet-type submarines were employed: *I-2, I-7, I-31, I-34, I-35, I-168, I-169,* and *I-171*.[15]

By May the Americans were prepared to push the Japanese out of the Aleutians. When the U.S. invasion of Attu began on 12 May, there were only three Japanese submarines operating in the vicinity. Because of thick fog around this small island, the Combined Fleet Headquarters felt it was impossible to use carrier aircraft or battleships. Moreover, Japanese forces in the area lacked radar. Thus, the high command decided to abandon Attu on 21 May. Before then, however, the *I-35* was damaged by ASW forces and the *I-31* was sunk. The Imperial Army garrison force was annihilated in a final "banzai attack" on 29 May.[16] The sacrifice of submarines in these Aleutian operations was to be more crushing at Kiska.

THE EVACUATION OF KISKA

On the same day the high command decided to abandon Attu, Imperial Headquarters decided also to evacuate its armed forces from Kiska. Thirteen submarines involved in the operation (*I-2, I-7, I-9, I-21, I-24, I-34, I-36, I-155, I-156, I-157, I-169, I-171,* and *I-175*) were assigned to the Commander Submarine Group (Submarine Squadron 1) of the Northern District Force. Rear Adm. Takerō Kōta planned and commanded the evacuation from Kiska to Paramushiro Island, the northeasternmost island in the Kurile chain. The difficult evacuation operations commenced on 27 May, the thirty-eighth anniversary of the Japanese victory over the Russians at the battle of Tsushima.[17]

The toll incurred by the submarine force mounted quickly. The *I-24* was sunk on 11 June by an American submarine chaser, and within a week, the *I-9* was lost during an attack by the USS *Frazier* (DD-607). Appalled by these staggering losses, Admiral Kōta called off the submarine operations because of the effectiveness of enemy ASW operations, but pressure from the high command forced him to resume the evacuation operations on the seventeenth.[18] At this crucial juncture, the submarine commander was not in control of the fate of his force.

Predictably, disaster followed. Soon another submarine engaged in the evacuation operations was lost. While on the surface, the *I-7* was surprised by U.S. ASW forces on 20 June. This big squadron-flagship type of submarine was heavily damaged and forced to beach at Vega Bay on the southern coast of Kiska.

A survivor who eventually became commanding officer during the attack, then twenty-two-year-old Lt. (jg) Hisao Shindō, described *I-7*'s ordeal. During the afternoon of 22 June, the *I-7* surfaced in a dense fog near Vega Bay, when suddenly the submarine came under a barrage of withering enemy gunfire. The commanding officer was immediately killed. There was much flooding, and damage to the main ballast tank prevented the large I-boat from submerging. After emergency repairs and under the command of the executive officer, the *I-7* began steaming for Paramushiro after dark on the same day. At a point about 10 miles south of Vega Bay, the submarine was again suddenly bombarded by the enemy, whom Japanese lookouts could not see (the submarine did not have radar equipment). The conning tower was hit, and the executive officer was killed.

Lieutenant Shindō took command and decided to return to Kiska. The *I-7* was severely hit several times by enemy gunfire; there was fire, heavy flooding, and many casualties. His pursuer was the USS *Monaghan* (DD-354). Shindō felt lucky to reach Vega Bay, and by running aground in the early morning of 22 June, the boat was saved from sinking in deep water. However, eighty-seven officers and crewmen, including the commanding, executive, and engineering officers, were lost.[19]

Clearly, the treacherous evacuation operations were extremely costly to the submarine force. Finally, after the loss of the third submarine in a two-week period, Vice Adm. Shirō Kawase, commander of the North District Force, decided to halt the submarine evacuation operations. About nine hundred of the seven thousand fighting men on Kiska were evacuated by submarine.[20]

New plans were drawn up at the end of June to resume evacuation operations, but this time they were to be carried out by cruisers and destroyers. Submarines were ordered to survey the waters of Kiska, Amchitka, Adak, and Atka and to attack any enemy ships detected during the patrols. Evacuation operations remained very difficult and extremely dangerous because the Japanese surface forces, unlike those of their enemy, lacked radar; thus, the Japanese had much difficulty in navigating through the prevailing fog and low visibility in the Aleutians. However, largely because of the tenacious and insightful leadership of Rear Adm. Masazumi Kimura, commander of Destroyer Squadron 1, the daring evacuation succeeded on 28 July, without American detection.[21] About six thousand troops were evacuated and taken safely to Paramushiro Island. Not until mid-August did a major force of American and Canadian troops land on what turned out to be a vacated Kiska. After these evacuation operations, submarines were temporarily detached from the Northern District Force and concentrated in southern areas.[22]

Submarine Patrols in the Pacific, Mid-1943

ADMINISTRATIVE CHANGES IN THE SUBMARINE FORCE

Japanese armed forces were increasingly hard-pressed by the Allies. Allied assaults in the Bismarck Sea were from two areas: from the central Solomons came the South Pacific Force, and along the northern coast of New Guinea advanced the Southwest Pacific Force. The pressure from the Allies appeared even worse in light of the Japanese total evacuation and abandonment of the Aleutians. The high command believed that an administrative shuffle and, in particular, the appointment of younger commanders might enable the submarine force to deal more effectively with future crises.[23] Therefore, Vice Adm. Takeo Takagi, two classes junior to his predecessor, was named commander of the Sixth Fleet, and all new squadron and division commanders were also junior to their predecessors (see appendix 7).[24] But administrative changes alone were insufficient to correct the deterioration of the submarine force.

SUBMARINE OPERATIONS IN THE SOUTH PACIFIC

Rather extensive submarine operations were undertaken in the South Pacific during the second half of 1943; a shockingly large number of submarines was sunk, whereas damage to Allied forces was limited. Two new submarines, the *I-177* and *I-180,* patrolled the waters of the central Solomons in July, but they did not report any attacks on enemy ships. These were the New *Kaidai* Type A—the *I-177* was completed in December 1942, and the *I-180* entered service in January 1943. The *I-180* rescued some of the survivors of the light cruiser *Jintsū,* sunk in the battle of Kolombangara (Solomons) on the night of 12 July. Afterward, until near the end of August, four submarines of the First Submarine Group (*I-11, I-19, I-17,* and *I-25*) patrolled the waters of Santa Cruz, Espiritu Santo, Fiji, and New Caledonia. The *I-11* badly damaged the Australian cruiser *Hobart* in a torpedo attack on 20 July. HMAS *Hobart* underwent temporary repairs in Espiritu Santo for a month, but full repairs were not completed in Sydney until the end of the year. The *I-19* sank a cargo vessel. But Japanese submariners paid a high price for their successes—two boats were sunk. The *I-17* was sunk by the New Zealand corvette *Tui* and shore-based U.S. Navy aircraft on 19 August; then, five days later, the *I-25* was sunk. Four more submarines of the First Submarine Group (*I-20, I-39, RO-35,* and *I-182*) sortied for patrols starting in late August. They too were largely unsuccessful. The *I-20* damaged a cargo vessel, and the *I-39* sank a similar craft. Overall, however, the group was devastated—three of the four submarines were sunk. The *RO-35* was not heard from after 25 August, the *I-20* was last heard from at the end of August, and the *I-182* on 3 September. Thus, five boats were sunk in the South Pacific in two weeks late in August and early September.[25] By comparison, damage to the enemy was minor.

The Japanese submarine force was being thinned out rapidly. In October only seven submarines were on patrol in the South Pacific, and rather surprisingly, there were no losses to the force. However, the results of their deployment were not notable. Two enemy vessels were sunk. The *I-176* sank an enemy submarine near Truk on 17 October,[26] *I-21* sank a cargo ship in the vicinity of Fiji, and *I-32* conducted a reconnaissance patrol near Pago Pago, American Samoa.

The submarine force nevertheless remained on call to meet the demands of surface admirals. For example, submarines were immediately called upon because of the U.S. Carrier Task Force air strike on Wake Island during the first week of October. The high command asked the commander of the Sixth Fleet, Vice Adm. Takagi, to have his submarines patrol the waters of Wake. Consequently, five submarines took up stations in the vicinity of the island, but they failed to make contact with any enemy forces.[27]

More significantly, the ability of the U.S. Navy to launch such an assault on Wake was of great concern to the Japanese high command. Combined Fleet Headquarters was, therefore, anxious in late 1943 to learn about the sort of strength the U.S. Navy might be assembling at distant Pearl Harbor. Thus, submarine reconnaissance planes were again sought for the mission to Hawaii on two occasions in late

1943.[28] The *I-36*, with Comdr. Michimune Inaba as its commanding officer, was selected for the first mission in October. But Inaba found that he could not get very close to Oahu because of aggressive radar surveillance, and on the night of 17 October he was forced to launch *I-36*'s little seaplane from a point about 150 miles south of Oahu. The reconnaissance plane radioed to its parent submarine that four aircraft carriers and four battleships were sighted inside Pearl Harbor, but the plane failed to return and rendezvous with the *I-36*. On the other hand, Americans at Pearl Harbor assumed that the reconnaissance mission was not particularly successful. As a Honolulu newspaper reported, during the night mission, the Japanese plane "immediately dived in an attempt to elude the [search] lights, reversed its course, and sped out to sea at low altitude."[29] Also, *I-19*'s reconnaissance plane made a successful flight and was fortunate to return with the report that a carrier and a battleship were sighted in Pearl Harbor on the night of 16 November.[30] The Japanese high command was made painfully aware of the buildup of U.S. naval strength and the foreboding shadows that it cast in the western Pacific.

SUBMARINE OPERATIONS DURING THE INVASION IN THE CENTRAL SOLOMONS

The pressure of mounting invasions weighed heavily on an already strained Japanese submarine force. When U.S. forces invaded Rendova Island (off the southwest central coast of New Georgia Island) on 30 June, Rear Adm. Kaku Harada, commander of Submarine Squadron 7, had only three coastal-defense-type submarines in Rabaul and two others out on patrol. Soon most of these submarines concentrated in the vicinities of Rendova and New Georgia, particularly in the Blanche Channel. As in other recent operations, enemy ASW forces held down the submarines: *LST-342* (Landing Ship Tank) was sunk by the *RO-106* on 18 July, and the *RO-108* sank an escort vessel, possibly the USS *Strong* (DD-467) on 5 July. However, the *RO-103* and *RO-107* were themselves sunk. The former boat last reported on 28 July, and the *RO-107* was probably sunk on 12 July in the central Solomons. And the enemy invasion was hardly deterred.[31]

Losses among submarines continued to mount in the South Pacific during the remainder of 1943 and in early 1944. The *RO-101* was sunk by a U.S. Navy vessel about 15 September, and the *RO-100* struck a mine and sunk off the south coast of Bougainville on 25 November. The *I-11* was lost after carrying out a reconnaissance patrol at Funafuti Atoll, Ellice Islands, on New Year's Eve; its final report was made on 11 January. Within hours after the *RO-37* sank the oil tanker *Cache* on 22 January 1944, the *Kaichū* Type 6 of submarine was sunk by the USS *Buchanan* (DD-484). And a few days earlier, 16 January, the *I-181* was sunk by U.S. surface ASW operations in Saint George's Channel, between New Britain and southern New Ireland Islands, after the submarine left Rabaul for transportation operations. Submarine losses in the South Pacific amounted to no fewer than seven boats sacrificed from late in 1943 to the opening weeks of January 1944, as U.S. military pressure mounted in the central Solomons.[32]

Submarine Patrols in the Indian Ocean, Mid-1943

Compared to Japanese submarine operations in the South Pacific, operations in the Indian Ocean, the Arabian Sea, and the Bay of Bengal remained lucrative in mid-1943. One reason was because Japanese submarines were deployed predominantly against merchant ships and supply lines rather than specifically against combat vessels. In addition, Allied ASW forces were not as numerous or as sophisticated as those in the Pacific. Sixteen enemy vessels were sunk, and five were damaged by six submarines between July and December 1943. The *I-10*, under a veteran commanding officer, Comdr. Kinzō Tonozuka, sank five cargo ships (slightly over 30,000 tons) and damaged a sixth one:

22 July 1943	Norwegian motorship *Alcides* (7,634 tons)
14 September 1943	Norwegian tanker *Bramora* (6,361 tons)
24 September 1943	American "Liberty ship" *Elias Howe* (7,176 tons)
1 October 1943	Norwegian steamer *Storviken* (4,836 tons)
5 October 1943	Norwegian tanker (damaged) *Anna Knudsen* (9,057 tons)
24 October 1943	British motorship *Congella* (4,533 tons)

The *I-27*, also with a veteran skipper, Comdr. Toshiaki Fukumura, sank 30,000 tons of shipping and damaged two additional merchantmen; *I-37* sank two cargo vessels and reconnoitered Diégo Suarez, Madagascar; and two smaller coastal-defense-type submarines in the Indian Ocean sank a cargo ship each. Furthermore, the *I-26* landed twelve Indian revolutionaries and their equipment near Karachi on the Arabian Sea for insurgency operations in India. Later, this submarine sank two cargo ships and damaged another.

* * *

Although these kinds of strategic operations in the Indian Ocean would have been significant if they were sustained throughout the long war of attrition, the high command remained hard-pressed by the immediate struggle with Allied forces. It is true that the German navy wanted the Imperial Navy to take a defensive stance in the Pacific against American naval forces, as a distinguished Japanese navy scholar has recently argued. Nevertheless, the reality of the war would not permit the Japanese to pursue such a course. Nor were the Japanese particularly eager to comply with German wishes that the Japanese navy concentrate on offensive operations against the British in the Indian Ocean.[33] There was also the traditional pattern of submarine deployment—submarines were always rushed in to help against new enemy offensives. Thus, the Japanese high command, pressured by the new Allied offensives in late 1943, reacted with alarm and immediately sought the assistance of the submarine force.[34]

The Gilbert Islands

The Combined Fleet Headquarters was plagued by Allied offensives in the central Solomons, eastern New Guinea, and especially on Bougainville Island. Large numbers of Japanese carrier- and land-based aircraft were lost in these campaigns. Under these severe conditions, news of the initial success (21 November 1943) of Adm. Chester Nimitz, U.S. Central Pacific Force, against Tarawa and, a hundred miles north, against Makin in the Gilberts, was particularly shocking to the Japanese high command. This was the first American amphibious landing vigorously opposed on the beach, and casualties were very heavy—of about eighteen thousand American assault troops, over one thousand were killed, and fewer than one hundred of about fifty-three hundred Japanese troops survived the three-day attack. Heaviest losses were around the Betio airfield. Highly skilled Japanese garrison forces on these two atolls were important to the high command; nevertheless, they were largely abandoned. Circumstances did not permit the deployment of any major Japanese fleet units—only land-based air groups from Truk and Kwajalein and submarines were assigned to attack American forces.[35] Adm. Mineichi Koga, commander in chief,

The Attrition of War and Submarine Operations   125

Combined Fleet, wanted large numbers of submarines to concentrate in the Gilbert Islands, whereas the Sixth Fleet commander, Vice Admiral Takagi, had only nine submarines of various types available for operations in the Gilberts: *I-19, I-21, I-35, I-39, I-40, I-169, I-174, I-175*, and *RO-38*.[36]

How the submarines were deployed proved devastating to the force. The high command failed to learn from the mistakes in handling submarines at Midway, during the struggle for Guadalcanal, and in the central Solomons. Again, because of the stress and confusion within the high command, submarines were repeatedly ordered to dash about, almost daily, between 19 and 30 November. Whole picket lines were also shifted frequently—first established east of Tarawa in a northeast-southwest direction, then on each side of Makin in east-west lines. This high command formula for disaster resulted in the loss of six of the nine submarines, and only one enemy ship was sunk[37] (see map 8).

The six submarines sunk in the last two weeks of November were the victims of skillful Allied ASW operations:

1. The *I-19* was lost en route to Tarawa from a reconnaissance mission to the Hawaiian Islands. Its final message was received on 17 No-

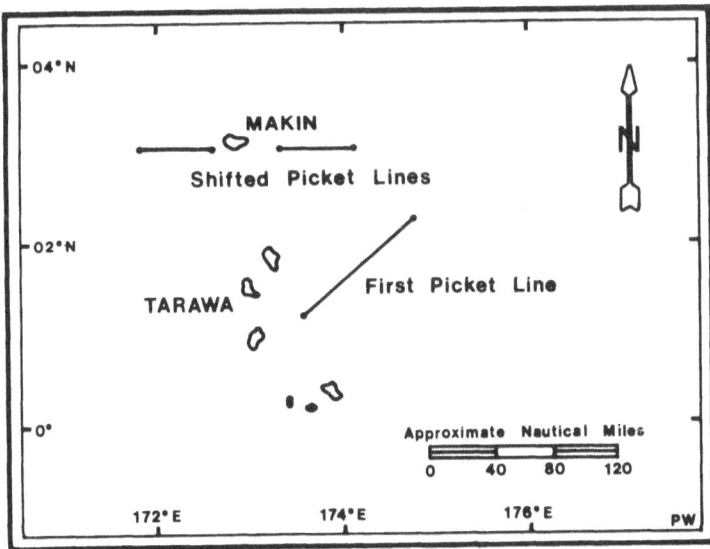

Map 8. Submarine picket lines in the vicinity of Tarawa. (Source: Bōeichō Bōeikenshūjo Senshibu, ed., *Sensuikan shi,* 278)

vember, but the boat was probably sunk by the USS *Radford* (DD-446) in the Gilberts on 25 November.
2. The *I-21* was also lost off the Gilberts after its final message was received on 27 November.
3. The *I-35* was sunk on 22 November by the U.S. Navy destroyers *Frazier* (DD-607) and *Meade* (DD-602).
4. The *I-39* was sunk in much the same fashion on the night of 26 November, probably by the USS *Boyd* (DD-544).
5. The *I-40* was lost without a sign after it sortied from Truk for the Gilberts on 22 November. The USS *Radford* (DD-446) was responsible for sinking the 2,600-ton I-boat on 25 November.
6. The *RO-38* was lost very similarly after it sortied from Truk on 19 November—it was possibly sunk by the USS *Cotten* (DD-669).

There was, however, one major submarine attack during the defense of the Gilbert Islands. The escort aircraft carrier USS *Liscome Bay* (CVE-56) was sunk off Makin Island, with heavy loss of life, by the *I-175* on 24 November. However, the toll taken against the submarine force was so heavy and the mission considered so futile that the head of the Combined Fleet, Admiral Koga, discontinued the Tarawa-Makin operation on 4 December.[38] This disaster—the loss of the six submarines in late November—made such an indelible impression on the high command that early the next year when U.S. forces invaded the Marshall Islands, the Combined Fleet Headquarters decided not to send extensive submarine reinforcements.[39] Only the *I-175* and *RO-39* were ordered to the Marshalls to rescue downed Japanese aviators, and both submarines were sunk by U.S. Navy ASW units: the *RO-39* was sunk by the USS *Walker* (DD-517) on 1 February, and the *I-175* was sunk in an attack by the USS *Charrette* (DD-581) and the *Fair* (DE-35) on 17 February 1944.[40]

* * *

The submarine campaign in 1943 was obviously disastrous. This was not only because of the misuse of submarines, weak submarine tactics, and the remarkable tactical and technological developments of the U.S. Navy in the field of ASW, but also because of the lack of significant developments in Japanese ASW countermeasures. The Imperial Japanese Navy had very little concern for the protection of Japanese shipping lanes or ASW tactics and operations. There was no Japanese navy policy for countering enemy ASW. Japanese submarines were designed as offensive weapons, and their defensive characteristics were very weak. Their generally big hulls, fast surface speeds, and powerful armaments were intended to assist them in offensive operations, but their lack of fully modern electronic sensors, slow submerged speed, shallow maximum test depth, and bad maneuverability, for example, helped make them relatively easy targets for astute ASW forces. As a result, Japanese submarine losses increased tragically throughout 1943.[41]

Other Submarine Expeditions to Europe

Not long after the Japanese entry into the war, Anglo-American intelligence developed an amazingly accurate grasp of German-Japanese plans for exchange of vital goods. Submarines would eventually become the sole means of physical transport between the European Axis powers and Japan. The following British Admiralty message of 25 June 1942 is a good example of the sophistication of Allied intelligence:

> There are strong grounds for believing plans have been made by Germany and Japan for large scale exchange of vital commodities. If these plans succeed, German's principal deficiencies, in particular, rubber, tin, wolfram, hemp, hides and vegetables oils will be largely made good by Japan. The latter will obtain in return chemical, specialised machinery, prototypes of naval and military material blueprints and instructions for plant and processes and expert technicians. Similar exchanges are believed to be contemplated with Italy.[42]

At that time, in 1942, blockade-running efforts, called Yanagi operations, were carried out by surface transport vessels; however, by early 1943 the losses of Axis surface runners became so severe that the Germans, with the advice of the Japanese ambassador in Berlin, decided to inaugurate submarine blockade-running operations.[43]

In 1942, the Japanese inaugurated a submarine expedition to Europe. Although the *I-30* struck a mine, as noted in chapter 4, during the final leg of its return voyage from German-occupied France in October 1942, the Imperial Headquarters was enthusiastic about more expeditions. Thus, four submarines set out for Europe in 1943 and 1944, but their fate, for the most part, was not unlike that of the *I-30*.[44]

Only the *I-8* (commanded by Cmdr. Shinji Uchino) successfully completed the treacherous journey. The *I-8*, in company with *I-10*, left Penang submarine base on 6 July 1943 with a cargo of much-needed quinine for the Germans and an extra crew of forty-eight sailors. The extra crew was supposed to sail back to Japan in a submarine Hitler planned to give the Japanese (*U-1224*). Sailing safely across the Indian Ocean, the *I-8* refueled from the *I-10* and rounded the Cape of Good Hope into the Atlantic. On 24 July the *I-8* received the first secret radio transmission from the German Naval Command—it included a welcome into the Atlantic Ocean, sailing instructions, and a warning about Allied radar searches and aircraft patrols. The big submarine, with an unusual twin 5.5-inch gun mount, crossed the equator on 2 August and rendezvoused with the *U-161* near the Azores in late August. The Japanese picked up a German officer in *I-8*'s rubber dinghy to assist them in entering port safely. The *I-8* finally slipped into the protection of a U-boat bunker at Brest some sixty-one days after leaving Penang. Loaded with much military machinery (even the torpedo tubes were filled) and carrying a dozen German officers, radar and hydrophone technicians, and civilian advisers, the *I-8* sailed from France on 5 October and arrived safely in Singapore on 5 December. The big Japanese submarine then sailed on safely to Kure, its home port, where it arrived 21 December.[45] This was a remarkable voyage that again effectively demonstrated the fine seamanship of Japanese submariners and the endurance qualities of large I-boats.

However, three other I-boats failed in the remaining years of the war to complete the east-west round trip. Two were sunk with their cargoes of rubber and tin before reaching France, and one was sunk near the end of the long return voyage.

The *I-34* was the first of these blockade runners to be lost, early into its voyage, as it turned out. The British submarine *Taurus* in the Strait of Malacca sank the *I-34* on 13 November 1943, after the fully loaded I-boat set sail for Europe from Singapore two days earlier.

The sinking of the second unsuccessful boat in this series was somewhat more involved. The *I-29* had already delivered Indian revolutionary Nationalist leader Bose safely to Singapore in May 1943, and in 1944 this veteran I-boat came very close to completing a round-trip Axis mission. The *I-29* left Singapore for Europe on 16 December 1943. Carrying a dozen scientists, engineers, and other Japanese specialists and a cargo of East Asian raw materials, the submarine refueled from a German supply ship in the Indian Ocean on 23 December, rounded the Cape of Good Hope in January 1944, and arrived safely in Lorient, France, on 10 March.

The *I-29*'s progress was plotted by ULTRA. For example, the U.S. Navy learned from enemy-enciphered communications intelligence that on 8 January 1944 the "Japanese sub will be approximately at 39 S–42 E on 11 January."[46] Several days later ULTRA reported that "*I-29* [was] estimated to be at approximately 30 S–10 E on 19 Jan., en route [to] Biscay," and the "estimated position [was] 06 S–05 E on 26 Jan."[47] In spite of this information, Allied forces were not available in time to attack the *I-29* before the large Japanese submarine safely reached the protection of German forces in the Bay of Biscay.

The return trip was quite different, although it appeared promising at the beginning. Loaded with very important German scientific equipment and vast quantities of blueprints for new secret weapons, the submarine blockade runner left France on 16 April and arrived safely at Singapore on 14 July.[48] Most significantly, after the three-month journey, some of *I-29*'s passengers disembarked at Singapore with their secret plans and documents from Germany and proceeded to Japan by air. Among these passengers was Technical Commander Iwaya, who carried plans for the rocket-powered Messerschmitt Me 163 Komet interceptor and the turbo-jet Messerschmitt Me 262. Another passenger, Captain Matsui, carried plans for two sets of exhaust turbo-superchargers, two sets of "R" apparatus for a rocket-type launching accelerator, and a set of parts for the pressure cabin and complete plans for the Henschel Hs 130C high-altitude aircraft.[49] These plans were delivered safely in Japan.

Because of the effectiveness of Allied communications intelligence, the rest of *I-29*'s prize German scientific cargo did not reach Japan. The *I-29* had been tracked since leaving Lorient in April, but usually with little specificity. Moreover, the information about the submarine's progress in the Atlantic and Indian Oceans was usually dated and of little use by the time the deciphered messages reached combat intercept forces. For example, U.S. naval intelligence learned only on 15 July that the *I-29* had arrived safely in Singapore the day before. Soon, however, an intercepted message from Berlin to Tokyo listed *I-29*'s cargo in greater detail. Included were "5 'special weapons,' various radar apparatus, 20 Enigma coding machines, ordnance parts, rocket-type launching apparatus, bombsight plans, [and] pressure cabin parts and plans."[50] It suddenly became clear that the cargo was of considerable strategic value to Japan. Therefore, three available U.S. Navy submarines—*Tilefish* (SS-307), *Rock* (SS-274), and *Sawfish* (SS-276)—were alerted through ULTRA about the impending passage of the surfaced *I-29* from Singapore to Japan. The American search for the Japanese submarine was aided immeasurably when *I-29* radioed its detailed itinerary to Japan on 20 July. Intercepted and deciphered on the same day, the commander in chief, Pacific, sent the three American submarines the following bulletin four days later:

> *I-29* recently arrived Singapore from Europe carrying samples and plans of many recent German developments in fields of radar, communications, gunnery, aeronautics and medicine. [*I-29*] left Singapore 22 July en route [to] Kure. Believe above very important cargo very likely still aboard. Will pass through posit[ion] 15 N., 117 E., at 251400, and *through Balintang Channel at 261200* [emphasis in the original], speed 17 [knots], arriving western channel of Bungo Channel at 291000.[51]

Thus, the three U.S. submarines were lying in wait, and it was the USS *Sawfish* that fired its torpedoes first. The *I-29* reeled from the enormous explosions of three torpedoes hitting fore and aft of the conning tower, followed quickly by heavy secondary explosions. The submarine sank almost immediately.[52] As the *Sawfish* radioed on the morning of 26 July, "He did not pass. . . . Put three fish into . . . [*I-29*] which disintegrated in a cloud of smoke and fire."[53]

By this point in the war, U.S. submarines were imposing a blockade on Japan, and ULTRA messages, often intercepted and deciphered while en route to Japanese blockade runners, were particularly timely and often exact. In this instance the Japanese routing message to the *I-29* provided crucial information to nearby American submarines in enough time for them to execute a carefully planned ambush.

The *I-52* was the last I-boat to attempt the voyage to Europe. Like the *I-34* in November 1943, the *I-52* was also sunk while en route to German-occupied France, although its fate was not sealed until near the end of the European-bound leg of the difficult voyage. The *I-52*, a new submarine completed in December 1943, sortied from Singapore on 23 April 1944. It had a cargo of rubber in bales; quantities of wolfram, molybdenum, and quinine; and fourteen passengers. After rendezvousing with the *U-530* off the Azores and taking on board a German liaison officer in mid-June, the Japanese submarine was sunk by aircraft from the escort carrier USS *Bogue* (CVE-9) the next day.[54]

However, the sinking of the *I-52* was a far more sophisticated operation than the previous brief account would suggest. Anglo-American communication intelligence, highly efficient by this point in the war, was largely responsible for the destruction of Axis submarine blockade running. As an August 1944 TOP SECRET ULTRA report claimed, during the past year or more, Germany and Japan have made strenuous efforts to transport strategic materials, technical information and technical personnel between Europe and Asia by the use of blockade running submarines. . . . Thanks in no small measure to the contributions made by [ULTRA] communication intelligence, the results of these blockade running attempts have been relatively poor, and are growing progressively worse.[55]

I-52's blockade-running voyage was jeopardized by ULTRA intelligence from the outset.[56] In early March 1944 the U.S. Fleet Radio Unit, Pacific (FRUPac) in Pearl Harbor intercepted and deciphered a key ULTRA message from Tokyo. It read: "The *I-52* will depart Kure the middle of March. While docked at Singapore, preparations will be made for her trip to Germany. Arrange space for a cargo of 270 tons, including 80 tons of rubber." Secret information about the large I-boat continued to be assembled as *I-52*'s journey across the Indian Ocean and into the Atlantic was monitored by the British and Americans. Finally, in early June Anglo-American intelligence specialists intercepted German instructions radioed from Berlin to the *I-52:*

> Anglo-American forces have landed on French coast between Le Havre and Cherbourg, but your destination is still Lorient. The *rendezvous will be at 15 N., 40 W., at 2115 (G.M.T.) on 22 June* [to receive a German liaison officer]. *After rendezvous, you will proceed due North to 38 N., 40 W.,* [emphasis in the original] and thence to 43 N., 30 W. From the latter point, you will make for the Spanish coast as directed by the German liaison officer. Special precautions must be taken against enemy aircraft, particularly since two German subs have recently been sunk by carrier aircraft in the vicinity of 15 N., 30 W.

On 16 June the *I-52* further endangered itself by transmitting in cipher the following message: "On 11 June we were in posit[ion] 10 N., 31 W. Proceeding at 11 knots, have sufficient fuel remaining for 12,000 miles." Not surprisingly, then, a U.S. Navy communications intelligence log entry for 24 June 1944 noted, "Enemy sub, probably MOMI [cover name for *I-52*], believed sunk by USS *Bogue early on 24 June in the vicinity of 15–15 N., 40–00 W* [emphasis in the original]."

Cryptologic intelligence proved to be the nemesis of Axis submarines in World War II, not only in terms of the specific sinkings of the *I-52* and *I-29,* for example, but also in terms of strategic developments in Axis submarine warfare. By intercepting and deciphering radio traffic that Japanese Ambassador Hiroshi Ōshima in Berlin sent to Tokyo,

Allied intelligence analysts discovered the alarming information in January 1943 that Hitler planned to transfer two U-boats to Japan. The purpose was to encourage and help facilitate the building of a new type of Japanese submarine. If new Japanese submarines were modeled after the Type IXC or IXC-40 German U-boat, the Germans believed that the new boats would be better suited for raiding Allied supply lines in the Pacific and Indian Oceans. The Germans had little faith in the much larger I-boats. Moreover, there was some concern among U.S. Navy strategic thinkers that the Germans might convince the Japanese to switch to a more effective type of submarine warfare focused primarily on Allied lines of communication. This was probably a groundless concern. Nevertheless, Vice Adm. Naokuni Nomura, who had represented Japan on the Tripartite military commission in Berlin since 1941, left Germany in early April 1943 aboard the *U-511*, one of the U-boats to be transferred to the Japanese navy. The *U-511*, Hitler's personal gift to Emperor Hirohito, reached Penang with its German crew and then sailed to Kure with a Japanese crew, arriving safely on 7 August. There the craft was renamed *RO-500* on 16 September 1943. Through cipher intercepts, U.S. intelligence analysts watched this transfer with alarm. However, Allied naval and air forces were unable to intercept the submarine.[57]

The second submarine transferred to the Imperial Japanese Navy was not so lucky. The *U-1224*, renamed *RO-501* when taken over by a Japanese crew on 15 February 1944, sailed from Kiel on 30 March. Allied radio intelligence soon started to plot the course and approximate daily positions of Hitler's submarine gift to the Japanese. Not surprisingly, then, within six weeks the new Japanese submarine was sunk by an American destroyer escort in the mid-Atlantic on 13 May; all members of the Japanese crew were lost—they had sailed to Germany the year before in the *I-8*.[58] Coincidentally, it was the *I-8* that in July had waited in vain for *RO-501* at predesignated refueling locations in the Indian Ocean.

In spite of very heavy losses sustained by Axis submarines, including a few Italian boats engaged in east-west expeditions, recently declassified U.S. intelligence documents suggest that a surprisingly large amount of strategically important commodities intended for the Japanese was shipped by submarine from Europe after March 1943. While much of this matériel was sunk en route to Japan, a significant portion arrived safely. For example, the following commodities were shipped during the war: eight sets of Würzburg FuSe 62 (ground radar) (four sets were sunk en route); twenty-six code machines and accessories (twenty machines were sunk); 325 metric tons of lead (129.96 metric tons were sunk); one ball bearing polishing machine (arrived safely); and two sets of Naxos Borkum (German electric countermeasure equipment to detect Allied radar transmission) (both sets were sunk en route). It is clear, however, that the Germans were prepared to send much more important military material, and it would have reached the Japanese if a fully reliable east-west transport system could have been established. A few months after the landings at Normandy in June 1944, Allied investigations of warehouses and factories in Bordeaux and other Bay of Biscay French cities revealed that vast quantities of German technical aid intended for the Japanese were awaiting shipment.[59]

The employment of I-boats in these expeditions to Europe was symptomatic of larger problems in Axis relations as well as an example of the awkward use of submarines. Aside from a very few submarines and surface blockade runners after 1943, Japan and Germany had no means of communicating, except by radio. Increasingly after mid-1943 the round-trip railway route for Japanese travel (not German, of course) between Manchukuo, through the Soviet Union, and neutral Turkey was reduced. Furthermore, during the war, the Japanese government was afraid of offending Russia and being accused by Moscow of violating the 1941 Japanese-Soviet neutrality agreement. Indeed, Tokyo refused to approve a German plan in early 1945 to fly a German technical air delegation to Japan because the proposed flight plan included passage over some Soviet territory. Thus, submarines were the sole means of transporting goods and personnel between Japan and Germany in the closing days of this grand war of attrition. These I-boats were designed as warships, not as long-range transport vessels, and their deployment as blockade runners proved to be as hazardous as their use in transport and supply operations to isolated islands. More significantly, as one author observed in the early 1980s about cryptologic intelligence, the blockade-running Axis vessels were sailing "straight into the meshes of the Allied signal intelligence net. Magic (with its command of the diplomatic signals and the Japanese-German naval attaché code) and . . . the British ability to read the German Enigma cipher contributed intelligence about the Yanagi operations which, cumulatively but decisively, aborted them."[60]

6
Submarine Operations and Plans for the Decisive Battle, 1944

The Mariana Islands

On 1 September 1943, Imperial Headquarters issued a new and complex set of strategic plans that were intended to achieve the increasingly elusive victory. Titled *Sensō shidō no taikō* (General principles for conduct of the war), the document emphasized the need for the armed forces to assume a defensive strategy in the central and South Pacific. The strategy for victory, however, dictated that Japanese forces seize the initiative in a decisive battle in what was called the *Zettai kokubō ken* (zone of absolute national defense). The outer perimeter of this zone ran from the northern end of the Marianas to the southern tip of western New Guinea. Reinforcements of every kind, especially carrier and land-based air groups, were prepared for the decisive battle. Preparations were scheduled for completion by May 1944. Until then all of the frontier areas were to be held, for example, the Bismarck Barrier of Rabaul and eastern New Guinea as well as the Marshall and Gilbert Islands of the central Pacific. Thus, 1944 was to become the year when the Combined Fleet sought victory through a decisive battle against the United States and its allies within the boundaries of this imperative zone. Explicit in the new strategy was the assumption that the subma-

Plans for the Decisive Battle, 1944

rine force would continue to serve any role demanded by the battle fleet, no matter how ineffective or detrimental the assignments might be to the silent service.[1]

However, strategic conditions changed quickly, and in early 1944 the Japanese were thrown off balance by a series of Allied assaults—the high command would have to modify plans in light of severe setbacks. The Bismarck Barrier was penetrated when the Allied Southwest Force invaded New Britain and central New Guinea—the Gilbert (November 1943) and Marshall (February 1944) Islands were also lost. Moreover, Truk naval base was destroyed by U.S. carrier task force operations on 17–18 February, and its function as a Japanese advance base was lost. In addition, the Sixth Fleet's flagship, the light cruiser *Katori*, was sunk by surface gunfire, and the auxiliary submarine tender *Heian Maru* (11,614 tons), with its valuable cargo of submarine spare parts and supplies, was sunk during the air assaults.[2] U.S. intelligence fully understood the significance to Vice Adm. Takeo Takagi of the loss of his flagship and concluded that "it is not surprising that he [Takagi] was unable to mount an effective submarine attack against [U.S.] carrier task forces."[3] Additional Allied advances were made to the Admiralty Islands in February and to Hollandia, central New Guinea, in April. There was also a major air assault against Japanese facilities at Palau, western Caroline Islands. Another setback came when the commander in chief of the Combined Fleet, Adm. Mineichi Koga, and many of his staff officers were killed on 31 March when Koga's plane crashed in bad weather.[4] Thus, the original strategic plans of September 1943 were completely unrealistic in view of recent Allied gains.

In the aftermath of this series of disastrous events, the newly appointed commander in chief of the Combined Fleet, Adm. Soemu Toyoda, ordered Operation A-Gō (*A-Gō sakusen*) to set in motion the decisive battle in the "zone of absolute national defense." The plan came from the Naval General Staff (*Gunreibu*) and was issued to the Combined Fleet; it called for the full force of the enemy to be drawn unswervingly and unsuspectingly into a Japanese trap for the decisive battle. The site would be of Japanese choosing inside the imperative zone. Not surprisingly, the role envisaged for submarines was dictated by the needs of the Combined Fleet. All available forces were especially organized for the strategic mission and decisive battle outlined in Operation A-Gō (see appendix 8).

SUBMARINE DEPLOYMENT AND OPERATIONS BEFORE U.S. INVASIONS IN EARLY 1944

With the loss of the Gilbert and Marshall Islands in late 1943 and early 1944, thus permitting enemy penetration of the Bismarck Barrier, the submarine force was called upon to wear down the enemy before the decisive engagement between the battle fleets. Submarines concentrated primarily in the central and South Pacific areas. Four submarines patrolled the waters east and northeast of Truk after the U.S. carrier assault on 17 February, but they failed to catch the retreating enemy's fast carrier force. Similarly, seven submarines patrolled the Marianas after another U.S. carrier strike a few days later in February; again, to no avail.

The weight of these failures was compounded by the continuous loss of submarines, some while engaged in dangerous transportation operations. The *I-181*, as noted earlier, was sunk near Rabaul on 16 January, and the *I-43*, while carrying reinforcing troops to Truk, was sunk by the American submarine USS *Aspro* (SS-309) on 15 February. The *RO-40* was sunk the next day off Kwajalein by the USS *Phelps* (DD-360) and the minesweeper USS *Sage*. The toll taken on the submarine force was alarmingly heavy, and Japanese submarines accomplished so little in comparison to their losses.[5]

Japanese submariners realized that U.S. ASW forces were more persistent than ever. The high command knew that the enemy was using the Marshall Islands as an advance base for preparing invasion forces, but submarine reconnaissance was restricted because of ASW patrols. Nevertheless, *RO-106* successfully carried out a reconnaissance mission at Eniwetok on 4–5 March. At Majuro, *RO-44* was also involved in a reconnaissance mission, and *RO-42* sighted a carrier task force in the vicinity of Majuro and Jaluit during the morning of 15 March. Thus, eight submarines (*I-32, I-42, RO-36, RO-40, RO-42, RO-44, RO-105,* and *RO-106*) were sent to the Marshalls to watch, report, and oppose the American buildup, but ASW forces held these submarines down; Japanese reports were limited, whereas their losses were high. The *I-32* was sunk by a U.S. hunter-killer group during the night of 24 March by the USS *Manlove* (DE-36) and *PC-1135*, and the *I-42* was sunk, with the aid of ULTRA intelligence, by the U.S. submarine *Tunny* (SS-282) the day before. The *I-42* was en route from Palau to Rabaul on a supply mission when it was caught on the surface during *Tunny*'s night attack.[6]

The pattern was much the same in April and May. Several submarines patrolled the central Pacific, but no damage to U.S. ships was reported. Yet at least three submarines were lost: the *I-174* was not heard from after 10 April—it was sunk on 29 April south of Truk by the USS *MacDonough* (DD-351) and the USS *Stephen Potter* (DD-538); the *I-2*, a veteran from the beginning of the war, was sunk near the Admiralties on 7 April by the USS *Saufley* (DD-465); and the *RO-45* was sunk near Truk at the end of April. As Admiral Ugaki lamented in his diary entry of 16 April, "Now we have only thirty-six submarines in the Sixth Fleet [immediately available].... Look how vainly they have been employed, after having been sent to the east or to the west as they saw some possibility of enemy onslaught, only to be completely exhausted! A steadier and more efficient method of using them must be found."[7]

At this bleak point in the war, Navy General Headquarters came up with a curious plan for the use of submarines. A small 17-foot amphibious tanklike vehicle (*Toku 4-shiki Naikatei*) was built and armed with two torpedoes. The intention was to attack enemy ships anchored inside atolls. Its 62-horsepower gasoline engine was fitted with a watertight pressure box. The plan was for a parent submarine to carry this contraption to the outer reef of an atoll anchorage where the self-propelled weapon would disembark, creep along the reef on its treads, enter the lagoon, motor slowly to an anchored target, and finally attack with its torpedoes.

This plan to develop amphibious tanks for launching from I-boats was promoted by Rear Adm. Kameto Kuroshima, a former staff operations officer with Admiral Yamamoto and later head of a readiness branch of the Naval General Staff. Kuroshima was assisted by Comdr. Yasuo Fujimori, a staff submarine operations officer. The Navy General Headquarters wanted to use five new fleet-type submarines as parent undersea carriers in this highly unusual operation. Most submarine officers opposed the idea; nevertheless, Admiral Kuroshima persisted in the matter. Finally, however, he was forced to cancel the entire operation because of insoluble technical problems with the amphibious tank.

Admiral Kuroshima's scheme was a sign of the desperation that permeated the submarine force by early 1944. Submariners wanted to do something of import on their own, rather than merely to act out the role of the servile followers of battle fleet interests. Yet, as discussed in the previous chapter, the breadth and pace of the war was an unchanging burden that would eventually impair the submarine force beyond redemption.

Submarine Deployment and Operations in the Southwest Pacific

The Japanese Naval General Staff recognized clearly that an enemy invasion was imminent after observing the very heavy U.S. radio traffic and air reconnaissance missions around U.S. advance bases. However, the Japanese believed that the invasion would be aimed at Palau in the western Caroline Islands. If the enemy invasion were successful there at the outset, the operation would then be extended to the Philippines. Thus, the Combined Fleet concentrated its strength in the waters connecting the western Carolines and western New Guinea and Mindanao, the so-called Great Triangle (see map 9). However, American strike forces did not behave as the Japanese high command anticipated, and this miscalculation was to have long-range and disastrous repercussions for Japanese fighting forces.[8]

The interests of the Combined Fleet were foremost; it was natural, therefore, for Admiral Takagi to order his submarines of the First Submarine Group to take up stations according to the requirements of the battle fleet. The *I-41, I-43, I-53,* and *RO-47* were deployed between the Admiralty Islands and Wewak, on the coast of northeast New Guinea. In the Marshall Islands the *RO-42* reconnoitered Kwajalein and Majuro Atolls, and *RO-44* searched the area around Eniwetok Atoll. The latter boat reported on 10 June that the Eniwetok anchorage was empty. Moreover, the *I-10* reported similar information concerning Majuro on 12 June, and the seaplane of the *I-38* searched Kwajalein at about the same time—the enemy fleet was not discovered. It was clear to the Japanese high command that the U.S. invasion forces had sortied and were en route to the invasion site.[9]

Rear Adm. Noboru Ōwada ordered his submarines of the Seventh Submarine Group to form picket lines designed to warn the Combined Fleet of the approach of American battle forces. Seven submarines of "A (*Kō*)" Unit deployed to the south of the Caroline Islands along picket line "N" (see map 10). The center of picket line "N" crossed the equator at meridian 150 E. It was about 200 miles north of New Ireland, 200 miles long, and ran in a northeast to southwest direction. Submarines of "B (*Otsu*)" Unit continued transportation operations near central New Guinea. (Two of them were lost before the invasion:

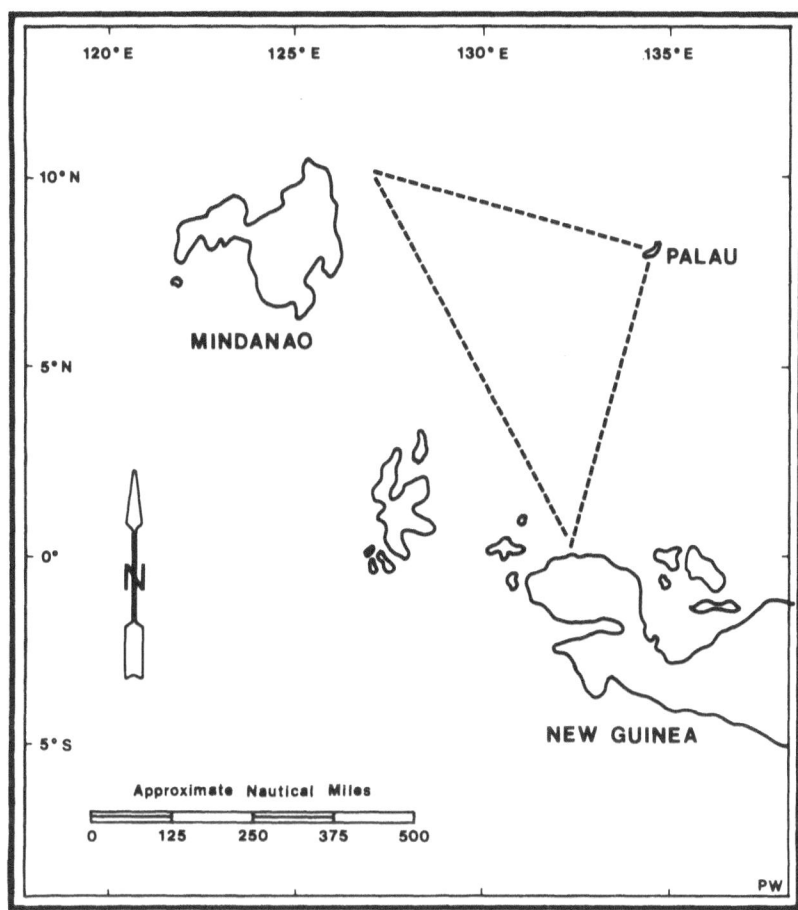

Map 9. The Great Triangle. (Source: Japan, Bōeichō Bōeikenshūjo Senshibu, (Defense Ministry, Defense Research Institute, War History Branch), ed., *Daihon'ei kaigunbu, Rengō kantai,* 5 (Imperial General Headquarters, Navy Division, Combined Fleet, part 5), Senshi Sōsho (War history series), vol. 71 [Tokyo: Asagumo Shimbunsha, 1974], 557)

the *I-176* was running supplies to Buka when it was attacked and sunk by U.S. ASW forces north of Bougainville on 16 May; three days later the *I-16*, also carrying supplies to Buka, was sunk in the same general vicinity by the USS *England* [DE-635].) Thus, four submarines of the First Submarine Group and seven of "A (*Kō*)" Unit of the Seventh Submarine Group were concentrated for the purpose of intercepting, attacking, and weakening the enemy fleet before the decisive battle.

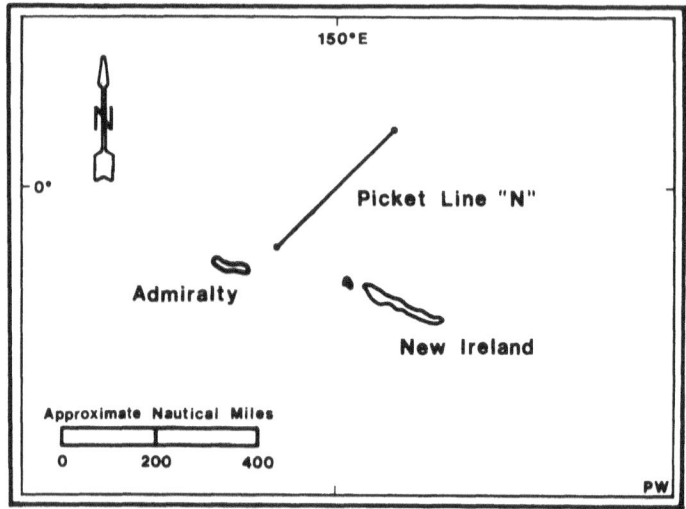

Map 10. Submarines of "A (Kō)" Unit. (Source: Bōeichō Bōeikenshūjo Senshibu, ed., *Sensuikan shi*, 318)

However, these eleven submarines were ineffective, and the force suffered heavy losses.[10]

Submarine Redeployment and Operations in the Mariana and Western Caroline Islands

The air assault against Saipan, Tinian, and Guam on the morning of 11 June 1944 caught the Japanese high command completely by surprise. The Japanese had misjudged the enemy's intentions. They expected the U.S. invasion to be directed against targets in the Great Triangle, not nearly a thousand miles away in the Marianas. Combined Fleet Headquarters did not know if the air assault by the U.S. carrier task force was the prelude to a major invasion or simply a probing type of air assault like the previous ones at Truk and Palau. Consequently, execution of Operation A-Gō was delayed for two days, until the morning of 13 June, when U.S. assault forces started bombardment and minesweeping operations. This delay brought enormous disadvantage to all of the Japanese fighting units.[11]

For the Sixth Fleet this miscalculation required a rapid shift of all submarines from the area of the Great Triangle to the vicinity of the Marianas, where the Imperial Combined Fleet Headquarters now expected the decisive battle to occur. The order came on 13 June, by which time U.S. ASW forces were heavily deployed and fully prepared to support the invasion forces. The submarine force was the first to pay dearly for the high command's error about the site and time of the U.S. invasion.

Orders of the commander in chief, Combined Fleet, to the Sixth Fleet commander, Vice Adm. Takeo Takagi, set in motion the dangerous dashes of Japanese submarines through waters infested with ASW forces. The *I-10, I-38, I-184, RO-41, RO-42,* and *RO-44* were to redeploy as quickly as possible to the east of Guam; *I-41, I-53,* and several submarines of the Seventh Submarine Group were ordered to dash to the south of Guam; and *I-6* and *RO-47* were sent to the area west of Saipan.[12]

Disaster quickly befell the submarine force. On the morning of 15 June, U.S. amphibious forces landed on Saipan and soon established a strong beachhead. The Japanese command post of the submarine Advance Expeditionary Force was in the town of Garapan on the west coast of Saipan, and soon the American invasion rendered the submarine command ineffective. Thus, overall command of submarine operations was transferred from Admiral Takagi on Saipan to Rear Adm. Noboru Ōwada, stationed at Truk. By this point during the American invasion the Japanese had some twenty-one submarines available for patrol and picket duty in the vicinity of the Marianas:[13] Unit "A" (*I-10, I-38,* and *I-53*); Unit "B" (*RO-41, RO-42, RO-43, RO-44,* and *RO-47*); Unit "C" (*I-5, I-6, I-41, I-184,* and *I-185*); and Unit "D" (*RO-36, RO-109, RO-111, RO-112, RO-113, RO-114, RO-115,* and *RO-117*).

Initially, three picket lines were stationed east of Guam, while the remaining eight boats patrolled around Saipan. Unit "A" formed picket line "Z," some 500 miles east of Guam along a 100-mile, nearly north-south line. Unit "B" formed picket line "Y," some 300 miles east of Guam along a 200-mile, nearly north-south line. The five boats of Unit "C" formed picket line "X," about 200 miles east of Guam along a 300-mile, nearly north-south line. Unit "D" patrolled waters surrounding Saipan.

After the initial deployment of submarines along the three picket lines and in the vicinity of Saipan (see map 11), new orders were issued, which sent the boats dashing about. Moreover, the battle developed so quickly and the ASW offensives were so intense that the submarines had great difficulty forming the picket lines (also called "NA" lines) or disrupting enemy operations. The submarines of these units

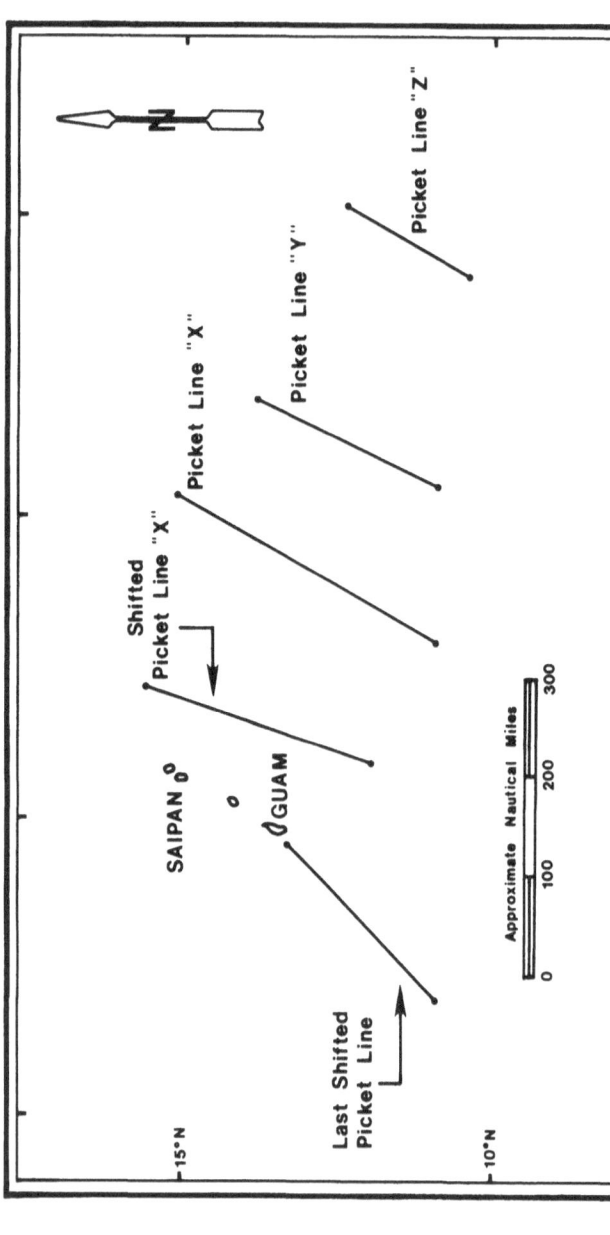

Map 11. Submarine redeployment on picket lines after U.S. invasion. (Source: Bōeichō Bōeikenshūjo Senshibu, ed., *Sensuikan shi*, 326)

and others were themselves devastated by ASW forces. They were largely victims of American intelligence estimates and sophisticated ASW operations. No fewer than fourteen submarines were sunk in May and June.

The most impressive series of attacks was carried out by the USS *England* (DE-635) and two other destroyer escorts of a hunter-killer group (*Raby* [DE-698] and *George* [DE-697]). In late May the *England* sank six submarines in the waters northwest of New Ireland: *I-16* (the nineteenth), *RO-106* (twenty-second), *RO-104* (twenty-third), *RO-116* (twenty-fourth), *RO-108* (twenty-sixth), and *RO-105* (thirty-first). The *England*, knowing from intercepted ULTRA messages the area designated for one of the shifted picket lines, arrived at the northern end and systematically worked its way southward along much of the picket line. During the urgency of movement of the picket lines, various Japanese submarines took up different stations, and newly available submarines also entered the foray. American intelligence concluded that this sinking of six submarines in less than two weeks by one ASW vessel was "the most brilliant antisubmarine operation in history."[14] Eight additional Japanese submarines were sunk during a comparable period in June (Table 2).[15] Once again the Japanese submarine force was the victim of changing orders from the high command, of superior U.S. Navy ASW activities, and of the effectiveness of American intelligence.

Submarine Operations and the Destruction of the Japanese Carrier Force

The Japanese high command had available a considerable number of land-based aircraft, but the planes were not deployed very effectively, and a counterattack on American forces on Saipan was delayed. The Land Based Air Force (First Air Fleet) was deployed not only in the Marianas, but also in Palau, Mindanao, and the western Caroline Islands. The air groups deployed in the Marianas were largely destroyed on 11 June at the outset of the struggle, but another part of the Land Based Air Force remained in good condition. Nevertheless, an effective counterattack failed to materialize, because of a general shortage of qualified substitute pilots, some of whom were incapacitated by illness. The Carrier Mobile Force (First Mobile Fleet) could possibly have intervened by sailing earlier from Tawitawi, southwest Sulu Archipelago in the Philippines, but MacArthur's advance against Biak in

Table 2. Sinking of Japanese submarines near the Marianas, June 1944

RO-111	10 June	Sank after attack by USS *Taylor* (DD-468) north of Admiralty Islands
RO-42	10 June	Sank during a night attack by USS *Bangust* (DE-739) near Kwajalein
RO-36	13 June	Sank during night gun attack by USS *Melvin* (DD-680) off Eniwetok
RO-44	16 June	Sank after hedgehog attack from USS *Burden R. Hastings* (DE-19) about 120 miles from Eniwetok
RO-114	17 June	Destroyed early in the morning in depth-charge attacks from USS *Melvin* (DD-680) and the *Wadleigh* (DD-689) off Saipan
RO-117	17 June	Caught on the surface and sunk by American aircraft from Eniwetok
I-184	19 June	Sunk by carrier planes from USS *Suwannee* (CVE-27) near Saipan
I-185	22 June	Probably sunk during the night by USS *Newcomb* (DD-586) and the fast minesweeper *Chandler* (DMS-9) east of Saipan

the Schouten Islands off the north coast of Netherlands New Guinea (27 May) also delayed the decision to counterattack. Some carrier force was detached to the vicinity of Biak, only later to be recalled because refueling was essential before the Japanese carriers could advance into the waters west of Saipan. The carriers were finally in position in the afternoon of 18 June for launching a belated counterattack. Some Japanese critics referred to the carriers of the fleet not as a *Kidō butai* (mobile or fast-moving force), but as a *Chidō butai* (slow-moving force).[16]

The air counterattack was doomed to failure from the outset. On the morning of 19 June Vice Adm. Jisaburō Ozawa, Commander, First Mobile Fleet, launched his full air strength to strike the enemy carrier task force about 350 miles away. He followed what were called "out-of-range tactics" in the belief that the Americans, by the time they determined the source of the Japanese attack, would not be able to launch counterattacks from such a long-distance, because the U.S. Navy planes could not return safely to their carriers. After attacking American carriers, the Japanese planes planned to continue on to the Marianas and land on Guam, an additional hundred miles' flight.

There they planned to refuel and rearm before taking off for a second attack on U.S. forces on the way back to their own carriers. The Japanese aircraft were to be joined in the attack by land-based planes from Guam, flown there specifically to take part in this operation. But Admiral Ozawa was unaware that heavy U.S. carrier air strikes had already whittled the Guam-based Japanese strength down to a fraction. Consequently, the unexpected action of the U.S. carrier task force rendered Japanese tactics ineffective. Instead of an effective Japanese counterattack, the "Marianas Turkey Shoot" developed during the June 1944 battle of the Philippine Sea, and the Japanese carrier air groups were devastated. Japanese search planes made errors in reports of the locations of the American carriers, and prolonged searches by the carrier air groups consumed precious fuel. Bombs were sometimes jettisoned to save fuel or in preparation for landing on Guam. Whirling U.S. air intercepts often caught Japanese planes at the most inopportune times. Furthermore, because of good radar fighter direction, American aircraft downed some three hundred Japanese planes at a cost of only thirty-one U.S. aircraft; there was no damage to U.S. ships.

Shades of disaster could be seen early during the Japanese counterattack. Japanese carriers were also confronted by U.S. submarines while their planes were the victims in the "Turkey Shoot." Although Admiral Ozawa's flagship, the new heavy carrier *Taihō*, was hit by only one torpedo fired from the U.S. submarine *Albacore* (SS-218) on the morning of 19 June, the explosion locked a flight elevator in an awkward position and caused some aviation fuel tanks to leak. Gasoline vapor accumulated inside the ship after the attack and ignited some five hours later; a massive explosion sank Ozawa's flagship. During that five-hour period the carrier *Shōkaku*, veteran of Pearl Harbor, was also attacked and sunk by an American submarine, the USS *Cavalla* (SS-244). On the next day, the U.S. carrier task force, having steamed hard to close the distance between the two fleets, launched its counterattack and sank the carrier *Hiyō*. (The *Hiyō* had been converted into a carrier after being built originally as a luxury passenger liner for the Tokyo Olympic Games planned for 1940.)

The loss of three of Admiral Ozawa's carriers at this low point in the war was a telling severe blow to the Japanese high command, but any lessons to be drawn from such a setback for the surface force were not likely to benefit the submarine force. Indeed, the Naval General Staff and the Combined Fleet continued to expect the submarine force to carry out elaborate missions. Such assignments were always designed from the battle fleet's perspective. Then came an additional humiliation for the submarine force—the failure of the mission to rescue its own chief and the staff members of the Sixth Fleet Headquarters from Saipan.

Destruction of Sixth Fleet Headquarters on Saipan

Japanese armed forces suffered widespread devastation as a result of the high command's miscalculation about the site of the enemy's forthcoming invasion. The submarine force was particularly hard hit, not only because of the loss of some fourteen submarines, but also through the destruction of Sixth Fleet Headquarters.

As already observed, the Japanese naval high command anticipated the U.S. assault against the Great Triangle. Therefore, Vice Admiral Takagi thought that Saipan, roughly 1,000 miles northeast of Palau at the eastern tip of the Great Triangle, would be the best place for the command post of his Advance Expeditionary Force. Moreover, Takagi reasoned that Truk was the best place for Rear Adm. Noboru Ōwada and his Seventh Submarine Group. Takagi and his large staff established temporary headquarters in facilities of the Central Pacific District Fleet on Saipan, in the coastal town of Garapan.[17]

The U.S. invasion was in the Marianas, not the Carolines; thus Saipan became a battlefield. The besieged island was quickly rendered ineffective as a site from which submarine operations might be directed. During the early days of the invasion, the submarine staff hid in the mountains of Saipan. Command of submarine operations, as noted earlier, was passed to Admiral Ōwada on Truk. Under these circumstances, the commander in chief of the Combined Fleet ordered the rescue of Admiral Takagi and his submarine staff officers as well as some pilots who were isolated on Saipan after their planes were destroyed. These evacuation missions were assigned to the *I-10* for Saipan and to the *I-41* for Guam.[18]

Conditions were extremely hazardous, and only the *I-41* was successful, with the rescue of about one hundred aviators from Guam. But the *I-10* was sunk in depth-charge attacks carried out by the USS *Riddle* (DE-185) and the USS *David W. Taylor* (DD-551) during the evening of 4 July. Two other submarines were assigned to the Saipan mission, but they were unable to reach the embattled island. The *I-6* was sunk by the USS *William C. Miller* (DE-259) and the *Gilmer* (APD-11) some 70 miles west of Saipan on 13 July. The other rescue boat, *I-38*, failed in its attempt to save Admiral Takagi, but it survived to return to Kure. Orders were then issued to cancel any additional rescue attempts, and the head of the submarine force and his staff died in the mountains of Saipan. Yamamoto's former chief of staff recorded in his diary Takagi's last message of 6 July sent from embattled Saipan. It was heroic, but with limited perspective: "I am pleased to have defended Saipan to the death and eyewitnessed the brilliant achievements of the submarines under my command. Commanding all Sixth Fleet personnel remaining[,] . . . I am going to charge into an enemy position. Banzai!"[19] Admiral Ōwada continued to direct submarine operations from Truk, but on 13 July Vice Adm. Shigeyoshi Miwa, who as a submarine squadron commander was in an I-boat off Pearl Harbor when the war began, became commander of the Sixth Fleet.[20]

Submarines continued to patrol the Marianas until mid-July. The chief hope was to rescue any Japanese survivors on isolated islands or in the water, but none was found. In addition to the loss of the *I-10* and *I-6* off Saipan, the *RO-48* was sunk in the same area on 14 July, probably by the U.S. Navy destroyer escort *William C. Miller*. And on 19 July, not long after midnight, the *I-5* sank during a hedgehog attack carried out by the USS *Wyman* (DE-38). A fifth submarine, *I-55*, also became one of the *Wyman*'s victims near Tinian on 28 July. At the conclusion of the operations in the Marianas, four key islands were lost by mid-August—Saipan, Tinian, Guam, and Rota.[21] Moreover, another major command, Vice Adm. Kakuji Kakuta and air wing staffs, was lost on Tinian. About a year later, Tinian served as the airstrip from which the B-29 Superfortresses carrying atomic bombs to Hiroshima and Nagasaki took off.[22]

Assigning the Blame

Losses to the submarine force were catastrophic. By July nearly half of some forty submarines deployed in the Marianas campaign were lost; other submarines were damaged. Yet no enemy ships, according to American records, were damaged by submarine torpedoes. *I-41*'s evacuation of aviators from Guam was the only success claimed by the submarine force.[23] Lt. Comdr. Kennosuke Torisu, staff operations officer of the Sixth Fleet, missed the fate of his submarine comrades on Saipan because at the time of the U.S. invasion he was serving on a special liaison mission at Kure. Commander Torisu later recalled that

> I was questioned closely by Rear Admiral Keizō Komura, Chief of Staff to Admiral Ozawa, about why I was still alive; about why Japa-

nese submarines were so ineffective; and about why American submarines could sink two of our carriers. I had no answers at the time, but I was full of resentment about being asked such questions. I asked myself the rhetorical questions: 'Who indeed is responsible for bringing such misery to the submarine force? Who is genuinely responsible for the deaths of so many Japanese submariners?'[24]

In many ways the Japanese submarine force seemed at the breaking point as an effective fighting force after defeats in the Gilberts, the Marshalls, and the Marianas. Vice Adm. Shigeaki Yamazaki (recently promoted), former commander of Submarine Squadrons 1 and 2, was superintendent of the Submarine School at the time. He took the lead by writing a critical document titled *Sensuikan senka zōshin ni kansuru iken* (Opinions for increasing the effectiveness of submarines). It was sent for review to the navy minister, the chief of staff of the Navy General Headquarters, and to the commander in chief, Combined Fleet. The document had very widespread support among submariners; nevertheless, Admiral Yamazaki was reprimanded and accused of stirring up bitter feelings in the navy. The high command persisted. The same type of submarine operations that was so costly and ineffective continued to be demanded by the high command until the end of the war.[25] Yet deteriorating conditions demanded some change.

Another report, circulated in September 1944 by Vice Adm. Tadashige Daigo (who in May 1945 replaced Admiral Miwa as commander of the Sixth Fleet), was the result of a massive investigation following the debacle of the Marianas. Eight hundred copies of "Operation 'A' Submarine Campaign, 20 May 1944–19 July 1944," were published by the Battle Lessons Investigation Committee of the Bureau of Submarines on 28 September 1944. The study was a lament of traditional doctrine, an analysis of enemy ASW capabilities, and a corrective for future submarine operations.

At the outset of the report, past naval regulations were criticized. "Actual naval operations were thought of as decisive fleet-actions focused upon the battleship," the report recounted. "However, it was obvious that changes finally had to be made in the tactical methods pertaining to submarine warfare."[26]

The overwhelming success of American forces in taking Saipan, Tinian, Guam, and Rota during the last few months highlighted the weakness of the Navy Battle Regulations (*Kaisen yōmurei*) concerning the role of submarines. The report observed that anti-submarine methods used by the American navy in the area of main attack, at the present stage of the war, are ferocious and thorough. No matter how strong spiritual valor may be, it is pointless to return to a reliance upon it. Submarines are now unable to fulfill their missions with complete success by using the group-submarine methods, which are in accord with former tactical concepts.... A formation in which a large number of submarines is arranged in a straight line, and in which each submarine occupies a fixed position, is very likely to be discovered if it is in the vicinity of enemy air bases which have been specially strengthened in anti-submarine devices.[27]

In addition to recognizing the effectiveness of enemy ASW forces in the Marianas, the investigative report also cited a crucial shortcoming of Japanese submarine operations. The USS *England* (DE-635) and other ASW vessels were equipped with new, highly effective explosive weapons thrown ahead (hedgehogs). Moreover, the behavior of individual submarine commanders assisted the *England* in rolling up the picket line of Japanese submarines. The Japanese submarine commanders failed to communicate with each other. They were picked off one by one. Indeed, only after *England*'s feat was completed did Japanese radio intelligence detect the pattern of attacks. As an American intelligence officer wrote later, "Takagi radioed a warning to the NA [picket] line. The *RO-109* and *RO-112* fled the area and were saved."[28] The wartime Japanese account of this battle lesson is explicit.

> It is natural that submarines stationed on patrol line 'NA' would keep their presence a secret as long as possible, but once they had received a thorough attack from enemy anti-sub boats and aircraft, since their positions were then discovered, they should have sent a message concerning their present condition. However, none did so. The high command, on the other hand, learned this through enemy radio intelligence and ordered the patrol line moved.[29]

In addition to new emphasis placed on communications among individual submarines operating together on a common mission, greater initiative for submarine commanding officers was recommended by the Battle Lesson Investigation Committee. Commanding officers were urged to take "action in keeping with the fundamental outline of the [squadron commander's] orders," but they were expected to grasp every opportunity for battle and to reach beyond the high command's directives when operational circumstances demanded unanticipated, immediate action.[30]

However, the committee's long-range recommendations were tempered by growing reservations about Japan's circumstances and prospects after nearly three years of war. While submarines had traditionally been dispersed for strategic use and then diverted quickly to another strategical point for defense purposes, after the battle of the Marianas the submarine force was too weak to be similarly used on future missions. The solution recommended was "to make up this deficiency by carrying out mass production of small type submarines, for example, Type A midget submarines, or special equipment for those [midget boats] already built."[31] A certain desperation started to shade the Japanese submariner's view of the future, but the dilemma was nationwide and affected Japan's ability as a whole to continue the war. The armed forces of the highly industrialized United States were an overwhelming giant.

The Coming of the Decisive Battle and Submarine Operations at Leyte Gulf

A great portion of the "zone of absolute national defense" vanished when the Japanese lost the Marianas, and a new defense line had to be drawn. It included the Japanese homeland itself. The new Japanese counterstroke was called *Shō* (victory). There were four *Shō* plans, one for each of the probable areas of Allied attack. *Shō-Gō 4* covered Hokkaido and the Kurile Islands; *Shō-Gō 3* covered Honshu; *Shō-Gō 2* covered Formosa (Taiwan) and the Ryūkyū Islands; and *Shō-Gō 1* was the plan for the Philippines. *Shō-Gō 1* was emphasized because it was believed throughout the army and navy that the Philippines would be the site of the next American invasion.

Shō-Gō 1 was built primarily around land-based air groups and the surface force, including the giant battleships *Yamato* and *Musashi*, since the carrier and submarine forces were so badly weakened in the Marianas. The newly organized Second Air Fleet, commanded by Vice Adm. Shigeru Fukudome (former chief of staff to Admiral Koga), was deployed in southern Japan and on Formosa. What remained of the First Air Fleet was deployed in the Philippines under the command of Vice Adm. Kimpei Teraoka (successor to Vice Admiral Kakuta). The surface force was commanded by Vice Adm. Takeo Kurita at Lingga Roads, southeast of Singapore. By July the submarines that survived the Marianas sailed to base facilities in the home islands for repair and reconstruction. Other forces also withdrew to home waters for repair and reconstruction. These included the aircraft carrier force that had suffered badly at the Marianas, and the air groups that were decimated in the "Marianas Turkey Shoot." Of course, it was impossible to replace the vast losses of experienced pilots in the short time before *Shō-Gō 1* was implemented.[32]

While emergency work was going on in all areas to collect and prepare for the great battle, the commander in chief of the Combined Fleet, Adm. Soemu Toyoda, set 1 August 1944 as the date of readiness for *Shō-Gō 1*. It was anticipated that land-based air forces deployed to the Philippines would strike the enemy fleet; the Japanese battle surface force would dash from its anchorage in Brunei Bay, northern coast of Borneo, to the enemy's landing beaches in the Philippines and destroy the invasion forces. The submarine force was again assigned familiar missions: ambush, reconnaissance, and transportation operations.[33]

Admiral Miwa organized his submarine force so that it could respond as quickly as possible to sudden orders from Combined Fleet Headquarters. The First Submarine Group was under his direct command. It was made up of five ocean-cruising-type, six fleet-type, and four coastal-defense-type submarines, totaling fifteen submarines: *I-12, I-26, I-36, I-37, I-38, I-41, I-44, I-45, I-53, I-54, I-177, RO-41, RO-43, RO-46,* and *RO-47.* Plans were for these submarines to ambush enemy ships and, if possible, coordinate attacks with Japanese surface units. The Seventh Submarine Group was under the command of Rear Adm. Noboru Ōwada. His three submarines, the *RO-112, RO-113,* and *RO-115,* remained at Truk and were prepared for ambush and transportation operations.[34]

Imperial Headquarters was showing more signs of desperation—by this point in the war, it was starting to grab almost forlornly for any glimmer that seemingly held the promise of victory. The high command became obsessed with panaceas for victory, which usually rested on belief in the uniqueness of the Japanese warrior and his extraordinary fighting ability to persevere against all odds.

In this instance the high command seized on the fame of an elite group in the Second Air Fleet called the "T" Air Wing. "T" was the abbreviation for Typhoon, suggesting that this air wing was as strong as a typhoon and that it could therefore change things drastically. Imperial Headquarters placed much confidence in the ability of the "T" Air Wing when U.S. carrier forces struck Formosa on 13 October. The Second Air Fleet, including the "T" Air Wing, intercepted the enemy in the largest single air battle of the war, the battle off Formosa, 13–16 October 1944.[35]

Initial Japanese estimates claimed a magnificent victory for the Second Air Fleet, and this was seemingly confirmed by what appeared to be the retreat of the U.S. carrier task force on the sixteenth. Euphoria swept the high command. The Navy General Headquarters embraced erroneous and greatly exaggerated estimates of the damage inflicted on the enemy: Claimed as sunk were eleven enemy aircraft carriers, two battleships, three cruisers; claimed as damaged were eight enemy aircraft carriers and four cruisers. Many Japanese admirals believed that the U.S. carrier force had been dealt a deadly blow and was routed. In fact, Japanese land-based planes never sank a ship in this battle, although the new heavy cruiser *Canberra* (CA-70) and the light cruiser *Houston* (CL-81) were severely damaged. Both ships were taken under tow and eventually fully repaired. More significantly, errors of assessment in the battle off Formosa dimmed the judgment and ability of the high command to come to grips with the swift and startling new show of enemy strength. As a result, the Navy General Headquarters was psychologically unprepared to deal with the military reality of the early morning of 17 October: U.S. amphibious forces appeared off Suluan, the small island at the entrance of Leyte Gulf. Within a few days, more than seven hundred U.S. ships steamed into Leyte Gulf, and 103,000 troops were landed on Leyte by the end of 21 October.[36]

Finally, after much hesitation and delay, during the evening of 18 October the perplexed high command ordered the execution of *Shō-Gō 1*. The day to concentrate attack on the enemy's landing forces at Leyte, "X" day, started at dawn on 25 October. All forces were deliberately scattered, but they were to conform to a strict timetable. The once glorious carrier task force now comprised only four carriers, with little more than a hundred aircraft among them—most of the pilots were inexperienced recruits, fresh from an inadequate training program in the Inland Sea. The most promising role for Japanese carriers in this battle was to act as bait—to draw U.S. carrier air strength to them, thus diverting enemy aircraft away from launching attacks against Vice Adm. Takeo Kurita's main surface force. His force, made up of five battleships (including the *Yamato* and *Musashi*, 70,000-ton behemoths) and more than two dozen cruisers and destroyers, converged eastward into Philippine waters in preparation for a "general decisive battle."[37]

Plans for the Decisive Battle, 1944   153

The battle for Leyte Gulf (24–26 October 1944) started on an ominous note for the Japanese. Admiral Kurita's surface force was attacked by U.S. submarines while it was en route to the Philippines on 23 October. Kurita's flagship, the cruiser *Atago,* was sunk; so was a second cruiser, the *Maya.* A third cruiser, the *Takao,* was so severely damaged that it was forced to withdraw and return to its Borneo base. Nevertheless, four Japanese battle groups continued to converge on the Philippines. Over the next forty-eight hours all of them would engage enemy forces and lose in each of the four separate battles making up the battle for Leyte Gulf: the battles of the Sibuyan Sea, Cape Engano, Samar, and Surigao Strait. The battle for Leyte Gulf was fought to a near-ultimate defeat for Japan. Losses included the super-battleship *Musashi.* So long planned and so ardently desired by at least two generations of Imperial Japanese Navy officers, the decisive battle had at last taken place.[38]

SUBMARINE DEPLOYMENT AND OPERATIONS

While submarines were still to serve the interests of the Combined Fleet, Admiral Miwa was more persuasive with Combined Fleet Headquarters than his predecessors. The high command agreed with Sixth Fleet Headquarters that submarines were not to establish picket lines; rather, they were to patrol in designated sectors. Nevertheless, the Combined Fleet Headquarters continued to insist that it could still call on submarines, if necessary, to dash to the vicinity of the landings in what would amount to a kind of helter-skelter charge.[39]

Submarines sortied at first with the intention of intercepting and chasing the enemy carriers thought by the high command to be retreating on 16 October. Events soon proved otherwise—Adm. William Halsey's message would become famous: I am "retiring at high speed towards the enemy." Submarines available for *Shō-Gō 1* included "A" Unit (*I-26, I-45, I-54,* and *I-56*); "B" Unit (*I-38, I-41, I-44, I-46, RO-41, RO-43,* and *RO-46*); and "C" Unit (*RO-109* and *RO-112*). Admiral Miwa ordered these submarines to take up assigned sectors for patrolling.[40] This change from the usual deployment along picket lines to sector assignments is suggested in the maps 12, 13, and 14.

The role played by submarines was completely different from the one long envisaged by Admiral Miwa. Submarines were deployed very briefly to assigned sectors, 20–24 October, but on 27 October, by which time the battle fleet had already lost the decisive battle, subma-

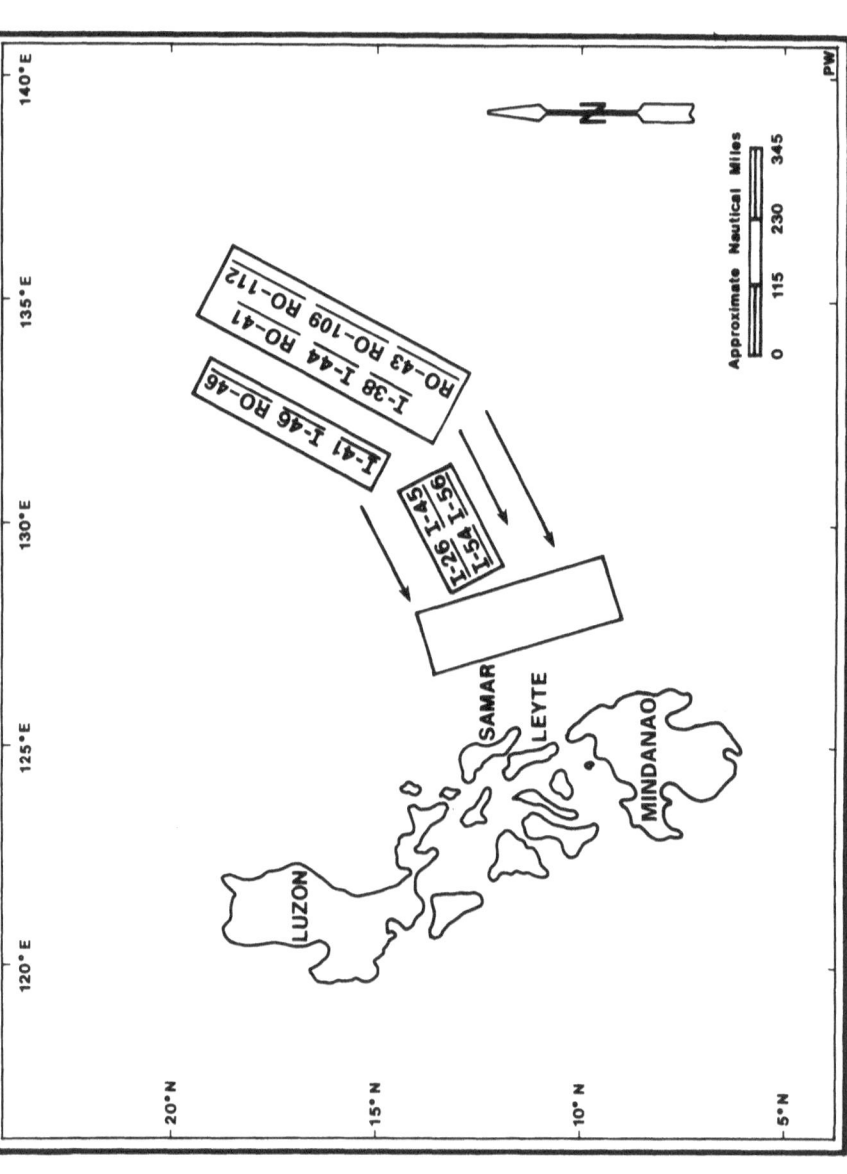

Map 12. Submarine initial deployment as ordered on 18 October 1944. (Source: Bōeichō Bōeikenshūjo Senshibu, ed. *Sensuikan shi*, 370)

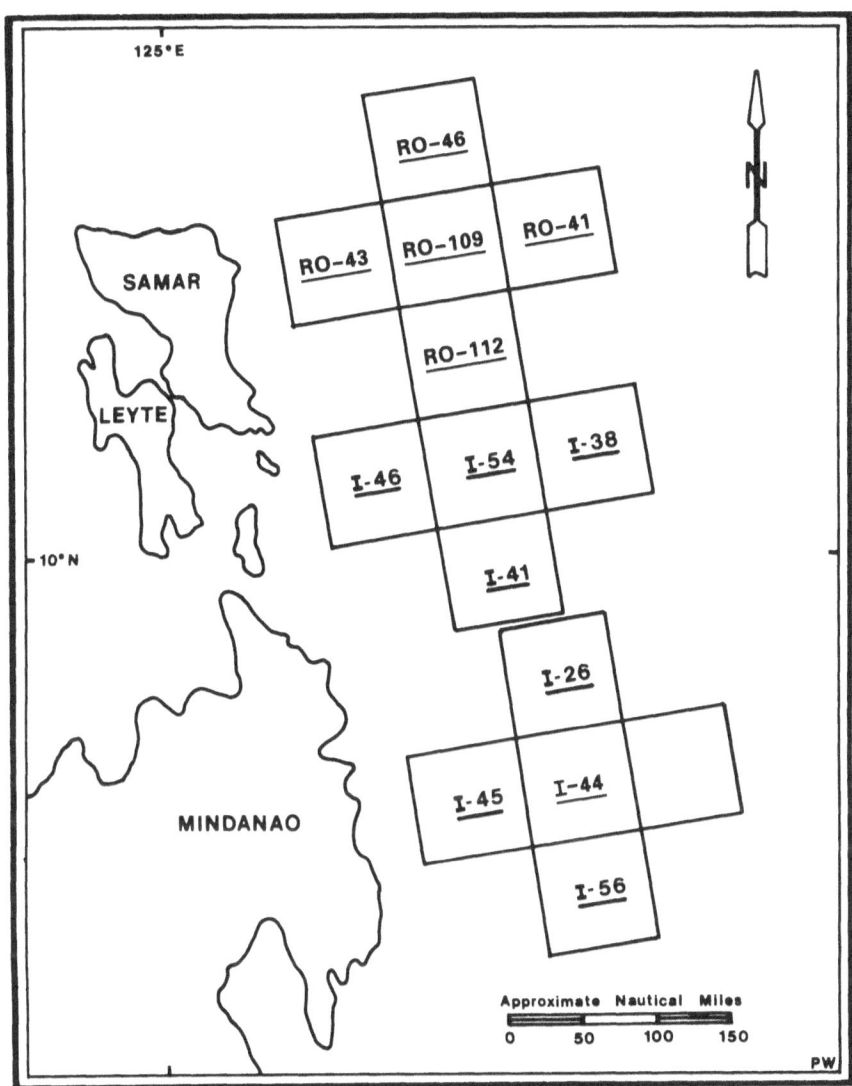

Map 13. Submarine deployment, 20–24 October 1944. (Source: Bōeichō Bōeikenshūjo Senshibu, ed., *Sensuikan shi*, 372)

rines were ordered by the high command to deploy for a charge against the enemy[41] (see maps 13 and 14).

For several weeks after the battle, submarines continued to patrol in assigned areas off the eastern coast of the Philippine Islands.[42] Their success was very limited in view of the large number of Allied invasion

156 The Japanese Submarine Force

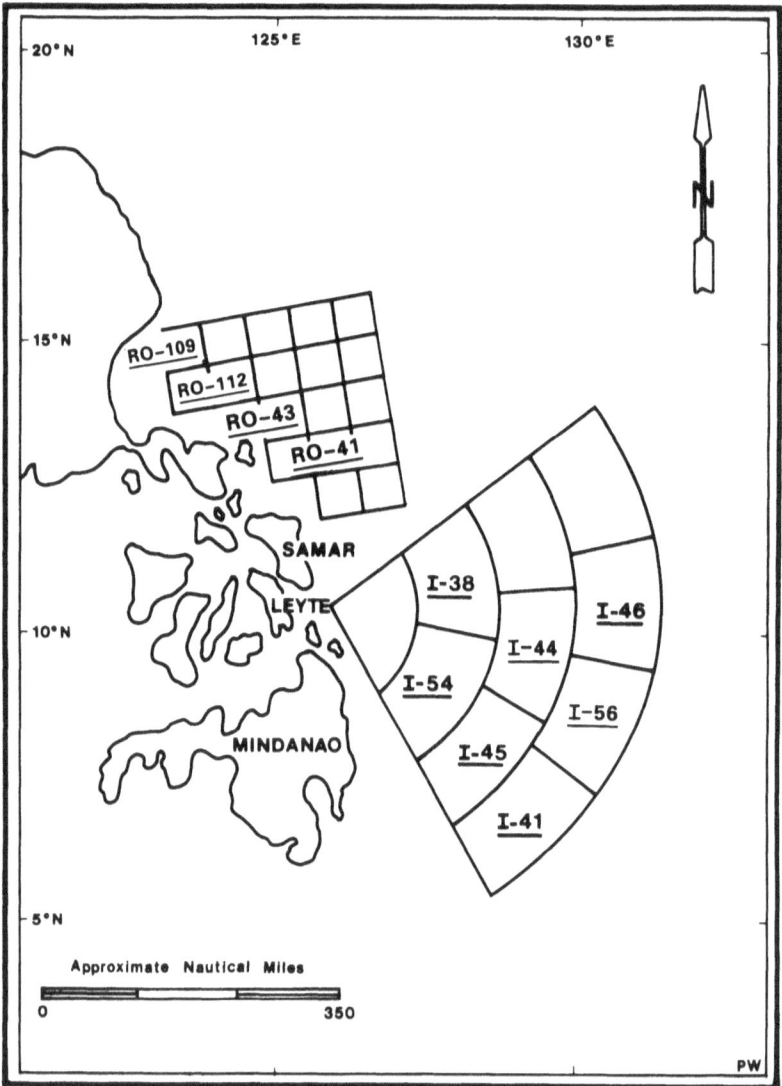

Map 14. Final deployment of submarines, 27 October 1944. (Within a day, three submarines were sunk: *I-45*, *I-46*, and *I-54*.) (Source: Bōeichō Bōeikenshūjo Senshibu, ed., *Sensuikan shi*, 375)

support ships in the area; however, Japanese submarines were more effective in their operations than during the Marianas campaign. The *I-56*'s torpedoes damaged the USS *Santee* (CVE-29) on 25 October, and the USS *Reno* (CL-96) was also damaged in *I-41*'s attack of 3 November. Moreover, the *I-45* sank the USS *Eversole* (DE-404) in an early morning attack on 29 October. During the same period, however, six submarines were sunk near Leyte, hard evidence of the effectiveness of American ASW forces. Indeed, *I-56* barely escaped destruction during a heavy depth charging following its attack on the escort carrier *Santee*. An American intelligence officer learned that when the attacking U.S. Navy destroyer retired, "the Japanese submarine surfaced and the *I-56* found an unexploded hedgehog on her deck; a piece of ordnance that aroused intense interest in Japan."[43] The *I-26* was sunk probably by hedgehogs fired from the USS *Richard M. Rowell* (DE-403) on 25 October east of Leyte. And the *I-54* was lost three days later during an attack by two destroyers, the USS *Helm* (DD-388) and USS *Gridley* (DD-380). The *I-46* last reported on 26 October and was sunk, probably by the *Helm*, on about 28 October. The USS *Whitehurst* (DE-634) sank *I-45* at dawn on 29 October, after the sinking of the USS *Eversole*. And in little more than two weeks, two more I-boats were lost: the *I-38* was sunk by the USS *Nicholas* (DD-449) on 12 November near Palau, western Caroline Islands, and the *I-41* was sunk probably by the USS *Lawrence C. Taylor* (DE-415) and carrier planes from the USS *Anzio* (CVE-57) on 18 November.

The year 1944 was disastrous for the Japanese submarine force. Its demise was of course symptomatic of the destruction of the navy as a whole. Nevertheless, the threadbare plans for the decisive battle were particularly feeble in 1944, when the elusive set-piece confrontation was expected to occur in the so-called zone of absolute national defense. If the Japanese failed to bring about this decisive battle at the beginning of the war, when the Imperial Navy was an estimated 70 percent of the strength of the U.S. Navy in the Pacific, what likelihood was there in 1944 that a vastly superior U.S. Navy could be tricked into fighting a largely contrived decisive battle? The Allies would choose the most advantageous circumstances in which to bring to bear their overwhelming forces, and inevitably the site drew closer to the Japanese home islands.

7
Submarine Operations Near the War's End

Aside from the Mariana and Leyte Gulf operations discussed in the previous chapter, Japanese submarine operations in the last year and a half of the Pacific War were extremely diverse. There was no grand operational scheme to direct the submarine force, to coordinate operations, or to concentrate submarines at critical times and places. Overall, operations were directed in an almost unstructured fashion in attempts to resolve frequent crises as the Allied power mounted in preparation for amphibious attacks on the home islands. In the waning months of the war a sort of crisis management seized Japanese submarine operations, particularly when battle fleet interests dictated assignments. The Japanese never had a comprehensive submarine strategy similar in scope and purpose to those implemented by Vice Adm. Charles A. Lockwood, Commander of Submarines, Pacific, or German Adm. Karl Dönitz in their respective submarines forces.[1] And the Japanese paid dearly for this failure in strategy.

The Indian Ocean

In the first half of 1944, several submarines of the Eighth Submarine Group continued to operate in the Indian Ocean, but the days when that area proved easy and relatively safe hunting for Japanese submarines were coming rapidly to a close. For example, the *I-27*, commanded by a noted submariner, Comdr. Toshiaki Fukumura, sortied from Penang on 4 February to sink the troop transport *Khedive Ismail* (7,513 tons) with two torpedoes—nearly twelve hundred passengers and crew were lost. The escorting British destroyers of this troop convoy K.R.8, the *Paladin* and *Petard*, immediately commenced a search. They later caught the *I-27* on the surface and finally sank the large submarine with a torpedo after a two-hour duel just south of the Maldive Islands on 12 February. (Fukumura was given the distinction of being promoted posthumously to the rank of captain.) A few hours earlier, the *RO-110*, a *Kaishō*-type boat, smaller and newer than the *I-27*, damaged the cargo ship *Asphalion* (6,274 tons) in convoy JC36 sailing from Colombo to Calcutta about 7.30 A.M. on 11 February. The Japanese submarine was soon discovered, and after a series of depth-charge attacks by the Indian sloop *Jumna* and the Australian minesweepers *Ipswich* and *Launceston*, the submarine's destruction was confirmed later that day.[2]

Some other submarines operating in the Indian Ocean, however, were more successful. They all survived their patrols in the Indian Ocean. The *I-8*, a veteran boat from the beginning of the war, sank four vessels:

26 March 1944	Dutch steamer *Tjisalak* (5,787 tons)
30 March 1944	British steamer *City of Adelaide* (6,589 tons)
16 April 1944	small sailing vessel was sunk by gunfire
2 July 1944	American steamer *Jean Nicolet* (7,176 tons)

The *I-26* and *I-37* each sank three. Two old fleet-type submarines, *I-162* and *I-165*, each sank one cargo ship. The *RO-111*, temporarily modified to lay mines off Ceylon, also sank a cargo vessel. Up to mid-1944, submarines sank well over a dozen enemy cargo ships in the Indian Ocean, yet the loss of two submarines was ample evidence that Allied ASW forces were becoming more powerful in the somewhat remote Indian Ocean. There were no longer any easy hunting areas with great prizes for Japanese submarines. Furthermore, the situation in the Pacific was such that the bulk of the Japanese submarine force had to be concentrated there to coordinate operations against the American fleet.

Submarines in the Indian Ocean were much less effective in the second half of 1944 and early 1945 because of strengthened Allied

ASW forces. Only one submarine, the *RO-113,* sank a cargo ship, but two submarines were lost. The *I-166* was sunk by the British submarine HMS *Telemachus* in the Strait of Malacca on 17 July.

The North Pacific

A very few submarines continued to operate in the North Pacific after the loss of Attu and the evacuation of Kiska. No American vessels were damaged, but the *I-180* was sunk during a late night attack in the vicinity of Kodiak by the USS *Gilmore* (DE-18) on 26 April 1944.

The South and Southwestern Pacific

When U.S. amphibious forces invaded Peleliu in the Palau Islands and at Morotai off Halmahera in September 1944, five Japanese submarines were ordered to take up stations in nearby waters. Again, the full weight of enemy ASW operations was felt. The *RO-41* sank the USS *Shelton* (DE-407) on 3 October and survived an immediate counterattack by the USS *Richard M. Rowell* (DE-403) to escape eventually back to Kure. Otherwise, submarine action was insignificant, but two submarines were lost. The *RO-47* was listed as missing on 2 October—this boat was probably sunk by the USS *McCoy Reynolds* (DE-440) west of Yap on 26 September. And the *I-177* was sunk by the *Samuel B. Miles* (DE-183) off Palau on 3 October. Obviously, such a two-to-one ratio was devastating to the Japanese. Moreover, U.S. Navy destroyer escorts were being mass produced by this point in the war, whereas the capacity of Japanese shipyards was greatly reduced by the attrition of war.

The Last of Submarine Operations in Hawaiian Waters

Many Japanese submarine operations after the defeat at the battle for Leyte Gulf in late 1944 seemed to fritter away precious strength. The nature of the assignments and their widely scattered objectives and purposes were characteristic of the withering Sixth Fleet. By the end of July there were only twenty-six fully operational Japanese submarines. Nevertheless, Admiral Miwa sent the *I-12* on an adventurous mission to Hawaiian waters in late 1944. The submarine sortied from Japan on 4 October and was ordered to attack enemy commerce. It sank a cargo vessel between Hawaii and San Francisco on 29 October; however, the

I-12 was caught and sunk on 13 November by the U.S. Coast Guard cutter *Rockford* (PF-48) and the minesweeper *Ardent*. The Japanese defense perimeter was being constantly reduced, and it became increasingly dangerous for submarines to operate in distant waters. At every turn it seemed that Japanese submarines fell prey to highly experienced and efficient enemy ASW forces, although *I-12*'s foray into the eastern Pacific caught Americans off guard since the focus of the war had long been thousands of miles to the west.

Submarine Transportation Operations

The Seventh Submarine Group, after suffering badly in two big operations with the Combined Fleet, abandoned the advance submarine base at Truk and returned to Japan. Rear Adm. Noboru Ōwada continued to command the group; however, after mid-1944 its chief purpose was to carry out transportation operations to isolated islands. A new type of submarine, the *Sen-tei* Type D1, was built for this purpose. Several submarines of this type transported some 350 troops and about 700 tons of military supplies, mostly ammunition, from late 1944 until early 1945, but these transport submarines paid a high price. Six submarines of this new series were soon sunk. The *I-364*, on its maiden voyage, was torpedoed by the U.S. submarine *Sea Devil* (SS-400) off Honshu on 15 September. The *I-365* was also torpedoed by an American submarine, the USS *Scabbardfish* (SS-397), southeast of Tokyo Bay on 29 November. This transport I-boat was returning from a mission to Truk. The *I-362*, on a transport mission to Woleai, was missing since early January 1945—it was probably sunk by the USS *Fleming* (DE-32) on 13 January. The *I-371* sortied from Truk with evacuees on 31 January and was not heard from thereafter. It was probably sunk on 24 February by the USS *Lagarto* (SS-371) off Bungo Suidō between Kyushu and Shikoku. The *I-370* was sunk by the USS *Finnegan* (DE-307) south of Iwo Jima on 26 February 1945, and the same day, the *I-368* fell victim to attacks by planes from the escort carrier *Anzio* (CVE-57). At the time of these last two attacks, the submarines had abandoned transport operations, were refitted, and were then engaged in *kaiten* operations.

The toll taken on submarines engaged in supply or evacuation operations was heavy because of Allied access to Japanese secret radio traffic through the ULTRA intercept system, although a precise estimate of how much this access to Japanese radio traffic affected ASW cannot be made. Invariably these operations involved much planning and coordination; therefore, a lot of radio traffic was required. Thus, through communication intelligence the crucial role of submarines was emphasized. For example, ULTRA messages in late May 1944 declared that the Japanese 18th Army desperately needed supplies at Wewak on the northern coast of eastern New Guinea. Japanese headquarters in Manila urged Tokyo on 28 May to "please rush to Wewak as absolutely necessary supplies by the end of June the allotment (28 metric tons) of two *RO* submarines."[3] In these kinds of operations, the submarines could easily be targeted. Although available evidence is insufficient to assign ULTRA its full responsibility for the sinking of Japanese submarines during the war, it is clear that this special communication intelligence was extremely important. As the U.S. Navy commander of submarines, Pacific, wrote to the commander in chief, Pacific, in a TOP SECRET DISPATCH of 14 April 1945, a "high percentage of submarine sinkings is based on ULTRA information."[4]

* * *

Affecting Japanese submarine operations in the Pacific theater were some aspects of German–Japanese relations. Toward the end of the war, Allied intelligence of the exchange between the Axis powers ultimately brought about the demise of Axis submarine operations.

The Collapse of Germany and the Legacy to Japan

The Pacific Strategic Intelligence Section (PSIS) was established in Washington, D.C., late in 1944 to study, compile, and disseminate Japanese strategic intelligence based on ULTRA and available collateral information. An early PSIS series in January 1945 focused on the impact the demise of Hitler's Germany would have on Japan, the sole remaining power of the Axis coalition. Not only had Germany on previous occasions shipped a considerable amount of strategic matériel to Japan, but U.S. naval intelligence observed a marked increase in German-Japanese discussions after mid-1944 for the transfer of highly sophisticated German electronic equipment to Japan. Submarines were the only means of transport, and American intelligence analysts were extremely apprehensive and watchful concerning the German-Japanese exchange.

American intelligence analysts believed that the Germans wanted to assist the Japanese as much as possible to maintain the war against the Allies in the Pacific. By September 1944, U.S. naval intelligence learned that "according to a recent order from Commander-in-Chief of the German Navy, based on Hitler's decision, the exchange of practical knowledge with the Japanese is to be carried out on the broadest basis without disguise or deceit."[5]

With the failure of the German Ardennes offensive in December 1944, U-boats scheduled to sail for Japan were keenly watched by Allied intelligence. Since it was becoming extremely difficult for U-boats to operate from their home bases, the Japanese proposed that "as many U-boats as possible be transferred to East Asia."[6] The Japanese promised to provide full services for the German U-boats. Nevertheless, the Germans informed the Japanese on 16 March 1945, as an American intelligence report stated, that they could "count on only 2 more [submarine] arrivals in the Far East in [the next] four months at the earliest. The *U-234* ([commanded by Johann-Heinrich] Fehler), a 1600-tonner, departed Kristiansand [in Norway] 16 April for Batavia; the other, *U-876* ([commanded by] Bahn) presumably a 1200-tonner, has not yet left the Baltic."[7] News of the *U-234* was first noted in an intercepted German Admiralty message of 14 April from Berlin to Tokyo.[8] Soon, however, more detailed information was known about German eleventh-hour attempts to send submarines to Japan. "Since the sinking of *U-864* (Wolfram) on 9 February [1945]," an intelligence report read, "only two U/B's [U-boats] are known to be, or to have been, destined for the Far East." Information about the departure of Fehler's *U-234* was repeated, although this report "believed that Gen. [Ulrich] Kessler, German Air Attaché [to] Tokyo, is on board. His route may be via Cape Horn." There were also two Japanese officers on the *U-234*. The report then added that the trip for Bahn's *U-876* was "cancelled because of damage from A/C [aircraft] attack. German Naval Attaché [to] Tokyo has been informed."[9] Only the *U-234* was left of the submarines bound for Japan in the final weeks of the Third Reich.

The *U-234* proved unique among all the U-boats that sailed for East Asia during the war. Despite a series of setbacks, the German submarine arm continued its struggle to regain supremacy at sea. A last-ditch effort was made in late 1944 to resume the offensive by using steadily increasing numbers of submarines fitted with the snorkel. The *U-234* was such a submarine.

More significantly, the *U-234* was fitted with the new *Kurier* communications system, which the U.S. Navy did not want to fall into Japanese hands. Experiments were made in January 1945 with a new type of transmission in an attempt to prevent Allied interception of U-boat messages. The *Kurier* system employed an ultra-high-speed or flash transmission, in which a brief but complete message was sent in a fraction of a second.[10] A naval intelligence report stated specifically that "it is of interest that *U-234* (Fehler) is one of these boats."[11]

In an ULTRA TOP SECRET U-boat intelligence summary of 19 May 1945, the account of the *U-234*'s final voyage seemingly ended in an anticlimax:

> *U-234*, a 1600-tonner en route to Japan with General Kessler (new air attaché to Tokyo), two Japanese commanders and 8 other technical, naval and air personnel, reported her position in plain language about 600 miles NNW of Azores 12 May and was taken to Portsmouth, N.H. The two Japanese committed suicide before the escort arrived. Cargo included a/c [aircraft] drawings, arms, medical supplies, instruments, *lead*, mercury, caffeine, steel, optical glass and brass.[12]

In fact, the end of the *U-234* saga was anything but anticlimactic, for the submarine carried a cargo of uranium intended to aid the Japanese in building an atomic bomb.

THE VOYAGE OF *U-234* AND U^{235}

Five hundred and fifty kilograms of uranium, U^{235}, the most deadly consignment for the Imperial Japanese Army, was secretly loaded aboard the *U-234* at Kiel in late February 1945.[13] The exact characteristics of the U^{235} prepared for the Japanese remain unknown and open to speculation, but almost certainly, the uranium was not weapons-grade quality. Nevertheless, American intelligence specialists during the war were taking no chances, and they gave the matter very high priority. It is possible that the Japanese request for the German isotope was not made through radio communications; rather, the request was perhaps carried by Japanese officers aboard the *I-29* when it arrived in France in March 1944.[14] Two Japanese technical officers, naval Captain Hideo Tomonaga, a submarine architect, and air force Colonel Genzō Shōji, an aeronautical engineer, painted the inscription "U-235" on each of the fifty or so 9-by-9-by-9-inch radioisotope lead cubes before they carefully stored them in cargo hatches forward on the large minelayer U-boat. After awaiting the arrival of escort vessels and three small Type XXIII U-boats, the flotilla started a gauntlet-like voyage from Kiel to Kristianland on 26 March. They faced mine-infested areas and were under constant threat of air attack in waters too shallow, particularly for the large *U-234,* to dive for protection. Safe arrival in Norway came three days later, and after repairs were completed for damage caused in an accidental collision with another U-boat, the fatal trip continued on 16 April. After Germany's capitulation on 8 May, the *U-234* surrendered to the U.S. Navy destroyer escort *Sutton* (DE-771) several days later in the western Atlantic. U.S. sailors boarded the German submarine to take it to Portsmouth, New Hampshire, where the giant minelayer was moored on 19 May alongside three other U-boats that had surrendered a few days earlier.[15] The *U-234* was also put in a drydock.

The surrender of the *U-234* caused quite a stir. American inspectors learned immediately that the submarine was bound for Japan with a German general and several other passengers. "Gen. Kessler Caught on U-boat" read a newspaper caption the day before the *U-234* arrived at Portsmouth.[16] It was also known that the two Japanese officers had committed suicide and that the Germans had buried them at sea shortly before the American boarding party arrived. Found aboard the German submarine were the newest electric torpedoes and two Me 262 jet fighters in crates with the technical data for assembling the revolutionary new aircraft. After the submarine was moored in Portsmouth, American scientists using Geiger counters confirmed that the boat's cargo included uranium, and the material was carefully removed. The story, unfortunately, ends there, for as a recent author demonstrates, even fifty-year-old matters relating to atomic energy affairs retain a high-security classification, and "no further information of any nature has ever been elicited from US Government sources in respect of the uranium."[17]

Aside from being the last German attempt to communicate with Tokyo by submarine, the story of the *U-234*'s maiden voyage also highlights the extreme sophistication of Anglo-American ULTRA intelligence operations against U-boats in the Atlantic. It is not surprising, therefore, that with the German surrender came U.S. Navy interest in transferring some Atlantic ULTRA submarine expertise to the Pacific to be used against Japanese submarines. For example, in June 1945 a key intelligence officer in the Office of Chief of Naval Operations in Washington, D.C., wrote to his counterpart in Hawaii at the Joint Intelligence Center, Pacific Ocean Area (JICPOA). He offered to transfer an officer to JICPOA from the Atlantic Section of Combat Intelligence whose experience included three years "in the tracking room working with ULTRA." However, the differences between the two theaters had to be considered. Therefore, it was suggested that the officer to be transferred would "be particularly valuable in dealing with the Japanese submarine picture, although it would of course be necessary for him to have a short period of training in Japanese ULTRA and in the general Pacific picture."[18] Capt. W. J. Holmes in JICPOA heartily endorsed the proposal from Washington and added tellingly that the forthcoming officer "will probably find enemy submarine warfare in the Pacific a dull business after his experiences in the Atlantic."[19] But Japan's surrender came in August before any appreciable American experience gained through the defeat of the U-boat could be transferred to the Pacific.

Although no U-boats destined for Japan in 1945 succeeded in getting out of the Atlantic, six Axis submarines already in east and southeast Asian waters were taken over by the Japanese. These transfers were watched carefully by U.S. naval intelligence from 8 to 21 May 1945. The European Axis submarines taken over by the Japanese were the former Italian *Commandante Alfredo Cappellini*, which became the German *UIT-24* in 1943 and the Japanese *I-503* in 1945; the former *Luigi Torelli* became the *UIT-25* and then the *I-504*. They were cargo submarines undergoing overhaul in Kobe, Japan, at the end of the war in Europe. There were also two U-boats in Singapore in May 1945: the *U-181* (renamed the *I-501* by the Japanese) and the *U-862* (renamed the *I-502*). Two other German submarines were taken over by the Japanese: the *U-219* in Batavia was renamed the *I-505*, and the *U-195* in Surabaya became the *I-506* in the Imperial Japanese Navy.[20] No evidence has been found that suggests these submarines actively engaged the Allied forces in the remaining brief weeks of the Pacific War.

Waters around the Philippine Islands after the Battle for Leyte Gulf

Like the German U-boats in late 1944, Japanese submarines carried out last-ditch efforts in their fateful struggle. In the aftermath of the Leyte Gulf defeat, they engaged in various schemes and widely different types of operations in order to save their force. Their efforts were a desperate quest for effective ways to fight an overpowering enemy. As a distinguished Japanese naval historian has recently concluded, by mid-1944, "all submarines were frantically thrown into local areas such as the Philippine Sea, the Leyte Gulf, Iwo Jima, and Okinawa, attacking well-protected assault forces regardless of the losses."[21]

A very few coastal-defense-type submarines continued to patrol around the northern and central Philippines after October, but they caused little damage. The *RO-46* torpedoed an enemy transport ship, the *Cavalier*, on 30 January 1945 off the west coast of Luzon, but the vessel did not sink; rather, it was towed to Leyte. On the other hand, the *RO-55* was sunk by the USS *Thomason* (DE-203) off Luzon during the night of 7 February. Several nights later three somewhat smaller coastal-defense *Kaishō*-type submarines were sunk in the same general area off Luzon. The *RO-115* was en route from its patrol area of Manila to Takao, Formosa, when on the night of 9 February 1945 it was intercepted and sunk by the American submarine *Batfish* (SS-310). The *RO-112* and *RO-113*, which had been sent to northern Luzon to rescue downed Japanese pilots, were sunk by the U.S. submarine *Batfish*. The *RO-112* was sunk on the night of 10 February, and the *RO-113* was sunk early in the morning of 12 February. Thus the *Batfish*, which of course was privy to ULTRA intelligence, sank three submarines in four days.[22]

Furthermore, midget submarines were again brought into service after the defeat at Leyte. They had not been used since late 1943 because they were not effective and appeared to be easy targets for enemy ASW forces. Now, however, the new role of midget submarines was for defense purposes against enemy invaders. Newly trained and organized midget submarine units were located at Cebu, east central Philippines, and at Davao and Zamboanga, Mindanao. But there is no evidence that these units caused any damage—all of these midget submarines were lost or scuttled by early 1945.

Human Torpedoes—*Kaiten* Operations

A few desperate-minded Japanese submariners promoted the idea of developing a suicide weapon, a human torpedo called the *kaiten*, for over a year before the first *kamikaze* ("divine wind") was introduced in combat off the coast of Leyte on 25 October 1944. Some young submariners were responsible for putting forth the human torpedo idea during the struggle for Guadalcanal in very early 1943. These submariners, anxious about the future of the Japanese Empire, suggested the development of some sort of ultimate weapon that would be operated by suicide pilots, but their suggestions were not very concrete or specific.

More specific suggestions came from two young officers, engineering Lt. (jg) Hiroshi Kuroki and Ens. Sekio Nishina. They were trained in midget submarines and were already psychologically prepared to die, if necessary, for the purpose of carrying out an effective mission against the enemy. They proposed that a Type 93 torpedo for surface ships, the so-called Long Lance torpedo, could be converted into a kind of homing, human-driven torpedo. The human torpedoes could be carried on the deck of submarines to the vicinity of the target. They could then be launched after getting torpedo firing data about the target—range, course, speed, and angle on the bow. Their suggestions were not given much consideration in 1943, in part because Kuroki's and Nishina's proposal did not include an escape mechanism to ensure the pilot's survival. But Lieutenant Kuroki persisted to promote his human torpedo idea, and eventually, in February 1944, he presented plans to central naval authorities in Tokyo.

By early 1944, after a year of discouraging news about the course of the war, it is not altogether surprising that at least some naval authorities in Tokyo became more receptive to the human torpedo idea than they had been earlier. Indeed, Comdr. Tamori Yoshimatsu, officer in charge of submarine readiness in the navy ministry, accepted Lieutenant Kuroki's proposal. He thought it was at least worthy of further investigation, and ordered the top secret manufacturing of an experimental human torpedo.[23]

There were many initial problems. The biggest was the limited maximum depth that the human torpedo could endure—80 meters, or 264 feet (most I-boats that were refitted to carry the *kaiten* had a maximum diving depth of 330 feet). Thus, the diving range of the parent submarine carrying the new weapon to the scene of combat could be restricted in emergency situations. This factor was of no small concern to some submarine planners at the time because of the growing sophistication of enemy ASW forces and the increased need to dive deeper. Nevertheless, the shocking defeat Japanese forces suffered in the Marianas tended to encourage planners of this new weapon to rationalize earlier views about the vehicle's weaknesses and to push ahead for the development and use of the human torpedo.[24]

The term *kaiten* had special meaning in wartime Japan. It conveyed a broad feeling about making the impossible possible, such as turning impending defeat in 1945 into victory (see chapter 2). The First Special Submarine Training Base Group for the *kaiten* was organized in Ōtsujima, Tokuyama Bay, on the Inland Sea on 10 July 1944. The facility was commanded by Rear Adm. Mitsuru Nagai. Not surprisingly, there was great enthusiasm for the *kaiten* program, which enjoyed no shortage of volunteers.

Training was hard in special attack (*tokkō*) suicide units, but young officers and enlisted men, mainly from reserved officer corps and petty officer aviation training groups, volunteered eagerly. To drive a *kaiten* at speeds up to 40 knots was extremely difficult, and accidents were not infrequent. Engineering Lieutenant Kuroki was killed in an accident during trials in September 1944. The craft was often unstable; to employ it successfully was always a trying experience. Use of the periscope to steer or to reconnoiter was difficult because of the nature of the projectile, especially during a night attack made at high speed.

There were many delays before the weapon became operational. The first *kaiten* operation was planned for meeting the enemy in the Marshall Islands in September, especially against ships in anchorages at Kwajalein, Majuro, and Eniwetok. Because of technical problems, however, the first *kaiten* operations were delayed until November 1944.

THE FIRST *GEN* OPERATION

The first *Gen* operation, the use of the *kaiten*, was planned with the engagement of three ocean-cruising submarines—the *I-36*, *I-37*, and *I-47*. With four *kaiten* on each parent submarine, attacks were planned on enemy ships anchored in atolls of the western Carolines.

The first *Gen* operation was perhaps a qualified success, but it carried with it a considerable price. The three parent submarines sortied from Ōtsujima on 8 November. Among the twelve *kaiten* drivers was Lt. (jg) (formerly Ens.) Sekio Nishina, closely associated with the *kaiten* program from the outset. After reconnoitering, the *I-36* and *I-47* approached the entrance to Ulithi Atoll, where the *I-36* launched one *kaiten* and the *I-47* launched four, including Lieutenant Nishina's craft, at dawn on 20 November 1944. Explosions were heard, and through the periscopes of the parent submarines huge flames were seen when the fleet oiler *Mississinewa* (AD-39) blew up with a load of aviation gasoline. However, the ASW forces at Ulithi sighted some of the *kaiten* and sank them before their attacks could be completed. All of the *kaiten* launched at Ulithi were lost, but the *I-36* and *I-47* returned safely to Japan. The third *kaiten*-carrying submarine was not so lucky. The *I-37* proceeded to Palau but was sunk before launching its *kaiten* group by ASW forces, probably the USS *Conklin* (DE-439) and *McCoy Reynolds* (DE-440), during the afternoon of 19 November.

THE SECOND *GEN* OPERATION

Japanese naval authorities were desperate. They failed to evaluate the results of the first *Gen* operation very realistically; the high command claimed that the operation was a success and planned immediately for a second *kaiten* operation on a grander scale. Six parent submarines made up the second *Gen* operation at the end of the year: the *I-36* and *I-48* were assigned to Ulithi; *I-47* to Hollandia; *I-53* to Palau; *I-56* to the Admiralty Islands; and *I-58* was assigned to Guam. These submarines sortied from the Inland Sea in late December 1944 and very early January 1945; "X" day, the day of the attack, was 12 January. The *I-36* launched four *kaiten* near the entrance of the Ulithi Atoll at dawn on "X" day—four explosions occurred. The *I-47* launched four *kaiten* near Hollandia at dawn on "X" day—flames from the attack were sighted. At Palau, also early on "X" day, *I-53* launched three *kaiten* (one blew up accidentally soon after being launched), and two explosions were heard from inside the parent submarine, presumably during attacks against enemy ships. The *I-56*, because of the presence of strong enemy ASW forces, was unable to approach Seeadlar Harbor, Manus, in the Admiralties, and could not launch any *kaiten*. The *I-58* launched four *kaiten* near Apra Harbor, Guam, at dawn on "X" day and reported seeing black smoke from two separate attacks. The sixth submarine of the second *Gen* operation, the *I-48*, was delayed. It finally sortied for Ulithi on 9 January, but an enemy ASW group caught and sank the 2,557-ton I-boat on the morning of 22 January with a full *kaiten* load. This ASW group included the *Conklin*, which had helped in the sinking of the *I-37* in mid-November, and the USS *Corbesier* (DE-438) and *Raby* (DE-698).

As with the first *Gen* operation, Sixth Fleet Headquarters exaggerated the effectiveness of the *kaiten* in the second *Gen* operation, especially before the loss of the *I-48*. Indeed, no ships were sunk, but as a U.S. naval intelligence officer noted, "The Japanese assessed the results as eighteen vessels sunk, including one converted aircraft carrier, nine large transports, one oil tanker, one cruiser, and six other large ships including aircraft carriers, battleships, and transports. Such optimistic estimates can only be the result of inexcusably poor staff work."[25]

More *kaiten* attacks against enemy atoll anchorages were immediately planned—the high command anticipated that *kaiten* operations would become extremely widespread and soon dominate the entire submarine force. Yet the submarine commanding officers returning from the first two *Gen* operations complained about how difficult it was for them to approach well-protected anchorages to a suitable point for launching the *kaiten*. Rather than employing the *kaiten* like midget submarines in operations at Pearl Harbor, Madagascar, Sydney, and elsewhere, I-boat skippers recommended, to no avail, that the best tactics for using the *kaiten* would be to deploy the new weapon like an ordinary torpedo and launch it against moving targets in the open sea.

Submarine Operations off Iwo Jima

After the loss of the Philippines, the Japanese high command reluctantly concluded that the final and decisive battle would have to take place on the Empire's home islands. To gain time for making defense preparations it seemed essential to strengthen the defenses of Formosa, the Ryūkyū Islands, and other islands off the Japanese home islands.[26]

The Japanese assumed that Iwo Jima, part of the Tokyo Metropolitan Prefecture, was the next target for an Allied invasion, including the Bonin Islands. However, the Imperial Japanese Navy was a naval force of desperation—its chief remaining strength consisted of land-based air units, landing forces, and the submarine force. As a result of the great losses suffered in the Marianas and at Leyte and a very serious shortage of fuel, submarines were the only vessels in the Imperial Navy still capable of operating very extensively on the open seas. Nevertheless, there were only a few submarines available to oppose the powerful U.S. amphibious forces off Iwo Jima on 19 February 1945.[27]

Admiral Miwa knew the next day that the odds were heavily against him when he ordered four submarines from the Inland Sea to sortie for Iwo Jima. Between 20 and 23 February, the following boats set out on their perilous mission: the *RO-43* and three *kaiten*-carrying submarines, the *I-44* with four, and the *I-368* and *I-370* with five *kaiten* each. They had little prospect of being effective against the powerful enemy whose ASW skills were well honed by this point in the war. Only the *RO-43* was able to launch an attack with conventional torpedoes, damaging a destroyer on 21 February, according to Japanese records, but such an attack remains unconfirmed in American accounts. However, this boat was sunk near Iwo Jima by aircraft from the escort carrier *Anzio* (CVE-57) on 26 February. The same day, as noted earlier, about 120 miles south of Iwo Jima, the *I-370* (with its entire *kaiten* group still aboard) was sunk by the destroyer escort *Finnegan* (DE-307). Similarly, the *I-368* was sunk 26 February by *Anzio*'s planes. This attack occurred about 35 miles west of Iwo Jima.

The fourth submarine of this group, the *I-44*, also failed to launch any *kaiten*. Commanded by Lt. Comdr. Genbei Kawaguchi, who tried repeatedly to maneuver for attacks on enemy ships off Iwo Jima, the *I-44* was kept submerged for nearly forty hours by aggressive ASW forces. Commander Kawaguchi decided that it was impossible to launch any *kaiten* and slowly withdrew from the dangerous waters off Iwo Jima. Upon reporting the dilemma and his decision to withdraw, the high command immediately ordered Kawaguchi to return to the assigned area off Iwo Jima. Again, the *I-44* approached the invasion site, but U.S. ASW forces remained vigilant: it was still impossible for Kawaguchi to make a *kaiten* attack. In these severe circumstances, the Combined Fleet Headquarters finally realized that *kaiten* attacks against enemy ships in the well-protected waters off Iwo Jima were impossible, and the *kaiten* operation off Iwo Jima was officially canceled on 6 March. Nevertheless, when Commander Kawaguchi returned from his mission to Iwo Jima, he was relieved of command and relegated to a land assignment because his superiors maintained that the I-boat skipper failed to obey his original orders.[28] (The garrison force on Iwo Jima, an isolated island, continued to fight to the bitter end under the command of Lt. Gen. Tadamichi Kuribayashi.)[29]

Submarine Operations off Okinawa

It was obvious to the Japanese high command that the next Allied invasion would be aimed at Okinawa in the Ryūkyū Islands, but there was a conflict between the army and navy about the design of Japanese strategic defense of Okinawa. The Imperial Army regarded the defense of Okinawa as a kind of delaying operation in which more time would be earned for preparing for the defense of the home islands, for *Ketsu-Gō*, meaning a decisive, unified operation. On the other hand, the Imperial Navy regarded the Okinawa operation not only as an opportunity to earn time for preparing for *Ketsu-Gō*, but also as an opportunity to inflict enormous damage on U.S. invasion forces. The conflict was never fully resolved before the American landings began on

1 April 1945. Thus, Japanese defenses of Okinawa were not as strong as they could have been. In particular, the Thirty-Second Army Corps abandoned the defense of air bases and entrenched itself in fortified strong points near Naha and Shuri in southern Okinawa. Therefore, U.S. amphibious forces were more effective and made greater advances at the outset than they might have, were there no conflict within the Japanese high command. In particular, the land air bases (Yontan and Kadena), which the navy intended to use for launching *kamikaze* attacks, were overrun by nightfall of L-day (landing day), occupied, and used by American units. Indeed, the first Vought F4U Corsair of Marine Aircraft Group 31 landed on Yontan airfield on 7 April; Marine Aircraft Wing 33 began tactical operations from Kadena airfield on 9 April; and a 7,000-foot runway expansion to Yontan airfield was completed on 17 June 1945. In spite of the early capture of these airfields, others were used extensively by the Japanese, particularly Naha airfield, which was not captured until June. The *kamikaze* attacks were massive, taking a heavy toll on enemy ships off Okinawa. Thirteen American ships were sunk in air attacks, usually *kamikaze*, off Okinawa in the month of April alone, another fifty-six ships were heavily damaged, and American casualties soared to 1,433 killed and 2,275 wounded as a result of *kamikaze* attacks during the thirty-day period.[30]

The Japanese fought desperately. The super battleship *Yamato*, in an attempt to reach Okinawa, made a final sortie from the Inland Sea in early April. This surface special attack force around the *Yamato* consisted of only one light cruiser and eight destroyers. There was a sacrificial air about this group as it sought chiefly to keep alive the glorious tradition of the Imperial Japanese Navy.[31] Indeed, so short of oil was the Imperial Navy at this time that the *Yamato* had only enough fuel to reach Okinawa—once there, the plan was to beach the giant battleship and to use its big guns in support of Japanese ground units on Okinawa. But in a four-hour battle 175 miles south of Kyushu, only four destroyers survived nearly continuous attacks by waves of hundreds of American planes, and nearly thirty-seven hundred Japanese sailors were killed. And although some four thousand suicide planes were used in *kamikaze* attacks, Okinawa was lost by the end of June after three months of battle.[32]

Like the *Yamato*, four submarines were deployed for the defense of Okinawa, and they too accomplished nothing because of the overwhelming strength of U.S. naval and air forces. The Japanese boats first sortied to intercept the U.S. carrier task force after assaults on the big naval bases at Kure and Kobe on 19 March. After they failed to catch the fast carriers, Admiral Miwa redirected them to the waters around Okinawa. There they ran into a solid wall of powerful ASW defenses—the submarines carried out a few torpedo attacks against American warships, but they failed to score any hits, and all four submarines were sunk. The *RO-41* was sunk during the night of 22 March, after the USS *Haggard* (DD-555) depth charged and later rammed the battered submarine. The *RO-49,* after its final report was received on 25 March, was sunk in a depth-charge attack on the morning of 5 April by the destroyer *Hudson* (DD-475). And the *RO-56* was sunk on 9 April as a result of attacks carried out by the USS *Mertz* (DD-691) and *Monssen* (DD-798).33

The *I-8* was the largest submarine sent to Okinawa at this time, a *Junsen* Type 3 specially equipped as a squadron flagship. This veteran boat that had made the remarkable round trip to Brest in 1943 was on the surface some 65 miles southeast of Okinawa on the night of 31 March when the USS *Stockton* (DD-646) made radar contact. The *I-8* soon submerged, but a depth-charge attack by both the *Stockton* and the USS *Morrison* (DD-560) forced the damaged I-boat to the surface again. Then, as described in a reliable American account, "the destroyers pounded the stricken submarine with gunfire for half an hour before the shattered hull sank."34

As long as the government in Tokyo continued the war, all Imperial Japanese armed forces would continue to fight, but Sixth Fleet Headquarters believed that *kaiten* operations still held promise. Thus, after the disastrous submarine operations off Okinawa, Admiral Miwa planned still another suicide mission. This one used four fleet-type submarines loaded with six *kaiten* each. Again, intense ASW forces ensured failure for the submarines. The *I-56* was sunk in a series of depth-charge attacks by several U.S. destroyers west of Okinawa on 18 April, and the *I-44* was sunk southeast of Okinawa on 29 April, probably by carrier planes. These two submarines were lost before they had an opportunity to launch *kaiten* attacks. Similarly, the *I-47* was damaged during an ASW attack, but it escaped to return to base with all *kaiten* still aboard. The *I-58* also returned to base on 29 April because strong ASW forces kept the boat submerged during most of the patrol. Unlike what occurred with the *I-44* in February, *I-58*'s actions were approved by the high command because the submarine was unable to charge batteries sufficiently for attack maneuvering.

Kaiten operations off Okinawa, like those earlier off Iwo Jima, had to be canceled because of the effectiveness of enemy ASW forces. Admiral Miwa finally recognized that the *kaiten* could not be used effectively in the well-protected waters. He reverted to more traditional and ordinary assignments for submarines, but the pattern of sacrifice and failure remained unchanged. Of the three *Kaichū* submarines (without *kaiten*) available to attack enemy warships and supply vessels off Okinawa, only one, *RO-50,* survived the mission, but it was unable to attack any enemy vessels. The *RO-46* was last heard from on 17 April and was probably sunk in a bombing attack by U.S. aircraft off Okinodaitō-Jima, South Ryūkyū. The *RO-109* was sunk by the light transport *Horace A. Bass* (ex-DE-691) 200 miles south of Okinawa on 25 April. Thus, the net result of submarine operations around Okinawa was the loss of eight of the eleven Japanese submarines deployed there; most of them were sunk in April, one of the worst months experienced by Japanese submariners.[35]

The chief reason for such staggering losses rested with the character of high command leadership. A siege mentality swept through the Combined Fleet Headquarters. The fundamental response to bad military news was to order repeated offensives until nothing was left. Blind fanaticism and suicidal perspectives too often dominated the decision-making process; orders to make senseless assaults resulted in the disintegration of an already destitute submarine force, and the wretched death of ships such as the *Yamato*.[36]

Operations of the Giant Submarines

The *I-400*-class submarine, with a standard displacement of over 5,000 tons surfaced, was designed to carry three *Seiran* dive-bomber seaplanes (Aichi M6A1s). Converted from "Judy" dive-bombers, the planes and their large parent submarines were designed originally with the intent of attacking the Panama Canal or ports on the west coast of mainland United States. The completion of both the submarines and the aircraft in this 1942 project was delayed due to the stringencies of war, and the *I-400* and *I-401* were not completed until the end of 1944. The *I-402* was nearly completed by August 1945, but other submarines of this class, up to *I-417*, were canceled or never laid down before surrender. In addition to the two *I-400*-class submarines, the *I-13* and *I-14* could also carry two aircraft each. These four submarines were organized into Submarine Squadron One under the command of Capt. Tatsunosuke Ariizumi, whose flag was aboard the *I-401* (Comdr. Shinsei Nambu was its skipper).[37] The four submarines sortied from Honshu in mid-July, with the expectation of attacking Ulithi on 17 August.

Originally, the units of the Submarine Squadron One trained for an attack on the Panama Canal, and American intelligence sources watched developments closely. However, limitations imposed by the war forced a change in plans; the threat of an American invasion of the home islands was overwhelming. Therefore, the squadron, with a total of six *Seiran* aircraft, was assigned to attack U.S. Navy task forces assembling at Ulithi Atoll.[38] The *I-13* and *I-14* were each loaded with two *Saiun* reconnaissance seaplanes (Navy Nakajima C6Ns), dubbed "Myrt" by American intelligence officers. These airplanes were crated and could easily be reassembled. Thus, the *I-13* and *I-14* were prepared to transport the four planes to Truk as reinforcements for the reconnaissance unit there and for specific reconnaissance missions to Ulithi before 17 August, but the *I-13*, which departed from Ōminato for Truk on 11 July, was sunk en route, possibly on 16 July by the USS

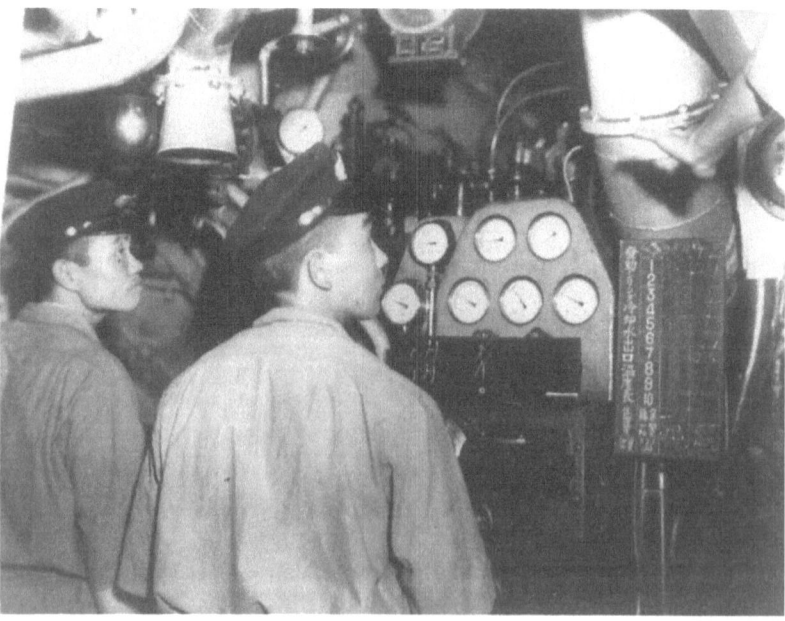

Port auxiliary engine room of the *I-14*. The *I-14* was completed at Kobe on 14 March 1945. (Naval Historical Center, NR&L [M] 30926)

Submarine Operations Near the War's End 177

The water-tight hangar door on the *I-400*. This submarine was completed at Kure Navy Yard on 30 December 1944. (Naval Historical Center, NR&L [M] 30947)

An inside view of *I-400*'s hangar designed to hold three seaplanes. (Naval Historical Center, NR&L [M] 30942)

Looking forward from the bridge of the *I-14*. This photograph taken 29 August 1945 shows the catapult for launching the two seaplanes carried by this submarine. Along the port side of the submarine is a retracted crane, which when raised was used to hoist the aircraft back aboard. (Courtesy of the Mariners' Museum, Newport News, Virginia)

Lawrence C. Taylor (DE-415) and aircraft from the escort carrier *Anzio* (CVE-57) some 550 miles east of Yokosuka.[39] Before the three remaining aircraft-carrying I-boats could accomplish their missions, however, the war finally ended and they were ordered to surrender and return to Japan.

Captain Ariizumi deliberately shot himself to death while his squadron was being escorted by U.S. naval vessels to Yokosuka. Evidence later demonstrated that Ariizumi was responsible for the massacre of more than one hundred unarmed survivors of merchantmen he had sunk earlier while commanding the *I-8* in the Indian Ocean or while he was chief of staff, Submarine Squadron 8, at Penang in 1944. Evidence of atrocities was overwhelming, particularly during the sinking of the Dutch steamer *Tjisalak* on 26 March 1944 and the American steamer *Jean Nicolet* on 2 July 1944. Concern about his earlier activities in the Indian Ocean may have contributed to Ariizumi's decision to commit suicide.[40]

The Sinking of the USS *Indianapolis* (CA-35)

The Imperial Japanese Navy's submarine force was practically ruined by the summer of 1945. It had no spectacular successes after the Japanese surrendered Guadalcanal, and it had suffered through the Gilberts and Marshalls, the Marianas, Leyte, then Iwo Jima and Okinawa without achieving a remarkable strike at a major enemy warship. Yet in the eleventh hour of the war there occurred the controversial sinking of the heavy cruiser USS *Indianapolis* by the *I-58*.

The *I-58*, under the command of Lt. Comdr. Mochitsura Hashimoto, sortied from the Inland Sea on 18 July. American signal intelligence units knew about *I-58*'s movements. The U.S. Navy Seventh Fleet Intelligence Center concluded in a TOP SECRET ULTRA report on 27 July 1945 that there were at least four Japanese submarines in the general area of the Philippine Sea. I-boats carrying the *kaiten* seemed ominous in the report. "An Allied destroyer escort was sunk on 24 July on the Leyte to Okinawa shipping route, presumably by a *kaiten* launched from *I-53*," ULTRA estimated. Sunk was the USS *Underhill* (DE-682). Furthermore, it was known from ULTRA that

> this sub had sortied from the Inland Sea on 14 July for a patrol station between Leyte and Okinawa. No Allied ships have made contacts with the other three subs which sortied at about the same time as the *I-53* to patrol along the Okinawa-Palau and Okinawa-Marianas lines, but it is believed all these subs are on their patrol stations by now.[41]

Hashimoto's *I-58* was among the submarines cited in this report barely three days before the *Indianapolis* was sunk.

Hashimoto patrolled in the vicinity of the cross point of lines connecting Guam and Leyte and Okinawa and Palau.[42] He claimed to have damaged an enemy destroyer with one of his *kaiten* on 28 July. By 29 July U.S. intelligence knew the identity of the four Japanese submarines patrolling in the Philippine Sea, the *I-53*, *I-58*, *I-47*, and *I-367*. It was near midnight on the same date when Hashimoto sighted a large warship sailing unescorted.

This situation was nearly unbelievable to Commander Hashimoto. Not only was there no escort with this target then caught in the moonlight, but he thought the ship was actually larger than a heavy cruiser. Moreover, at a range of about 5 miles it appeared to Hashimoto that the target was nearly dead ahead and on a steady course (not zigzagging). He was required to maneuver to open the angle on the bow—the official Japanese record cites the following data concerning *I-58*'s attack on the *Indianapolis*:

> Launch time: 2332 (JST, India) (Japanese Standard Time, 9 hour East)
> Target course: south (straight on)
> Target speed: twelve knots
> Angle on the bow: sixty degrees, starboard
> Range: 1500 meters [1650 yards]
> Divert angle: twenty-eight degrees, right
> Angle of torpedo spread: three degrees
> Interval of torpedo firing: three seconds
> Number of torpedoes fired: six
> Depth of torpedo run: four meters [13 feet][43]

Through *I-58*'s periscope Hashimoto saw his torpedoes strike the target's side a minute after firing—a flame shot up near "A" turret, and he saw three plumes of water. Fifteen minutes later he saw flames from near the center of the ship and soon heard a series of explosions. An hour later, at 0030 on 30 July, Hashimoto brought the *I-58* to the surface, but he did not see his target or any evidence that it had been sunk. He soon sped north for two hours before submerging when an enemy aircraft was sighted. Not long afterward, the *I-58* returned to the surface, and Hashimoto radioed to naval headquarters in Tokyo that he had sunk an *Idaho*-class battleship with three torpedo hits. Hashimoto's report was intercepted by the U.S. Navy's Fleet Radio Unit, Pacific, deciphered, and passed to the commander in chief, Pacific, about sixteen hours after the sinking. As one of the most important

U.S. Navy intelligence officers in the Pacific theater wrote many years later, Hashimoto's message was viewed, however,

> as just another of the many Japanese messages exaggerating their successes. It also was given very limited distribution [since it was ULTRA derived], and probably no one had both essential bits of information—the position of the *Indianapolis* and the *I-58*'s report of sinking a battleship at that position.[44]

Enormous casualties were suffered in the sinking of the *Indianapolis;* only 316 survivors were eventually rescued out of a ship's company of 1,199 men, and a court martial was convened to try the warship's commanding officer, Capt. Charles B. McVay III. Neither McVay nor the members of the court were authorized to have access to ULTRA. Commander Hashimoto was called to the court martial in Washington, D.C., in December 1945, to describe how he had sunk the ship. Hashimoto testified that he had not used the *kaiten*, because Type 95 torpedoes, propelled by oxygen, were considered sufficient to

A view of the forward torpedo room of the *I-58* in January 1946. This Japanese submarine was responsible for sinking the USS *Indianapolis* (CA-35) in late July 1945. The *I-58* was completed at Yokosuka on 7 September 1944. (National Archives, USMC 139986)

sink the enemy vessel, and the official Japanese history supports his account. There were many twists to this tragedy of war, not the least of which the *Indianapolis*'s having transported the major parts of the atomic bombs, including the fissionable core, to Tinian and left them there a few days before the sinking. The bombs were later dropped on Japanese cities.

In the minds of some Japanese warriors, a peculiar type of justice seems to have been spun out. The uncompromising high command assured defeat of the erstwhile Imperial Japanese Navy submarine force, yet it was a submarine that doomed the American cruiser that had transported the devastating atomic bombs destined for Japan. The death and untold misery suffered by three-fourths of the 1,199 sailors aboard the *Indianapolis* were seen by some as poetic justice for the horror unleashed on the citizens of Hiroshima and Nagasaki.[45]

The Seventh Fleet Intelligence Center made specific reference to the danger of the *kaiten* in a report of 3 August.

> The Japanese are placing increasing emphasis on attacks on Blue [U.S. Navy] ships by *kaiten* launched from submarines. The four I-class subs already patrolling the routes from Okinawa to Leyte, Palau and the Marianas, are being augmented by one which left the Inland Sea on 1 August and another which will leave on 6 August to patrol those lines south of the Ryukyus. Each of these subs carries 5 to 6 *kaiten*. The sinking of the CA INDIANAPOLIS, following closely on the heels of the sinking of the DE UNDERHILL, is testimony of the effectiveness of Japanese submarine warfare at this time.[46]

This report also explained the surprising endurance of the *kaiten*, secret information contained in Japanese communications and revealed to the Allies through ULTRA.

How the *Indianapolis* was sunk continues to be debated in some circles, particularly in the United States. It has been suggested that Commander Hashimoto employed the *kaiten* in the attack on the *Indianapolis*. Capt. Edward L. Beach, USN (ret.), a distinguished submariner and naval historian, first publicly set forth the *kaiten* case in his introduction to the 1954 English edition of Hashimoto's book, *Sunk*. But the official Japanese history denies that the *kaiten* was used, and the wall of silence in Japanese naval circles appears impregnable. Thus, whatever previous weight might have been behind the *kaiten* case, with the passage of time and no new evidence, one must conclude that the *I-58*'s conventional torpedoes did in fact sink the *Indianapolis*.[47]

Submarines on Their Final Patrols

The available submarines in the Imperial Japanese Navy continued operations after the loss of Okinawa. Some of them were loaded with the new *kaiten* weapons, and they most frequently patrolled the waters east of the Philippines, where the *Indianapolis* was sunk. Other submarines were engaged in transportation operations, including the transport of the *kaiten* weapon to shore bases in Japan.

The submarines fought to the bitter end, but their efforts were without any prospect of changing the course of the war, even though the boats now carried *kaiten* weapons. The *I-361* was sunk off Okinawa on 30 May 1945 by planes from the USS *Anzio* (CVE-57), and the veteran fleet-type submarine *I-165* was sunk off Saipan on 27 June by land-based U.S. Navy aircraft. The *kaiten* operations of these two submarines did not accomplish anything. The dying submarine force could offer little resistance to the sweep of powerful Allied ASW forces.[48]

Other submarine operations near the close of the war were also of little consequence. The *I-366* and *I-367* carried out patrols in July—no enemy ships came under attack—and they were able to return safely to Japan. The *I-369* transported supplies to Truk, and the *I-372* operated similarly to Wake. The *I-351* and *I-373* were converted into aviation fuel tankers and operated mainly out of Singapore shortly before the war ended. Both were sunk by U.S. submarines: the *I-351* was sunk by two torpedoes fired from the USS *Bluefish* (SS-222) off Borneo on 15 July, and the *I-373* was sunk by the USS *Spikefish* (SS-404) in the East China Sea at daybreak on 14 August 1945, shortly before the war ended. The *I-373* was the 127th Japanese submarine (I and RO classes) lost since the attack on Pearl Harbor and the final victim of American ASW forces in the war.[49]

In sharp contrast to the Imperial Japanese Navy submarine force, the U.S. Navy submarine force remained amazingly strong and effective throughout the war, especially after defective torpedoes were improved. Vice Adm. Charles A. Lockwood, Commander of Submarines, Pacific, during the war, wrote in a TOP SECRET report in 1947 that

> in early 1945 it was learned from a Japanese prisoner of war that it was a common saying in Singapore that you could walk from that port to Japan on American periscopes. This feeling among the Japanese was undoubtedly created, not by the great number of submarines on patrol, but rather by the fact, thanks to Communication

Intelligence, the submarines were always at the same place as Japanese ships.[50]

Midget Submarines and Other Special Attack Weapons

After the loss of the Philippines and then Okinawa, the Japanese army and navy began preparations for the final battle in the Japanese home islands. The intent of the *Ketsu-Gō*, the decisive operation, was to have all navy and army forces assume defensive positions in caves and trenches and then fight to the death. With the mandate of such a desperate scheme, the navy found that the deployment of some types of special attack or small suicide units would be feasible at this late point in the war. Thus, small vessels, for example, were hidden in trenches and caves for protection from bombing and shore bombardment. They were to remain hidden until the chance came to launch the classic final "*banzai* charge." Various special attack suicide forces rallied to defend the Japanese homeland during the summer of 1945—this was to be a modified decisive battle, certainly not as envisioned by Japanese decisive battle enthusiasts in earlier decades.[51]

In addition to the *kaiten*, Japanese suicide forces included the *Kōryū*, a midget submarine with performance characteristics similar to those of the A-targets (*Kō hyōteki*) used from the beginning of the war. There was also the *Kairyū*, a smaller submarine combining characteristics of the midget submarine and the *kaiten*. It carried two small torpedoes or an explosive head for ramming. And there was the *Shin-yō*, a small wooden motor boat loaded with an explosive head for ramming. Each special attack (*tokkō*) unit of suicide weapons was well organized and deployed along much of the coast of the southern home islands and in southern Korea.[52] U.S. naval intelligence estimated in a November 1945 report the number of suicide attack units the Japanese had available for defense of the home islands: 161–180 *kaiten*, 59 *Kōryū*, 140–160 *Kairyū*, and 1,658–1,954 *Shin-yō*.[53]

But these suicide units were never fully reliable or genuinely effective as weapon systems. A U.S. Navy veteran of several engagements with Japanese naval forces wrote eloquently that

> in a rising sea of troubles, the Imperial Navy resorted to suicide missions: the *kaitens*, the *kamikazes*, the *Ōka* bombs, the suicide motorboats, the nautical *banzai* charge of the *Yamato* group. It is interesting to note that the *kaiten* program antedates the others. But other than

tie up valuable men and equipment, kill some very brave and dedicated pilots, and bring about the loss of eight submarines fitted for carrying *kaitens,* what did this strange program accomplish? . . . It deprived the U.S. Navy of the tanker *Mississinewa* and the destroyer escort *Underhill,* which was finished off by friendly forces. This could hardly be called a profitable enterprise. In fact, the Imperial Navy did a lot better with its torpedoes *before* the human guidance system was added.[54]

Surviving Submarines and Their Fate

The tattered survivors of the Japanese submarine force were wrenched by the attrition of war.[55] These included fifteen I-class submarines that were operational (excluding seven *Kaidai* training I-boats), a handful of former German and Italian submarines, only five smaller RO-class boats, and various transport or high-speed types of submarines of the once-powerful submarine force of the Imperial Navy. They surrendered and were held in various ports of the Japanese home islands (mostly Kure and Maizuru) and a few foreign ports such as Batavia, Surabaja, and Singapore. Most of them were scrapped or sunk off the coast of Japan by Americans within a few months of surrender, but a few I-boats were taken over by the U.S. Navy. In such cases a few members of the former Japanese crews would usually remain aboard, including the former commanding officer, to assist with the transfer.[56] The officer in charge was always a U.S. Navy officer. American submarine officers were interested in only the latest large and fast designs; therefore, submarines transferred included the *I-14, I-400,* and *I-401* and the *I-201* and *I-203* (high-submerged-speed submarines). ULTRA reported much advanced information on these new designs of Japanese submarines during the war, and U.S. naval investigators knew before surrender which features of Japanese submarines they wanted specifically to inspect.[57] In addition to all types of midget submarines, the following classes of Japanese submarines were studied after the war by the U.S. Navy: *I-200, I-361, HA-101,* and *HA-201*. Moreover, many Japanese submarine specialists, particularly at Sasebo and Kure, were carefully interviewed.[58]

Nevertheless, Japanese submarines did not long hold much interest among American submariners. Paul Schratz, who sailed the *I-203* from Sasebo to Pearl Harbor in January and February 1946, wrote about his difficult voyage in the former enemy submarine.

186 The Japanese Submarine Force

The *I-14*, *I-401*, and *I-400* at Guam in November 1945 while en route from Japan to Pearl Harbor. (Naval Historical Center, NH 82107)

The snorkel device fitted on an *I-400*-class submarine at Yokosuka Naval Base, 7 September 1945. The *I-400* as well as the *I-14* and *I-401* seen in the illustrations above and right were surrendered submarines then under the control of the U.S. Navy. (National Archives, 80-G-339822)

Submarine Operations Near the War's End 187

An aerial view of part of the Pearl Harbor Submarine Base, 27 February 1946. The three large Japanese submarines, *I-14, I-401,* and *I-400,* are tied up together, with the submarine escape training tank to their left and several smaller U.S. Navy submarines at the finger piers in front. Across Magazine Loch to their right is the survey ship USS *Bowditch* (AGS-4). (National Archives, 80-G-361745)

> Without question a high speed target submarine would be invaluable for training antisubmarine forces. The real issue, yet to be faced, was whether the Japanese models, brought up to minimum American standards, would be more costly than a new model built from the keel up. Our experiences at sea under considerable stress went a long way to furnish the answers.[59]

Not surprisingly, therefore, the *I-201* and *I-203* were deliberately torpedoed by USS *Caiman* (SS-323) off Pearl Harbor in March 1946. These exercises involved a test of a new torpedo exploder, and witnesses noted that the two *I-200*-class Japanese submarines "sank in about 10–13 seconds."[60]

The sinking of a Japanese submarine during U.S. Navy scuttling operations off Sasebo in April 1946. Another Japanese submarine is waiting to be sunk while a U.S. Navy PBM Mariner patrol bomber flies overhead. (National Archives, 80-G-260221)

Epilogue

By the beginning of 1945, the Japanese submarine force, like the rest of the Imperial Navy, was a shambles. Submarine policy had not been effectively focused since the outset of the war; therefore, nothing could be saved near the end. Adm. Shigeru Fukudome, chief of the First Bureau of the Naval General Staff at the time of the Pearl Harbor attack, wrote later that

> it was my belief that, even if the Task Force's aerial attack ended in failure, the Submarine Force's operation would not fail. . . . Furthermore, I expected that more damage would be inflicted by submarine attacks, which would be continued over a longer period, than by the air attacks.[61]

However, writing the conclusion to Hashimoto's work on Japanese submarines, Admiral Fukudome reflected on the entire war.

> The Japanese Navy expected much from its submarines, and for this reason alone both officers and men were carefully selected and put through the most rigorous training. They considered themselves superior in technique in the field of submarine warfare to any in other navies. But when it came to the test of actual warfare, the results were deplorable.[62]

The Japanese submarine force made prewar training as realistic as possible, but the realities of the war increasingly surpassed the capacity of the force to adapt. The mind-set and command structure in the Imperial Navy prevented complete identification of the problems that plagued the submarine force. Moreover, rapidly changing circumstances of the war, in which the powerful U.S. Navy was the pacesetter, inhibited the implementation of fresh and crucial alternatives. Thus, the Japanese were a prisoner of their past, and the legacy of prewar thinking offered only a grim fate for the Japanese submarine force after 1941.

Japanese submarine operations were frequently widely scattered during the war. When they were concentrated to take part in major Combined Fleet operations early in the war—at Pearl Harbor and Midway, for example—submarines failed to live up to the expectations of Japanese operation planners.

Submarine effectiveness against American warships during the Guadalcanal campaign, particularly in September 1942, was quite distinguished. Yet submarines did not inflict enough damage to force an American withdrawal from Guadalcanal; nor were the Japanese air and surface naval forces capable of accomplishing the high command's goal.

Immediately after the Pearl Harbor attack, the Japanese navy should have concentrated *all* ocean-going and fleet-type submarines in Hawaiian waters and off the U.S. mainland. Operations like those of the *I-25* in October 1942, including more aggressive action than the mere incendiary bombing of Oregon forests, ought to have been emphasized. The large submarines ought to have been rotated systematically, and these two war patrol areas (Hawaii and the U.S. west coast) should have been maintained at least throughout 1942. That is, one-third of the available submarines should have been on station, one-third en route, and one-third being refitted. Only Japanese submarines could chance operations around the Hawaiian Islands and eastward after 7 December 1941. While manning these two patrol areas, the submarines could have obstructed quite effectively the flow of American reinforcements being rushed westward, and at least in the early part of 1942, they would have been ideally situated to attack American warships en route to the U.S. mainland for permanent repairs after suffering damage during the Pearl Harbor attack.

As a corollary to a focus for submarine operations on the areas of the Hawaiian and California coasts, *I-25*-like operations should have included a large tanker I-boat for refueling in order to continue I-boat–aircraft operations in the Panama Canal area. Bombing the canal locks would have been the goal, and even if there were no hits on the vital waterway, such an attack would have alarmed the American public. Thus, the U.S. Congress would have voted enormous defense expenditures, funds that would not have been available for the American buildup in the South Pacific in 1942.

After the Pearl Harbor attack, Japanese air and surface naval forces should have focused exclusively on the southern and westward areas of expansion *without* demanding the heavy involvement of the Sixth Fleet. The major enemy capital ships in those areas, HMS *Prince of Wales* and *Repulse,* for example, were sunk by air power in early December 1941. Other available British battleships of the Eastern Fleet were the four old World War I "Rs"—the *Ramillies, Resolution, Revenge,* and *Royal Sovereign* and the 1913 *Warspite,* at Sydney in March 1942. These capital ships, with the much newer fleet aircraft carriers HMS *Indomitable* and *Formidable,* were incapable of effective opposition to Japanese expansion. And surely the Japanese air and surface naval forces could have overwhelmed the ABDA (American, British, Dutch, and Australian) cruisers and lesser warships without, as it turned out, the modest aid of the submarine force. At a minimum, the medium-range RO-class submarines could have served as an arm of Combined Fleet operations in southern and westward expansion during the first thirteen months of the war. As it turned out, Japan's submarine force never had a chance to prove itself as a strategic arm, but was always subordinated to local needs and tactical situations.

Appendix 1
Imperial Japanese Navy Instructions for Submarine Warfare and the Decisive Battle

Note: Excerpts in this appendix are from old Japanese documents composed in an archaic style; they are rendered into English sometimes loosely with the primary purpose of providing the modern reader with an accurate description of the Japanese text, but without distorting the meaning or intent of the original material.

General Battle Instructions, 1934*

1. Submarines are deployed effectively for the purpose of achieving their main goal: surprise attack on the enemy's main force.
2. The intent is to achieve repeated attacks on the enemy's main force. Operational preliminaries, such as types of submarines deployed, consideration of enemy intelligence, and weather conditions, are weighed carefully to help achieve these repeated attacks.
3. Except for a few submarines attached directly to the main force, most submarines constitute an advance expeditionary force. These

---

*Japan, Bōeichō Bōeikenshūjo Senshibu, *Kaisen yōmurei* (Navy battle regulations) (1934), par. II-5-102-120. The 1934 edition of the *Kaisen yōmurei*, the last one published, is cited here; however, information from a handwritten draft of 1940, located in the National Institute for Defense Studies library in Tokyo, is incorporated into the first section of this appendix.

advance submarines launch early attacks on the enemy's main force while also coordinating their operations with other Japanese units.

4. The submarine squadron commanders plan and organize the operation with much care before deployment. The purpose is to maximize the possibilities for contact with the enemy.
5. The submarine squadron commander's orders for deployment include the time and area for rendezvous and instructions for submarine commanders to report on the movement and action of enemy ships.
6. The submarine squadron commander is to be kept fully informed, communication conditions permitting, about submarine action throughout the deployment.
7. Submarines are expected to attack key targets at close range. Indeed, a submarine commander is expected to be fully prepared for attack before penetrating the antisubmarine screen protecting the enemy's battleships; torpedoes are not to be fired from great distances simply to avoid enemy antisubmarine warfare (ASW) forces.
8. Submarines are expected to make high-speed runs on the surface in order to achieve a better position on the enemy's course of advance or return. In the latter instance, the enemy's retreat to safety is possibly prevented.
9. Submarines are always ready to dive quickly during poor visibility or night attacks when enemy destroyers are present.
10. Good coordination of air-sea communications is to be established in areas of submarine operation.
11. After submarines are deployed, their squadron flagship acts as a communications control station; however, care is urged in order to prevent the enemy from intercepting messages or otherwise gaining information about submarine deployment.
12. When the submarine squadron flagship services are no longer needed or the flagship is out of communication range of the submarines, it joins the main force or operates independently until the submarines once again need and are within range to receive assistance from the flagship.
13. When a major redeployment of a submarine squadron becomes necessary, the squadron flagship is expected to proceed in advance of the submarines to a forward area.
14. Submarine and air forces, minefields, and the advantage of geo-

graphical features are to be used to full advantage when a weaker Japanese fleet is forced to fight a stronger enemy fleet. Nevertheless, the inferior fleet ought to be ready to seize the offensive quickly if combat conditions warrant such a switch.

Combined Fleet Tactical Instructions of 1943: The Specific Tactical Role of Submarines in a Decisive Battle between the Main Fleets†

1. Submarines, aided by naval aircraft, reconnoiter enemy bases or anchorages. If the enemy sorties, submarines and aircraft attempt to intercept the enemy fleet and maintain contact. Moreover, these submarines direct other submarines and aircraft to concentrate along the enemy's course.
2. When the enemy main fleet emerges from under its own land-based air cover into a Japanese sphere, the tracking submarines threaten the enemy's rear in order to prevent the enemy fleet from retreating and returning once again to the protection of its own air cover. Japanese land-based air units should attack the enemy repeatedly in the vicinity of the anticipated decisive battle. Japanese auxiliary forces systematically reduce the enemy strength by launching torpedo night attacks—at dawn, the big guns of the Japanese main fleet open the decisive assault.
3. Intercept operations are divided into five stages:
    a. In the surveillance stage, submarines take up the best possible station in order to reconnoiter the enemy fleet in its ports or anchorages.
    b. In the sortie stage, submarines maintain contact and track the enemy fleet while constantly communicating with squadron flagships or the main force.
    c. In the stage when the enemy fleet is under the protection of its own air cover, submarines maintain contact and track the enemy's main force while also intercepting any enemy forces trying to join the main force.
    d. During the torpedo attack stage, it is crucial for the submarine force to seize the initiative through aggressive attacks. The purpose is to prevent the enemy from retreating and to force the

†Japan, Bōeichō Bōeikenshūjo Senshibu, ed., *Rengō kantai sensaku* (Combined fleet tactical instructions), rev. ed. (1943), pars. I-1-3-19, I-3-2-28(9), I-3-3-29(8), I-3-3-33(3), I-5-3-66(7), and I-5-5-73(6).

enemy to move toward the Japanese main force. Submarines are also to maintain communications with the main fleet during this stage.

   e. In the stage when contact is lost with the enemy fleet, submarine commanders commence routine surveillance operations in an assigned area.
4. Procedures for submarines in decisive battles between the main fleets. Most submarines concentrate in the vicinity of the anticipated battle to launch torpedo attacks. Submarines station themselves at the enemy's rear to prevent retreat while the main fleets are engaged in a running daylight battle on a parallel course. When the main fleets are firing on each other while running on opposite courses, surfaced submarines seek to race ahead of the enemy, then submerge, and launch torpedo attacks when the enemy fleet comes within firing range. If confronted by strong ASW forces during the high-speed race to get ahead of the enemy's main fleet, attack is to be avoided by submerging quickly, but the surface race must be resumed as soon as possible. Torpedo attacks are thought to be most promising when launched at dawn or dusk, especially when air support is available. During the night, submarines track the enemy's main fleet until Japanese destroyers and cruisers can launch their night torpedo attacks. At that time submarines are expected to assist those surface vessels by preventing the enemy's retreat.
5. The command relationship. The command relationships between submarine forces attached to the fleet and those attached to a district garrison are intended to be cooperative; operations are coordinated, and operational boundaries are established in order to avoid confusion. Operation command of air and submarine forces in the same area belongs to the senior commander present or to a coordinated command resulting from a mutual agreement. These command relationships are determined by the senior authority.
6. Reconnaissance operations. The role of submarines on reconnaissance operations emphasizes the reconnoitering of enemy harbors, attacking the enemy fleet as it enters or leaves harbor, and the tracking and, thereafter, repeated attacking of the enemy fleet.

   a. The primary mission of submarines engaged in reconnaissance operations is to sight the enemy as soon as possible and to radio Japanese forces full information about the enemy, composition, formation, course, and speed, for example. Such an enterprising submarine is then expected to track and maintain contact with the enemy while continuing to relay vital information.

b. A portion of submarines assigned to reconnaissance operations also perform the following services: guard and watch all around the Japanese battle fleet formation, reconnoiter and radio information about weather conditions in the operational area, and search for and rescue the pilots of any downed Japanese aircraft.

Appendix 2
The Pearl Harbor Carrier Strike Force*

Vice Adm. Chūichi Nagumo, Commander of the First Air Fleet

Mission: On "X" day, with full air power, launch a surprise attack at Pearl Harbor and in Hawaiian waters and destroy the enemy naval and air fleets.

Task Force Organization (*Guntai-Kubun*)
Carrier Group: *Akagi, Kaga, Sōryū, Hiryū, Shōkaku,* and *Zuikaku*—six fast carriers and their full carrier air groups.
Screen Group: One light cruiser and nine destroyers.
Support Group: *Kirishima* and *Hiei*—two fast battleships—and *Tone* and *Chikuma*—two heavy cruisers with seaplanes.
Advance Submarine Screen Unit: *I-19, I-21,* and *I-23*—three new ocean-cruising submarines.
Midway Bombardment Unit: Two destroyers.

Advance Expeditionary Force
Vice Adm. Mitsumi Shimizu, Commander Sixth Fleet

*Japan, Bōeichō Bōeikenshūjo Senshibu (Defense Ministry, Defense Research Institute, War History Branch), ed., *Daihon'ei kaigunbu, Rengō kanta, 2,* (Imperial General Headquarters, Navy Division, Combined Fleet, part 2), Senshi Sōsho (War history series), vol. 82 (Tokyo: Asagumo Shimbunsha, 1979), 77–78.

Mission: Reconnoiter Hawaiian waters and ambush the enemy fleet, blockade the entrance to Pearl Harbor, and intercept any enemy ships attempting to sortie.

Submarine Organization and Mission Details†

Flagship Unit: Light cruiser *Katori,* anchored at Kwajalein, was in charge of all submarine operations.
First Submarine Group: Rear Adm. Tsutomu Satō, Commander Submarine Squadron 1. Four ocean-cruising submarines, *I-9, I-15, I-17,* and *I-25,* were stationed northeast of Oahu to support the carrier task force by intercepting any enemy ships in the area.
Second Submarine Group: Rear Adm. Shigeaki Yamazaki, Commander Submarine Squadron 2. Seven older ocean-cruising submarines, *I-7, I-1, I-2, I-3, I-4, I-5,* and *I-6,* were stationed between Oahu and Kauai and between Molokai and Oahu to reconnoiter and to attack any enemy ships attempting to sortie from Pearl Harbor.
Third Submarine Group: Rear Adm. Shigeyoshi Miwa, Commander Submarine Squadron 3. Nine submarines (one ocean-cruising submarine and eight fleet-type submarines, *I-8, I-74, I-75, I-68, I-69, I-70, I-71, I-72,* and *I-73,* were stationed south of Oahu to reconnoiter, attack any enemy ships attempting to escape from Pearl Harbor, and to rescue any Japanese pilots forced into the sea. Moreover, some boats of this group also had the assignment of carrying out a preliminary reconnaissance patrol of the Lahaina Roads, where U.S. Navy ships anchored sometimes.
Special Attack Unit: Capt. Hanku Sasaki, Commander Submarine Division 3. Five ocean-cruising submarines, *I-16, I-18, I-20, I-22,* and *I-24,* each with a midget submarine "Type A Target (*Kō hyōteki*)," were stationed at the entrance of Pearl Harbor to launch their five midget submarines for surprise attacks against enemy ships inside the harbor, to reconnoiter, and to attack any ships attempting to sortie.
Reconnaissance Unit: Two ocean-cruising submarines, *I-10* and *I-26,* were sent to enemy waters in the South Pacific and Aleutians for reconnaissance missions.

†Japan, Bōeichō Bōeikenshūjo Senshibu (Defense Ministry, Defense Research Institute, War History Branch), ed., *Sensuikan shi* (History of submarines), Senshi Sōsho (War history series), vol. 98 (Tokyo: Asagumo Shimbunsha, 1979), 93–94.

Appendix 3

Reconnaissance Operations with Submarine-Borne Aircraft, November 1941 through November 1942*

Date	Submarine	Place
30 November 1941	I-10	Suva Bay, Fiji
17 December 1941	I-7	Pearl Harbor
5 January 1942	I-19	Pearl Harbor
7 February 1942	I-25	Sydney, Australia
24 February 1942	I-9	Pearl Harbor
26 February 1942	I-25	Melbourne, Australia
1 March 1942	I-25	Hobart, Tasmania
8 March 1942	I-25	Wellington, New Zealand
13 March 1942	I-25	Auckland, New Zealand
19 March 1942	I-25	Suva Bay, Fiji
7 May 1942	I-30	Aden, Hadhramaut (Yemen)
8 May 1942	I-30	Djibouti, French Somaliland (Afars and Issas)
19 May 1942	I-30	Zanzibar & Dar es Salaam, Tanganyika (Tanzania)
19 May 1942	I-21	Suva Bay, Fiji
23 May 1942	I-29	Sydney, Australia
24 May 1942	I-21	Auckland, New Zealand

*U.S. Strategic Bombing Survey (Pacific), *Japanese Military and Naval Intelligence* (Washington, D.C.: U.S. Government Printing Office, 1946), 91.

Reconnaissance Operations with Aircraft

Date	Submarine	Place
25–26 May 1942	*I-9*	Kiska & Amchitka, Aleutian Islands
27 May 1942	*I-19*	Bogoslof, Aleutian Islands
27 May 1942	*I-25*	Kodiak, Alaska
29 May 1942	*I-21*	Sydney, Australia
30 May–1 June 1942	*I-10*	Diégo Suarez, Madagascar
29 August 1942	*I-29*	Seychelles Islands (NE of Madagascar)
9 September 1942	*I-25*	Oregon, U.S.
29 September 1942	*I-25*	Oregon, U.S.
2 October 1942	*I-21*	Espiritu Santo, New Hebrides
13 October 1942	*I-7*	Espiritu Santo, New Hebrides
19 October 1942	*I-19*	Nouméa, New Caledonia
30 October 1942	*I-9*	Nouméa, New Caledonia
2 November 1942	*I-8*	Efate Island, New Hebrides
4 November 1942	*I-31*	Suva Bay, Fiji
4 November 1942	*I-9*	Nouméa, New Caledonia
11 November 1942	*I-7*	Vanikoro Island, Solomon Islands
11 November 1942	*I-21*	Nouméa, New Caledonia
11 November 1942	*I-9*	Espiritu Santo, New Hebrides

Appendix 4
Southern Expeditionary Main Force (Second Fleet)*

Vice Adm. Nobutake Kondō, Commander

Philippines Invasion Force (Third Fleet)
  Vice Adm. Ibō Takahashi

Malaya Invasion Force (Southern Expeditionary Fleet)
  Vice Adm. Jisaburō Ozawa

Dutch East Indies Invasion Force (Third Fleet—after conquest of the Philippines)
  Vice Adm. Ibō Takahashi

General Support Land Based Air Force (Eleventh Air Fleet)
  Vice Adm. Nishizō Tsukahara

*Bōeichō Bōeikenshūjo Senshibu, ed., *Daihon'ei kaigunbu, Rengō kantai*, 2:137.

Appendix 5
Imperial Japanese Navy Task Force Organization (*Guntai-Kubun*) against Midway, the Aleutians, and Port Moresby*

Surface Forces

Main and General Support Force (First Fleet)
 Adm. Isoroku Yamamoto, Commander in Chief, Combined Fleet
 Vice Adm. Mitsumi Shimizu, Commander First Fleet

Midway Assault Force (Second Fleet), Vice Adm. Nobutake Kondō

Carrier Strike Force (First Air Fleet), Vice Adm. Chūichi Nagumo

Advance Expeditionary Force (Sixth Fleet), Vice Adm. Teruhisa Komatsu

Northern Assault Force (Fifth Fleet), Vice Adm. Boshirō Hosokaya

Land Based Air Force (Eleventh Air Fleet), Vice Adm. Nishizō Tsukahara

Southern Pacific Force (Fourth Fleet), Vice Adm. Shigeyoshi Inoue

---

*Bōeichō Bōeikenshūjo Senshibu, ed., *Daihon'ei kaigunbu, Rengō kantai*, 2:345, 418–19.

Appendix 5

Battle Orders for Submarines of the Advance Expeditionary Force and the Northern Assault Force†

Third Submarine Group: Rear Adm. Chimaki Kōno, Commander Submarine Squadron 3. Four new fleet-type submarines: *I-169, I-171, I-174,* and *I-175.*

Fifth Submarine Group: Rear Adm. Tadashige Daigo, Commander Submarine Squadron 5. Seven old fleet-type submarines: *I-156, I-157, I-158, I-159, I-162, I-164,* and *I-166.*

Submarine Division 13, Capt. Takeji Miyazaki, Commander. Two minelaying submarines (*I-121* and *I-123*) were assigned the mission of refueling two Type 2 Flying Boats ("Emily") at French Frigate Shoals so that the aircraft could carry out reconnaissance missions at Pearl Harbor before the Japanese attack at Midway.

The *I-168,* commanded by Lt. Comdr. Yahachi Tanabe, sailed independently from Japan to reconnoiter in the vicinity of Midway.

First Submarine Group: Rear Adm. Shigeaki Yamazaki, Commander Submarine Squadron 1. Six new ocean-cruising submarines, *I-9, I-15, I-17, I-19, I-25,* and *I-26,* were assigned to reconnaissance missions off Seattle, Kodiak, Dutch Harbor, and in the western Aleutians.

---

†Bōeichō Bōeikenshūjo Senshibu, ed., *Sensuikan shi,* 141–45.

Appendix 6
Sixth Fleet Submarines in the Eastern Solomons, Late 1942*

Submarine Organization

Vice Adm. Teruhisa Komatsu, Commander Sixth Fleet (Truk)

First Submarine Group (Submarine Squadron 1)
Rear Adm. Shigeaki Yamazaki
(Twelve new ocean-cruising-type submarines: *I-9, I-15, I-17, I-19, I-21, I-22, I-24, I-25, I-26, I-31, I-32,* and *I-33*)

Second Submarine Group (Submarine Division 7)
Capt. Tomejirō Tamaki
(Seven mostly old ocean-cruising-type submarines: *I-1, I-2, I-3, I-4, I-5, I-7,* and *I-8*)

Third Submarine Group (Submarine Squadron 3)
Rear Adm. Chimaki Kōno
(One ocean-cruising-type and four fleet-type submarines: *I-11, I-172, I-174, I-175,* and *I-176*)

Seventh Submarine Group (Submarine Squadron 7)
Rear Adm. Setsuzō Yoshitomi
(Two minelaying-type and one coastal-defense-type submarines: *I-121, I-122,* and *RO-34*)

*Bōeichō Bōeikenshūjo Senshibu, ed., *Sensuikan shi*, 194–95.

Appendix 7
Leadership of the Sixth Fleet, Mid-1943*

Submarine Organization

Vice Adm. Takeo Takagi, Commander Sixth Fleet

First Submarine Group (Submarine Squadron 1)
  Rear Adm. Takerō Kouta
(Fourteen submarines of various types: *I-11, I-16, I-17, I-19, I-20, I-21, I-25, I-26, I-34, I-35, I-36, I-39, I-182,* and *RO-35*)

Third Submarine Group (Submarine Squadron 3)
  Rear Adm. Katsumi Komazawa
(*I-169, I-171,* and *I-175*)

Eighth Submarine Group (Submarine Squadron 8)
  Rear Adm. Hisashi Ichioka
(Five ocean-cruising submarines: *I-8, I-10, I-27, I-29,* and *I-37*)

Others, mainly old-type submarines, were attached to each of the district forces:

*Bōeichō Bōeikenshūjo Senshibu, ed., *Sensuikan shi*, 259.

Southeast District Force
Seventh Submarine Group (Submarine Squadron 7)
   Rear Adm. Kaku Harada
(Six ocean-cruising and fleet-type submarines: *I-32, I-34, I-174, I-176, I-177,* and *I-180;* two minelaying I-boats and five coastal-defense-type submarines were originally attached: *I-121, I-122, RO-100, RO-101, RO-103, RO-106,* and *RO-107.* Initially, *I-168* was assigned to the Southeast District Force in the new organization, but while it was en route to Rabaul it was torpedoed and sunk by the U.S. submarine *Scamp* (SS-277) on 27 July 1943.)

Southwest District Force
   Capt. Toyojirō Ōyama, Submarine Division 30
(*I-162, I-165,* and *I-166*)

Northern District Force
   Capt. Yūsaku Okada, Submarine Division 7
(*I-2, I-5,* and *I-6*)

Appendix 8
Task Force Organization for Operation A-Gō sakusen*

Combined Fleet

Commander in Chief, Adm. Soemu Toyoda

Carrier Mobile Force (First Mobile Fleet)
  Vice Adm. Jisaburō Ozawa
(Nine regular and light carriers, six battleships, thirteen heavy and light cruisers, thirty-nine destroyers, eleven fleet oilers, 450 carrier-based aircraft)

Land Based Air Force (First Air Fleet)
  Vice Adm. Kakuji Kakuta
(Four Air Wings: about one thousand various types of land-based aircraft)

Advance Expeditionary Force (Sixth Fleet)
  Vice Adm. Takeo Takagi
(Thirty-nine various types of submarines)

---

*Bōeichō Bōeikenshūjo Senshibu, ed., *Daihon'ei kaigunbu, Rengō kantai*, 5:510–23, 593–42.

Central Pacific Force (Central Pacific District Fleet)
Vice Adm. Chūichi Nagumo
(Army Corps [five divisions], Navy Land Base Group for the defense of the Marianas, Carolines, and Palau)

Submarine Task Force Organization[†]

First Submarine Group
(under direct command of Vice Adm. Takeo Takagi)
(Eight ocean-cruising-type, eleven new fleet-type, and eight new coastal-defense-type submarines, totaling twenty-seven submarines: *I-2, I-5, I-10, I-26, I-32, I-35, I-36, I-38, I-41, I-42, I-43, I-53, I-169, I-171, I-174, I-175, I-181, I-184, I-185, RO-36, RO-37, RO-38, RO-39, RO-40, RO-42, RO-44,* and *RO-47*)

Seventh Submarine Group
Rear Adm. Noboru Ōwada, Commander Submarine Squadron 7

"A (*Kō*)" Submarine Unit
Capt. Yoshinosuke Katō, Commander Submarine Division 51
(Seven new coastal-defense-type submarines: *RO-104, RO-105, RO-106, RO-108, RO-109, RO-113,* and *RO-114*)

"B (*Otsu*)" Submarine Unit
(under direct command of Rear Adm. Noboru Ōwada)
(One ocean-cruising type, two new fleet-type, and two new coastal-defense-type submarines: *I-16, I-176, I-183, RO-41,* and *RO-115*)

[†]Bōeichō Bōeikenshūjo Senshibu, ed., *Sensuikan shi,* 311.

Appendix 9

Summary of Japanese Submarine Losses in World War II and the Surviving Submarines

Note: The tabulation of data here is based chiefly on information and estimates contained in dozens of primary and secondary sources, particularly Japanese and ULTRA-based, cited in the bibliography. The authors have done their best to reconcile this information from these various and often contradictory sources. Errors are inevitable—exact times, sites, identity of the attackers, and the identity of many submerged submarines under attack frequently differ. We would like a precise accounting, but perhaps only a fairly reliable yardstick is all that is possible.

I-boats

I-1: At night on 29 January 1943, this veteran boat was damaged in gun combat with HMNZS *Kiwi* and *Moa*, New Zealand corvettes, and beached near the northwest tip of Guadalcanal. Most of the crewmen were guided by the executive officer and survived.

I-2: At 0630 on 7 April 1944, this I-boat was lost in ASW action of the U.S. destroyer *Saufley* (DD-465) near the Admiralties.

I-3: At night on 9 December 1942, this old submarine was lost in ASW action of U.S. *PT-59* off Guadalcanal.

Summary of Submarine Losses 209

I-4: No sign after last communication report on 20 December 1942; probably lost in torpedo attack by U.S. submarine *Seadragon* (SS-194) south of Rabaul, New Ireland, Bismarcks.

I-5: At 0130 on 19 July 1944, lost in ASW action of destroyer escort USS *Wyman* (DE-38) some 200 miles east of Saipan.

I-6: Sortied from Yokosuka for Saipan on 15 June 1944, for the mission of rescue of Sixth Fleet Headquarters staff members. No sign after 30 June; in fact, this submarine was sunk by the U.S. Navy ships *William C. Miller* (DE-259) and *Gilmer* (APD-11) west of Saipan on 13 July 1944.

I-7: At 2300 on 21 June 1943, this large submarine was damaged twice by bombardment from U.S. destroyer and ran ashore at Vega Bay, Kiska. Many crewmen and the commanding and executive officers were killed.

I-8: During the night of 31 March 1945, lost in ASW action of U.S. destroyers *Stockton* (DD-646) and *Morrison* (DD-560) south of Okinawa.

I-9: At 1758 on 13 June 1943, this submarine squadron flagship was sunk in ASW action of the USS *Frazier* (DD-607) off Kiska.

I-10: At 1828 on 4 July 1944, this 1941 submarine was sunk in ASW action of U.S. destroyer *David W. Taylor* (DD-551) and destroyer escort *Riddle* (DE-185) east of Saipan.

I-11: No sign after final report on 11 January 1944, off Funafuti, Ellice Island in the South Pacific.

I-12: During afternoon of 13 November 1944, this year-old submarine was sunk in ASW action of U.S. Coast Guard cutter *Rockford* (PF-48) and the minesweeper USS *Ardent* northeast of Kauai.

I-13: No sign after sortie from Ōminato, Honshu, on 11 July 1945 to Truk for transport mission of reconnaissance seaplanes—evidence is uncertain, but the *I-13* was possibly the victim of attacks on 16 July carried out by the USS *Lawrence C. Taylor* (DE-415) and aircraft from the *Anzio* (CVE-57) some 550 miles east of Yokosuka.

I-14: Survived the war. Transferred to the United States and later scuttled.

I-15: No sign after final report on 3 November 1942, south of Guadalcanal.

I-16: At 1325 on 19 May 1944, this 1940 submarine was sunk in ASW action of U.S. destroyer escort *England* (DE-635) north of Bougainville Island in the Solomons.

I-17: During evening on 19 August 1943, this mass-produced I-boat was lost in ASW action of New Zealand corvette *Tui* and shore-based U.S. Navy aircraft off Nouméa.

I-18: During morning of 11 February 1943, this Pearl Harbor veteran was lost in ASW action of U.S. destroyer *Fletcher* (DD-445) and aircraft in the area of the eastern Solomons.

I-19: No answer or sign after ordered to sail to Gilberts from reconnaissance mission to Pearl Harbor on 17 November 1943. Probably sunk by the USS *Radford* (DD-446) on 25 November.

I-20: No sign after final report on 30 August 1943, off Espiritu Santo Island in the South Pacific. Probably sunk by the USS *Saufley* (DD-465).

I-121: Survived the war. Scuttled by occupation forces.

I-122: At 1145 on 10 June 1945, this minelaying I-boat was lost in torpedo attack of U.S. submarine *Skate* (SS-305) in the Sea of Japan.

I-123: At 0829 on 28 August 1942, sunk in ASW action of U.S. light minelayer *Gamble* (DM-15) off Savo Island, eastern Solomons.

I-24: During the afternoon of 20 January 1942, sunk primarily by depth charges dropped by the minesweeper HMAS *Deloraine* and with assistance from the USS *Edsall* (DD-219) off Darwin, Australia.

I-21: No sign after final report on 27 November 1943, off Gilbert Islands.

I-22: No sign after final report on 4 October 1942, off eastern Solomon Islands.

I-23: No sign after final report in February 1942, off Oahu—probably lost through a diving accident or another type of marine casualty.

I-24: On 11 June 1943, lost in ASW action and ramming carried out by the U.S. submarine chaser *PC-487* off the Near Islands in the western Aleutians.

I-25: No sign after reconnaissance of Espiritu Santo Island on 24 August 1943. Probably sunk by the USS *Patterson* (DD-392).

I-26: No sign after final report on 25 October 1944, east of Leyte. Probably lost during a hedgehog attack from the USS *Richard M. Powell* (DE-403) on the same day of the submarine's final report.

I-27: Near noon on 12 February 1944, this mass-produced I-boat was lost after being rammed by the British destroyer *Paladin* and finally blown up by a torpedo from the destroyer *Petard* off Maldive Island, Indian Ocean.

I-28: On 17 May 1942, lost in torpedo attack of U.S. submarine *Tautog* (SS-199) south of Truk.

Summary of Submarine Losses 211

I-29: On 26 July 1944, sunk in torpedo attack delivered by the U.S. submarine *Sawfish* (SS-276) in the South China Sea.

I-30: During the morning of 13 October 1942, hit a mine off Singapore on the final leg of a return trip from Europe.

I-31: At night on 13 May 1943, lost in ASW action probably carried out by the U.S. destroyers *Edwards* (DD-619) and *Farragut* (DD-348) and aircraft off Attu.

I-32: At 0420 on 24 March 1944, lost in ASW action of U.S. hunter-killer group off Wotje Island, Marshall Islands.

I-33: On 26 September 1942, sunk accidentally at Truk, refloated, towed to Japan, repaired, and lost accidentally during trials on 13 June 1944, in the Inland Sea.

I-34: During early morning of 13 November 1943, lost in torpedo attack of submarine HMS *Taurus* off Penang, Malaya, en route to Europe. There were about thirteen survivors.

I-35: During afternoon on 22 November 1943, lost by ramming of U.S. destroyer *Frazier* (DD-607), which was assisted by the USS *Meade* (DD-602) in ASW action off Tarawa, Gilbert Islands.

I-36: Survived the war. Scuttled by occupation forces.

I-37: On 19 November 1944, lost in ASW action of U.S. destroyer escorts *Conklin* (DE-439) and *McCoy Reynolds* (DE-440) off Palau, western Caroline Islands.

I-38: At 2235 on 12 November 1944, sunk in ASW action of U.S. destroyer *Nicholas* (DD-449) off Palau, western Caroline Islands.

I-39: At 2140 on 26 November 1943, lost in ASW action carried out by a U.S. destroyer, probably the USS *Boyd* (DD-544), off Makin Island, Gilbert Islands.

I-40: No sign after sortie from Truk on 22 November 1943—this submarine was sunk by the USS *Radford* (DD-446) three days later.

I-41: At 0559 on 18 November 1944, this year-old submarine was lost in ASW action probably led by the U.S. destroyer escort *Lawrence C. Taylor* (DE-415) and aircraft from the USS *Anzio* (CVE-57) east of Samar.

I-42: At 2300 on 23 March 1944, sunk during a torpedo attack from the U.S. submarine *Tunny* (SS-282) south of Palau, western Carolines.

I-43: On 15 February 1944, this New *Kaidai* Type B1 I-boat was lost in torpedo attack of U.S. submarine *Aspro* (SS-309) off Truk.

I-44: On 29 April 1945, lost during an ASW bombing probably by carrier planes southeast of Okinawa.

I-45: At 0545 on 28 October 1944, sunk by the USS *Whitehurst* (DE-634) east of Leyte.

I-46: No sign after final report on 26 October 1944. Probably sunk by the USS *Helm* (DD-388) on 28 October 1944 east of Leyte.

I-47: Survived the war. Scuttled by occupation forces.

I-48: At 0936 on 22 January 1945, lost in ASW action of U.S. destroyer escorts *Conklin* (DE-439), *Corbesier* (DE-438), and *Raby* (DE-698) off Ulithi, western Carolines.

(Hull numbers I-49 to I-51 and I-57 were never assigned.)

I-52: Near 0100 on 24 June 1944, lost in bombing patrol by U.S. aircraft in the Atlantic.

I-53: Survived the war. Scuttled by occupation forces.

I-54: At 1228 on 28 October 1944, this big submarine was lost in ASW action of U.S. destroyers *Helm* (DD-388) and *Gridley* (DD-380) off Leyte.

I-55: No sign after final report on 14 July 1944, off Tinian, Marianas—this submarine was sunk during a hedgehog attack by the USS *Wyman* (DE-38) in the Marianas on 28 July 1944.

I-56: On 18 April 1945, this *kaiten*-carrying submarine was lost in ASW action carried out in prolonged attacks by several U.S. destroyers off Okinawa.

I-58: Survived the war. Scuttled by occupation forces.

I-153 to *I-159:* These oldest fleet-type (*Kaidai*) submarines (pre-1930) were used only for training or transportation missions. All survived the war. Scuttled by occupation forces.

I-60: During the afternoon of 17 January 1942, this submarine was lost in gun combat with the British destroyer *Jupiter* in Sunda Strait, Java.

I-61: Lost in accidental collision before the war (2 October 1941).

I-162: Survived the war. Scuttled by occupation forces.

I-63: Lost in accidental collision before the war (2 February 1939).

I-64: During night of 17 May 1942, this old *Kaidai* Type 4 I-boat was lost in torpedo attack of U.S. submarine *Triton* (SS-201) south of Shikoku.

I-165: On 27 June 1945, this 1932 submarine was lost east of Saipan in a bombing patrol of U.S. Navy aircraft from Tinian.

I-166: At night on 17 July 1944, lost in torpedo attack of British submarine *Telemachus* (P-321) in the Strait of Malacca.

Summary of Submarine Losses   213

I-67: Lost accidentally for unknown reason before the war (29 August 1940).

I-168: At about 1800 on 27 July 1943, sunk in torpedo attack of U.S. submarine *Scamp* (SS-277) northwest of Rabaul, New Britain, Bismarck Islands.

I-169: On 4 April 1944, lost at Truk during a quick dive to escape an air raid. One of *I-169*'s torpedo doors was accidentally left open. All attempts failed to raise the submarine and rescue the crew.

I-70: On 10 December 1941, sunk by planes from the USS *Enterprise* (CV-6) about 200 miles northeast of Oahu.

I-171: During the night of 1 February 1944, lost in ASW action of U.S. destroyers *Guest* (DD-472) and *Hudson* (DD-475) near Rabaul.

I-172: At 0200 on 11 November 1942, sunk by the U.S. fast minesweeper *Southard* (DMS-10, formerly DD-207) off San Cristobal Island, eastern Solomons.

I-73: On 27 January 1942, lost in a torpedo attack by the submarine USS *Gudgeon* (SS-211) near Midway.

I-174: No sign after final report on 10 April 1944 in the Marianas—this submarine was sunk on 29 April 1944 south of Truk by U.S. destroyers *MacDonough* (DD-351) and *Stephen Potter* (DD-538).

I-175: On 17 February 1944, sunk by the USS *Charrette* (DD-581) and USS *Fair* (DE-35) east of Wotje, Marshall Islands. This was the first Japanese submarine sunk by hedgehogs.

I-176: At 2213 on 16 May 1944, lost in ASW action of U.S. destroyers, probably the USS *Haggard* (DD-555) and USS *Franks* (DD-554), north of Bougainville in the Solomons.

I-177: At 0440 on 3 October 1944, sunk by the USS *Samuel B. Miles* (DE-183) some 100 miles north of Palau in the western Carolines.

I-178: No sign after sortie from Truk en route to the eastern coast of Australia. No response to communications call on 17 June 1943.

I-179: Lost accidentally during trials on 14 July 1943 in the Inland Sea.

I-180: At 2330 on 26 April 1944, lost in ASW action of U.S. destroyer escort *Gilmore* (DE-18) south of Kodiak, Aleutians.

I-181: At unknown time on 16 January 1944, lost in ASW action carried out by U.S. destroyers and PT boats in Saint George's Channel off the east coast of New Britain, south of New Ireland Islands.

I-182: At 2059 on 3 September 1943, sunk in ASW action of U.S. destroyers north of Espiritu Santo Island in the eastern Solomons.

I-183: During the night on 28 April 1944, this submarine, only in service since November 1943, was lost during attack by U.S. submarine *Pogy* (SS-266) east of Kyushu.

I-184: At unknown time on 19 June 1944, lost in bombing patrol of U.S. aircraft from the USS *Suwannee* (CVE-27) east of Saipan.

I-185: At 1144 on 22 June 1944, lost in ASW action of U.S. destroyer *Newcomb* (DD-586) and the fast minesweeper *Chandler* (DMS-9) east of Saipan.

I-201: Survived the war. Transferred to the United States and later scuttled.

I-203: Survived the war. Transferred to the United States and later scuttled.

I-351: During night of 15 July 1945, lost in torpedo attack of U.S. submarine *Bluefish* (SS-222) off Borneo.

I-361: At 1200 on 30 May 1945, lost in bombing attack of U.S. aircraft from the USS *Anzio* (CVE-57) east of Okinawa.

I-362: At 1900 on 13 January 1945, sunk in ASW action of U.S. destroyer escort, probably the USS *Fleming* (DE-32), off the eastern Carolines.

I-363: Survived the war; however, this submarine was damaged by a mine off Kyushu on 29 October 1945 and later scuttled by occupation forces.

I-364: During night of 15 September 1944, lost in torpedo attack of U.S. submarine *Sea Devil* (SS-400) east of Honshu.

I-365: During night of 29 November 1944, lost in torpedo attack of U.S. submarine *Scabbardfish* (SS-397) southeast of Tokyo Bay; one POW was recovered.

I-366: Survived the war. Scuttled by occupation forces.

I-367: Survived the war. Scuttled by occupation forces.

I-368: At unknown time on 26 February 1945, lost in bombing patrol of aircraft from the USS *Anzio* (CVE-57) off Iwo Jima.

I-369: Survived the war. Scuttled by occupation forces.

I-370: At 0659 on 26 February 1945, sunk in ASW action of U.S. destroyer escort *Finnegan* (DE-307) off Iwo Jima.

I-371: No sign after sortie from Truk on 31 January 1945. Probably sunk by USS *Lagarto* (SS-371) on 24 February 1945 near Kyushu.

I-372: On 18 July 1945, lost in bombing patrol of U.S. aircraft while the submarine was moored at Yokosuka.

I-373: At daybreak on 14 August 1945, lost in torpedo attack of U.S. submarine *Spikefish* (SS-404) in the East China Sea.

I-400: Survived the war. Transferred to the United States and later scuttled.
I-401: Survived the war. Transferred to the United States and later scuttled.
I-402: Survived the war. Scuttled by occupation forces.

RO-Boats

RO-33: On 29 August 1942, this 1935 boat was lost in an ASW attack carried out by an Australian destroyer *Arunta* off Port Moresby, New Guinea.
RO-34: At 0218 on 5 April 1943, this 1937 submarine was lost in ASW action of U.S. destroyer *O'Bannon* (DD-450) off Santa Isabel Island in the Solomons.
RO-35: At 1923 on 25 August 1943, lost in ASW action of U.S. destroyer, probably the *Ellet* (DD-398), north of Espiritu Santo, New Hebrides.
RO-36: At 2239 on 13 June 1944, lost in ASW gunfire from the U.S. destroyer *Melvin* (DD-680) off Eniwetok, Marshall Islands.
RO-37: On 22 January 1944, this submarine was sunk by the USS *Buchanan* (DD-484) off Santa Cruz Island, eastern Solomons.
RO-38: No sign after sortie from Truk for Gilbert Island on 19 November 1943. Possibly sunk by the USS *Cotten* (DD-669).
RO-39: On 1 February 1944, lost in ASW action of U.S. destroyer *Walker* (DD-517) east of Wotje, Marshall Islands.
RO-40: At 1742 on 15 February 1944, lost in ASW action of U.S. destroyer *Phelps* (DD-360) and the minesweeper USS *Sage* off Kwajalein, Marshall Islands.
RO-41: At 2333 on 22 March 1945, sunk by the U.S. destroyer *Haggard* (DD-555) south of Okinawa.
RO-42: At 2335 on 10 June 1944, this new submarine was lost in ASW action of U.S. destroyer escort *Bangust* (DE-739) south of Kwajalein, Marshall Islands.
RO-43: On 26 February 1945, lost in bombing patrol of U.S. aircraft from the USS *Anzio* (CVE-57) off Iwo Jima.
RO-44: At 0337 on 16 June 1944, lost in ASW action of U.S. destroyer escort *Burden R. Hastings* (DE-19) off Eniwetok, Marshall Islands.
RO-45: Probably lost in ASW action of U.S. destroyer and aircraft south of Truk on 30 April 1944.

RO-46: Last heard from on 17 April 1945—probably lost in bombing patrol of U.S. aircraft off Okinodaitō-Jima, South Ryūkyū.

RO-47: At 0230 on 26 September 1944, sunk, probably by the USS *McCoy Reynolds* (DE-440), north of Palau in the western Carolines.

RO-48: At 0720 on 14 July 1944, lost in ASW action of U.S. destroyer escort, probably the USS *William C. Miller* (DE-259), north of Saipan.

RO-49: No sign after final report on 25 March 1945, off Kyushu—in fact, this submarine was attacked and sunk by the USS *Hudson* (DD-475) off Okinawa on 5 April 1945.

RO-50: Survived the war. Scuttled by occupation forces.

(Hull numbers RO-51 to RO-54 were never assigned.)

RO-55: At 2327 on 7 February 1945, this improved *Kaichū* Type 6 boat was lost in ASW action of U.S. destroyer escort *Thomason* (DE-203) off Mindoro Island in the Philippines.

RO-56: At 0546 on 9 April 1945, lost in ASW action of U.S. destroyers *Mertz* (DD-691) and *Monssen* (DD-798) off Okinodaitō-Jima, South Ryūkyū.

RO-60: At 0200 on 29 December 1941, this 1923 boat wrecked on a reef off Kwajalein after returning from an invasion operation against Wake Island.

RO-61: At unknown time on 31 August 1942, this 1924 submarine was lost in ASW action of U.S. destroyer *Reid* (DD-369) and American patrol aircraft.

RO-62: Survived the war. Scuttled by occupation forces.

RO-63: Survived the war. Scuttled by occupation forces.

RO-64: On 12 April 1945, this small 1925 boat hit a mine and sank in Hiroshima Bay.

RO-65: On 4 November 1942, this 1926 boat was lost in 90 feet of water near Kiska during a U.S. air attack.

RO-66: During the night of 17 December 1941, this small 1927 submarine was lost in an accidental collision with *RO-62* off Wake Island during invasion operations.

RO-67: Survived the war. Scuttled by occupation forces.

RO-68: Survived the war. Scuttled by occupation forces.

RO-100: On 25 November 1943, hit a mine off Bougainville Island, central Solomons.

RO-101: About 15 September 1943, this new submarine was lost in

ASW action of a U.S. destroyer off San Cristobal Island in the eastern Solomons; it is possible that this submarine was sunk by the USS *Eaton* (DD-510).

RO-102: No sign after final report on 9 May 1943, south of New Guinea; this boat was sunk by *PT-150* and *PT-152* on 14 May 1943.

RO-103: No sign after final report on 28 July 1943, north of New Georgia Island, Bismarck Islands.

RO-104: On 23 May 1944, lost in ASW action of U.S. destroyer escort *England* (DE-635) north of the Admiralty Islands.

RO-105: On 31 May 1944, lost in ASW action carried out by the USS *England* (DE-635) north of the Admiralty Islands.

RO-106: At dawn on 22 May 1944, sunk by the USS *England* (DE-635) north of the Admiralty Islands.

RO-107: At 0450 on 12 July 1943, lost in ASW action of a U.S. destroyer, off Kolombangara Island, central Solomons.

RO-108: At 2303 on 26 May 1944, sunk by the U.S. destroyer escort *England* (DE-635) north of the Admirality Islands.

RO-109: On 25 April 1945, lost in ASW action of U.S. light transport ship *Horace A. Bass* (formerly DE-691) some 200 miles south of Okinawa.

RO-110: On 11 February 1944, lost in ASW action of an Indian gunboat and two Australian minesweepers in the Bay of Bengal.

RO-111: At unknown time on 10 June 1944, lost in ASW action of U.S. destroyer *Taylor* (DD-468) north of the Admiralties.

RO-112: At 2204 on 10 February 1945, lost in torpedo attack of U.S. submarine *Batfish* (SS-310) north of Luzon, Philippines.

RO-113: At 0449 on 12 February 1945, lost in torpedo attack of U.S. submarine *Batfish* (SS-310) north of Luzon, Philippines.

RO-114: At 0115 on 17 June 1944, lost in ASW action of U.S. destroyers off Saipan.

RO-115: At night on 9 (31?) February 1945, lost in a torpedo attack by the USS *Batfish* (SS-310) between Manila and Formosa.

RO-116: At dawn on 24 May 1944, lost in ASW action of U.S. destroyer escort *England* (DE-635) north of the Admiralty Islands.

RO-117: At unknown time on 17 June 1944, lost in bombing patrol of U.S. aircraft east of Saipan.

RO-500: Survived the war. Scuttled by occupation forces.

RO-501: At 1900 on 13 May 1944, lost in ASW action of U.S. destroyer escort *Francis M. Robinson* (DE-220) in the Atlantic.

Appendix 9

Midget Submarines (*Kō hyōteki* or *Kōryū*)

Midget submarines were lost chiefly in the following five operations, four in which the midget submarines were launched from parent submarines and one in the Philippines, where shore bases were used.

Pearl Harbor: Before dawn on 7 December 1941 (Hawaiian time), five midget submarines were launched to attack Pearl Harbor. All five were lost, at least one inside the harbor.

Sydney: During the afternoon of 31 May 1942, three midget submarines were launched to attack Sydney (Jackson) Harbor. All three were lost; two got inside the harbor and the other became caught in the antitorpedo net near the harbor entrance.

Diégo Suarez, Madagascar: During the evening of 30 May 1942, two midget submarines were launched. Both were lost inside the harbor.

Guadalcanal: In November 1943, eight midget submarines were transported to the base on Shortland Island, off the south end of Bougainville. From there they were carried by parent submarines and launched near enemy landing sites on Guadalcanal. By the end of December, three of the midget submarines were lost in ASW action, three were lost accidentally, and two remained inactive.

Philippine Islands: In the fall of 1944, ten midget submarines were sent to shore bases in the central and southern Philippines. All small craft were lost in combat, accidentally, and by scuttling when U.S. forces invaded.

Appendix 10
Biographies of Key Members of the Imperial Japanese Navy Submarine Force*

Note: This list is arranged alphabetically by family name within the category of the officer's highest rank, excluding any posthumous promotions. Not all officers under the rank of captain are included—selections have been made based on an officer's special duty as a submariner. All biographic information is limited to submarine assignments, although an officer's naval academy graduation class is added.

Vice Admiral

Daigo, Tadashige: Class of 1913; Commander, Sixth Fleet; Superintendent, Submarine School; Commander, Submarine Squadron (hereafter cited as Subron.) 5, Subron. 11, and Kure Subron.
Higuchi, Shūichirō: Class of 1910; Superintendent, Submarine School.
Ichioka, Hisashi: Class of 1915; Superintendent, Submarine School; Commander, Subron. 8, Subron. 2, and Kure Subron.
Komatsu, Teruhisa: Class of 1910; Commander, Sixth Fleet.
Miwa, Shigeyoshi: Class of 1912; Chief, Bureau of Submarines (newly organized in 1944); Head, Submarine Department, Bureau of Ships and Weapons; Commander, Sixth Fleet; Commander, Subron 3.

*Bōeichō Bōeikenshūjo Senshibu, ed., *Sensuikan shi*, table.

Shimizu, Mitsumi: Class of 1907; Commander, Sixth Fleet.
Takagi, Takeo: Class of 1912; Commander, Sixth Fleet. Killed in action, Saipan.
Takatsu, Mizurō: Class of 1910; Head, Submarine Department, Bureau of Ships and Weapons.
Yamazaki, Shigeaki: Class of 1914; Chief, Bureau of Submarines; Superintendent, Submarine School; Commander, Subron. 1, Subron. 2, and Kure Subron.

Rear Admiral

Harada, Kaku: Class of 1914; Commander, Subron. 7.
Ishizaki, Noboru: Class of 1915; Commander, Subron. 11, and Subron. 8.
Komazawa, Katsumi: Class of 1915; Commander, Subron. 3.
Kōno, Chimaki: Class of 1915; Commander, Subron. 3 and Subron. 6.
Kōta, Takerō: Class of 1914; Commander, Subron. 1.
Mito, Hasashi: Class of 1915; Commander, Subron. 1; Chief of Staff, Sixth Fleet.
Nishina, Kōzō: Class of 1917; Chief of Staff, Sixth Fleet; Commander, Subron. 11.
Ōnishi, Shinzō: Class of 1915; Commander, Subron. 7.
Ōwada, Noboru: Class of 1917; Commander, Subron. 7.
Sasaki, Hanku: Class of 1918; Chief of Staff, Sixth Fleet; Commander, Submarine Division (hereafter cited as Subdiv.) 3.
Satō, Tsutomu: Class of 1913; Commander, Subron. 1.
Shimamoto, Kyūgorō: Class of 1917; Chief of Staff, Sixth Fleet; Commander, Subdiv. 7.
Uozumi, Jisaku: Class of 1915; Commander, Subron. 8.
Yoshitomi, Setsuzō: Class of 1912; Commander, Subron. 4.

Captain

Ageta, Kiyoo: Class of 1923; Commander, Subdiv. 1, Subdiv. 34, and Subdiv. 51.
Aku, Eitarō: Class of 1923; Commander, Subdiv. 33; Commanding Officer (hereafter cited as CO), *I-1*, and *I-38*.
Ariizumi, Tatsunosuke: Class of 1924; Commander, Subdiv. 1; Staff Operations Officer (submarine), Navy General Headquarters; Staff

Operations Officer, Subron. 8, and Subron. 11; CO, *I-8*. Suicide at end of war.

Fujii, Akiyoshi: Class of 1922; CO, *I-9*. Killed in action.

Fujimoto, Tsutau: Class of 1921; Commander, Subdiv. 13, Subdiv. 19, and Subdiv. 21.

Fukaya, Sōkichi: Class of 1919; Commander, Subdiv. 27. Killed in action.

Hamano, Motoichi: Class of 1920; Commander, Subdiv. 19, and Subdiv. 26.

Horinouchi, Miyoshi: Class of 1923; Staff Operations Officer, Sixth Fleet; Officer in Charge for Submarine Readiness, Ministry of the Navy; Staff Operations Officer, Subron. 7. Killed in action, Saipan.

Imaizumi, Kijirō: Class of 1917; Commander, Subdiv. 1, Subdiv. 2, and Subdiv. 16; Commander, Submarine Base Group, Yokosuka.

Imazato, Hiroshi: Class of 1918; Commander, Subdiv. 1, and Subdiv. 2.

Iura, Shōjirō: Class of 1924; Staff Operations Officer, Sixth Fleet; Staff Operations Officer (submarine), Navy General Headquarters; Staff Operations Officer, Subron. 3, and Subron. 8.

Iwagami, Eiju: Class of 1919; Commander, Subdiv. 1, Subdiv. 2, and Subdiv. 11.

Katō, Ikuo: Class of 1920; Commander, Subdiv. 28. Killed in action.

Katō, Yoshinosuke: Class of 1921; Commander, Subdiv. 6, Subdiv. 33, and Subdiv. 51. Accidental death.

Katsuta, Haruo: Class of 1919; Commander, Subdiv. 14.

Kijima, Moritsugu: Class of 1917; Commander, Subdiv. 15, and Subdiv. 18.

Kobayashi, Hajime: Class of 1921; Commander, Subdiv. 12, and Subdiv. 26. Killed in action.

Koizumi, Kiichi: Class of 1922; Commander, Subdiv. 19, and Subdiv. 33; CO, *I-7*.

Maejima, Yasuhide: Class of 1922; Commander, Subdiv. 22. Killed in action.

Makihara, Yasuchika: Class of 1922; Commander, Subdiv. 19, and Subdiv. 22; CO, *I-10*. Killed in action.

Maruyama, Hanzō: Class of 1925; Staff Operations Officer, Subron. 2, and Subron 8; Commander, Submarine Base Group 11.

Matsumura, Hiroji: Class of 1923; Commander, Subdiv. 34; CO, *I-21*. Killed in action.

Minokuchi, Hyōe: Class of 1919; Commander, Subdiv. 2, and Subdiv. 11.
Miyazaki, Takeji: Class of 1919; Commander, Subdiv. 2, and Subdiv. 13. Killed in action.
Nagai, Mitsuru: Class of 1918; Commander, Subdiv. 4.
Nagai, Takeo: Class of 1920; Commander, Subdiv. 15, and Subdiv. 33.
Nakaoka, Nobuki: Class of 1918; Commander, Subdiv. 12.
Nanau, Tsuneo: Class of 1922; Commander, Subdiv. 6; CO, *I-5*, *I-11*, and *I-25*.
Narahara, Shōgo: Class of 1921; Commander, Subdiv. 6, Subdiv. 7, Subdiv. 12, Subdiv. 26, and Subdiv. 33; CO, *I-19*.
Nishino, Kōzō: Class of 1920; Commander, Subdiv. 19, and Subdiv. 22; CO, *I-17*.
Oda, Tameharu: Class of 1916; Commander, Subdiv. 4.
Okada, Yūsaku: Class of 1920; Commander, Subdiv. 7, and Subdiv. 15.
Okamoto, Yoshisuke: Class of 1920; Commander, Subdiv. 6, and Subdiv. 12. Killed in action.
Ono, Ryōjirō: Class of 1921; Commander, Subdiv. 2, and Subdiv. 19.
Ōta, Shinsuke: Class of 1920; Commander, Subdiv. 1, and Subdiv. 19. Killed in action.
Ōtake, Yasuo: Class of 1918; Commander, Subdiv. 20. Killed in action.
Ōtani, Kiyonori: Class of 1922; Commander, Subdiv. 33; CO, *I-18*, and *I-37*.
Ōyama, Toyojirō: Class of 1922; Commander, Subron. 30.
Shimizu, Tarō: Class of 1921; Commander, Subdiv. 34. Killed in action.
Takahashi, Chōjirō: Class of 1922; Staff Operations Officer, Sixth Fleet; Staff Operations Officer, Subron. 5; Commander, Subdiv. 15, and Subdiv. 30.
Takezaki, Kaoru: Class of 1918; Commander, Subdiv. 8.
Tamaki, Tomejirō: Class of 1918; Commander, Subdiv. 7, and Subdiv. 29. Killed in action.
Teraoka, Masuo: Class of 1919; Commander, Subdiv. 14, and Subdiv. 30.
Uchino, Shinji: Class of 1922; Senior Instructor, Submarine School; Staff Operations Officer, Kure Subron.; CO, *I-8*.
Yamada, Takashi: Class of 1922; Commander, Subdiv. 34; CO, *I-10* and *I-20*.

Yokota, Minoru: Class of 1925; Commander, Subdiv. 52; Staff Operations Officer, Subron. 1, and Subron. 11; CO, *I-26*.

Commander

Emi, Tetsushirō: Class of 1923; CO, *I-8*.
Endō, Keiyu: Class of 1919; Commander, Subdiv. 9. Killed in action.
Endō, Shinobu: Class of 1925; CO, *I-30*, and *I-43*. Killed in action.
Fujimori, Yasuo: Class of 1929; Staff Operations Officer (submarine), Navy General Headquarters; CO, *I-121*, and *RO-60*.
Fukumura, Toshiaki: Class of 1924; CO, *I-27*, and *I-159*. Killed in action.
Hanabusa, Hiroshi: Class of 1924; CO, *I-24*. Killed in action.
Harada, Tamae: Class of 1925; CO, *I-17*, and *I-165*. Killed in action.
Hori, Takeo: Class of 1923; CO, *I-6*, *I-32*, and *I-157*.
Ikezawa, Masayuki: Class of 1925; Staff Operations Officer, Subron. 3; CO, *I-32*, and *I-174*.
Inaba, Michimune: Class of 1924; CO, *I-6*, *I-36*, and *I-121*.
Inada, Hiroshi: Class of 1924; CO, *I-21*. Killed in action.
Inoue, Noriki: Class of 1924; CO, *I-31*, and *I-175*. Killed in action.
Irie, Tatsu: Class of 1924; CO, *I-34*. Killed in action.
Ishikawa, Nobuo: Class of 1922; CO, *I-15*. Killed in action.
Iuchi, Shirō: Class of 1928; Staff Operations Officer, Kure Subron.
Izu, Hisaichi: Class of 1924; CO, *I-11*, and *I-29*. Killed in action.
Izumi, Masaji: Class of 1926; Officer in Charge for Submarine Readiness, Ministry of the Navy; Staff Operations Officer, Subron. 3, and Subron. 7.
Kawasaki, Mutsurō: Class of 1924; CO, *I-4*.
Kinashi, Takaichi: Class of 1924; CO, *I-19*, *I-29*, and *I-162*. Killed in action.
Kohiga, Masaru: Class of 1923; CO, *I-25*, and *I-157*. Killed in action.
Koike, Koreitsu: Class of 1925; Staff Operations Officer (submarine), Combined Fleet; Staff Operations Officer, Subron. 1. Killed in aircraft accident.
Koizumi, Kiichi: Class of 1922; CO, *I-7*.
Kōno, Masamichi: Class of 1925; CO, *I-37*, and *I-122*.
Kudō, Kameo: Class of 1929; CO, *I-12*, *I-20*, *I-155*, and *RO-65*. Killed in action.
Kusaka, Toshio: Class of 1926; CO, *I-26*, *I-174*, *I-180*, and *I-400*.
Matsumura, Midori: Class of 1921; Staff Operations Officer, Sixth Fleet.

Matsuo, Yoshiyasu: Class of 1920; Commander, Subdiv. 26.
Muraoka, Tomiichi: Class of 1925; CO, *I-18*. Killed in action.
Nakagawa, Hajime: Class of 1923; CO, *I-4*, *I-37*, and *I-177*.
Nakajima, Seiji: Class of 1927; CO, *I-10*, and *I-155*.
Nakamura, Otoji: Class of 1925; CO, *I-5*, *I-168*, and *I-402*.
Nakamura, Shōzō: Class of 1927; CO, *I-6*, and *I-16*.
Ogawa, Tsunayoshi: Class of 1923; CO, *I-33*, *I-42*, and *I-164*. Accidental death.
Ōhashi, Katsuo: Class of 1926; CO, *I-13*, *I-54*, and *I-181*. Killed in action.
Ōhira, Masajirō: Class of 1925; Staff Operations Officer, Subron. 6.
Sekito, Yoshimitsu: Class of 1930; Staff Operations Officer, Subron. 7; CO, *I-5*, *I-45*, *I-156*, and *I-185*. Later Rear Admiral in Japanese Maritime Self-Defense Force.
Shibata, Genichi: Class of 1924; CO, *I-23*. Killed in action.
Shibuya, Tatsumi: Class of 1925; Staff Operations Officer (submarine), Combined Fleet; Staff Operations Officer, Subron. 1, Subron. 2, and Subron. 5.
Tagami, Akeji: Class of 1924; Commander, Subdiv. 34; CO, *I-11*, *I-25*, and *I-45*.
Takahashi, Katsuichi: Class of 1927; Staff Operations Officer, Kure Subron.
Takatsuka, Tadao: Class of 1922; Staff Operations Officer, Subron. 7.
Tanaka, Makio: Class of 1925; CO, *I-39*, and *I-166*. Killed in action.
Tonoue, Ichirō: Class of 1924; CO, *I-3*, and *I-172*. Killed in action.
Tonozuka, Kinzō: Class of 1923; CO, *I-3*, *I-10*, *I-34*, and *I-168*.
Tsutsumi, Michizō: Class of 1921; Staff Operations Officer, Subron. 4.
Uno, Kameo: Class of 1926; CO, *I-52*, and *I-175*. Killed in action.
Utsuki, Hidejirō: Class of 1925; CO, *I-5*, *I-122*, and *I-178*.
Yamada, Kaoru: Class of 1923; CO, *I-16*.
Yokota, Minoru: Class of 1924; CO, *I-44*.
Yoshimatsu, Tamori: Class of 1928; Officer in Charge for Submarine Readiness, Ministry of the Navy; CO, *I-41*, and *I-159*. Later Vice Admiral in Japanese Maritime Self-Defense Force.
Yoshimura, Iwao: Class of 1924; CO, *I-20*, and *I-27*.

Lieutenant Commander

Arai, Atsushi: Class of 1936; CO, *I-185*, and *RO-108*. Killed in action.
Doi, Mareshige: Class of 1933; CO, *I-5*, and *I-162*. Killed in action.

Fujita, Hidenori: Class of 1935; CO, *I-180*, and *RO-103*. Killed in action.
Fumon, Shōsō: Class of 1936; CO, *I-6*, and *RO-49*. Killed in action.
Hashimoto, Mochitsura: Class of 1932; CO, *I-58*, and *RO-44*.
Imoto, Masayuki: Class of 1931; CO, *I-32*, *I-153*, and *RO-67*. Killed in action.
Itakura, Mitsuyoshi: Class of 1934; CO, *I-2*, *I-41*, and *I-176*.
Izutsu, Monshirō: Class of 1930; CO, *I-6*, *I-55*, *I-153*, and *RO-68*. Killed in action.
Kanmoto, Nobuo: Class of 1929; CO, *I-37*, and *I-156*. Killed in action.
Kawaguchi, Genbei: Class of 1937; CO, *I-44*.
Kitamura, Sōshichi: Class of 1928; CO, *I-27*, and *I-158*.
Kobayashi, Shigeo: Class of 1929; CO, *I-19*, and *I-171*. Killed in action.
Kondō, Fumitake: Class of 1934; CO, *I-41*, and *RO-112*. Killed in action.
Masuzawa, Kiyoji: Class of 1938; CO, *I-44*, *I-158*, and *RO-109*. Killed in action.
Morinaga, Masahiko: Class of 1932; CO, *I-2*, *I-5*, *I-56*, *I-159*, and *RO-34*. Later Vice Admiral in Japanese Maritime Self-Defense Force.
Nagai, Katsuhiko: Class of 1930; CO, *I-7*, *I-174*, and *RO-63*. Killed in action.
Nakayama, Denshichi: Class of 1934; CO, *I-54*, and *I-165*. Killed in action.
Nambu, Nobukiyo: Class of 1934; CO, *I-174*, and *I-401*. Later Rear Admiral in Japanese Maritime Self-Defense Force.
Narusawa, Sunao: Class of 1925; CO, *I-22*. Killed in action.
Nishiuchi, Shōichi: Class of 1933; CO, *I-26*, *RO-47*, and *RO-105*. Killed in action.
Ōba, Saichi: Class of 1935; CO, *I-53*, *I-162*, *RO-49*, and *RO-105*. Later Captain in Japanese Maritime Self-Defense Force.
Okada, Hideo: Class of 1934; CO, *I-176*, and *RO-36*. Killed in action.
Orita, Zenji: Class of 1932; CO, *I-47*, *I-177*, and *RO-101*. Later Captain in Japanese Maritime Self-Defense Force.
Ōtsuka, Tadasu: Class of 1929; CO, *I-20*, and *I-158*. Killed in action.
Rikihisa, Matsuji: Class of 1931; CO, *I-184*, and *I-122*. Killed in action.

Saiki, Takeo: Class of 1932; CO, *I-183, I-157*, and *RO-106*. Killed in action.
Sakamoto, Eiichi: Class of 1930; CO, *I-1, I-154*, and *RO-33*. Killed in action.
Shimizu, Tsuruzō: Class of 1931; CO, *I-14, I-165*, and *I-153*. Later Rear Admiral in Japanese Maritime Self-Defense Force.
Shimose, Kichirō: Class of 1931; CO, *I-6, I-38, I-162*, and *I-176*.
Shinohara, Shigeo: Class of 1935; CO, *I-6, I-8*, and *I-169*. Killed in action.
Shōda, Keiji: Class of 1935; CO, *I-56, I-159*, and *RO-104*. Killed in action.
Sugamasa, Tetsuaki: Class of 1938; CO, *I-36*, and *RO-49*.
Suzuki, Shōkichi: Class of 1935; CO, *I-47*, and *RO-46*.
Tabata, Naoshi: Class of 1931; CO, *I-7*, and *I-175*. Killed in action.
Takeuchi, Yoshitaka: Class of 1932; CO, *I-16*, and *I-158*. Killed in action.
Tanabe, Yahachi: Class of 1929; CO, *I-168*, and *I-176*.
Taoka, Kiyoshi: Class of 1928; CO, *I-181*, and *RO-500*. Killed in action.
Teramoto, Iwao: Class of 1932; CO, *I-36*, and *I-156*.
Torisu, Kennosuke: Class of 1931; Staff Operations Officer, Sixth Fleet; CO, *I-165*, and *RO-65*.
Tōyama, Masanobu: Class of 1932; CO, *I-38, I-48*, and *I-169*. Killed in action.
Toyomasu, Seihachi: Class of 1932; CO, *I-53*, and *I-159*.
Ueno, Toshitake: Class of 1929; CO, *I-4*, and *I-123*. Killed in action.
Wada, Mutsuo: Class of 1934; CO, *I-33*, and *I-153*. Killed in action.
Watanabe, Katsuji: Class of 1928; CO, *I-40, I-168*, and *I-169*. Killed in action.
Yajima, Yasuo: Class of 1924; CO, *I-28*. Killed in action.
Yamaguchi, Kazuo: Class of 1934; CO, *I-2, I-154, I-176*, and *RO-67*. Killed in action.
Yamaguchi, Kōzaburō: Class of 1932; CO, *I-46, I-154*, and *I-176*. Killed in action.
Yonehara, Minoru: Class of 1932; CO, *I-182*, and *I-156*. Killed in action.
Yuasa, Hiroshi: Class of 1932; CO, *I-179*, and *I-154*. Killed in action.

Notes

Introduction

1. Nippon Dempo News Agency, ed., *Japan Illustrated, 1934* (Tokyo: Nippon Dempo News Agency, 1934), 88, and W. H. Beehler, "A Review of Japanese Naval Financial Policy," U.S. Naval Institute *Proceedings* 37 (1911): 802.
2. Japan, Bōeichō Bōeikenshūjo Senshibu (Defense Ministry, Defense Research Institute, War History Branch), ed., *Daihon'ei kaigunbu, Rengō kantai, 1, kaisen made* (Imperial General Headquarters, Navy Division, Combined Fleet, part 1: To the start of the war), Senshi Sōsho (War history series), vol. 91 (Tokyo: Asagumo Shimbunsha, 1975), 100–103. Sadao Asada ("The Revolt against the Washington Treaty: The Imperial Japanese Navy and Naval Limitation, 1921–1927," *Naval War College Review* 46, no. 3 [Summer 1993], 83) observes insightfully that "the conception of the United States as the IJN's 'hypothetical enemy' had first appeared in the Imperial National Defense Policy of 1907. At that time, however, the U.S. amounted to little more than a 'budgetary enemy,' a convenient pretext for demanding greater building appropriations."
3. Bōeichō Bōeikenshūjo Senshibu, ed., *Daihon'ei kaigunbu, Rengō kantai*, 1:168.
4. Ibid., 319.
5. Ibid., 322.
6. Japan, Bōeichō Bōeikenshūjo Senshibu, ed., *Kaigun gunsenbi ichi: Shōwa jūrokunen jūichigatsu made* (The navy's war preparations, part 1: To November 1941), Senshi Sōsho (War history series), vol. 23 (Tokyo: Asagumo Shimbunsha, 1969), 127. Emphasis added. The authors are indebted to David C.

Evans for this important citation. (Japanese proper names have been inverted for the convenience of most English readers; that is, the personal name is followed by the surname. A macron is used over a long vowel in all Japanese terms in *rōmaji* except well-known place-names, for example, Tokyo.)

7. Stephen E. Pelz, *Race to Pearl Harbor: The Failure of the Second London Naval Conference and the Onset of World War II* (Cambridge: Harvard University Press, 1974), 35.
8. Japan, Bōeichō Bōeikenshūjo Senshibu, ed., *Kaisen yōmurei* (Navy battle regulations) (1934), pars. II-1-5, II-1-7-13.
9. Pelz, *Race to Pearl Harbor*, 35.
10. Bōeichō Bōeikenshūjo Senshibu, ed., *Kaisen yōmurei*, par. II-1-11.
11. Ibid., par. II-1-5.
12. See Arthur J. Marder, *From the Dreadnought to Scapa Flow: The Royal Navy in the Fisher Era, 1904–1919* (London: Oxford University Press, 1966), 3:38, where he observes that "although no U-boats were actually present during the battle itself, there were thirteen U-boat reports. These were largely, no doubt, a by-product of the 'submarinitis' in the fleet."
13. Asada, "The Revolt against the Washington Treaty," 92.
14. Pelz, *Race to Pearl Harbor*, 28–29; Arthur E. Tiedemann, introduction to "The London Naval Treaty, 1930," by Kobayashi Tatsuo, in *Japan Erupts: The London Naval Conference and the Manchurian Incident, 1928–1932*, ed. James William Morley (New York: Columbia University Press, 1984), 8–9; and Shigeru Fukudome, "The Air Battle off Taiwan," in *The Japanese Navy in World War II*, 2nd ed., ed. David C. Williams (Annapolis, Md.: Naval Institute Press, 1986), 340–41.
15. John J. Stephan, *Hawaii under the Rising Sun: Japan's Plans for Conquest after Pearl Harbor* (Honolulu: University of Hawaii Press, 1984), 72.
16. Japan, Bōeichō Bōeikenshūjo Senshibu, ed., *Sensuikan shi* (History of submarines), Senshi Sōsho (War history series), vol. 98 (Tokyo: Asagumo Shimbunsha, 1979), 29–32.
17. Quoted in Michael A. Barnhart, *Japan Prepares for Total War: The Search for Economic Security, 1919–1941* (Ithaca: Cornell University Press, 1987), 39.

Chapter 1

1. The technical information in this chapter, unless specifically documented otherwise, is compiled from Bōeichō Bōeikenshūjo Senshibu, ed., *Sensuikan shi*, 1–3, 7–12, 55–61, and 174–75; Shizuo Fukui, *Nihon no gunkan* (Warships of the Japanese navy), 9th ed. (Tokyo: Kyōdō Shuppansha, 1956), tab. 10; and *Shashin shū Nihon no sensuikan* (Photograph collection of submarines of the Japanese navy) by the editors of *Maru Magazine* (Tokyo: Kōjinsha, 1973), 182–83.
2. *Conway's All the World's Fighting Ships, 1906–1921* (London: Conway Maritime Press, 1985), 126; see also Frank T. Cable, "The Submarine Torpedo Boat *Holland:* The Submarine to Become a Part of the United States Navy," U.S. Naval Institute *Proceedings* 69 (February 1943): 173–80.

3. Bōeichō Bōeikenshūjo Senshibu, ed., *Sensuikan shi*, 1–3.
4. *Conway's Ships, 1906–1921*, 245.
5. Bōeichō Bōeikenshūjo Senshibu, ed., *Sensuikan shi*, 3–5.
6. Ibid., 5.
7. Ibid., 7.
8. "Japanese Submarine Service," Office of Naval Intelligence File, Naval Attaché Reports, 1886–1939, Register no. 19650, P-10-1, Records of the Office of the Chief of Naval Operations, Record Group 38, National Archives, Washington, D.C. (hereafter cited as ONI Reports, with filing designations).
9. "German Submarines Allotted to Japan," Office of the Chief of Staff, Military Intelligence Division, War Department General Staff, Military Attaché Reports, 15 July 1919, microfilm reel no. 26:0628, U.S. Army Center of Military History, Washington, D.C. (hereafter cited as MID Reports, with filing designations).
10. C. Burnett, U.S. Army Military Attaché, Tokyo, to the Director of Military Intelligence, Washington, D.C., ONI Reports, Register no. 12164, C-10-j. This information is also found in a report titled "Japanese Submarine Construction," filed under Register no. 6452, P-10-1. Here, however, there is the added observation that "the Japanese have not yet tried out the German submarines, as they do not yet understand the mechanism."
11. "Japanese Submarines," ONI Reports, Register no. 6452, P-10-1. Similar information is included in a report titled "Submarines in the Japanese Navy," 11 September 1919, under the same register number.
12. "Japanese Policy—Pacific War Plans, Notes, etc., 1921–1923," ONI Reports, Register no. 13247-A, U-1-b.
13. C. A. Willoughby, U.S. Army Military Attaché, Caracas, Venezuela, to G-2, Washington, D.C., 1 May 1927, MID Reports, microfilm reel no. 26:0774.
14. Edward Carpenter, U.S. Army Military Attaché, Berlin, to G-2, Washington, D.C., 19 November 1929, MID Reports, microfilm reel no. 26:0781–82.
15. "Employment of German Experts in Japan," ONI Reports, Register no. 6452-R, P-10-1.
16. Ibid.
17. Hector C. Bywater, *Sea-Power in the Pacific: A Study of the American-Japanese Naval Problem* (London: Constable, 1921), 231–32.
18. Ibid., 234–35.
19. U.S. Army Military Attaché, Tokyo, to G-2, Washington, D.C., 23 August 1924, MID Reports, microfilm reel no. 27:0936.
20. C. Burnett, U.S. Army Military Attaché, Tokyo, to G-2, Washington, D.C., 17 January 1927, MID Reports, microfilm reel no. 28:0989.
21. Ibid., 16 May 1929, MID Reports, microfilm reel no. 29:0587.
22. *RO-29* to *RO-32*, completed in 1923 and 1924, were based on French Schneider-Laubeuf plans and designated *Kaitoku chū*.
23. Norman Friedman, *Submarine Design and Development* (Annapolis, Md.: Naval Institute Press, 1984), 42.
24. Hajime Fukaya, "Three Japanese Submarine Developments," U.S. Naval Institute *Proceedings* 78 (August 1952): 863.

Chapter 2

1. Bōeichō Bōeikenshūjo Senshibu, ed., *Sensuikan shi*, 64. (Weapons and aircraft of the Imperial Japanese Navy were named after the year of an emperor's reign. The reign of Emperor Taishō, for example, was from 1912 to 1926; thus a 1917 weapon model would be named for the sixth year of Taishō's reign, that is, Type 6. Beginning in 1928, the year of the model was based on the traditional Japanese calendar; thus, a model produced in 1928 was referred to as Type 88 from the old Japanese calendar of 2588. The traditional date for the beginning of the reign of Emperor Jimmu was 660 B.C.; thus, 660 + 1928 = 2588.)
2. John D. Alden, *The Fleet Submarine in the U.S. Navy: A Design and Construction History* (Annapolis, Md.: Naval Institute Press, 1979), 15, 46.
3. Excluding specific references to other works, the following sections through "Navy Yards and Private Shipbuilding Companies" are based on Bōeichō Bōeikenshūjo Senshibu, ed., *Sensuikan shi*, 38, 64, 66–68, 72–73, 76–78, 80–82, and 407–10.
4. Friedman, *Submarine Design and Development*, 40.
5. Reports of the U.S. Naval Technical Mission to Japan, 1945–1946, "Lead-Acid Storage Batteries Used by the Japanese Navy," (Washington, D.C.: Naval Historical Center), microfilm reel JM-200-I, report no. S-92(N), 13.
6. Shizuo Fukui, *Shūsen to teikoku kantai* (Japanese naval vessels at the end of the war) (Tokyo: Kyōdō Shuppansha, 1961), 11, 48–49. The carrier survived the war and was scrapped at Kure in 1946.
7. Bōeichō Bōeikenshūjo Senshibu, ed., *Sensuikan shi*, 83.
8. Ibid.
9. Ibid., 475.
10. Alden, *The Fleet Submarine*, 96, and U.S. Navy Crews of *I-201* and *I-203* at Sasebo, Kyushu, Japan, 1946, "General Information Book: *I-200*-class Japanese Submarines," USS *Bowfin* Submarine Museum and Park, Honolulu, Hawaii, 44–47. The latter reference was kindly made available to the authors by the late Paul R. Schratz, who with three other U.S. Navy officers from the end of the World War II era, edited and revised the document in 1992.
11. Bōeichō Bōeikenshūjo Senshibu, ed., *Sensuikan shi*, 473, 475–78, and 483–85.
12. U.S. Navy, Naval History Division, ONI, *German Technical Aid to Japan: A Survey* (Washington, D.C., 15 June 1945), 1–51.
13. Bōeichō Bōeikenshūjo Senshibu, ed., *Sensuikan shi*, 251.
14. This and the next two paragraphs are based on ibid., 79 and 251–54.
15. Shizuo Fukui, *Naval Vessels, 1887–1945, Mitsubishi Zosen Built* (Tokyo: Hosokawa, 1956), 74. See also idem, *Japanese Naval Vessels at the End of War* (Old Greenwich, Conn.: WE, 1960), 196.
16. U.S. Navy, Naval History Division, Office of Naval Intelligence, *Japanese Naval Vessels of World War Two as Seen by U.S. Naval Intelligence*, introduction by A. D. Baker III (Annapolis, Md.: Naval Institute Press, 1987).
17. See Paul R. Schratz, *Submarine Commander: A Story of World War II and Korea* (Lexington: University Press of Kentucky, 1988), 205–21, and Reports of the U.S. Naval Technical Mission to Japan, 1945–1946, "Characteristics of

Japanese Naval Vessels—Submarines" (Washington, D.C.: Naval Historical Center), microfilm reel JM-200-I, report no. S-01-1, 7–10.

Chapter 3

1. Japan, Bōeichō Bōeikenshūjo Senshibu (Defense Ministry, Defense Research Institute, War History Branch), ed., *Chūgoku Hōmen kaigun sakusen, 1* (Naval operations in the China theater, part 1), Senshi Sōsho (War history series), vol. 72 (Tokyo: Asagumo Shimbunsha, 1974), 243.
2. This and the next paragraph are based on ibid., 249, 274, 431, and 479.
3. Stephan, *Hawaii under the Rising Sun*, 80.
4. Records of the National Security Agency, National Archives, Washington, D.C., Record Group 457 (hereafter cited as NSA, RG 457, with filing designations), "The Role of Radio Intelligence in the American-Japanese Naval War, August 1941–June 1942," vol. 1, SRH-012, 171.
5. Bōeichō Bōeikenshūjo Senshibu, ed., *Sensuikan shi*, 98.
6. Excluding specific references to other works as well as references to the remarks of two Japanese navy officers, this and the following five paragraphs are based on Bōeichō Bōeikenshūjo Senshibu, ed., *Sensuikan shi*, 98–104, and 111.
7. Ibid., 103.
8. Shigeru Fukudome, "Hawaii Operation," U.S. Naval Institute *Proceedings* 81 (December 1955): 1326.
9. W. J. Holmes, *Undersea Victory: The Influence of Submarine Operations on the War in the Pacific* (Garden City, N.Y.: Doubleday, 1966), 58.
10. Bōeichō Bōeikenshūjo Senshibu, ed., *Sensuikan shi*, 111.
11. Jean K. Lambert, "Recollections of Pearl Harbor" (paper presented at the Tenth Naval History Symposium, United States Naval Academy, Annapolis, Md., 11 September 1991).
12. Ibid., and Bōeichō Bōeikenshūjo Senshibu, ed., *Sensuikan shi*, 101.
13. Sakamaki's submarine was in Chicago at the end of the war; eventually it was sent to the U.S. Navy Submarine Base in Key West, Florida. Displayed there until 1964, it was then transferred on loan to the Mariner's Lighthouse Museum in Key West, near Ernest Hemingway's home. However, in early 1991 this craft was moved to the Admiral Nimitz Museum, Fredericksburg, Texas. There it is currently exhibited, separated into the three pieces just as it was manufactured, and painted anew similar to its paint scheme at the time of the Pearl Harbor attack. Sakamaki again saw the little boat he formerly commanded when he attended the Nimitz Museum Symposium in May 1991.
14. J. F. Riley and B. L. Delanoy, "The Last of the Midgets," U.S. Naval Institute *Proceedings* 87 (December 1961): 127–28.
15. See Charles L. Jackson, *On to Pearl Harbor and Beyond* (Dixon, Calif.: Pacific Ship and Shore, 1982), 43–51, and Peggy Warner, "Arms and Men: The Secret Weapon That Failed," *MHQ: The Quarterly Journal of Military History* 4, 1 (Autumn 1991): 44–49.
16. Bōeichō Bōeikenshūjo Senshibu, ed., *Sensuikan shi*, 106.
17. Ibid.

18. Edward P. Stafford, *The Big E: The Story of the USS* Enterprise (New York: Random House, 1962), 22–27.
19. Bōeichō Bōeikenshūjo Senshibu, ed., *Sensuikan shi*, 111–12.
20. Matome Ugaki, *Fading Victory: The Diary of Admiral Matome Ugaki, 1941–1945*, trans. Masataka Chihaya (Pittsburgh, Pa.: University of Pittsburgh Press, 1991), 73–74.
21. Ibid., 75.
22. Holmes, *Undersea Victory*, 59.
23. The battleships *New Mexico* (BB-40), *Mississippi* (BB-41), and *Idaho* (BB-42) had been on neutrality patrols in the Atlantic Ocean until late November and early December, and in January 1942 they were en route to the Pacific Fleet.
24. Bōeichō Bōeikenshūjo Senshibu, ed., *Sensuikan shi*, 106–7.
25. Ibid., 108–9. See also Bert Webber, *Retaliation: Japanese Attacks and Allied Countermeasures on the Pacific Coast in World War II* (Corvallis: Oregon State University Press, 1975), and Adam B. Siegel, "The Wartime Diversion of U.S. Navy Forces in Response to Public Demands for Augmented Coastal Defense" (professional paper of the Center for Naval Analyses, Alexandria, Va., no. 472, November 1989).
26. NSA, RG 457, "Japanese Submarine Operations, 23 January to 25 March 1942," SRH-064, 2.
27. Stephan, *Hawaii under the Rising Sun*, 122–34.
28. Quoted in ibid., 125.
29. Clark G. Reynolds, "Submarine Attacks on the Pacific Coast, 1942," *Pacific Historical Review*, 33, 2 (May 1964): 187–89.
30. Stephan, *Hawaii under the Rising Sun*, 125, 127.
31. Edwin T. Layton, *"And I Was There": Pearl Harbor and Midway—Breaking the Secrets* (New York: William Morrow, 1985), 360.
32. Allied Translator and Interpreter Section, South West Pacific Area, Enemy Publications, "Characteristics of Submarines and Anti-Submarine Operations," no. 288 (Naval Historical Center, Washington, D.C., 19 January 1945), 22.
33. Excluding specific references to other works, information on the Japanese submarine operations at Wake Island, the Bismarck Islands, and the "Southern Important Territories" is based on Bōeichō Bōeikenshūjo Senshibu, ed., *Sensuikan shi*, 123–27, 132–35, and 137–38.
34. David Jenkins, *Battle Surface! Japan's Submarine War against Australia, 1942–44* (Sydney: Random House Australia, 1992), 94–108.
35. Quoted in Arthur J. Marder, Mark Jacobsen, and John Horsfield, *The Pacific War*, vol. 2 of *Old Friends, New Enemies: The Royal Navy and the Imperial Japanese Navy* (Oxford: Clarendon Press, 1990), 14.
36. NSA, RG 457, "Combat Intelligence Unit, Fourteenth Naval District Traffic Intelligence Summaries with Comments by CINCPAC War Plans/Fleet Intelligence Sections, 16 July 1941–30 June 1942," part 2, "1 January–31 March 1942," SRMN-012, 557, 584, and 590.
37. Bōeichō Bōeikenshūjo Senshibu, ed., *Daihon'ei kaigunbu, Rengō kantai*, 2:203.
38. Bōeichō Bōeikenshūjo Senshibu, ed., *Sensuikan shi*, 135–36.

39. Bōeichō Bōeikenshūjo Senshibu, ed., *Daihon'ei kaigunbu, Rengō kantai*, 2:204. The first ship to be designed specially as an aircraft carrier, HMS *Hermes* was launched in 1919 and finally completed in 1924.
40. John Robertson and John McCarthy, *Australian War Strategy, 1939–1945: A Documentary History* (St. Lucia, Australia: University of Queensland Press, 1985), 311.
41. Excluding specific references to other works, this and the following seven paragraphs are based on the source in note 39 above, 143, 146, 154, and 343–44. On 20 May 1942, old fleet-type and minelaying submarines before *I-176* had 100 added to their hull numbers; thus, *1-75* was renamed *I-175*.
42. See Layton, "And I Was There," 372–74, and Carl Boyd, "American Naval Intelligence of Japanese Submarine Operations Early in the Pacific War," *Journal of Military History* 53 (April 1989): 177–81.
43. NSA, RG 457, SRH-012, vol. 2:328.
44. Bōeichō Bōeikenshūjo Senshibu, ed., *Daihon'ei kaigunbu, Rengō kantai*, 2:147–48.
45. Ibid., 149–50.
46. Ibid., 429–30.
47. NSA, RG 457, SRH-012, vol. 2:33.
48. Bōeichō Bōeikenshūjo Senshibu, ed., *Sensuikan shi*, 152.
49. Ibid.
50. Ibid., 154–55.
51. Ibid., 156.
52. This and the following three paragraphs are based on ibid., 156–58 and 160–61.
53. G. Hermon Gill, *Royal Australian Navy, 1942–1945* (Canberra: Australian War Memorial, 1968), 61–74.
54. Robert C. H. Courtney (Australian War Memorial, Canberra) to A. Sendzikas (Pacific Fleet Submarine Memorial Association, Honolulu), 11 September 1991, Midget Submarine File, USS *Bowfin* Submarine Museum and Park, Honolulu, Hawaii. The midget submarine referred to here is a composite craft incorporating two of the vessels sunk in Sydney Harbor. It includes the bow section from one midget submarine and the center and stern sections from another.
55. Lew Lind, *The Midget Submarine Attack on Sydney* (Sydney: Bellrope Press, 1990), 29–45; Malcolm Brown, "Claim Laid to Wrecked Sub in Harbour Mud," *Sydney Morning Herald*, 30 March 1978, p. 3; and "The War's Final Mystery," *Weekend Australian* (Sydney), 17–18 September 1988, p. 4.
56. Bōeichō Bōeikenshūjo Senshibu, ed., *Sensuikan shi*, 159.
57. Carl Boyd, *Hitler's Japanese Confidant: General Ōshima Hiroshi and MAGIC Intelligence, 1941–1945* (Lawrence: University Press of Kansas, 1993), 53–55.
58. Bōeichō Bōeikenshūjo Senshibu, ed., *Sensuikan shi*, 163.
59. Lind, *The Midget Submarine*, 66.
60. Bōeichō Bōeikenshūjo Senshibu, ed., *Sensuikan shi*, 164–66.
61. Lind, *The Midget Submarine*, 52–58.
62. Bōeichō Bōeikenshūjo Senshibu, ed., *Sensuikan shi*, 170–71.

Chapter 4

1. Bōeichō Bōeikenshūjo Senshibu, ed., *Daihon'ei kaigunbu, Rengō kantai,* 3:99–100.
2. Bōeichō Bōeikenshūjo Senshibu, ed., *Sensuikan shi,* 178–81.
3. Ibid.
4. Ugaki, *Fading Victory,* 201.
5. Bōeichō Bōeikenshūjo Senshibu, ed., *Sensuikan shi,* 178–81.
6. Bōeichō Bōeikenshūjo Senshibu, ed., *Daihon'ei kaigunbu, Rengō kantai,* 3:193–96.
7. W. J. Holmes, *Double-Edged Secrets: U.S. Naval Intelligence Operations in the Pacific during World War II* (Annapolis, Md.: Naval Institute Press, 1979), 110; see also F. A. Rhoades, *Diary of a Coastwatcher in the Solomons* (Fredericksburg, Tex.: Admiral Nimitz Foundation, 1982).
8. Bōeichō Bōeikenshūjo Senshibu, ed., *Sensuikan shi,* 181–82.
9. Ibid., 182.
10. Ibid., 186.
11. Earl S. Boyd, interview with Carl Boyd, Scottsburg, Ind., 26 December 1962.
12. Bōeichō Bōeikenshūjo Senshibu, ed., *Sensuikan shi,* 186.
13. Ibid., 191–92.
14. John C. Reilly, Jr., comp. and ed., *Operational Experience of Fast Battleships: World War II, Korea, Vietnam* (Washington, D.C.: Naval Historical Center, 1989), 220–29.
15. Ben W. Blee, "Whodunnit," U.S. Naval Institute *Proceedings* 108 (July 1982): 42–47; idem, "Enemies No More," U.S. Naval Institute *Proceedings* 113 (February 1987): 57–63.
16. Bōeichō Bōeikenshūjo Senshibu, ed., *Daihon'ei kaigunbu, Rengō kantai,* 3:239–40.
17. Bōeichō Bōeikenshūjo Senshibu, ed., *Sensuikan shi,* 191.
18. Bōeichō Bōeikenshūjo Senshibu, ed., *Daihon'ei kaigunbu, Rengō kantai,* 3:285, 313–15.
19. Bōeichō Bōeikenshūjo Senshibu, ed., *Sensuikan shi,* 196–97.
20. Ibid., 199–202.
21. Ibid., 202.
22. Bōeichō Bōeikenshūjo Senshibu, ed., *Daihon'ei kaigunbu, Rengō kantai,* 3:354–62.
23. Bōeichō Bōeikenshūjo Senshibu, ed., *Sensuikan shi,* 204.
24. Ibid., 205.
25. Ibid., 206.
26. John Costello, *The Pacific War* (New York: Rawson, Wade, 1981), 368.
27. Bōeichō Bōeikenshūjo Senshibu, ed., *Sensuikan shi,* 206–7.
28. Carl Boyd, "The Role of Cryptologic Intelligence in the Pacific War, 1941–1943," in *America at War, 1941–1945,* ed. Robert Wolfe (Carbondale: Southern Illinois University Press, forthcoming).
29. Holmes, *Double-Edged Secrets,* 124. See Translation of Captured Japanese Documents, Naval Historical Center, Washington, D.C., "Log Taken from Submarine *I-1* Sunk off Guadalcanal," April 27, 1943, item no. 508 (S-951).

The corvettes were the HMNZS *Kiwi* and *Moa* (1941), 600 tons displacement, one 4-inch gun, 13 knots. The *Moa* was sunk during a Japanese air attack near Tulagi on 7 April 1943. The *I-1* was a more formidable vessel with its 2,135 tons surfaced displacement, two 5.5-inch deck guns, and 18 knots. The *Tui*, which helped to sink the *I-17* in August 1943, was the third member of the *Kiwi* class of trawlers, as they are cited in *Conway's All the World's Fighting Ships, 1922–1946*. However, these three New Zealand vessels are most frequently referred to as corvettes; indeed, they resembled corvettes in appearance and differed from most trawlers because they burned oil and not coal.

30. Bōeichō Bōeikenshūjo Senshibu, ed., *Sensuikan shi*, 207–8.
31. Yoshimitsu Sekito, *Kōjutsu kiroku* (Oral history record), Bōeichō Bōeikenshūjo Senshibu (Defense Ministry, Defense Research Institute, War History Branch) Tokyo, Japan, 1977.
32. Bōeichō Bōeikenshūjo Senshibu, ed., *Daihon'ei kaigunbu, Rengō kantai*, 3:516–17.
33. Bōeichō Bōeikenshūjo Senshibu, ed., *Sensuikan shi*, 344.
34. Ibid., 345.
35. NSA, RG 457, "Blockade-Running between Europe and the Far East by Submarines, 1942–44," SRH-019, 13–19.
36. Ugaki, *Fading Victory,* 234.
37. Excluding specific references to other works, the remainder of this chapter is based on Bōeichō Bōeikenshūjo Senshibu, ed., *Sensuikan shi*, 218–21, 224–25. See also Kevin Don Hutchison, *World War II in the North Pacific: Chronology and Fact Book* (Westport, Conn.: Greenwood Press, 1994).
38. Bert Webber, *Silent Siege: Japanese Attacks against North America in World War II* (Fairfield, Wash.: Ye Galleon Press, 1983), 167, 172; see also "Japanese Bomb Found in Oregon Is Linked to Unidentified Seaplane," *New York Times*, 15 September 1942, pp. 1, 10.
39. Webber, *Retaliation,* 21–24, 63–78, and Holmes, *Double-Edged Secrets*, 169.

Chapter 5

1. NSA, RG 457, "The Role of Communication Intelligence in Submarine Warfare in the Pacific, January 1943–October 1943," SRH-011, vol. 2, 40–41.
2. Ibid., "Op-20-G Exploits and Commendations: World War II," SRH-306, 111–12.
3. Edward J. Drea, *MacArthur's ULTRA: Codebreaking and the War against Japan, 1942–1945* (Lawrence: University Press of Kansas, 1992), 68–72.
4. Bōeichō Bōeikenshūjo Senshibu, ed., *Sensuikan shi*, 228.
5. Ibid., 229.
6. Ibid., 230–31.
7. Dorr Carpenter and Norman Polmar, *Submarines of the Imperial Navy* (Annapolis, Md.: Naval Institute Press, 1986), 30–31, 53.
8. Bōeichō Bōeikenshūjo Senshibu, ed., *Daihon'ei kaigunbu, Rengō kantai*, 4:76–79.
9. Bōeichō Bōeikenshūjo Senshibu, ed., *Sensuikan shi*, 232–33.

10. Bōeichō Bōeikenshūjo Senshibu, ed., *Daihon'ei kaigunbu, Rengō kantai*, 4:428.
11. Yōichi Hirama, "Sensuikan sensenka zōshin ni kansuru ikensho" (A paper on the effective use of submarines), *Gunji shigaku* (Journal of military history) 29, 3 (December 1993): 41.
12. Bōeichō Bōeikenshūjo Senshibu, ed., *Sensuikan shi*, 234–35.
13. Werner Musenberg, "Unbekannter Passagier auf *U-180*," *Der Frontsoldat erzählt* 19 (1955): 181–82.
14. Bōeichō Bōeikenshūjo Senshibu, ed., *Sensuikan shi*, 235.
15. Ibid., 235–36.
16. Ibid., 239, and Bōeichō Bōeikenshūjo Senshibu, ed., *Daihon'ei kaigunbu, Rengō kantai*, 4:279.
17. Bōeichō Bōeikenshūjo Senshibu, ed., *Sensuikan shi*, 242.
18. Ibid., 243. Since at least August 1942, the chief of staff of the Combined Fleet was painfully aware of the great effectiveness of U.S. ASW operations. See Ugaki, *Fading Victory*, 201.
19. Bōeichō Bōeikenshūjo Senshibu, ed., *Sensuikan shi*, 245–46.
20. Ibid., 247.
21. Holmes, *Double-Edged Secrets*, 137.
22. Bōeichō Bōeikenshūjo Senshibu, ed., *Daihon'ei kaigunbu, Rengō kantai*, 4:319–20.
23. Ibid., 431.
24. By comparing the dates of graduation from the naval academy (appendix 10) for the squadron and division commanders (appendix 6) and their replacements (appendix 7), one observes that the new appointees were junior to their predecessors; that is, on the average the new group of officers was 1.2 classes later than their predecessors.
25. Bōeichō Bōeikenshūjo Senshibu, ed., *Sensuikan shi*, 257–61.
26. Ibid., 264. Japanese records probably err about the date of the sinking of an enemy submarine near Truk. American records suggest that the USS *Corvina* (SS-226) was sunk by a Japanese submarine near Truk on 16 November 1943. This was the only American submarine sunk by a Japanese submarine during the war. See Theodore Roscoe, *United States Submarine Operations in World War II* (Annapolis, Md.: U.S. Naval Institute, 1949), 287, and Samuel Eliot Morison, *Aleutians, Gilberts and Marshalls, June 1942–April 1944*, vol. 7 of *History of United States Naval Operations in World War II* (Boston: Little, Brown, 1951), 188.
27. Bōeichō Bōeikenshūjo Senshibu, ed., *Daihon'ei kaigunbu, Rengō kantai*, 5:89.
28. Ibid.
29. Eugene Burns, "Craft, Detected Sunday, Believed from Submarine," *Honolulu Star-Bulletin* 18 October 1943, p. 1.
30. Bōeichō Bōeikenshūjo Senshibu, ed., *Sensuikan shi*, 263.
31. Ibid., 266.
32. Ibid., 267.
33. Yōichi Hirama, "The Indian Ocean and the Pacific War: Why the Axis Could Not Establish a Joint Strategy" (paper presented at the World War II in the Pacific Conference, Crystal City, Va., 10–12 August 1994), 2.

34. Bōeichō Bōeikenshūjo Senshibu, ed., *Sensuikan shi*, 270–74.
35. Bōeichō Bōeikenshūjo Senshibu, ed., *Daihon'ei kaigunbu, Rengō kantai*, 5:143.
36. Bōeichō Bōeikenshūjo Senshibu, ed., *Sensuikan shi*, 275.
37. Ibid., 276–79.
38. Ibid., 277.
39. Bōeichō Bōeikenshūjo Senshibu, ed., *Daihon'ei kaigunbu, Rengō kantai*, 5:202.
40. Bōeichō Bōeikenshūjo Senshibu, ed., *Sensuikan shi*, 280.
41. Ibid., 280–81.
42. NSA, RG 457, "Admiralty—COMINCH ULTRA Message Exchange, 25 June 1942–17 October 1944," SRMN-035, 1–2.
43. Boyd, *Hitler's Japanese Confidant*, 48.
44. Bōeichō Bōeikenshūjo Senshibu, ed., *Sensuikan shi*, 344.
45. Ibid., 346–48. See also Shinji Uchino, "Die erfolgreiche Faht des japanischen U-Bootes *I-8*," *Marine-Rundschau* 81 (1984): 224–27.
46. NSA, RG 457, "Op-20-G File of Memoranda, Reports and Messages on German Blockade Runners, World War II, 1943–1944," SRH-260, 18.
47. Ibid., 22, 25.
48. Ibid.
49. Ibid., "Op-20-GI Memoranda to COMINCH F-21 on German U-boat Activities, October 1943–May 1945," SRMN-051A, 208–11.
50. Ibid., SRH-306, 89.
51. Ibid., 90.
52. Vernon J. Miller, *Analysis of Japanese Submarine Losses to Allied Submarines in World War II* (Bennington, Vt.: Merrian Press, 1988), 17, and Holmes, *Double-Edged Secrets*, 183.
53. NSA, RG 457, SHR-306, 90.
54. Bōeichō Bōeikenshūjo Senshibu, ed., *Sensuikan shi*, 345–46.
55. NSA, RG 457, SRH-306, 88.
56. This account of the sinking of *I-52* is based on ibid., 91–92.
57. NSA, RG 457, SRDJ [Individual Translations, Japanese Diplomatic Messages] nos. 31305–6, 31267, 42716, and U.S. Navy, Naval History Division, ONI, *German Technical Aid to Japan: A Survey* (Washington, D.C.: 15 June 1945), 184.
58. See NSA, RG 457, "Battle of the Atlantic, Vol. II, U-boat Operations, December 1942–End of War," SRH-008, 252, and Theodore Roscoe, *United States Destroyer Operations in World War II* (Annapolis, Md.: U.S. Naval Institute, 1953), 308.
59. NSA, RG 457, SRH-019, D-1 to D-7.
60. Ronald Lewin, *The American Magic: Codes, Ciphers and the Defeat of Japan* (New York: Farrar Straus Giroux, 1982), 205.

Chapter 6

1. Bōeichō Bōeikenshūjo Senshibu, ed., *Daihon'ei kaigunbu, Rengō kantai*, 5:54–55.

2. Ibid., 245–46.
3. Holmes, *Double-Edged Secrets*, 168.
4. Bōeichō Bōeikenshūjo Senshibu, ed., *Daihon'ei kaigunbu, Rengō kantai*, 5:445–46, 453. Koga's predecessor, Admiral Yamamoto, also died in his plane nearly a year earlier on 18 April. However, Yamamoto's death was the result of an ambush by sixteen P-38s that intercepted his plane over the jungles of Bougainville during a visit to forward military installations. The American attack was a trap based on communications intelligence from which the projected flight and exact schedule of the commander in chief were learned. Yamamoto had designated Koga to be his successor; not surprisingly, there was no change in the decisive battle strategy and the deployment of submarines. Indeed, the same strategy also remained largely in place after Koga's death. See Paul S. Dull, *A Battle History of the Imperial Navy, 1941–1945* (Annapolis, Md.: Naval Institute Press, 1978), 273, 298, and Ugaki, *Fading Victory*, 330–33.
5. Excluding specific references to other works, this and the following five paragraphs are based largely on Bōeichō Bōeikenshūjo Senshibu, ed., *Sensuikan shi*, 294–96, 301, 314–16.
6. See also NSA, RG 457, SRH-306, 45.
7. Ugaki, *Fading Victory*, 350.
8. Bōeichō Bōeikenshūjo Senshibu, ed., *Daihon'ei kaigunbu, Rengō kantai*, 5:557.
9. Bōeichō Bōeikenshūjo Senshibu, ed., *Sensuikan shi*, 319.
10. Ibid., 317–18.
11. Bōeichō Bōeikenshūjo Senshibu, ed., *Daihon'ei kaigunbu, Rengō kantai*, 5:559. Admiral Ugaki's diary entry of 24 June 1944 points out the "fault of judging the enemy would come to Palau and not to the Marianas." See Ugaki, *Fading Victory*, 419.
12. Bōeichō Bōeikenshūjo Senshibu, ed., *Sensuikan shi*, 322–23.
13. Ibid., 325.
14. Holmes, *Double-Edged Secrets*, 170.
15. Bōeichō Bōeikenshūjo Senshibu, ed., *Sensuikan shi*, 328–29.
16. This and the next three paragraphs are based largely on Bōeichō Bōeikenshūjo Senshibu, ed., *Daihon'ei kaigunbu, Rengō kantai*, 5:546, 557–58, 563.
17. Bōeichō Bōeikenshūjo Senshibu, ed., *Sensuikan shi*, 332.
18. Ibid., 329.
19. Ugaki, *Fading Victory*, 428.
20. Bōeichō Bōeikenshūjo Senshibu, ed., *Sensuikan shi*, 329, 332.
21. Ibid., 331–32. In view of the importance of cryptologic intelligence to the Allies in the Pacific War, it is worth noting that the Japanese "Jade" Cipher Machine— 97 *Shiki injiki-1, 2 gata*—was captured on Saipan. It was part of the opening exhibit in 1993 of the National Cryptologic Museum, Fort George G. Meade, Maryland.
22. Bōeichō Bōeikenshūjo Senshibu, ed., *Daihon'ei kaigunbu, Rengō kantai*, 5:572.
23. Bōeichō Bōeikenshūjo Senshibu, ed., *Sensuikan shi*, 329.
24. Kennosuke Torisu, *Kōjutsu kiroku* (Oral history record), Japan, Bōeichō

Bōeikenshūjo Senshibu (Defense Ministry, Defense Research Institute, War History Branch) Tokyo, Japan, 1977.
25. Bōeichō Bōeikenshūjo Senshibu, ed., *Sensuikan shi*, 334–35.
26. Reports of the U.S. Naval Technical Mission to Japan, 1945–1946, "Battle Lessons of the Greater East Asia War," vol. 7, "Submarines" (Washington, D.C.: Naval Historical Center), microfilm reel JM-200-I, report no. S-17 (hereafter JM-200-I, report no. S-17), 30. Classified "Military—Very Secret," this copy no. 157 of 800 copies was intercepted in Japanese mail not long after publication.
27. Ibid., 30–31.
28. Holmes, *Undersea Victory*, 331.
29. JM-200-I, report no. S-17, 41.
30. Ibid., 39.
31. Ibid., 33.
32. Bōeichō Bōeikenshūjo Senshibu, ed., *Daihon'ei kaigunbu, Rengō kantai*, 6:244–45.
33. Ibid., 246.
34. Bōeichō Bōeikenshūjo Senshibu, ed., *Sensuikan shi*, 355.
35. Bōeichō Bōeikenshūjo Senshibu, ed., *Daihon'ei kaigunbu, Rengō kantai*, 6:437–40.
36. Ibid., 459–60.
37. Ibid., 475.
38. Ibid., 530–31.
39. Bōeichō Bōeikenshūjo Senshibu, ed., *Sensuikan shi*, 364–67.
40. Ibid., 368–69.
41. Ibid., 371.
42. Ibid., 375–76.
43. Holmes, *Undersea Victory*, 390.

Chapter 7

1. See, for example, Charles A. Lockwood and Hans Christian Adamson, *Hellcats of the Sea* (New York: Greenburg, 1955), and Karl Doenitz, *Memoirs: Ten Years and Twenty Days,* trans. R. H. Stevens (Annapolis, Md.: Naval Institute Press, 1990).
2. Excluding specific reference material, such as the names of Allied warships, this and the following six paragraphs are largely based on Bōeichō Bōeikenshūjo Senshibu, ed., *Sensuikan shi,* 141–43, 340–41, 361–62, and 378–85.
3. NSA, RG 457, "Selected Examples of Commendations and Related Correspondence Highlighting the Achievements and Value of U.S. Signals Intelligence during World War II," SRH-059, 53.
4. NSA, RG 457, SRH-306, 111.
5. NSA, RG 457, "Op-20-GI-A Reports on Japanese/German Radar and Electronics, July 1943–March 1945," SRMN-052, 89.
6. NSA, RG 457, "COMINCH File: U-boat Intelligence Summaries, January 1943–May 1945," SRMN-037, 642.

7. Ibid. These submarines were larger than U.S. naval intelligence estimates. *U-234*'s displacement was 1,763 tons surfaced, 2,177 tons submerged; the *U-864* was 1,616 tons surfaced, 1,804 tons submerged.
8. NSA, RG 457, "Japanese Reaction to German Defeat," SRH-075, 2–3.
9. NSA, RG 457, "Op-20-GI Reports on U-boat Disposition and Status, December 1942–2 May 1945," SRMN-048, 185.
10. NSA, RG 457, "Selections from the Cryptologic Papers Collection of Rear Admiral J. N. Wenger, USN," SRH-403, 75.
11. NSA, RG 457, SRMN-048, 187.
12. NSA, RG 457, SRMN-037, 650. Emphasis added. Several months earlier the Germans wanted to send General Kessler and his party to Tokyo by air, but the Japanese objected strongly because the proposed trip would include flight over Russian territory, and the Japanese feared that if discovered, for example, in a forced landing, Japanese cooperation with Germany would jeopardize the delicate Soviet-Japanese neutrality pact. See NSA, RG 457, "The Problem of the Prolongation of the Soviet-Japanese Neutrality Pact, 12 February 1945," SRH-069, 29, and SRH-075, 10–11.
13. See Geoffrey Brooks, *Hitler's Nuclear Weapons: The Development and Attempted Deployment of Radiological Armaments by Nazi Germany* (London: Leo Cooper, 1992), 141–73, an account based on the contemporary dairy kept by Wolfgang Hirschfeld, the senior radio operator aboard the *U-234* in the spring of 1945.
14. Jürgen Rohwer, letters to Carl Boyd, 27 November and 20 December 1993.
15. William M. Blair, "Big U-boat Arrives with High General," *New York Times*, 20 May 1945, p. 20.
16. Ibid., "Gen. Kessler Caught on U-Boat," 18 May 1945, p. 18.
17. Brooks, *Hitler's Nuclear Weapons*, 168.
18. NSA, RG 457, "JICPOA/F-22 File of Administrative Letters/Correspondence, January 1942–September 1945," SRMD-009, 392.
19. Ibid., 394.
20. NSA, RG 457, "Op-20-GI Reports on German U-boats East of Capetown, July 1944–May 1945," SRMN-053, 73–75. See also ibid., "U.S. Navy (CINCPAC/CINCPOA) Post War Summaries of Status of Japanese Naval Vessels (Sunk and Afloat), November 1945," SRMN-025, 3, 37.
21. Hirama, "The Indian Ocean and the Pacific War," 8–9.
22. NSA, RG 457, SRH-059, 45.
23. Bōeichō Bōeikenshūjo Senshibu, ed., *Sensuikan shi*, 386–87. See also Yutaka Yokota and Joseph D. Harrington, "*Kaiten* . . . Japan's Human Torpedoes," U.S. Naval Institute *Proceedings* 88 (January 1962): 55–67.
24. Excluding specific reference material, such as the names of Allied warships, this and the following six paragraphs are based on Bōeichō Bōeikenshūjo Senshibu, ed., *Sensuikan shi*, 387, 389–91, and 393–98.
25. Holmes, *Undersea Victory*, 432.
26. Bōeichō Bōeikenshūjo Senshibu, ed., *Daihon'ei kaigunbu, Rengō kantai*, 7:150–54.
27. Ibid., 219.
28. Bōeichō Bōeikenshūjo Senshibu, ed., *Sensuikan shi*, 417–20.

29. Bōeichō Bōeikenshūjo Senshibu, ed., *Daihon'ei kaigunbu, Rengō kantai*, 7:222.
30. Morison, *Victory in the Pacific, 1945*, vol. 14 of *History of United States Naval Operations in World War II*, 390–91. For the total Okinawa campaign, ending officially on 2 July, Morison (p. 282) notes that "thirty [American] naval ships and craft had been sunk, mostly by *kamikaze* attack, and 368 ships and craft had been damaged. The Fleet lost 763 aircraft. Over 4900 sailors were killed or went missing in action, and an additional 4824 were wounded. This was by far the heaviest loss incurred in any naval campaign in the war."
31. See Yoshida Mitsuru, *Requiem for Battleship* Yamato, trans. Richard H. Minear (Seattle: University of Washington Press, 1985).
32. Bōeichō Bōeikenshūjo Senshibu, ed., *Daihon'ei kaigunbu, Rengō kantai*, 7:255–60, 301–2.
33. Bōeichō Bōeikenshūjo Senshibu, ed., *Sensuikan shi*, 424–25.
34. Holmes, *Undersea Victory*, 441. The *Morrison* was sunk with very heavy casualties five weeks later in a series of air attacks in the same waters.
35. Bōeichō Bōeikenshūjo Senshibu, ed., *Sensuikan shi*, 425–26.
36. Bōeichō Bōeikenshūjo Senshibu, ed., *Daihon'ei kaigunbu, Rengō kantai*, 7:301.
37. Bōeichō Bōeikenshūjo Senshibu, ed., *Sensuikan shi*, 432.
38. NSA, RG 457, SRMD-009, 423–26. The movement of all submarines, especially the giant *I-400* class, was detailed in this ULTRA Special Submarine Summary of 3 August 1945. See NSA, RG 457, "Joint Intelligence Center, Pacific Ocean Area, Summary of ULTRA Traffic, 1 July–31 August 1945," pt. 4, SRMD-007, 45, 75, and 140.
39. Bōeichō Bōeikenshūjo Senshibu, ed., *Sensuikan shi*, 433.
40. *United States of America v. Hisashi Ichioka, et al.*, "Yokohama Trials," Naval Historical Center, Washington, D.C., International Prosecution Section Document no. 3146-A (Exhibit 3841) 17 April 1946, and Defense Document no. 1896 (Exhibit 3064) 6 December 1945; Thomas O. Paine, "The Transpacific Voyage of His Imperial Japanese Majesty's Submarine *I-400:* Journal, July–December 1945," USS *Bowfin* Submarine Museum and Park, Honolulu, Hawaii; "International Military Tribunal for the Far East," proceedings, University of California, Berkeley, pp. 15,148–51, 15,193, and 27,267; and Hirama, "The Indian Ocean and the Pacific War," 12–13.
41. NSA, RG 457, "U.S. Navy Estimated Disposition of Japanese Fleet, Aircraft, Merchant Shipping and Economic Notes, 2 December 1944–3 August 1945," SRMN-027, 477.
42. NSA, RG 457, SRMD-007, pt. 4, 45, 75.
43. Bōeichō Bōeikenshūjo Senshibu, ed., *Sensuikan shi*, 431.
44. Holmes, *Double-Edged Secrets*, 211. The restricted distribution of ULTRA information in the sinking of the *Indianapolis* is thoughtfully discussed by Richard A. von Doenhoff, in "ULTRA and the Sinking of the USS *Indianapolis*" (paper presented at the Eleventh Naval History Symposium, U.S. Naval Academy, Annapolis, Md., 21–23 October 1993).
45. See, for example, Richard F. Newcomb, *Abandon Ship!* (London: Constable, 1960); Thomas Helm, *Ordeal by Sea: The Tragedy of the U.S.S.* Indianapolis

(New York: Dodd, Mead, 1963); Raymond B. Lech, *All the Drowned Sailors* (New York: Stein and Day, 1982); Dan Kurzman, *Fatal Voyage: The Sinking of the USS* Indianapolis (New York: Atheneum, 1990); and Kennosuke Torisu and Masataka Chihaya, "Japanese Submarine Tactics," U.S. Naval Institute *Proceedings* 87 (February 1961): 78–83.

46. NSA, RG 457, SRMN-027, 498.
47. See Carl Boyd, "Attacking the *Indianapolis:* A Re-examination," *Warship International* 13, 1 (1976): 15–25, where the *kaiten* versus conventional torpedo arguments are discussed.
48. Bōeichō Bōeikenshūjo Senshibu, ed., *Sensuikan shi*, 430–31.
49. Ibid., 436.
50. NSA, RG 457, "COMINT Contributions: Submarine Warfare in WW II," SRH-235, [3].
51. Bōeichō Bōeikenshūjo Senshibu, ed., *Sensuikan shi*, 440–41.
52. Ibid., 441–43.
53. NSA, RG 457, SRMN-025, 70–75.
54. Bruce McCandless, "Comment and Discussion," U.S. Naval Institute *Proceedings* 88 (July 1962): 120.
55. NSA, RG 457, SRMN-025, 1, 3, 36–39.
56. Bōeichō Bōeikenshūjo Senshibu, ed., *Sensuikan shi*, 445.
57. See, for example, NSA, RG 457, SRMD-009, 419–20.
58. See Reports of the U.S. Naval Technical Mission to Japan, 1945–1946, Naval Historical Center, Washington, D.C., "Characteristics of Japanese Naval Vessels—Submarines," microfilm reel JM-200-G, S-01-1, S-01-6, and S-01-7.
59. Schratz, *Submarine Commander*, 217. See also Thomas O. Paine, "I Was a Yank on a Japanese Sub," U.S. Naval Institute *Proceedings* 112 (September 1986): 73–78.
60. U.S. Navy Crews of *I-201* and *I-203* at Sasebo, Kyushu, Japan, 1946, "General Information Book: *I-200*-class Japanese Submarines," 58. The original version of this document is available in the USS *Bowfin* Submarine Museum and Park in Honolulu. However, the authors are particularly grateful to the late Paul Schratz, who kindly offered a new edition of this work revised in 1992 by himself and three other U.S. Navy officers responsible for sailing the two *I-200*-class submarines from Sasebo to Pearl Harbor after the war.
61. Fukudome, "Hawaii Operation," 1326.
62. Mochitsura Hashimoto, *Sunk: The Story of the Japanese Submarine Fleet, 1941–1945*, trans. E. H. M. Colegrave (New York: Henry Holt, 1954), 245.

Bibliography

Unpublished Documents

LIBRARY SOURCES

BŌEICHŌ BŌEIKENSHŪJO SENSHIBU (DEFENSE MINISTRY, DEFENSE RESEARCH INSTITUTE, WAR HISTORY BRANCH), TOKYO

Kaisen yōmurei (Navy battle regulations). 1934.
Rengō kantai sensaku (Combined fleet tactical instructions). Rev. ed. 1943.
Sekito, Yoshimitsu. *Kōjutsu kiroku* (Oral history record). 1977.
Torisu, Kennosuke. *Kōjutsu kiroku* (Oral history record). 1977.

USS *BOWFIN* SUBMARINE MUSEUM AND PARK, PACIFIC FLEET SUBMARINE MEMORIAL ASSOCIATION, HONOLULU, HAWAII

"The Imperial Japanese Navy in World War II: A Graphic Presentation of the Japanese Naval Organization and List of Combatant and Non-Combatant Vessels Lost or Damaged in the War." Report.
"Midget Submarine." File.
"Midget Submarines at Pearl Harbor, 7 December 1941." File.
"*Monaghan* Incident." File.
Paine, Thomas O. "The Transpacific Voyage of His Imperial Japanese Majesty's Submarine *I-400:* Journal, July–December 1945."
"Sakanaki's Submarine." File.
U.S. Army. Military History Section, Special Staff, General Headquarters, Far

East Command. "The Imperial Japanese Navy in World War II." February 1952.

U.S. Navy Crews of *I-201* and *I-203* at Sasebo, Kyushu, Japan, 1946. "General Information Book: *I-200*-class Japanese Submarines."

UNIVERSITY OF CALIFORNIA LIBRARY, BERKELEY

"International Military Tribunal for the Far East (1946–1948)." Proceedings.

GOVERNMENT SOURCES

NAVAL HISTORICAL CENTER, WASHINGTON, D.C.

Allied Translator and Interpreter Section, South West Pacific Area. Enemy Publications, no. 288. "Characteristics of Submarines and Anti-Submarine Operations." 19 January 1945.

"Documents Relating to the Japanese Submarine Squadron 8 Operations." Case J, 1507, Dr. 4. Miscellaneous—International Reports.

"Japanese Submarine Locations, 7–10 August 1942." Washington Document Center (WDC) no. 161701.

"Log Taken from Submarine *I-1* Sunk off Guadalcanal." Translation of Captured Japanese Documents, April 27, 1943. Item no. 508 (S-951).

Reports of the U.S. Naval Technical Mission to Japan, 1945–1946. Microfilm reels JM-200-B, G, H, and I.

"Submarine Operations, October 1944." Washington Document Center (WDC) no. 161011.

"Summary of the Major Japanese Submarine Operations." Case J, 1504, Dr. 3. U.S. Strategic Bombing Survey—Interrogations—Japanese Submarines.

United States of America v. Hisashi Ichioka, et al. "Yokohama Trials." International Prosecution Section Document no. 3146-A (Exhibit 3841), 17 April 1946; and Defense Document no. 1896 (Exhibit 3064), 6 December 1945.

U.S. Fleet, ASW Operations Research Group, Tenth Fleet. "Anti-Submarine Operations in the Pacific." Research Report 68. June–August 1944.

"War Diary of the Sixth Fleet for 1942." Washington Document Center (WDC) no. 160268.

NAVAL WAR COLLEGE, NEWPORT, R.I.

Riffer, William J. "A Study in Operational Failure: Japanese Submarine Operations in World War II." 1989. Photocopy.

U.S. ARMY CENTER OF MILITARY HISTORY, WASHINGTON, D.C.

Office of the Chief of Staff, Military Intelligence Division. War Department General Staff. Military Attaché Reports. Microfilm reels nos. 26–29.

Headquarters, 441st Counter Intelligence Corps Detachment, Special Operations. "German-Japanese Naval Operations in World War II." 3 May 1946.

U.S. NATIONAL ARCHIVES AND RECORDS ADMINISTRATION, WASHINGTON, D.C.

Record Group 38. Records of the Office of the Chief of Naval Operations. Office of Naval Intelligence (ONI) Files, Naval Attaché Reports, 1886–1939.

Record Group 165. Records of the War Department General and Special Staffs. Assistant Chief of Staff, G-2, Intelligence Division. Captured Personnel and Material Branch, 1943–1945: Enemy POW Interrogation File and Subject File.

Record Group 226. Records of the Office of Strategic Services (OSS). Seventh Army Interrogation Center. Japanese-German Cooperation.

Record Group 457. Records of the National Security Agency/Central Security Service.

- Individual Translations, Japanese Diplomatic Messages. SRDJ nos. 31305–42716.
- Special Research Histories (hereafter cited as SRH), no. SRH-008. "Battle of the Atlantic." Vol. 2, "U-boat Operations, December 1942–End of War."
- SRH-009. "Allied Communication Intelligence and the Battle of the Atlantic." Vol. 1, "December 1942–May 1945."
- SRH-011. "The Role of Communication Intelligence in Submarine Warfare in the Pacific, January 1943–October 1943." Vols. 1 and 2.
- SRH-012. "The Role of Radio Intelligence in the American-Japanese Naval War, August 1941–June 1942." Vols. 1 and 2.
- SRH-019. "Blockade-Running between Europe and the Far East by Submarines, 1942–44."
- SRH-020. "Narrative: Combat Intelligence Center, Joint Intelligence Center, Pacific Ocean Area."
- SRH-025. "Battle of the Atlantic." Vol. 4.
- SRH-059. "Selected Examples of Commendations and Related Correspondence Highlighting the Achievements and Value of U.S. Signals Intelligence during WW II."
- SRH-064. "Japanese Submarine Operations, 23 January to 25 March 1942."
- SRH-069. "The Problem of the Prolongation of the Soviet-Japanese Neutrality Pact, 12 February 1945."
- SRH-075. "Japanese Reaction to German Defeat."
- SRH-080. "Compilation of Intelligence Data, Japanese Submarine Forces (U.S. Navy/British Admiralty Letter), 9 February 1945."
- SRH-104. "Enemy Combat Ship Losses, 1 August 1945."

246 Bibliography

SRH-197. "U.S. Navy Communication Intelligence Organization, Liaison and Collaboration, 1941–1945."

SRH-235. "COMINT Contributions: Submarine Warfare in WW II."

SRH-254. "The Japanese Intelligence System, MIS/WDGS, 4 September 1945."

SRH-260. "Op-20-G File of Memoranda, Reports, and Messages on German Blockade Runners, World War II, 1943–1944."

SRH-263. "Japanese Submarine Sinkings during World War II, Op-23."

SRH-264. "A Lecture on Communications Intelligence by Capt J. N. Wenger, USN, 14 August 1946."

SRH-265. "Status of Japanese Naval Vessels as of November 1945, CINCPAC/CINCPOA."

SRH-266. "Japanese Signal Intelligence Service." 3rd ed. SSA, 1 November 1944.

SRH-305. "The Undeclared War 'History of R.I.,' 15 November 1943." By L. F. Safford, Capt., U.S. Navy.

SRH-306. "Op-20-G Exploits and Commendations: World War II."

SRH-403. "Selections from the Cryptologic Papers Collection of Rear Admiral J. N. Wenger, USN."

Discrete Records of Historical Cryptologic Import, Joint Military Services/U.S. Government Cryptologic Agencies (hereafter cited as SRMD), no. SRMD-007. "Joint Intelligence Center, Pacific Ocean Area, Summary of ULTRA Traffic, 1 July–31 August 1945." Part 4.

SRMD-009. "JICPOA/F-22 File of Administrative Letters/Correspondence, January 1942–September 1945."

Discrete Records of Historical Cryptologic Import, U.S. Navy (hereafter cited as SRMN), no. SRMN-005. "U.S. Navy Op-20-G File of Memoranda and Reports Relating to the Battle of Midway."

SRMN-007. "Japanese Espionage Activities in the United States, 1941–1943."

SRMN-012. "Combat Intelligence Unit, Fourteenth Naval District, Traffic Intelligence Summaries with Comments by CINCPAC War Plans/Fleet Intelligence Sections, 16 July 1941–30 June 1942." Part 2. "1 January–31 March 1942."

SRMN-018. "U.S. Navy (Op-20-G) West Coast Communications Intelligence Activities, Policies and Procedures, 20 June 1942–26 December 1943."

SRMN-025. "U.S. Navy (CINCPAC/CINCPOA) Post War Summaries of Status of Japanese Naval Vessels (Sunk and Afloat), November 1945."

SRMN-027. "U.S. Navy Estimated Disposition of Japanese Fleet, Aircraft, Merchant Shipping, and Economic Notes, 2 December 1944–3 August 1945."

SRMN-035. "Admiralty—COMINCH Ultra Message Exchange, 25 June 1942–17 October 1944."
SRMN-037. "COMINCH File: U-boat Intelligence Summaries, January 1943–May 1945."
SRMN-039. "COMINCH Pacific Strategic Intelligence Section (PSIS) File, March 1944–December 1945."
SRMN-040. "COMINCH File: Assessment of U-boat Fleet at the End of WW II, June–October 1945."
SRMN-042. "COMINCH File: Anti-Submarine Warfare Actions against Japanese Submarines, 12 September 1944–25 October 1945."
SRMN-048. "Op-20-GI Reports on U-boats Disposition and Status, December 1942–2 May 1945."
SRMN-051A. "Op-20-GI Memoranda to COMINCH F-21 on German U-boat Activities, October 1943–May 1945."
SRMN-052. "Op-20-GI-A Reports on Japanese/German Radar and Electronics, July 1943–March 1945."
SRMN-053. "Op-20-GI Reports on German U-boats East of Capetown, July 1944–May 1945."
SRMN-058. "Radio Intelligence Publication Related Documents, RIP 5."

Published Sources and Reference Materials

Alden, John D. *The Fleet Submarine in the U.S. Navy: A Design and Construction History.* Annapolis, Md.: Naval Institute Press, 1979.
———. *U.S. Submarine Attacks during World War II (Including Allied Submarine Attacks in the Pacific Theater).* Annapolis, Md.: Naval Institute Press, 1989.
Anderson, Frank J. *Submarines, Submariners, Submarining.* Hamden, Conn.: Shoe String Press, 1963.
———. *Submarines, Diving, and the Underwater World.* Hamden, Conn.: Archon Books, 1975.
Bagnasco, Erminio. *Submarines of World War Two.* Annapolis, Md.: Naval Institute Press, 1977.
Bray, Jeffrey K., ed. *Ultra in the Atlantic.* Vol. 2, *U-Boat Operations.* Laguna Hills, Calif.: Aegean Park Press, 1994. An edited version of SRH-008.
———. *Ultra in the Atlantic.* Vol. 3, *German Naval Communications Intelligence.* Laguna Hills, Calif.: Aegean Park Press, 1994. An edited version of SRH-024.
———. *Ultra in the Atlantic.* Vol. 4, *Technical Intelligence from Allid Communications Intelligence.* Laguna Hills, Calif.: Aegean Park Press, 1994. An edited version of SRH-025.
———. *Ultra in the Atlantic.* Vol. 6, *Appendices.* Laguna Hills, Calif.: Aegean Park Press, 1994.

Carpenter, Dorr, and Norman Polmar. *Submarines of the Imperial Japanese Navy.* Annapolis, Md.: Naval Institute Press, 1986.

Conway's All the World's Fighting Ships, 1906–1921. London: Conway Maritime Press, 1985.

Conway's All the World's Fighting Ships, 1922–1946. Annapolis, Md.: Naval Institute Press, 1980.

Doenitz, Karl. *Memoirs: Ten Years and Twenty Days.* Translated by R. H. Stevens. Annapolis, Md.: Naval Institute Press, 1990.

Evans, David C., ed. and trans. *The Japanese Navy in World War II: In the Words of Former Japanese Naval Officers.* 2nd ed. Annapolis, Md.: Naval Institute Press, 1986.

Friedman, Norman. *Submarine Design and Development.* Annapolis, Md.: Naval Institute Press, 1984.

Fukui, Shizuo. *Naval Vessels, 1887–1945, Mitsubishi Zosen Built.* Tokyo: Hosokawa, 1956.

———. *Nihon no gunkan* (Warships of the Japanese navy). 9th ed. Tokyo: Kyōdō Shuppansha, 1956.

———. *Japanese Naval Vessels at the End of the War.* Old Greenwich, Conn.: WE, 1960.

———. *Shūsen to teikoku kantai* (Japanese naval vessels that survived). Tokyo: Kyōdō Shuppansha, 1961.

Goldstein, Donald M., and Katherine V. Dillon, eds. *The Pearl Harbor Papers: Inside the Japanese Plans.* Washington, D.C.: Brassey's (U.S.), 1993.

Helm, Thomas. *Ordeal by Sea: The Tragedy of the U.S.S. Indianapolis.* New York: Dodd, Mead, 1963.

Hutchison, Kevin Don. *World War II in the North Pacific: Chronology and Fact Book.* Westport, Conn.: Greenwood Press, 1994.

Japan. Bōeichō Bōeikenshūjo Senshibu (Defense Ministry, Defense Research Institute, War History Branch), ed. *Chūgoku Hōmen kaigun sakusen* (Naval operations in the China theater). Senshi Sōsho (War history series), vol. 72, part 1. Tokyo: Asagumo Shimbunsha, 1974.

———. *Daihon'ei kaigunbu, Rengō kantai, 1, kaisen made* (Imperial General Headquarters, Navy Division, Combined Fleet, part 1: To the start of the war). Senshi Sōsho (War history series), vol. 91. Tokyo: Asagumo Shimbunsha, 1975.

———. Part 2. Vol. 82. Tokyo: Asagumo Shimbunsha, 1975.

———. Part 3. Vol. 77. Tokyo: Asagumo Shimbunsha, 1974.

———. Part 4. Vol. 39. Tokyo: Asagumo Shimbunsha, 1970.

———. Part 5. Vol. 71. Tokyo: Asagumo Shimbunsha, 1974.

———. Part 6. Vol. 45. Tokyo: Asagumo Shimbunsha, 1971.

———. Part 7. Vol. 93. Tokyo: Asagumo Shimbunsha, 1976.

———. *Kaigun gunsenbi ichi: Shōwa jūrokūnen jūichigatsu made* (The navy's war preparations, part 1: to November 1941). Senshi Sōsho (War history series), vol. 23. Tokyo: Asagumo Shimbunsha, 1969.

———. *Sensuikan shi* (History of submarines). Senshi Sōsho (War history series), vol. 98. Tokyo: Asagumo Shimbunsha, 1979.

Jentschura, Hansgeorg, Dieter Jung, and Peter Mickel. *Warships of the Imperial Japanese Navy, 1869–1945.* Translated by Antony Preston and David Brown. Annapolis, Md.: Naval Institute Press, 1986.

Kimble, David L. *Chronology of U.S. Navy Submarine Operations in the Pacific, 1939–1942.* Bennington, Vt.: Merriam Press, 1988.

Kurzman, Dan. *Fatal Voyage: The Sinking of the USS* Indianapolis. New York: Atheneum, 1990.

Lech, Raymond B. *All the Drowned Sailors.* New York: Stein and Day, 1982.

Miller, David. *Submarines of the World.* New York: Orion Books, 1991.

Miller, Vernon J. *Analysis of Japanese Submarine Losses to Allied Submarines in World War II.* Bennington, Vt.: Merriam Press, 1988.

Newcomb, Richard F. *Abandon Ship!* London: Constable, 1960.

Nippon Dempo News Agency, ed. *Japan Illustrated, 1934.* Tokyo: Nippon Dempo News Agency, 1934.

Preston, Antony, and John Batchelor. *The Submarine, 1578–1919.* N.p.: Marshall Cavendish, n.d.

———. *The Submarine since 1919.* N.p.: Marshall Cavendish, 1974.

Rhoades, F. A. *Diary of a Coastwatcher in the Solomons.* Fredericksburg, Tex.: Admiral Nimitz Foundation, 1982.

Rohwer, Jürgen. *Axis Submarine Success, 1939–1945.* Translated by John A. Broadwin. Annapolis, Md.: Naval Institute Press, 1983.

Scanlon, Val, Jr. *USS* Spadefish *(SS-411) in World War II.* Bennington, Vt.: Merriam Press, 1988.

Tomonaga, Yō, and Tadatoshi Yokoi. *Shashin shū Teikoku Kaigun* (Photographs of the Imperial Japanese Navy). 2 vols. Tokyo: Kyōdō Shuppansha, 1960.

Ugaki, Matome. *Fading Victory: The Diary of Admiral Matome Ugaki, 1941–1945.* Translated by Masataka Chihaya. Pittsburgh, Pa.: University of Pittsburgh Press, 1991.

U.S. Military History Section, Headquarters, Army Forces Far East. Japanese Monograph no. 95. *Submarine Operations in the Philippines Area, September 1944–March 1945.*

———. Japanese Monograph no. 102. *Submarine Operations, December 1941–April 1942.*

———. Japanese Monograph no. 108. *Submarine Operations in First Phase Operations, December 1941–April 1942.*

———. Japanese Monograph no. 110. *Submarine Operations in Second Phase Operations. Part 1, April–August 1942.*

———. Japanese Monograph no. 111. *Submarine Operations in Second Phase Operations.* Part 2, August 1942–March 1943.

———. Japanese Monograph no. 163. *Submarine Operations in Operations Phase III.* Part 1, March–November 1943.

———. Japanese Monograph no. 171. *Submarine Operations in Third Phase Operations.* Part 2, November 1943–March 1944.

———. Japanese Monograph no. 184. *Submarine Operations in the Third Phase Operations.* Parts 3, 4, and 5, April 1944–August 1945.

———. *Operational History of Japanese Naval Communications, December 1941–August 1945.* Laguna Hills, Calif.: Aegean Park Press, 1985. (This study was written by former officers of the Japanese General Staff and War Ministry as a result of Instruction no. 126 to the Japanese government of 12 October 1945 from the Supreme Commander for the Allied Powers. Translation of the Japanese text was made by the Military Intelligence Service Group, G2, Headquarters, Army Forces Far East.)

U.S. Navy, Naval History Division, Chief of Naval Operations. *German, Japanese, and Italian Submarine Losses: World War II.* OpNav-P33-100. Washington, D.C., 1946.

———. *United States Naval Chronology, World War II.* Washington, D.C., 1955.

———. *United States Submarine Losses: World War II.* Washington, D.C., 1963.

U.S. Navy, Naval History Division, Office of Naval Intelligence. *Axis Submarine Manual* (Op-16-F20) (ONI-220-M). Washington, D.C., 1942.

———. *German Technical Aid to Japan: A Survey.* Washington, D.C., 15 June 1945.

———. *Japanese Naval Vessels of World War Two as Seen by U.S. Naval Intelligence.* Introduction by A. D. Baker III. Annapolis, Md.: Naval Institute Press, 1987. (This is a collection of wartime Office of Naval Intelligence studies.)

U.S. Strategic Bombing Survey (Pacific) (USSBS-Pacific) (Naval Analysis Division). *The Campaigns of the Pacific War.* Washington, D.C.: Government Printing Office, 1946.

———. *Interrogations of Japanese Officials.* 2 vols. Washington, D.C.: U.S. Government Printing Office, 1946.

———. *Japanese Military and Naval Intelligence.* Washington, D.C.: U.S. Government Printing Office, 1946.

Watts, Anthony J. *Japanese Warships of World War II.* Garden City, N.Y.: Doubleday, 1973.

Yoshida, Mitsura. *Requiem for Battleship* Yamato. Translated by Richard H. Minear. Seattle: University of Washington Press, 1985.

Bibliography 251

Secondary Works: Books

Barnhart, Michael A. *Japan Prepares for Total War: The Search for Economic Security, 1919–1941.* Ithaca, N.Y.: Cornell University Press, 1987.
Blair, Clay, Jr. *Silent Victory: The U.S. Submarine War against Japan.* Philadelphia: J. S. Lippincott, 1975.
Boyd, Carl. *Hitler's Japanese Confidant: General Ōshima Hiroshi and MAGIC Intelligence, 1941–1945.* Lawrence: University Press of Kansas, 1993.
Brice, Martin. *Axis Blockade Runners of World War II.* Annapolis, Md.: Naval Institute Press, 1981.
Brooks, Geoffrey. *Hitler's Nuclear Weapons: The Development and Attempted Deployment of Radiological Armaments by Nazi Germany.* London: Leo Cooper, 1992.
Burlingame, William "Burl" G., Jr. *Advance Force—Pearl Harbor: The Imperial Navy's Underwater Assault on America.* Kailua, Hawaii: Pacific Monograph, 1992.
Bywater, Hector C. *Sea-Power in the Pacific: A Study of the American-Japanese Naval Problem.* London: Constable, 1921.
Chapman, John W. M., ed. and trans. *The Price of Admiralty: The War Diary of the German Naval Attaché in Japan, 1939–1943.* 3 vols. to date. Ripe, East Sussex: Saltire Press, 1982–.
Costello, John. *The Pacific War.* New York: Rawson, Wade, 1981.
d'Albas, Andrieu. *Death of a Navy: Japanese Naval Action in World War II.* Translated by Anthony Rippon. New York: Devin-Adair, 1957.
Domville-Fife, Charles W. *Submarines of the World's Navies.* London: Francis Griffiths, 1910.
Drea, Edward J. *MacArthur's ULTRA: Codebreaking and the War against Japan, 1942–1945.* Lawrence: University Press of Kansas, 1992.
Dull, Paul S. *A Battle History of the Imperial Japanese Navy, 1941–1945.* Annapolis, Md.: Naval Institute Press, 1978.
Enright, Joseph F. *Shinano! The Sinking of Japan's Secret Supership.* New York: St. Martin's Press, 1987.
Fuchida, Mitsuo, and Masatake Okumiya. *Midway: The Battle That Doomed Japan.* Annapolis, Md.: U.S. Naval Institute, 1955.
Gill, G. Hermon. *Royal Australian Navy, 1942–1945.* Canberra: Australian War Memorial, 1968.
Gray, Edwyn. *Captains of War.* London: Leo Cooper, 1988.
Hashimoto, Mochitsura. *Sunk: The Story of the Japanese Submarine Fleet, 1941–1945.* Translated by E. H. M. Colegrave. New York: Henry Holt, 1954.
Hinsley, F. H., et al. *British Intelligence in the Second World War.* Vols. 1–3, *Its Influence on Strategy and Operations.* Vol. 4, *Security and Counter-*

Intelligence. By F. H. Hinsley and C. A. G. Simkins. Vol. 5, *Strategic Deception.* By Michael Howard. London: Her Majesty's Stationery Office, 1979–90.

Holmes, W. J. *Doubled-Edged Secrets: U.S. Naval Intelligence Operations in the Pacific during World War II.* Annapolis, Md.: Naval Institute Press, 1979.

———. *Undersea Victory: The Influence of Submarine Operations on the War in the Pacific.* Garden City, N.Y.: Doubleday, 1966.

Howarth, Stephen, ed. *Men of War: Great Naval Leaders of World War II.* New York: St. Martin's Press, 1992.

Hoyt, Edwin P. *Submarines at War: The History of the American Silent Service.* New York: Stein and Day, 1983.

Icenhower, Joseph B., comp. *Submarines in Combat.* New York: Franklin Watts, 1964.

Ito, Masanori. *The End of the Imperial Japanese Navy.* Translated by Andrew Y. Kuroda and Roger Pineau. New York: Macfadden-Bartell, 1965.

Jackson, Charles L. *On to Pearl Harbor and Beyond.* Dixon, Calif.: Pacific Ship and Shore, 1982.

Jenkins, David. *Battle Surface! Japan's Submarine War against Australia, 1942–44.* Sydney: Random House Australia, 1992.

Kemp, Paul J. *Midget Submarines.* London: Arms and Armour Press, 1990.

Layton, Edwin T. *"And I Was There": Pearl Harbor and Midway—Breaking the Secrets.* New York: William Morrow, 1985.

Lewin, Ronald. *The American Magic: Codes, Ciphers and the Defeat of Japan.* New York: Farrar, Straus, Giroux, 1982.

Lind, Lew. *The Midget Submarine Attack on Sydney.* Sydney: Bellrope Press, 1990.

———. *Toku-tai: Japanese Submarine Operations in Australian Waters.* Maryborough, Victoria: Kangaroo Press, 1992.

Lockwood, Charles A., and Hans Christian Adamson. *Hellcats of the Sea.* New York: Greenberg, 1955.

Marder, Arthur J. *From Dreadnought to Scapa Flow.* 5 vols. London: Oxford University Press, 1961–70.

Marder, Arthur J., Mark Jacobsen, and John Horsfield. *The Pacific War, 1942–1945.* Vol. 2 of *Old Friends, New Enemies: The Royal Navy and the Imperial Japanese Navy.* Oxford: Clarendon Press, 1990.

Martin, Bernd. *Deutschland und Japan im Zweiten Weltkrieg: Vom Angriff auf Pearl Harbor bis zur deutschen Kapitulation.* Göttingen: Musterschmidt-Verlag, 1969.

Morison, Samuel Eliot. *History of United States Naval Operations in World War II.* 15 vols. Boston: Little, Brown, 1947–62.

Oritz, Zenji, and Joseph D. Harrington. *I-Boat Captain.* Canoga Park, Calif.: Major Books, 1976.

Parillo, Mark P. *The Japanese Merchant Marine in World War II*. Annapolis, Md.: Naval Institute Press, 1993.

Parker, Frederick D. *Pearl Harbor Revisited: United States Navy Communications Intelligence, 1924–1941*. Fort George G. Meade, Md.: National Security Agency, 1994.

———. *A Priceless Advantage: U.S. Navy Communications Intelligence and the Battles of Coral Sea, Midway, and the Aleutians*. Fort George G. Meade, Md.: National Security Agency, 1993.

Pelz, Stephen E. *Race to Pearl Harbor: The Failure of the Second London Naval Conference and the Onset of World War II*. Cambridge: Harvard University Press, 1974.

Prange, Gordon W. *At Dawn We Slept: The Untold Story of Pearl Harbor*. New York: Penguin Books, 1982.

———. *Miracle at Midway*. New York: McGraw-Hill, 1982.

Reilly, John C., Jr., comp. and ed. *Operational Experience of Fast Battleships: World War II, Korea, Vietnam*. Washington, D.C.: Naval Historical Center, 1989.

Robertson, John, and John McCarthy. *Australian War Strategy, 1939–1945: A Documentary History*. St. Lucia: University of Queensland Press, 1985.

Roscoe, Theodore. *United States Destroyer Operations in World War II*. Annapolis, Md.: U.S. Naval Institute, 1953.

———. *United States Submarine Operations in World War II*. Annapolis, Md.: U.S. Naval Institute, 1949.

Schratz, Paul R. *Submarine Commander: A Story of World War II and Korea*. Lexington: University Press of Kentucky, 1988.

Showell, J. P. Mallmann. *U-Boats under the Swastika*. New York: Arco, 1974.

Stafford, Edward P. *The Big E: The Story of the USS* Enterprise. New York: Random House, 1962.

Stephan, John J. *Hawaii under the Rising Sun: Japan's Plans for Conquest after Pearl Harbor*. Honolulu: University of Hawaii Press, 1984.

Stripp, Alan. *Codebreaker in the Far East*. London: Frank Cass, 1989.

Torisu, Kennosuke. *Kaiten* (Human torpedo). Tokyo: Shinkōsha, 1981.

———. *Tokkō to Genbaku no Tatakai* (The struggles of special attack units versus nuclear bombs). Tokyo: Sankei Shuppan, 1986.

Treadwell, Terry C. *Submarines with Wings: The Past, Present and Future of Aircraft-Carrying Submarines*. London: Conway Maritime Press, 1985.

Trenowden, Ian. *The Hunting Submarine: The Fighting Life of HMS Tally-Ho*. London: William Kimber, 1974.

Trew, Antony. *Yashimoto's Last Dive*. New York: St. Martin's Press, 1987.

Warner, Peggy, and Sadao Seno. *The Coffin Boats: Japanese Midget Submarine Operations in the Second World War*. London: Leo Cooper, 1986.

Webber, Bert. *Retaliation: Japanese Attacks and Allied Countermeasures on the Pacific Coast in World War II.* Corvallis: Oregon State University Press, 1975.

———. *Silent Siege: Japanese Attacks against North America in World War II.* Fairfield, Wash.: Ye Galleon Press, 1983.

Yokota, Yutaka, and Joseph D. Harrington. *The Kaiten Weapon.* New York: Ballantine Books, 1962.

Yoshimura, Akira. *Build the* Musashi! *The Birth and Death of the World's Greatest Battleship.* Translated by Vincent Murphy. Tokyo: Kodansha International, 1991.

Secondary Works: Articles and Papers

Asada, Sadao. "The Revolt against the Washington Treaty: The Imperial Japanese Navy and Naval Limitation, 1921–1927." *Naval War College Review* 46, 3 (Summer 1993): 82–97.

Beehler, W. H. "A Review of Japanese Naval Financial Policy." U.S. Naval Institute *Proceedings* 37 (1911): 801–22.

Blair, William M. "Big U-Boat Arrives with High General." *New York Times,* 20 May 1945, p. 20.

Blears, James. "A Warcrime at Sea, 1944." *Command Magazine* 25 (November–December 1993): 67–71.

Blee, Ben W. "Enemies No More." U.S. Naval Institute *Proceedings* 113 (February 1987): 57–63.

———. "Torpedoes Galore: History's Most Destructive Submarine Attack." *Command Magazine* 31 (November–December 1994): 54–61.

———. "Whodunnit." U.S. Naval Institute *Proceedings* 108 (July 1982): 42–47.

Boyd, Carl. "American Naval Intelligence of Japanese Submarine Operations Early in the Pacific War." *Journal of Military History* 53 (April 1989): 169–89.

———. "Attacking the *Indianapolis*: A Re-examination." *Warship International* 13, 1 (1976): 15–25.

———. "Japanese Military Effectiveness: The Interwar Period." In *Military Effectiveness,* edited by Allan R. Millett and Williamson Murray. Vol. 2, 131–68. Boston: Allen and Unwin, 1988.

———. "The Japanese Submarine Force and the Legacy of Strategic and Operational Doctrine Developed between the World Wars." In *Selected Papers from the Citadel Conference on War and Diplomacy, 1978,* edited by Larry H. Addington et al., 27–40. Charleston, S.C.: Citadel Press, 1979.

———. "The Role of Cryptologic Intelligence in the Pacific War, 1941–1943." In *America at War, 1941–1945,* edited by Robert Wolfe. Carbondale: Southern Illinois University Press. Forthcoming.

Brown, Malcolm. "Claim Laid to Wrecked Sub in Harbour Mud." *Sydney Morning Herald*, 30 March 1978, p. 3.

Burns, Eugene. "Craft, Detected Sunday, Believed from Submarine." *Honolulu Star-Bulletin*, 18 October 1943, p. 1.

Cable, Frank T. "The Submarine Torpedo Boat *Holland:* The Submarine to Become a Part of the United States Navy." U.S. Naval Institute *Proceedings* 69 (February 1943): 173–80.

Doenhoff, Richard A. von. "ULTRA and the Sinking of the USS *Indianapolis*." Paper presented at the Eleventh Naval History Symposium, United States Naval Academy, Annapolis, Md., 21–23 October 1993.

Fukaya, Hajime. "Three Japanese Submarine Developments." U.S. Naval Institute *Proceedings* 78 (August 1952): 863–67.

Fukudome, Shigeru. "The Air Battle off Taiwan." In *The Japanese Navy in World War II*, edited and translated by David C. Evans, 334–54. 2nd ed. Annapolis, Md.: Naval Institute Press, 1986.

———. "Hawaii Operation." U.S. Naval Institute *Proceedings* 81 (December 1955): 1315–31.

Gibson, Charles Dana. "The Far East Odyssey of the *UIT-24*." *Naval History* 4, 1 (Winter 1990): 19–23.

Goldingham, C. S. "Japanese Submarines in the Second World War." *Journal of the Royal United Service Institution* 96 (February 1951): 93–100.

Hirama, Yōichi. "The Indian Ocean and the Pacific War: Why the Axis Could Not Establish a Joint Strategy." Paper presented at the World War II in the Pacific Conference, Crystal City, Va., 10–12 August 1994.

———. "Japanese Naval Preparations for World War II." *Naval War College Review* 44, 2 (Spring 1991): 63–81.

———. "Sensuikan sensenka zōshin ni kansuru ikensho" (A paper on the effective use of submarines). *Gunji shigaku* (Journal of military history) 29, 3 (December 1993): 41–52.

"Japanese Bomb Found in Oregon Is Linked to Unidentified Seaplane," *New York Times*, 15 September 1942, pp. 1, 10.

Katō, Tatsuo, ed. "I-Go-sensuikan" (I-boats). Maru Special no. 13. Nihon kaigun kantai series (Warships of the Imperial Japanese Navy series). Tokyo: Ushio Shobō, 1977.

———. "Nihon no sensuikan I" (Japanese submarines I). Maru Special no. 31. Nihon kaigun kantai series (Warships of the Imperial Japanese Navy series). Tokyo: Ushio Shobō, 1979.

———. "Nihon no sensuikan II" (Japanese submarines II). Maru Special no. 37, Nihon kaigun kantai series (Warships of the Imperial Japanese Navy series). Tokyo: Ushio Shobō, 1980.

———. "Nihon no sensuikan III" (Japanese submarines III). Maru Special no. 43. Nihon kaigun kantai series (Warships of the Imperial Japanese Navy series). Tokyo: Ushio Shobō, 1980.

Lambert, Jean K. "Recollections of Pearl Harbor." Paper presented at the Tenth Naval History Symposium, U.S. Naval Academy, Annapolis, Md., 11 September 1991.
Lautenschläger, Karl. "The Submarine in Naval Warfare, 1901–2001." *International Security* 11, 3 (Winter 1986–87): 94–140.
Long, E. John. "Japan's 'Underseas Carriers.'" U.S. Naval Institute *Proceedings* 76 (June 1950): 607–13.
Masland, John W. "Japanese-German Naval Collaboration in World War II." U.S. Naval Institute *Proceedings* 75 (February 1949): 179–87.
McCandless, Bruce. "Comment and Discussion." U.S. Naval Institute *Proceedings* 88 (July 1962): 119–20.
Musenberg, Werner. "Unbekannter Passagier auf *U-180.*" *Der Frontsoldat erzählt* 19 (1955): 181–82.
Ōi, Atsushi. "Why Japan's Anti-Submarine Warfare Failed." U.S. Naval Institute *Proceedings* 78 (June 1952): 587–601.
"Opium, Erz und Öle." *Der Frontsoldat erzählt* 18, 8 (1954): 245–47.
Paine, Thomas O. "I Was a Yank on a Japanese Sub." U.S. Naval Institute *Proceedings* 112 (September 1986): 73–78.
Reynolds, Clark G. "Submarine Attacks on the Pacific Coast, 1942." *Pacific Historical Review* 33, 2 (May 1964): 183–93.
Riley, J. F., and B. L. Delanoy. "The Last of the Midgets." U.S. Naval Institute *Proceedings* 87 (December 1961): 127–28.
Rivera, Carlos R. "Akiyama Saneyuki and Satō Tetsutarō: Preparing the Imperial Navy for the Hypothetical Enemy, 1906–1916." Paper presented at the Twenty-Nineth Annual Northern Great Plains History Conference, St. Paul, Minn., 28 September–1 October 1994.
Saville, Allison W. "German Submarines in the Far East." U.S. Naval Institute *Proceedings* 87 (August 1961): 80–92.
Shashin shū Nihon no sensuikan (Photograph collection of submarines of the Japanese navy). By the editors of *Maru* Magazine. Tokyo: Kōjinsha, 1973.
Siegel, Adam B. "The Wartime Diversion of U.S. Navy Forces in Response to Public Demands for Augmented Coastal Defense." Professional paper of the Center for Naval Analyses, Alexandria, Va. No. 472. November 1989.
Tanabe, Yahachi, and Joseph D. Harrington. "I Sank the *Yorktown* at Midway." U.S. Naval Institute *Proceedings* 89 (May 1963): 58–65.
Tanaka, Raizo, and Roger Pineau. "Japan's Losing Struggle for Guadalcanal." Parts 1 and 2. U.S. Naval Institute *Proceedings* 82 (July, August 1956): 687–99, 815–31.
Tiedemann, Arthur E. Introduction to "The London Naval Treaty, 1930," by Kobayashi Tatsuo. In *Japan Erupts: The London Naval Conference and the Manchurian Incident, 1928–1932*, edited by James William Morley, 3–10. New York: Columbia University Press, 1984.

Torisu, Kennosuke, and Masataka Chihaya. "Japanese Submarine Tactics." U.S. Naval Institute *Proceedings* 87 (February 1961): 78–83.

Toyama, Saburo. "The Outline of the Armament Expansion of the Imperial Japanese Navy during the Years 1930–1941." *Revue Internationale d'Histoire Militaire,* No. 73 (1991): 55–67.

Uchino, Shinji. "Die erfolgreiche Faht des japanischen U-Bootes *I-8*." *Marine-Rundschau* 81 (1984): 224–27.

Warner, Peggy. "Arms and Men: The Secret Weapon That Failed." *MHQ: The Quarterly Journal of Military History* 4, 1 (Autumn 1991): 44–49.

"The War's Final Mystery." *Weekend Australian* (Sydney), 17–18 September 1988, p. 4.

Yokota, Yutaka, and Joseph D. Harrington. "*Kaiten* . . . Japan's Human Torpedoes." U.S. Naval Institute *Proceedings* 88 (January 1962): 55–67.

Index

A-Gō (*A-Gō sakusen*): description of, 135; initiated by Adm. Toyoda, 135; task force organization for, 206–7
Aichi Aircraft, 40, 175
aircraft: E14Y1 reconnaissance plane, 40; flying boat refueling, American interdiction of (Midway), 81; Heinkel-carrying submarine, early experiments with, 21; Henschel Hs 130C, 129; I-25 seaplane bombs Oregon forest, 110; Kawanishi H8K flying boat (*Emily*), 81; Messerschmitt Me 262 (jet), 129, 165; Messerschmitt Me 163 (rocket), 129; *Seiran* seaplane dive bomber (Aichi M6A1), 40, 175. *See also* aircraft-carrying submarines
aircraft carriers (U.S.): *Anzio* (CVE-57), 157, 172, 178; *Enterprise* (CV-6), 65, 96, 101; *Hornet* (CV-8), 65, 78, 101; *Lexington* (CVE-2), 65; *Santee* (CVE-29), 157; *Saratoga* (CV-3), 64, 65, 98; *Wasp* (CV-7), 65, 99, 100; *Yorktown* (CV-5), 65, 84–86
aircraft-carrying submarines
—development of: Bureau of Naval Aviation (*Kaigun kōkū honbu*), 50; I-5 experimental boat, 21; *Kadai* Type 5, 20–21; Oppama Aviation Corps early experiments, 21; retractable hangars (on *I-5*), 21
—operational employment of: I-25 seaplane bombs Oregon forest, 110; original mission for (Panama Canal), 175, 176; reconnaissance operations (11/41–11/42), 198–99; ULTRA intelligence on, 241
—planes for: E14Y1 reconnaissance plane, 40; Nakajima C6N ("Myrt"), 176; *Seiran* seaplane dive bomber (Aichi M6A1), 40, 175
—*Sen-toku* Type (*I-400* class): construction history of, 29, 175; hangar, hangar doors, 177; launching catapult on (*I-14*), 178; port auxiliary engine room, 176; postwar

aircraft-carrying submarines, *Sen-toku* Type (*cont.*)
  transfer to U.S., 52, 185–87; snorkel device on (photo), 186; specifications for, 28–29
Akiyama, Vice Adm. Shinshi, 3
Aleutians operations
—1942: Attu and Kiska, Japanese decision to hold, 109–10; force organization and composition (*Guntai-Kabun*), 201–2; RO-boat garrison at Kiska, 110; submarine losses in, 110; USS *Casco* (AVP-12) damaged, 110
—1943: Attu, abandonment of, 118; heavy submarine losses in, 118–19; Kiska, evacuation of, 118–20, 119, 120; submarine forces in, 118
—1944: scattered submarine patrols, losses, 160
amphibious tanks (*Toku 4-shiki Naikatei*), 137
anechoic coatings: on *I-400* class *Sen-toku* boats, 29; on modified *Junsen* Type A boats, 27
"ant carrying transport" (*Dai hatsu*) operations, 115
Aoba (heavy cruiser), 69
Ariizumi, Capt. Tatsunosuke, 176, 179
armament, submarine. *See* deck guns; *kaiten*; mines/minelaying; torpedoes
ASW tactics/countermeasures: American excellence in, 86, 126, 143; hedgehogs, 149; Japanese indifference to, 126–27. *See also* codes and cryptology
atrocities (by Capt. Ariizumi), 179
attrition doctrine (*yōgeki sakusen*). *See* strategy and tactics
Attu. *See* Aleutians operations
Australian waters, operations in: effectiveness of, 90–91; HMAS *Kuttabul* torpedoed, 88; loss of *I-28*, 87; Lt. Chūman destroys submarine, self, 88; midget submarine crews buried by Australians, 88; Naval Task Force organization (*Guntai-Kabun*), 201–2; submarine force organization and objectives, 87; submarine patrols, summary of (6-7/42), 90–91; Submarine Unit "A" sorties to Madagascar, 88–89; USS *Chicago* (CA-29) attacked, 88

Ballard, USS (AVD-10), 81
Ban, Lt. Katsuhisa, 88
Bass, Horace A., USS (ex-DE-691), 175
Beach, Capt. Edward L., 182
Bismarck Barrier, 134, 135, 136
blockade running (*Yanagi*). *See also* German technology transfer
—and Allied intelligence operations, 133
—British awareness of, 127
—*I-29:* arrives Lorient, France (3/43), 128; progress tracked by ULTRA, 128–29; sunk by USS *Sawfish* (SS-276), 130
—*I-30:* arrives Lorient, France (8/42), 108; mined off Singapore on return, 109, 127; Adm. Ugaki comment on loss, 109
—*I-34:* lost on outward voyage, 128
—*I-52:* sorties from Singapore with raw materials, 130; rendezvous with German U-530, 130; sunk by USS *Bogue* (CVE-9), 130; ULTRA role in sinking, 130–31
—introduction to, 108
—postwar evaluation of, 132–33
Bose, Subhas Chandra, 117
Bräutigam, Robert, 14
British influence (on Japanese submarine design): K-class prototype for *Kaidai* Type 1, 15–16; report on early British submarines, 9; Vickers "C" and "L" boats, 11–12; Vickers diesel engine, 40; Whitehead torpedoes, 36
Bureau of Air (*Kōkū gijutsu shō*), 40
Bureau of Naval Aviation (*Kaigun Kōkū honbu*), 50

Index 261

Bureau of Submarines (*Kaigun Sensuikanbu*), 51–52. *See also* submarine forces (Japanese)
Bywater, Hector, 17

Carlman, Theodor, 21
Chin Yen (Chinese battleship), 10
Chitose (seaplane tender), 34–35
Chiyoda (seaplane tender), 34–35, 104
Chūman, Lt. Kenshi, 88
coastal/island defense boats: *Kaishō (Kaigun-shō)* Type, 32–33; *Sen-taka shō (Sensui-taka shō)* Type, 33
codes and cryptology
—Enigma machine: Enigma intelligence and blockade running, 133; on *I-29* blockade runner, 129; and ULTRA, 114
—intelligence organizations: JICPOA (Joint Intelligence Center, Pacific Ocean Area), 165–66; Pacific Strategic Intelligence Section (PSIS), 162
—MAGIC codebreaking program, 133
—submarine codes (Japanese): codes and cryptology for radio communications, 48; *I-1* beached, yields code books (Guadalcanal), 105, 106
—ULTRA intelligence: account of *U-234* final voyage, 164; background to, 114; and destruction of submarine picket line (Marianas), 143; enables destruction Japanese convey, 114; on high-speed submarines, 185; and Japanese transportation operations (1994–1945), 162; Japanese ULTRA, 114; and movement of *I-400* class submarines, 241; and sinking of *I-42*, 136; and sinking of USS *Indianapolis*, 179, 181, 241; tracks *I-29* blockade run to Europe, 128–29
communications, submarine (Japanese): codes used for, 48; Communication Groups (Tokyo, Kwajalein, etc.), 48–49; *Kurier* communication system (German), 163–64; submarine equipment for, 48; tactical constraints on, 48; VLF/HF transmissions in, 48
communications destruction, by Eighth Submarine Group patrol, 111
construction, submarine: of aircraft-carrying I-boat (*I-5*), 21; of *Holland*-type boats, 11; inefficiency of, 50–51; of *Kōryū* midget submarines, 34, 51
Cornwall, HMS (heavy cruiser), 77
cruisers, U.S.
—heavy: *Canberra* (CA-70), 152; *Chester* (CA-27), 102; *Chicago* (CA-29), 88; *Indianapolis* (CA-35), 181–83
—light: *Juneau* (CL-52), 104; *Reno* (CL-96), 157

aigo, Rear. Adm. Tadashige, 71, 73
ai hatsu landing craft, 115
ecisive Battle. *See also* Leyte Gulf, battle of; Marianas; strategy and tactics
-strategic background to: Adm. Toyoda orders Operation *A-Gō*, 135; *A-Gō* (*A-Gō sakusen*), task force organization for, 206–7; Allied successes, impact of, 135; Bismarck Barrier, 134, 135, 136; Combined Fleet Tactical Instructions (*Rengō kantai sensaku,* 1943), 193–95; General Principles for the Conduct of the War (*Sensō shidō no taikō*), 134; historical background, 5–6; Navy Battle Instructions (*Kaisen yōmurei,* 1934), 191–93; Zone of Absolute National Defense (*Zettai kokubō*), 134, 135, 150
-submarine role in: introduction, 4–5; Adm. Ugaki laments losses (4/15/44), 137; A-targets (*kō Hyōptek, Kōryū*), 33–34, 35; early deployment and operations (1943–44), 136–37; later deployment and operations (prior to Saipan assault),

Decisive Battle, submarine role in (*cont.*) 138–40; submarine-deployed amphibious tanks (*Toku 4-shiki Naikatei*), 137; epilogue: Leyte Gulf as the Decisive Battle, 153, 157

deck guns: general description of, 38–39, 128; on *I-5*, 21; on *I-8*, 128

destroyer escorts (U.S.): *Conklin* (DE-439), 170; *Corbesier* (DE-438), 170; *England* (DE-635), 139, 143; *Eversole* (DE-404), 157; *Fair* (DE-35), 126; *Finnegan* (DE-307), 172; *George* (DE-697), 143; *Gilmore* (DE-18), 160; *Lawrence C. Taylor* (DE-415), 157, 178; *Manlove* (DE-36), 136; *McCoy Reynolds* (DE-440), 160, 170; *Richard M. Rowell* (DE-403), 157, 160; *Riddle* (DE-185), 146; *Ruby* (DE-698), 143, 170; *Samuel B. Miles* (DE-183), 160; *Shelton* (DE-407), 160; *Underhill* (DE-682), 179, 182, 185; *Whitehurst* (DE-634), 157; *William C. Miller* (DE-259), 146, 147; *Wyman* (DE-38), 147

destroyers (U.S.): *Boyd* (DD-544), 126; *Buchanan* (DD-484), 123; *Charette* (DD-581), 126; *Cotten* (DD-669), 126; *David W. Taylor* (DD-551), 146; *Fair* (DD-35), 126; *Frazier* (DD-607), 118, 126; *Gridley* (DD-380), 157; *Haggard* (DD-555), 174; *Helm* (DD-388), 157; *Hudson* (DD-475), 174; *MacDonough* (DD-351), 137; *Meade* (DD-602), 126; *Mertz* (DD-691), 174; *Monaghan* (DD-354), 60, 61, 62, 119; *Monssen* (DD-798), 174; *Morrison* (DD-560), 174; *Nicholas* (DD-449), 157; *O'Brien* (DD-415), 99; *Phelps* (DD-360), 136; *Radford* (DD-446), 125–26; *Reid* (DD-369), 110; *Saufley* (DD-465), 137; *Stephen Potter* (DD-538), 137; *Stockton* (DD-646), 174; *Strong* (DD-467), 122; *Walker* (DD-517), 126

diesel engines: foreign engines purchased, 40–41; *Kanpon (Kansei honbu)* engines, 41

doctrine, submarine. *See* Decisive Battle; strategy and tactics

Doolittle raid, 78

Dorsetshire, HMS (heavy cruiser), 77

Dutch East Indies, invasion of: Dutch East Indies Invasion Force, formation and command of, 72; loss of *I-24* and *I-60*, 75–76; submarine activities, analysis of effectiveness, 73, 75–76; Submarine Group "A" (*Kō*), composition and activities of, 73, 74; Submarine Group "B" (*Otsu*), composition and activities of, 73, 74–75; Submarine Group "C" (*Hei*), composition and activities of, 73, 75; submarine operations, success of, 73

Enigma. *See* codes and cryptology

fleet boats. *See* submarine types: *Kaichū*; *Kaidai*

Formidable, HMS (aircraft carrier), 190

Formosa, battle of: Japanese estimates of success, 152; Navy General Headquarters misled, unprepared (for Leyte Gulf), 152; "T" Air Wing initial response, 151–52. *See also* Leyte Gulf, battle of

French Frigate Shoals, 81, 83

Fukaya, Capt. Sōkichi, 69, 70

Fukudome, Vice Adm. Shigeru, 150, 188–89

Fukumura, Comdr. Toshiaki, 123, 159

Furutaka (heavy cruiser), 69

Gamble, USS (DM-15), 98

General Principles for the Conduct of the War (*Sensō shidō no taikō*), 134

Gen operations. *See* kaiten

German influence (on Japanese submarine design): American awareness of/interest in, 14; Capt. Godo heads naval mission to Germany, 13–14; German submarine specialists in Japan, 13–15; MAN diesel engines, 41; U-boat reparations (1919), 12–13. *See also* German submarine transfers; German technology transfer

German submarine transfers
—WWI reparations: as basis for *Kaidai* Type 2, 16–17; as basis for *Kirai sen* Type minelayers, 18; design features of, 12; Hector Bywater comment on, 17; receipt of seven U-boats, 12
—WWII transfers (German): *U-181*, 166; *U-195*, 166; *U-219*, 166; *U-234*, 162–63; *U-511*, 132; *U-862*, 166; *U-876*, 162; *U-1224*, 132
—WWII transfers (Italian): *Commandante Alfredo Cappellini* (ex-*UIT-24*), 166; *Luigi Torelli* (ex-*UIT-25*), 166

German technology transfer: introduction to, 108; acoustic mines, 113; advanced aircraft/engine plans, 117, 129; bombsight plans, 129; electric torpedoes, 165; Enigma coding machines, 129; *Kurier* communication system, 163–64; Messerschmitt ME-262 jet fighters, 129, 165; postwar evaluation of, 132–33; radar equipment, 49, 129; uranium (U^{235}), 164–65, 240; V2 rocket plans, 117. *See also* blockade running; German influence; German submarine transfers

Gilbert Islands/Tarawa: ASW countermeasures, Japanese indifference to, 126; available submarine forces, 125; submarine deployment, errors in, 125; submarine losses, 125–26; Tarawa, attack on, 124; Tarawa-Makin operation discontinued, 126

Gilmer, USS (APD-11), 146

Godo, Capt. T., 13–14
Great Triangle, 138–39. *See also* Marianas
Guadalcanal: Adm. Yamamoto responds to U.S. landings, 93; BBs *Hiei*, *Kirishima* sunk, 103; BBs *Kongō*, *Haruna* shell Henderson Field, 101; carrier *Ryūjō* sunk, 96; *Chester* (CA-27) damaged, 102; combat intelligence, importance of (to U.S.), 94, 96; *Enterprise* (CV-6) damaged, 96; first counterattack: Battle of Savo Island, 92; first Japanese troop reinforcement, 94; Henderson Field, Japanese failure to retake, 98, 102, 103; I-boat reconnaissance, interdiction patrols, 103–4; initial submarine responses, 93; *I-123* sunk, 98; Japanese troop convoy annihilated, 103; *Juneau* (CL-52) sunk, 104; Maj. Gen. Kawaguchi, attacks by, 94, 99; midget submarines, ineffectiveness and losses of, 104, 218; *North Carolina* (BB-55) damaged, 99; *O'Brien* (DD-415) sunk, 99; picket lines, first deployment, 94, 95; picket lines, second deployment, 96, 97; picket lines, third deployment, 98; Rear Adm. Yamazaki assumes command submarine forces, 101; *RO-33* sunk, 98; Santa Cruz, battle of, 101, 102; *Saratoga* (CV-3) damaged, 98; *Shōkaku*, *Zuihō* (aircraft carriers) damaged, 101–2; submarine force mismanagement, 93, 96, 102, 105; submarine force organization, 93, 203; Thirty-Eighth Division (Japan) ordered to reinforce, 103; transport operations, submarine, 105; *Wasp* (CV-7) sunk, 99, 100; summary and afterword, 107

HA-boats: *Kaichū (Kaigun chūgata)*, 31, 32
Harada, Rear Adm. Kaku, 115, 122

Haruna (battleship), 101
Hashimoto, Lt. Comdr. Mochitsura, 179, 180, 181, 182
Hawaiian waters, submarines in
—I-boat actions: Capt. Shimamoto critique of, 59; disposition of forces (map), 56; ineffectiveness, analysis of, 57–59
—last operations in (1994), 160–61
—midget submarine actions: chronology and evaluation of, 59–60; Ens. Sakamaki, capture of, 60; Lt. (jg) Yokoyama *tora, tora, tora* report, 59; ramming by USS *Monaghan* (DD-354), 61, 62; Sakamaki submarine, disposition of, 60–61, 63, 231; salvaged two-man submarine (1960), 60, 61
—overall (in)effectiveness of, 65, 189–90
—patrol areas, shifting of, 61–62, 63
—pursuit of carrier ordered, 62–63
hedgehogs (ASW weapon), 149
Heian Maru (submarine tender), 135
Hermes, HMS (aircraft carrier), 77
Hiei (battleship), 103
high-speed boats: experimental boat (1938), 32–33; *Sen-taka (Sensuikan taka)* Type (fast attack class), 29–30; *Sen-taka shō (Sensui-taka shō)* Type, 33; U.S. interest in, 52, 185, 187
Hiryū (aircraft carrier), 69
Hiyō (aircraft carrier), 145
Hobart, HMAS (cruiser), 121
Holland-type boats. *See* submarine types

I-boats, tabulation of losses, 208–15
Ichioka, Rear. Adm. Hisashi, 73, 111
I-400 class submarines. *See* aircraft-carrying submarines
I-168 (Comdr. Tanabe): photograph of, 85; sinks USS *Yorktown* (CV-5), 84–86
Ide, Lt. Kenji, 9, 11
Inaba, Comdr. Michimune, 64, 122
Inada, Hiroshi, 77
Indianapolis, USS, sinking of: *I-58* sorties from Inland Sea, 181; *I-58* sights, torpedoes *Indianapolis*, 182; Capt. McVay court martial of, 181; Comdr. Hashimoto testimony, 181; heavy casualties result, 183; *I-58* forward torpedo room (photo), 182; irony of (Japanese viewpoint), 181; *I-58* sinking report dismissed by Navy Intelligence, 182–83; *kaiten* controversy regarding, 181–82; Lt. Comdr. Hashimoto book *Sunk*, 182; ULTRA intelligence regarding, 179, 181, 241
Indian Ocean, operations in
—1942: Allied strength, effect on, 77, 90; HMS *Cornwall, Dorsetshire,* sinking of, 77; HMS *Hermes,* sinking of, 77; merchant ship sinkings, 77; submarine patrols, summary of, 90–91, 111; submarine reconnaissance (Rear Adm. Hisashi), 76–77
—1943: rendezvous with German *U-180*, 117; strategic evaluation of, 124; submarine patrols, 116–17, 123–24
—1944: *I-27* sinks British troop transport, 159; lack of submarine operational plan, 158; submarine actions, losses, 159–60
Indian troops, German effort to recruit, 117
Indomitable, HMS (aircraft carrier), 190
induction tubes (snorkels): loss of *Holland*-type boat No. 6, 11; on *Sen-taka* Type submarines, 29–30; on *Sen-tei* Type D2 submarines, 30; on *Sen-toku (I-400*-class) submarines, 29, 186
Inoue, Vice Adm. Shigeyoshi, 69
interceptive operations (*yōgeki sakusen*), 6–7
Ipswich, HMAS (minesweeper), 159
Italian submarine transfers. *See* German submarine transfers

Iwaya, Technical Commander, 129
Iwo Jima: Adm. Miwa orders submarine sorties, 171; desperate Japanese situation, 171; Iwo garrison fights to annihilation, 172; *kaiten* losses, 172

Jade cipher machine (Japanese), 238. *See also* codes and cryptology
Jintsū (light cruiser), 120
Jupiter, HMS (destroyer), 76

kaiten (suicide torpedoes)
—carried by *Sen-tei* Type D2 (*I-372*), 30, 39
—genesis of: early developmental difficulties with, 169; early proposals (based on Type 93 torpedo), 169; *kaiten*, etymology of, 39, 169–70; Lts. (jg) Kuroki, Nishina, contributions of, 168, 169; training group established, 170; Types 1-4, description and performance of, 39
—operational use of: change in tactics, plea for, 171; in defense of Home Islands, 184; first *Gen* operation, 169–70; *Indianapolis* sinking, 182, 242; Japanese evaluation, 170; off Iwo Jima, 171, 172; off Okinawa, 174, 183; second *Gen* operation, 170; U.S. Seventh Fleet estimate of dangers from, 181
—transfer to Germany, 117
Kajioka, Rear Adm. Tadamichi, 69
Kako (heavy cruiser), 69
Kakuta, Vice Adm. Kakuji, 147
kamikaze (divine wind): introduction off Leyte, 167; U.S. losses from (Okinawa campaign), 173, 241
Kanpon (*Kansei honbu*): Kanpon diesel engine development, application, 41; organization and responsibilities, 50. *See also* submarine forces (Japanese)
Katō, Capt. Yoshinosuke, 110
Katori (light cruiser), 47, 135
Katsuta, Capt. Haruo, 87

Kawaguchi, Lt. Comdr. Genbei, 172
Kawaguchi, Maj. Gen. Kiyotake, 94, 99
Kawanishi Aircraft Company, 21, 81
Kawasaki Shipyard (Kobe), 11
Kawase, Vice Adm. Shirō, 119
Kessler, Gen. Ulrich, 163, 164, 240
Kimura, Rear Adm. Masazumi, 120
Kinashi, Comdr. Takaichi, 99–100
Kinugasa (heavy cruiser), 69
Kirishima (battleship), 103
Kiska. *See* Aleutians operations
Kitamura, Lt. Comdr. Sōshichi, 71
Koga, Adm. Mineichi, 126, 135, 238
Kokubō hōshin (Imperial Defense Policy). *See* strategy and tactics
Komatsu, Vice Adm. Teruhisa
—Guadalcanal: assigns submarines to transport mission, 105; commands submarine forces, 93, 104; orders pursuit of U.S. carriers, 97; spasmodic shifts of submarine forces, 96–97
—Midway: establishes picket line C, 83
Komazawa, Rear Adm. Katsumi, 114–15
Kondō, Vice Adm. Nobutake, 72
Kongō (battleship), 101
Kōno, Rear Adm. Chimaki, 72
Kōta, Rear Adm. Takerō, 114, 118
Kuribayashi, Lt. Gen. Tadamichi, 172
Kurita, Vice Adm. Takeo, 150, 153
Kuroki, Lt. (jg) Hiroshi, 168, 169
Kuroshima, Adm. Kameto, 137
Kuttabul, HMAS, 88

Launceston, HMAS (minesweeper), 159
Leyte Gulf, battle of
—as Decisive Battle, 147, 153
—execution of: Kurita flagship sunk, 153; *Musashi* lost, 153; submarine deployment, final (10/27/44), 153, 156; submarine deployment (10/20–24/44), 153, 155; sub-

266 Index

Leyte Gulf, battle of, execution of (cont.)
　marine patrols and losses, 155–57; U.S. forces land on Leyte, 152
—preparations for (Japanese): First, Second Air Fleets deployed, 150; First, Seventh Submarine Groups organized, 151; Shō Gō 1, details and readiness date for, 151; Shō Gō 1 executed, 152; Shō-Gō-1 submarine forces, 153; Shō plans, 150; submarine deployment, initial, 154; "T" (Typhoon) Air Wing attacks Formosa invasion forces, 151–52; Vice Adm. Miwa authorizes submarine patrols, 153
Lockwood, Vice Adm. Charles A., 158, 183
logistics support: bases/Base Support Units (Sensuikan kichitai), 45–46; navy yards/shipbuilding facilities, 46; submarine squadron flagships, 46–47; submarine tenders, 46–47
losses, submarine. See submarine forces (Japanese)

Madagascar, operations off: "A" Unit submarines arrive from Malaya, 88–89; HMS Ramilles torpedoed by midget submarine, 89; I-10 aircraft spots HMS Ramilles, 89; midget submarine grounds, crew lost to British, 89
MAGIC, 133. See also codes and cryptology
Malaya, invasion of: Malaya Invasion Force lands, 70; submarine reconnaissance in Malay waters, 71; submarines sight, attack, Repulse and Prince of Wales (1941), 71
Marianas. See also Decisive Battle; Leyte Gulf, battle of
—Japanese carrier force, destruction of: air counterattack strategy fails, 144–45; Carrier Mobile Force delayed in sailing, 143–44; land-based aircraft fail to counterattack, 143; "Marianas Turkey Shoot" develops, 145; three Japanese carriers lost, 145
—post-battle evaluation (Japanese): bleak estimate of future, 150; communications failures, importance of, 149; future emphasis on midget submarines, 150; Lt. Comdr. Torisu comment, 147–48; submarine losses, 147; tactical initiatives, importance of, 149; Vice Adm. Daigo report, 148; Vice Adm. Yamazaki critique, 148
—Saipan, loss of: Sixth Fleet headquarters established on Saipan, 146; evacuation unsuccessful, 146–47; staff dispersed, submarine operations command lost, 146; submarine losses during evacuation, 146, 147; Vice Adm. Miwa assumes command Sixth Fleet, 147; Vice Adm. Takagi, staff, lost, 147
—strategic background to: Allied successes, impact of, 135; Bismarck Barrier, 134, 135, 136; General Principles for the Conduct of the War (Sensō shidō no taikō), 134; the Great Triangle, 138–39; Operation A-Gō (A-Gō sakusen), 135, 206–7; Truk naval base, destruction of, 135; Zone of Absolute National Defense (Zettai kokubō), 134, 135, 150
—submarine operations (after Saipan invasion): catastrophic losses, 141, 142, 147; Operation A-Gō delayed, 140; rapid redeployment ordered (6/13), 140–41; Saipan command post neutralized, command transferred, 141, 146
—submarine operations (before Saipan invasion): "B (Otsu)" Unit continues transport operations, 138–39; deployment of "A (Kō)" Unit, 138–40
—Tinian: B-29 base established on, 147; Vice Adm. Kakuji lost, 147

Index 267

"Marianas Turkey Shoot," 145. *See also* Marianas
Matsuo, Lt. Keiu, 88
Matsuo, Yoshiyasu, 69–70
McVay, Capt. Charles B. III, 181
midget submarines. *See also* kaiten
—A-targets (*Kō hyōteki*): Type A (*Hō-Gata*), 33, 34; Type B (Otsu-Gata), 33, 34; Type C (Hei-Gata), 33, 34; Type D (*Kōryū*), Type D variant (*Kairyū*), 33, 34, 184; production of, 34, 51
—in Australian waters: Sidney Harbor, actions/losses in, 88
—emphasis on, post-Marianas, 150
—general ineffectiveness of, 89
—at Guadalcanal, 103–4
—Hawaiian actions (1941). *See* Hawaiian waters, submarines in
—Madagascar, operations off: HMS *Ramilles* torpedoed, 89; *I-20*'s midget grounds, crew lost to British, 89
—tabulation of losses, 218
—tactical deployment of (general): in Decisive Battle, 34–35; in defense of Home Islands, 184; on *Junsen* Type C boats, 35; in seaplane tenders, 34–35
—training for, 45
Midway (Operation MI): American carriers escape, 84; errors in timing and submarine deployment, 79, 81; flying boat refueling, American interdiction of, 81; force organization and composition (*Guntai-Kabun*), 201–2; Japanese intelligence, failures of, 79; Operation MI abandoned, 83; submarine picket lines (first deployment), 79, 80; submarine picket lines (redeployment westward), 82, 83; tactical assumptions of, 79; USS *Yorktown* (CV-5) sunk, 84–86
Mikawa, Vice Adm. Gunichi, 92
mines/minelaying: acoustic mines (from Germany), 113; deploying from submarines, 39; *I-23, I-24* lay mines off Darwin, 74; *I-21, I-22* mine Jahore Strait (Singapore), 71; *I-23, I-24* mine Manila Bay, Balabac Strait, 72; minelaying submarines: *Kirai sen (Kirai fusetsu sensuikan)* Type, 18; Type 88 submarine mine, 39
Mississinewa, USS (AO-39), 169, 185
Mito, Rear Adm. Hisashi, 103
Miwa, Vice Adm. Shigeyoshi: becomes Commander, Sixth Fleet, 147; initiates submarine sector patrols (Leyte), 153; orders Iwo Jima sortie, 171; orders submarines to Okinawa, 174; recognizes *kaiten* ineffectiveness, 175; reorganizes submarine forces (post Marianas), 150; sends *I-12* to Hawaii (1944), 160
Musashi (battleship), 150, 152, 153

Nagai, Capt. Takeo, 70
Nagano, Adm. Osami, 54–55
Nagumo, Vice Adm. Chūichi, 76, 77
Nakajima C6N ("Myrt"), submarine-borne aircraft, 176
Nambu, Comdr. Shinsei, 176
naming conventions (for weapons and aircraft), 230
Naval Technical Bureau (*Kansei honbu*). *See* Kanpon
Navy Battle Regulations (*Kaisen yōmurei*): genesis of (Vice Adm. Akiyama), 3; Russo-Japanese War, influence of, 3; text of (1934 edition), 191–93; weaknesses of (post-Marianas evaluation), 148–49
New Guinea, and submarine transport operations, 115–16
Nimitz, Adm. Chester W., 81
Nishima, Lt. (jg) Sekio, 168, 169
Nomura, Vice Adm. Naokuni, 132
North Carolina, USS (BB-55), 99

Oguri, Lt. Comdr. Kōzaburō, 9, 10
Okinawa: airfields captured, 173; controversy compromises defense prep-

Okinawa (*cont.*)
arations, 173; as Japanese delaying action, 172; *kaiten* attacks, 174; *kamikaze* attacks exact heavy toll, 173, 241; submarine attacks costly, ineffective, 173–74, 175; *Yamato* sorties, 173
Ōmori, PO Takeshi, 88
Oppama (Yokosuka) Aviation Corps, 21
Ōshima, Ambassador Hiroshi, 131–32
Ōwada, Rear Adm. Noboru, 141, 147
Ozawa, Vice Adm. Jisaburō, 144, 145

Pacific coast (U.S.), submarine operations off: American anxiety over, 67; Astoria, Oregon, shelling of (6/42), 84; Capt. Tamaki recommendations regarding, 86; *I-25* accidentally sinks Russian submarine, 111; ineffectiveness of, 67–68, 189–90; *I-25* sinks two tankers, 110; Oregon forest bombed (by *I-25* seaplane), 110, 189; patrol areas shifted eastward, 61–62; Santa Barbara, shelling of (2/42), 68; submarine deployment (12/41) (map), 66; technical explanation for failures (Comdr. Muraoka), 68
Paladin, HMS (destroyer), 159
Panama Canal, target for aircraft-carrying submarines, 175, 176
periscopes, 38
personnel, submarine. *See* submarine forces (Japanese)
Petard, HMS (destroyer), 159
Philippine Islands, Japanese invasion of: Lingayen landing (12/41), 72; midget submarines, tabulation of losses, 218; minelaying submarines, actions of, 72
Prince of Wales, HMS (battleship), 70, 71, 190
propulsion systems. *See* diesel engines

Rabaul, New Britain, submarine operations near, 70

radar: Japanese lack of, 49, 118; transfer of German equipment, 49, 132–33
Ramilles, HMS (battleship), 89, 190
reconnaissance operations
—submarine: Alaska areas (5/42), 83; Dutch East Indies (1942), 73; Guadalcanal, 94, 96, 101, 102; *I-36* attempts Pearl Harbor reconnaissance (10/43), 122; Indian Ocean (1942), 76–77; in Malayan waters, 71; Midway area, 83; search for USS *Saratoga*, 64; Wake Island, 69
—submarine-borne aircraft: *I-10* reconnaissance of Fiji, 59; *I-7* reconnaissance of Pearl Harbor (12/17/41), 58; *I-9* reconnaissance of Pearl Harbor (11/16/43), 122; *I-36* reconnaissance of Pearl Harbor (10/17/43), 122; plane from *I-10* spots HMS *Ramilles*, 89; summary of (11/41–11/42), 198–99
Repulse, HMS (battle cruiser), 70, 71, 190
Resolution, HMS (battleship), 190
Revenge, HMS (battleship), 190
RO-boats: Kaichū (Kaigun chūgata) Type 5, 31; Kaichū (Kaigun chūgata) Type 6, 31–32; Kaishō (Kaigun shō), 32; losses during Wake Island occupation, 69–70; RO-boat garrison at Kiska, 110; RO-100 class submarine off Rabaul (photo), 107; *RO-33* sunk (Guadalcanal), 98; tabulation of losses, 215–17
Rockford, USS (PF-48), 161
Royal Sovereign, HMS (battleship), 190
Russia: Russian submarine, accidental sinking of, 111; Russo-Japanese War, 1, 3; Soviet-Japanese Neutrality Pact, 240

Saipan, loss of. *See* Marianas
Sakamaki, Ens. Kazuo: captured (midget submarine, Hawaii), 60;

captured submarine, disposition of, 60–61, 63, 231
Santa Cruz, battle of, 101, 102
Sasaki, Capt. Hanku, 87, 88, 104
Savo Island, Battle of, 90
Schratz, Paul, 185, 187
seaplane tenders, and tactical deployment of midget submarines, 34–35
Seiran seaplane dive bomber (Aichi M6A1), 40, 175
Sekito, Comdr. Yoshimitsu, 105
Sensō shidō no taikō (General Principles for the Conduct of the War), 134
Shimamoto, Capt. Kyūgorō, 59
Shimizu, Vice Adm. Mitsumi, 61–62
Shindō, Lt. (jg) Hisao, 119
Shōkaku (carrier), 101–2, 145
Shō plans, 150, 151. See also Leyte Gulf, battle of
Sino-Japanese War: *Chin Yen* (captured Chinese battleship), 10; impetus to Japanese naval development, 1; naval/submarine experience in, 53–54
snorkels. See induction tubes
Solomon Sea, actions in. See Guadalcanal
Sōryū (aircraft carrier), 69
South Pacific, submarine operations in
—1943: heavy losses, small returns, 121, 122–23; HMAS *Hobart* damaged by *I-11*, 121; Sixth Fleet submarines, organization of, 203, 204–5; USS *Strong* (DD-467) sunk, 122; Wake Island, patrol of, 121
—1944: Peleliu/Palau, operations near, 160
Soviet Union. See Russia
strategy and tactics (Japanese). See also Decisive Battle; submarine forces (Japanese)
—ASW tactics/countermeasures, Japanese indifference to, 126–27
—attrition doctrine: interceptive operations (*yōgeki sakusen*), 6–7; as prelude to Decisive Battle, 4, 6–7, 15, 35; sea communications, destruction of, 5
—and mismanagement of submarine forces: Guadalcanal, 93, 96, 102, 105; Hawaiian waters, 58, 59, 67–68; I-boat refueling tanker, need for, 190; Marianas, 137–38, 141–43, 147–49; at Okinawa, 175; postwar summary and appraisal, 188–90; Tarawa/Gilberts, 125, 126–27; in waning months of war, 159, 160, 175, 188–90
—offense vs. expansion: expansion to southeast, Navy General Headquarters advocacy of, 78; expansion to southeast, strategic correctness of, 190; offensive operations, Navy General Headquarters opposition to, 78; offensive operations, Yamamoto advocacy of, 77–78
—strategy, early development of: Chinese conflict (1894–95), 1; force requirements (for defeat of U.S. Navy), 2; Imperial Defense Policy (*Kokubō hōshin*), 2; Navy Battle Regulations (*Kaisen yōmurei*), 3, 191–93; Russian conflict (1904–5), 1, 3; Tsushima, influence of, 6
—submarine roles, specifics of: A-targets (*Kō hyōteki, Kōryū*) Types, 33–34, 35; I-boat refueling tanker, need for, 190; *Junsen* Types, characteristics and mission of, 18–19, 27; *Kaidai* Types, characteristics and mission of, 18–19; *Sen-tei* Type D transports, 30
—tactical force organization: Midway/Aleutians/Port Moresby Task Force Organization (*Guntai-Kaibun*), 201–2; Operation *A-Gō sakusen* Task Force Organization, 206–7; Pearl Harbor Carrier Strike Force, 196–97; Sixth Fleet leadership (mid-1943), 204–5; Sixth Fleet submarines (Eastern Solomons), 203; Southern Expeditionary Main Force (Second Fleet), 200

strategy and tactics (Japanese) (cont.)
—war with U.S.: introduction and overview, xi–xiii, 7; Adm. Nagano argues for, 54–55; Adm. Yamamoto proposes Pearl Harbor strike, 55; final patrols (1945), 183; postwar summary and evaluation, 188–90

submarine forces (Japanese). *See also* strategy and tactics; submarine types
—key members, biographies of, 219–26
—losses, tabulations of: I-boats, 208–15; midget submarines, 218; RO-boats, 215–17
—personnel: education, 44–45; training, 45; volunteers, 43–44
—submarine development/construction: Bureau of Submarines (*Kaigun Sensuikanbu*), 51–52; submarine construction, inefficiency of, 50–51; submarine force development, overview of, 49–50; technology development, bureaucratic fragmentation of, 50

submarines (U.S.): *Albacore* (SS-218), 145; *Aspro* (SS-309), 136; *Bluefish* (SS-222), 183; *Cavalla* (SS-244), 145; *Corvina* (SS-226), 236; *Halibut* (SS-232), 113; *Rock* (SS-274), 129; *Sawfish* (SS-276), 129, 130; *Spikefish* (SS-404), 183; *Stingray* (SS-186), 113; *Tautog* (SS-19), 87; *Tilefish* (SS-307), 129; *Trigger* (SS-237), 113; *Tunny* (SS-282), 136

submarine types (Japanese). *See also specific types;* British influence; German influence; German submarine transfers
—A-targets (*Kō hyōteki*): Type A (*Kō Gata*), 33, 34; Type B (*Otsu-Gata*), 33, 34; Type C (*Hei-Gata*), 33, 34; Type D (*Kōryū*), Type D variant (*Kairyū*) 34, 184; production of, 34, 51
—classification system for, 12
—foreign designs: American, 8–10; French (Schneider-Laubeuf), 11; Italian (Fiat-Laurenti), 11
—high-speed experimental boat (1938), 32–33
—*Holland*-type boats: early specifications for (1899), 9; initial purchases of, 8–9; Japanese boats, specifications for (1905), 9–10; Japanese construction of, 11; loss of boat No. 6, 11; surfaced Japanese submarine (photo, *ca.* 1908), 10
—*Junsen (Junyō sensuikan)*: characteristics and mission of, 18–19, 27; MAN, *Kanpon* diesel engines in, 41; Type 1, 19; Type 2, 22; Type 3, 22–23; Type C refitted to carry A-targets, 34; Type 1M (*I-5*), 21–22; New Type A1, 23; New Type A2, 27; New Type A (Modified), 27, 175–76, 178; New Type B, 24–26; New Type C, 26
—*Kaichū (Kaigun chūgata)* (RO-boats): *Kanpon* diesel engines in, 41; Type 5, 31; Type 6, 31–32
—*Kaidai (Kaigun-dai)*: characteristics and mission of, 18–19; MAN, *Kanpon* diesel engines in, 41; Type 1, 16; Type 2, 16–17; Type 4, 20; Type 5, 20; Type C2, 28; Types 3a,3B, 19–20; Types 6a,6b, 20, 21; Types B1,B2, 28
—*Kaishō (Kaigun shō)* (RO-boats): specifications for, 32
—*Kirai sen (Kirai fusetsu sensuikan)* minelaying submarines: MAN diesel engines for, 41; mines for (Type 88), 39; specifications for, 18
—*Sen-ho (Sensuikan ho)* (*I-351*), 30
—*Sen-taka (Sensuikan taka)* Type (fast attack class), 29–30
—*Sen-taka shō (Sensui-taka shō)* Type, 33
—*Sen-tei (Sensuikan tei)* Types, 30
—*Sen-toku (Sensuikan toku)* Type (*I-400* class), 28–29

submersible stores vessel (*Unkatō*), 115–16

Suetsugu, Adm. Nobumasa, 6–7, 12
suicide torpedoes. *See kaiten*
Sullivan brothers, loss of (in *Juneau*), 104
supply and transport boats: Sen-ho *(Sensuikan ho) (I-351)*, 30; Sen-tei *(Sensuikan tei)* (D-Types), 30

Taihō (heavy carrier), 145
Takagi, Vice. Adm. Takeo: named Commander, Sixth Fleet, 120; ordered to patrol Wake Island, 121; yields Saipan submarine command, 141; dies on Saipan, 147
Takahashi, Vice Adm. Ibō, 72
Tamaki, Capt. Tomejirō, 86
Tanabe, Comdr. Yahachi, 84–86
Tarawa. *See* Gilbert Islands/Tarawa
Telemachus, HMS (submarine), 160
Teraoke, Vice Adm. Kimpei, 150
Tōgō, Adm. Heihachirō, 6
Tokkō units: in defense of Home Islands, 184; training for, 45; volunteers for, 43–44. *See also kaiten*
Tora, tora, tora report (Lt. [jg] Yokoyama), 59
Torisu, Lt. Comdr. Kennosuke, 147–48
torpedoes: air-ejection techniques (Type 95), 38; early British (Whitehead, 18-inch), 36; electric (German transfers), 165; 21-inch, types and performance, 37; Long Lance as basis for *kaiten*, 168; Long Lance (Type 93), 37, 168; oxygen propellant, dangers of, 37; torpedo data computer (TDC), 38. *See also kaiten*
Toyoda, Adm. Soemu, 135, 151
transportation operations, submarine. *See also* blockade running
—Guadalcanal: Adm. Komatsu orders operations, 105; Comdr. Sekito comment on, 105; *I-1* beached, yields code books, 105, 106
—late 1944–early 1945: desperation of Japanese force on New Guinea, 162; heavy submarine losses, 161; *Sen-tei* Type D-1 built for purpose, 161; to Truk and Wake Island, 183; ULTRA influence on ASW successes, 161–62
—New Guinea: *Dai hatsu* landing craft, 115; evaluation of, 116; *Unkatō* submersible stores vessel, 115–16
—supply and transport boats: Sen-ho *(Sensuikan ho) (I-351)*, 30; Sen-tei *(Sensuikan tei)* (D-Types), 30, 161
Tripartite Pact, 108
Truk naval base, destruction of, 135
Tsushima, battle of, 6

Uchino, Comdr. Shinji, 127–28
Ugaki, Adm. Matome, 64, 93, 109, 137
ULTRA. *See* codes and cryptology
Unkatō submersible stores vessel, 115–16
uranium (U^{235}), transfer from Germany (aboard *U-234*), 164–65, 240

Vancouver Island, B.C., 86
victory disease (*senshō-byō*), 68
volunteers, submarine service. *See* submarine forces (Japanese)

Wake Island
—Japanese defense of (1943), 121
—occupation of (1942): Heavy Cruiser Support Group, composition of, 69; RO-boat losses during, 69–70; submarine patrol and blockade, 69–70; submarine reconnaissance operations, 69; Wake Island Occupation Group, composition of, 69
Warspite, HMS (battleship), 190
Washington Naval Treaty, 2, 12, 15

Yamamoto, Adm. Isoroku
—advocates offensive operations, 77–78
—death of, 238

Yamamoto, Adm. Isoroku (*cont.*)
—Guadalcanal: moves to Truk in *Yamato*, 93; orders naval force concentration, 93; orders submarine transport missions, 105
—Midway: orders westward shift of picket lines, 83
—nomination of Adm. Koga as successor, 238
—proposes Pearl Harbor strike, 55
Yamato (battleship), 150, 152, 173
Yamazaki, Rear Adm. Shigeaki, 64, 101, 103
Yanagi. See blockade running
Yokota, Comdr. Minoru, 98
Yokoyama, Lt. (jg), writes *tora, tora, tora* report, 59
Yoshitomi, Rear Adm. Setsuzō, 70, 71, 73, 104

zone of absolute national defense (*Zettai kokubō ken*): outer perimeter of, 134

About the Authors

Carl Boyd is Louis I. Jaffé Professor Emeritus of History and Eminent Scholar Emeritus at Old Dominion University in Norfolk, Virginia, where he taught military, naval, and intelligence history. He has published articles in *Intelligence and National Security, Journal of Military History, Modern Asian Studies, The Enigma Bulletin, Cryptologia*, and numerous other periodicals and is the author of *The Extraordinary Envoy: General Hiroshi Oshima and Diplomacy in the Third Reich, 1934–1939*; *Hitler's Japanese Confidant: General Oshima Hiroshi and MAGIC Intelligence, 1941–1945*; and *American Command of the Sea through Carriers, Codes, and the Silent Service*. He served in U.S. Navy submarines from 1954 to 1958 before earning bachelor's and master's degrees at Indiana University and a Ph.D. in history at the University of California, Davis.

Akihiko Yoshida retired from the Japanese Maritime Self-Defsnse Force with the rank of captain. He completed much of the primary research in Japanese sources.

The Naval Institute Press is the book-publishing arm of the U.S. Naval Institute, a private, nonprofit, membership society for sea service professionals and others who share an interest in naval and maritime affairs. Established in 1873 at the U.S. Naval Academy in Annapolis, Maryland, where its offices remain today, the Naval Institute has members worldwide.

Members of the Naval Institute support the education programs of the society and receive the influential monthly magazine *Proceedings* and discounts on fine nautical prints and on ship and aircraft photos. They also have access to the transcripts of the Institute's Oral History Program and get discounted admission to any of the Institute-sponsored seminars offered around the country.

The Naval Institute also publishes *Naval History* magazine. This colorful bimonthly is filled with entertaining and thought-provoking articles, first-person reminiscences, and dramatic art and photography. Members receive a discount on *Naval History* subscriptions.

The Naval Institute's book-publishing program, begun in 1898 with basic guides to naval practices, has broadened its scope to include books of more general interest. Now the Naval Institute Press publishes about one hundred titles each year, ranging from how-to books on boating and navigation to battle histories, biographies, ship and aircraft guides, and novels. Institute members receive significant discounts on the Press's more than eight hundred books in print.

Full-time students are eligible for special half-price membership rates. Life memberships are also available.

For a free catalog describing Naval Institute Press books currently available, and for further information about subscribing to *Naval History* magazine or about joining the U.S. Naval Institute, please write to:

Membership Department
U.S. Naval Institute
291 Wood Road
Annapolis, MD 21402-5034
Telephone: (800) 233-8764
Fax: (410) 269-7940
Web address: www.navalinstitute.org

www.ingramcontent.com/pod-product-compliance
Lightning Source LLC
Chambersburg PA
CBHW030308080526
44584CB00012B/484